# The New First Dictionary
# of Cultural Literacy

# The New First Dictionary

**THIRD EDITION** • Revised and Updated

# of Cultural Literacy

## What Your Child Needs to Know

*Edited by* E. D. Hirsch, Jr.

*Associate Editors*
William G. Rowland, Jr.
and Michael Stanford

**Houghton Mifflin Company**
Boston • New York

For information about permission to reproduce selections from this
book, write to trade.permissions@hmhco.com or to Permissions, Houghton Mifflin
Harcourt Publishing Company, 3 Park Avenue, 19th Floor,
New York, New York 10016.

Visit our Web site: www.hmhco.com

*Library of Congress Cataloging-in-Publication Data*

The new first dictionary of cultural literacy : what your child needs to
know / edited by E. D. Hirsch, Jr. ; associate editors William G. Rowland, Jr.
and Michael Stanford. — 3rd ed., rev. and updated.
p.   cm.
Rev. ed. of: A first dictionary of cultural literacy. 2nd ed., rev. and updated © 1996.
Includes bibliographical references and index.
ISBN 0-618-40853-3
ISBN 978-0-618-40853-5
1. Children's encyclopedias and dictionaries.  I. Hirsch, E. D. (Eric Donald).
II. Rowland, William G.  III. Stanford, Michael.  IV. First dictionary
of cultural literacy.
AG5.N335 2004
031 — dc22   2004043659

Printed in the United States of America

DOC   15
4500794822

# Contents

# Maps

# Preface to the Third Edition

This new, updated edition reflects important changes that have occurred in the world since 1991, changes in history, science, and the arts that have become part of our common awareness, such as Harry Potter, the Persian Gulf War, El Niño, global warming, DVDs, laptop computers, and the recently named Southern Ocean.

Most of the entries that appeared in the 1989 edition still appear here, illustrating how durable literate culture is and how valid was the idea that gave rise to this book: namely, that we can communicate with one another in our national community only because we continue to share and take for granted the knowledge that we hold in common. To possess this shared knowledge is to be a member of the cultural community — to be an insider. Not to possess it is to be excluded from full communication with other members of the community — to be an outsider. In our democracy we want all children to have the opportunity to be insiders. That is why we have made this book.

That is also why my colleagues and I started the Core Knowledge Foundation (www.coreknowledge.org), whose mission is to bring this knowledge to all children through our schools. The entries in this book overlap with the topics studied in the early grades in Core Knowledge Schools.

The overlap of the topics in this book with the topics studied in good schools is especially important today, when schools, under the influence of the national No Child Left Behind Act, are spending more and more classroom time trying to improve children's reading abilities. For children to understand writings in textbooks, magazines, books, and newspapers, they must possess the background knowledge that such writings take for granted. Cultural literacy and literacy are intertwined. Knowing the information contained in this book is a big step toward being a good reader and being a full participant in our society.

Good luck!

E. D. Hirsch, Jr.
*Charlottesville, Virginia*
*March 2004*

# To Parents and Teachers

This dictionary outlines the knowledge that, in the opinion of several hundred teachers and parents across the nation, American children should acquire by the end of the sixth grade. Of course, children should know many more things as well, depending on their local situation and individual interests, but they should at least share this common core of knowledge with other children across the nation. This compilation has been continually revised on the basis of comments and suggestions from all fifty states and from hundreds of teachers, school administrators, and parents who belong to the Cultural Literacy Network. If you have young children in your care who are not making good progress toward learning most of the information gathered here, they are being cheated, with the best intentions, by, among other things, wrongheaded theories about the primary importance of teaching skills rather than traditional content — theories that have dominated instruction in American schools in the past few decades.

If that indictment sounds too sweeping, consider what a parent had to say in the following letter. (I have received hundreds of such letters since the publication in 1987 of my book *Cultural Literacy*.) The letter eloquently expresses the experience of hundreds of thousands of parents who have felt that something has been wrong in the schooling of their children.

For our children, the elementary school years were, with the exception of one teacher, a notable void. This still saddens me, as I suspect from my own experience that there is a luminosity to knowledge acquired in those years that is unique. I visit England twice a year and have a friend there with children the ages of our children. Informal comparisons of homework assignments came out as one might have expected; her children were *learning* things, like names of rivers and parts of a flower. Ours had reams of ugly, sparsely written upon, very faint ditto sheets. There was very little to be learned from them at all.

The frustrations of our conferences with a majority of our children's elementary school teachers are still surprisingly fresh. We were quickly put on the defensive. The gist of the teachers' arguments was the claim that knowledge changes so rapidly as to be swiftly outmoded. Our knowledge, then, was largely irrelevant to the wonderful new knowledge our children were being taught *how* to acquire. (Baloney! By the time our children finally got to high school, much of the knowledge of their AP [Advanced Placement] courses was the same as or an expansion of the knowledge we had acquired decades before.)

In *Cultural Literacy*, I explained why about eighty percent of the knowledge commonly shared by literate Americans has not changed for more than a hundred years and is not likely to be quickly outmoded. The remaining twenty percent of shared literate knowledge does indeed change year by year, and my colleagues and I have taken account of such changes in this book. But as least eighty percent of what is listed will probably be just as central and valid ten years from now as it is today.

The current emphasis on skills in the primary grades, combined with trivial, incoherent, and watered-down content, has caused American education to decline in absolute terms, as measured by comparisons with the achievements of children from other countries. In recent comparisons among developed nations, the United States ranks near the bottom in math, science, and world geography — subjects that are the same everywhere.

Our schools' emphasis on skills rather than knowledge has also had the unintended effect of injuring disadvantaged students more than advantaged ones. Since so-called skills are really based upon specific knowledge, those who have already received literate knowledge from their homes are better able to understand what teachers and textbooks are saying and are therefore better able to learn new things than are children from nonliterate backgrounds. Consequently, when schools emphasize skills above knowledge, they consistently widen the gap between the haves and have-nots instead of narrowing it. Such schools unwittingly heighten economic and social inequalities instead of helping to overcome them.

This dictionary cannot take the place of good parenting and teaching or of good books, tapes, and videos that convey literate knowledge coherently and vividly. The dictionary can only hope to indicate what should be known by the end of the sixth grade and to encourage parents, teachers, and students themselves to make sure that such knowledge is effectively taught and learned. My colleagues and I hope that putting such a compilation between the covers of a book will be helpful to those who desire guidance about the specific knowledge that is the true foundation of our children's academic skills. A selection of some books that will help children learn more about the main topics we cover is provided in the back of the dictionary.

The list on which the dictionary entries are based is constantly being revised as comments and criticisms are sent to the Core Knowledge Foundation. The present compilation reflects the composition of the sixth-grade list as of March 2003. Readers are invited to address their recommendations for improvements, additions, and deletions to the Core Knowledge Foundation, 801 East High Street, Charlottesville, Virginia 22902.

E. D. Hirsch, Jr.
*Charlottesville, Virginia*

# To Young Readers: How to Use This Dictionary

This dictionary is divided into twenty-one *sections,* each devoted to what you should know about a subject such as fine arts, mathematics, or world geography by the time you finish sixth grade. You can find out what you still need to learn about a subject by looking through a particular section, and you can find a list of the sections by looking at the *contents* page. You can also look up an item by using the *index* at the back of the book.

Reading a dictionary, however, isn't the best way to gain the knowledge you need. If you discover a subject that you want to learn more about, you should ask the school librarian to suggest a good book about it for your age. For instance, if you want to know more about the stories of the Greek gods and their amazing activities, you could read a book about Greek myths. If you are interested in the people and places of South America, you could read a history of South America, study an atlas, or do research on the Internet. In the back of the dictionary, we list good reference works that will help you learn more about what you need to know.

In the geography sections of the dictionary, you will find more maps to help you learn where places are in the world.

*Cross-references* occur throughout the dictionary and are printed in small capital letters (for example, ABRAHAM LINCOLN, EQUILATERAL TRIANGLE, FOLK SONG). A cross-reference is a related topic that is defined in this dictionary. Usually you will find the cross-reference in the same section. If you don't find it there, turn to the *index* in the back. It lists every entry in the dictionary and gives the page number where it is found.

This dictionary will be useful in giving you a general picture of what you already know and what you still need to learn. Knowledge builds on knowledge. The more you already know about many different things, the easier it will be to learn about new things. If you and your classmates know many things in common, you will find that your classes will be more interesting than before, and you will be better able to understand what your teachers and textbooks are saying. Learning will be faster and much more exciting for everybody.

If you and your teachers have ideas about how to make this dictionary better, we shall pay attention to your advice. Write to me at the Core Knowledge Foundation, 801 East High Street, Charlottesville, Virginia 22902.

This dictionary has been written and designed with you in mind. Enjoy making good use of it!

E. D. Hirsch, Jr.

# PRONUNCIATION SYSTEM

Some entries in this dictionary include a pronunciation guide, which shows you how to say a word. More than one pronunciation is given if a word can be pronounced properly in more than one way. The pronunciation guide, which appears in parentheses after the entry term, is easy to use and does not require any special symbols. Hyphens separate syllables, and the syllable that takes the primary stress in pronunciation is printed in capital letters. The following key explains how to pronounce the simple combinations of letters that are used in this system.

| When the sound appears as | It should be pronounced as in |
|---|---|
| a | pat |
| ay | pay, make |
| air | fare, pear, hair |
| ah | father, are, guard |
| b | bib |
| ch | church, cello |
| d | deed, filled |
| e | bet, berry, bury |
| ee | bee each, conceit |
| f | fife, phase, rough |
| g | gag, ghost |
| h | hat, who, Gila monster, José |
| i | bit, spinach, manage |
| eye | by, bite, aisle, buy |
| eer | ear, pier, clear, beer, weird, cereal |
| j | edge, gem, jelly, judge, manage |
| k | kick, cat, pique, chaos, crack |
| kw | choir, quart, acquire |
| l | lad, lull |
| m | mum, column, paradigm |
| n | no, sin, sudden |
| ng | sing, anchor, angle |
| o | pot, water, honest |
| oh | no, owe, sew, moan, broach, low |
| aw | all, flaw, caucus, talk, Utah, broad, bought |
| oo | book |
| ooh | boot, Peru |
| oy | noise, boy |
| ow | out, house, bough, fowl, hour |
| p | pop |
| r | roar, rhythm, wren |
| s | sauce, cellar |

| When the sound appears as | It should be pronounced as in |
|---|---|
| sh | ship, dish, addition, anxious |
| t | tight, stopped, bought |
| th | breath |
| thh | breathe, feather |
| u | cut, income, does |
| yoo | purée, your, purify, uranium |
| yooh | few, beautiful, feud, ukase |
| uh | about, item, edible, lemon, circus, attention |
| ur | urge, firm, term, word, heard |
| v | valve, of, love, Wagner (German) |
| w | with, one, guano |
| y | yes, onion, hallelujah |
| z | zebra, xylem, anxiety, does |
| zh | garage, pleasure, vision |

The letter **x** presents special problems because it has several possible pronunciations:

| | |
|---|---|
| z | xylophone (ZEYE-luh-fohn) |
| ks | box (BOKS), excessive (ek-SES-iv) |
| gz | exact (eg-ZAKT), exist (ig-ZIST) |
| gzh | luxury (LUG-zhur-ee), luxurious (lug-ZHOOR-ee-uhs) |
| ksh | anxious (ANGK-shuhs) |

A few foreign words that appear in this dictionary rquire special sounds not usually found in English. They are:

| The sound | As pronounced in | Appears as |
|---|---|---|
| ö | schön | eu |
| āo | São Paulo (sownn-POW-looh) | nn |
| ü | trün | uu |

# Proverbs

A proverb is an old, familiar saying that has been handed down over many years. So when we hear a proverb, it is as if we were hearing the advice of our ancestors.

Proverbs often express ideas about how to act in daily life. There are proverbs to fit almost any situation. If careful attention is needed for a task such as building a model or sewing with tiny stitches, someone might advise you that "haste makes waste" (that is, don't go too fast or you may ruin your work). In another situation, you might need to hurry. If there is only one day left to sell raffle tickets for the school fair or only two tickets left for a baseball game, the proverb "He who hesitates is lost" makes the most sense.

Many proverbs are as memorable for the way they sound as for the things they say. For instance, the use of rhyme helps us remember "An apple a day keeps the doctor away." So, too, a repeated sound ("pr") helps us remember "Practice what you preach."

Here are some of the most widely used proverbs in English and what they mean.

**Actions speak louder than words**   It is safer to rely on what people do than on what they say.

**All for one and one for all**   Every member supports the group and the group supports every member. This saying is used by members of a group when they want to express their loyalty to each other. The proverb itself comes from the book *The Three Musketeers*, by Alexandre Dumas, a nineteenth-century French author.

**All's well that ends well**   In any effort, what matters is a good outcome.

**An apple a day keeps the doctor away**   Apples help keep us healthy.

**April showers bring May flowers**   Unpleasant things may bring about good things, just as rainy days cause flowers to bloom later on.

**Beauty is only skin deep**   People should be judged not by their appearance but by their inner qualities.

**Beggars can't be choosers**   People who have very little can't be fussy about what they get.

**The best-laid plans of mice and men oft go awry**   No matter how carefully you plan, something may still go wrong.

**Better late than never**   It is better to do something after it was supposed to be done than not to do it at all.

**Better safe than sorry**   Be careful before you act, or you may suffer later.

**The bigger they are, the harder they fall**   The more powerful and successful people are, the more spectacular is their downfall.

**A bird in the hand is worth two in the bush**   What you already have is more dependable than something that you only hope to get.

**Birds of a feather flock together**   People are attracted to others who are like themselves.

**Count your blessings**   Be happy for what you have. Think of the good things in your life instead of the bad.

**Curiosity killed the cat**   People should mind their own business.

**Do unto others as you would have them do unto you**   Treat other people with the same kindness that you would like them to show to you. This saying comes from the BIBLE and is known as the Golden Rule. Similar sayings occur in CONFUCIANISM and BUDDHISM as well as in JUDAISM and CHRISTIANITY.

**A dog is man's best friend**   A dog is even more faithful to its owner than human friends are.

**Don't count your chickens before they hatch**   Don't assume that you'll get the things you want before you actually have them.

**Don't cry over spilt milk**   It doesn't do any good to be unhappy about something that has already happened.

**Don't cut off your nose to spite your face**   Don't take some action in anger that will hurt you more than it hurts someone else.

**Don't judge a book by its cover**   Don't judge the value of a thing simply by its appearance.

**Don't lock the stable door after the horse is stolen**   After the damage has already been done, it's pointless to take the actions that could have prevented it.

**Don't look a gift horse in the mouth**   If you get something for nothing, don't complain if it's not exactly what you want. The proverb refers to the practice of deciding how much a horse is worth by looking at its teeth to estimate its age.

**Don't put all your eggs in one basket**   Don't make all your plans depend on one thing, because that one thing could go wrong and destroy your plans. It's safer to depend on several things; it's better to depend on two friends than just one.

**Don't put the cart before the horse**   Begin at the beginning; do things in their proper order.

**The early bird catches the worm**   To achieve a goal, get an early start.

**Early to bed and early to rise/Makes a man healthy, wealthy, and wise**   This saying was written by BENJAMIN FRANKLIN in *Poor Richard's Almanack*.

**Every cloud has a silver lining**   There is something good in every misfortune.

**Fish out of water**   You can feel awkward when you are out of your familiar environment.

**A fool and his money are soon parted**   Foolish people spend their money as soon as they get it.

**A friend in need is a friend indeed**   Someone who helps us when we are in trouble is a real friend.

**God helps those who help themselves** Don't expect to get what you want without working hard for it yourself.

**The grass is always greener on the other side** Some people are never satisfied with what they have; they always think that others are more fortunate.

**Great oaks from little acorns grow** Great things or great people often have humble beginnings.

**Half a loaf is better than none** To have something is better than to have nothing at all.

**Haste makes waste** If you do something too quickly, you will make even more work for yourself.

**He who hesitates is lost** A person who spends too much time thinking about what to do misses the chance to act at all.

**He who laughs last laughs best** People may be laughed at when they try to achieve a goal, but when they succeed, they will be able to laugh at those who laughed at them.

**Hitch your wagon to a star** Aim high; hope for great things. This advice was written by the American poet and essayist RALPH WALDO EMERSON.

**If at first you don't succeed, try, try again** Never give up.

**If the shoe fits, wear it** If a description of you is true, then you must accept it—even if you don't like it.

**If wishes were horses, then beggars would ride** If wishing could make things happen, we would all have everything we wanted.

**Laugh, and the world laughs with you; weep, and you weep alone** Most people would rather be around happy people than sad ones; so happy people have many friends, and sad people are often alone.

**A leopard cannot change his spots** People cannot change their basic nature—that is, the way they are deep inside.

**Let bygones be bygones** Don't hold grudges; let past offenses stay in the past.

**Lightning never strikes twice in the same place** Good luck or bad luck never comes to the same person twice in exactly the same way. (In the actual world, lightning *can* strike twice in the same place.)

**Little strokes fell great oaks** Persistent effort can accomplish great things, just as a person can chop down even the largest tree by staying at the task long enough.

**Live and learn** We should learn from our mistakes.

**Live and let live** We should live the way we choose and allow others to do the same.

**Look before you leap** We should know what we are getting into before we act.

**Make hay while the sun shines** When you have a chance to do something, do it; you will not have the chance forever.

**Many hands make light work** Large tasks become easier when they are divided among several people.

**Mind your p's and q's** Be on your best behavior. This saying is taken from a teacher's warning to keep handwriting neat by not mixing up the lowercase letters *p* and *q*.

**A miss is as good as a mile** If you fail at a task, it doesn't matter if you almost succeeded; losing a game by one point is still losing.

**Money is the root of all evil** Most wrongdoing occurs because people are greedy for money and the things it will buy. This saying is taken from the NEW TESTAMENT, which says, "For the love of money is the root of all evils" (1 Timothy 6:10).

**The more the merrier** If many people take part in something, it will be more fun than if just a few participate. This saying is often used to welcome people who would like to join in an activity.

**Necessity is the mother of invention** When people really need something, they will think of a way to get it.

**It's never over till it's over** Until a competition (such as a game or an election) has come to an end, you can never predict the winner. Things can always change at the last minute. This proverb also appears as "It's not over till it's over."

**Never put off till tomorrow what you can do today** Don't put off doing the things you have to do.

**It's never too late to mend** It's never too late to change your ways.

**Nothing will come of nothing** You won't gain anything if you don't contribute or do your part. This proverb from ancient times was used by WILLIAM SHAKESPEARE in his play *King Lear.*

**Once bitten, twice shy** If you've done something that has made you suffer, you will avoid doing it in the future, just as you would shy away from an animal that had bitten you.

**One rotten apple spoils the whole barrel** One bad person can ruin a larger group of people.

**An ounce of prevention is worth a pound of cure** It's better to make the small effort to plan ahead so that things don't go wrong rather than do a lot of fixing up afterward. Another proverb that expresses the same idea is "A STITCH IN TIME SAVES NINE."

**A penny saved is a penny earned** Money not spent is money in one's pocket.

**A picture is worth a thousand words** A visual image can give people a better sense of something than the written word.

**A place for everything and everything in its place** Things should be kept in order.

**Practice makes perfect** Doing something over and over makes one better at it.

**Practice what you preach** You yourself should follow the advice you give others.

**Procrastination is the thief of time** Putting off doing something makes us lose valuable time. Procrastination is a "thief" because it "steals" time away from us.

**The proof of the pudding is in the eating** If you want to find out if something is good, you must try it yourself.

**The road to hell is paved with good intentions** Good intentions don't matter if wicked actions result. People should be judged by their actions, not their intentions.

**Rome wasn't built in a day** It takes a long time to achieve anything worthwhile.

**Seeing is believing** This proverb is usually said when you doubt a thing is true, but you will believe it when it is shown to be true.

**The show must go on** People are counting on us to do this, and we must not disappoint them. This proverb is an old show business saying, meaning that nothing must stop a performance from going on as scheduled.

**A stitch in time saves nine** It's easier to take precautions rather than try to fix things after they go wrong (just as, by putting a single stitch in a garment, a person may prevent a tear that would take nine stitches to close). The same idea is expressed in the proverb "AN OUNCE OF PREVENTION IS WORTH A POUND OF CURE."

**Strike while the iron is hot** You should act on an opportunity as soon as it arises, just as a blacksmith shapes iron by striking it with his hammer when it is red hot.

**There's more than one way to skin a cat** There are usually several ways to accomplish a particular task.

**There's no place like home** One's home is the best place to be.

**Time heals all wounds** As time passes, people get over insults, injuries, and hatreds.

**Truth is stranger than fiction** Sometimes the things that happen in real life are stranger than the things that take place in imaginary stories.

**Two heads are better than one** Some problems can be solved more easily by two people working together than by one person working alone.

**Two wrongs don't make a right** A wrongdoing shouldn't be answered by more wrongdoing. For example, if someone hurts you in some way, that doesn't mean that it's right for you to be hurtful in return.

**Waste not, want not** If we don't waste the things we have, we won't lack ("want") the things we need.

**A watched pot never boils** When we impatiently wait for something to happen, it seems to take forever.

**Well begun is half done** Getting off to a good start on some task means that you've already accomplished a lot.

**What will be, will be** Some things will happen no matter what we do, so we should accept life as it comes. This proverb appears in Spanish as *Lo que será, será* and in Italian as *Che sarà, sarà.*

**When in Rome, do as the Romans do** You should adapt yourself to the ways of the people around you.

**When it rains, it pours** When bad luck comes, it seems that a lot of bad things happen at once.

**Where there's a will, there's a way** If you really want to do something, you will find a way to accomplish it.

**You can lead a horse to water, but you can't make him drink** You can give someone an opportunity, but you can't make him take advantage of it.

**You can't teach an old dog new tricks** A person who has had one way of doing something for a long time won't want to do it any other way.

# Idioms

An idiom is a special word or phrase that always appears in a particular form. Many idioms use metaphors or comparisons to make simple ideas more vivid. For instance, to say "You're making a mountain out of a molehill" is a more interesting way of saying, "You're exaggerating." In the same way, "Let's take the bull by the horns" is a more vivid way of saying, "Let's face this problem."

It is important to remember that an idiom always appears in the same basic form. No one says, "Make a mountain out of an *ant*hill" or "Take the *cow* by the horns."

**aka** (ay-kay-ay)  *Aka* is an abbreviation that means "also known as." For example: "Clark Kent, aka Superman."

**as the crow flies**  "As the crow flies" describes the straightest, most direct route between two places. "It takes an hour to drive from Jonestown to Hamilton, though it's only twenty miles as the crow flies."

**back to the drawing board**  When someone says, "Back to the drawing board," it means that he or she has failed at a task and has to start all over again. "The boat we built sank as soon as we put it in the water, so I guess it's back to the drawing board."

**his bark is worse than his bite**  If a person sounds harsh or mean but does not really act that way, we say that "his bark is worse than his bite," which is the way some dogs behave. "Although Dad sounded angry when we came in late, I don't think he'll punish us. His bark is worse than his bite."

**beat around the bush**  When you're talking seriously with someone who keeps changing the subject or won't come to the point, that person is probably "beating around the bush." "I wish you'd stop beating around the bush and tell me what you think of my story."

**bee in his bonnet**  Someone who has a "bee in his bonnet" is always complaining about one particular thing. "Mr. Turner has a bee in his bonnet about kids who skate on the sidewalk."

**Between a rock and a hard place**  Someone who is faced with two difficult choices or situations is said to be "between a rock and a hard place."

**birthday suit**  When you are "in your birthday suit" you are completely naked (as you were when you were born). "Please close the door while I change into my swimming trunks. I don't want anyone to see me in my birthday suit."

**bite the dust** When someone is defeated or killed, he or she is said to "bite the dust." "Our soccer team is still undefeated. Every team we've played this year has bitten the dust."

**bite the hand that feeds you** When you attack someone who has been helping or supporting you, you may be said to "bite the hand that feeds you." "When Rita started criticizing her boss, I said, 'Don't bite the hand that feeds you.'"

**blow hot and cold** If you're constantly changing your mind about something, you're "blowing hot and cold." "First Mom said I could go to the party; then she said I couldn't. I wish she'd stop blowing hot and cold."

**break the ice** When people are shy or tense in a situation and something happens to make them feel more comfortable, it is said to "break the ice," just as the ice on rivers has to be broken to let ships get through in the winter. "It really broke the ice when Nate and I found out we both love stamp collecting."

**bull in a china shop** Someone who deals with a situation awkwardly or clumsily is said to be a "bull in a china shop." "I don't want my brother to help with our project—he's like a bull in a china shop."

**bury the hatchet** When you "bury the hatchet," you agree to end a quarrel or fight. "Oscar and Kevin have been avoiding each other since their argument, but I saw them together this morning, so they must have buried the hatchet."

**can't hold a candle to** When something "can't hold a candle to" something else, it is not nearly as good. "The other school may have a better football team, but their marching band can't hold a candle to ours."

**catch-as-catch-can** In a "catch-as-catch-can" situation, you must make do or get along with what you have. "We don't have enough textbooks for all the students, so it'll be catch-as-catch-can."

**chip on one's shoulder** Someone who has a "chip on his shoulder" is very touchy. "Joe really has a chip on his shoulder. Whenever I speak to him, he takes it the wrong way." In the past, a young boy would place a wood chip on his shoulder and dare anyone to knock it off as a way of showing how tough he was.

**clean bill of health** If you are given a "clean bill of health," you have been told you are perfectly healthy. "Margaret just had a checkup, and the doctor gave her a clean bill of health."

**cold feet** To have "cold feet" is to change your mind about doing something because it now seems unwise or dangerous. "I was going to compete in the race but got cold feet."

**the cold shoulder** Someone who deliberately avoids you is giving you "the cold shoulder." "At the party Isabel tried to talk to Will, but he gave her the cold shoulder."

**crocodile tears** A person who acts sad but does not really mean it is shedding "crocodile tears." This idiom comes from a legend that says crocodiles weep before they eat their victims. "You're not really sorry for Jean. You're just shedding crocodile tears."

**easier said than done** If you are advised to do something that is very difficult, you might say that it's "easier said than done." "The doctor told my father to lose thirty pounds, but that's easier said than done."

**eat crow** You "eat crow" when you have to take back something you once said. "The captain of the other team bragged that he would crush us. After we beat them, he was forced to eat crow."

**eat someone out of house and home** Someone who eats a great deal of food may be said to "eat you out of house and home." "Mrs. Goldstein complained that her three teenagers were eating her out of house and home."

**eleventh hour** The "eleventh hour" is the latest possible time—just before 12—at which something may be done. "The water bombers arrived at the eleventh hour just in time to keep the forest fire from spreading to the town."

**Eureka!** "Eureka!" is a Greek word that means "I have found it!" "When I finally found the quotation after looking through all those books, I yelled, 'Eureka!' "

**a feather in your cap** "A feather in your cap" is an accomplishment to be proud of. "I'm glad Maria won that science award. It's a real feather in her cap."

**few and far between** Things that are "few and far between" are very scarce. "Gas stations are few and far between for the next hundred miles, so make sure you have plenty of gas."

**first come, first served** "First come, first served" means that the people who arrive first will be waited on first. "The ad for the tickets said that it would be first come, first served, so we got in line early."

**fish out of water** When you are someplace you feel you don't belong, you may feel like a "fish out of water." "Everyone at the party was so much older than we were, I really felt like a fish out of water."

**follow your nose** When you "follow your nose," you're using instinct or common sense. "The job isn't complicated; just follow your nose."

**for the birds** Something that is "for the birds" is worthless. "That boring movie was for the birds."

**forgive and forget** When you "forgive and forget," you refuse to hold a grudge against someone. "They are still good friends because Barb was willing to forgive and forget."

**forty winks** "Forty winks" means a nap or a brief sleep during the day. "I want to grab forty winks. Please wake me up in half an hour."

**get a taste of one's own medicine** Someone who treats others badly and then gets treated the same way is "getting a taste of his own medicine." "Mark got a taste of his own medicine when everyone started playing practical jokes on him."

**get up on the wrong side of the bed** Someone who seems grouchy for no particular reason is said to have "gotten up on the wrong side of the bed." "Mr. Murphy has been in a bad mood all day. He must have gotten up on the wrong side of the bed this morning."

**give the devil his due** When you "give the devil his due," you are giving credit to an opponent. "I disagree with everything Henry says, but to give the devil his due, he is a good debater."

**go to pot** If something "goes to pot," it decays or becomes rundown. "It was sad to see how our old clubhouse had gone to pot."

**hit the nail on the head** When you "hit the nail on the head," you have gone straight to the heart of a matter. "Nancy hit the nail on the head when she said that my sister is a better student than I am."

**in hot water** When you are in deep trouble, you are "in hot water." "When Peter failed the math test, he knew he would be in hot water with his folks."

**keep your fingers crossed** People who hope that nothing will happen to ruin their plans are said to "keep their fingers crossed." "Anna will find out tomorrow whether she was chosen for the school play. In the meantime, she's keeping her fingers crossed."

**kill two birds with one stone** When you "kill two birds with one stone," you accomplish two goals with one action. "If we can buy gas and have lunch at the next rest stop, we will kill two birds with one stone."

**land of Nod**   When you go to the "land of Nod," you fall asleep. "The principal's speech was so boring that half the students went to the land of Nod." The land of Nod was a real region mentioned in the Bible, but this idiom just plays with that name, because "nod" is what your head does when you fall asleep.

**the last straw**   "The last straw" is also referred to as "the straw that broke the camel's back." It is the last in a series of problems that finally forces you to lose patience. "I've had nothing but trouble since I joined the football team, and now I've sprained my knee! Well, that's the last straw: I quit!"

**let the cat out of the bag**   When you "let the cat out of the bag," you reveal a secret. "We planned a surprise party for José, but someone let the cat out of the bag." In early America or EUROPE, a dishonest person might offer to sell someone a pig (a valuable farm animal) in a bag but put a cat in the bag instead. Someone who let the cat out would be revealing the deception.

**lock, stock, and barrel**   "Lock, stock, and barrel" means everything or the whole thing. "The store looks completely different since I shopped there last; they've changed it lock, stock, and barrel." The three items in this idiom are the parts of an old type of rifle.

**make a mountain out of a molehill**   When you "make a mountain out of a molehill," you act as if something is very important when actually it is trivial. "You shouldn't call your sister a thief because she borrowed one of your shirts. You're making a mountain out of a molehill."

**make ends meet**   When you "make ends meet," you are earning enough money to provide for your basic needs. "Since my father lost his job, we can barely make ends meet."

**money burning a hole in your pocket**   If you have money that you can't wait to spend, you can say that it's "burning a hole in your pocket." "The day I got my allowance, I rushed down to the bookstore with the money burning a hole in my pocket."

**nose out of joint**   When your "nose is out of joint," you're annoyed because someone else is in the limelight or you feel unappreciated. "Bill's nose is out of joint because his brother Tim made the baseball team and he didn't."

**off the cuff**   If you say something "off the cuff," you have spoken without thinking too hard about it. "Off the cuff, I'd say we ate about two dozen apples."

**old hat**   If something is "old hat," it is old-fashioned or out of date. "Mom, those clothes are old hat!"

**on its last legs**   Something that is "on its last legs" is almost worn out. "I wouldn't bother to repair that bicycle; it's on its last legs."

**on tenterhooks**   Someone who is "on tenterhooks" is nervously awaiting news. "When we heard about the accident, we were on tenterhooks until we knew that David was all right." Tenterhooks were a kind of hook used long ago in cloth making; wet wool would be stretched on tenterhooks and left to dry.

**on the warpath**   Someone who is "on the warpath" is very angry and inclined to take some hostile action. "Watch out! Alicia just heard that her vacation plans were canceled and she's on the warpath today."

**once in a blue moon**   When you do something "once in a blue moon," you do it very rarely. "Sarah writes to me only once in a blue moon."

**out of the frying pan into the fire**   When you go "out of the frying pan into the fire," you're going from a bad situation to one that is even worse. "It was bad enough that Mrs. Norris scolded me, but now that I have to go see the principal it's out of the frying pan into the fire."

**the pot calling the kettle black**  A person who criticizes someone else for the very faults he or she possesses is "the pot calling the kettle black." "Jeff says Emily talks too much, but he's never quiet himself. It's the pot calling the kettle black." When this idiom first appeared, all pots and kettles were black because they were made of blackened iron.

**raining cats and dogs**  When it's "raining cats and dogs," it's raining very hard. "We wanted to play outdoors, but now it's raining cats and dogs."

**read between the lines**  When you "read between the lines," you try to figure out what somebody really means. "You can't take everything Hannah says literally. You have to read between the lines."

**rule of thumb**  A "rule of thumb" is an inexact but useful rule for doing something. "As a rule of thumb, figure three cookies per person when you are planning the picnic."

**rule the roost**  A person who dominates a group of people may be said to "rule the roost." "Even though she's the youngest child, Gracie really rules the roost in her family."

**run-of-the-mill**  "Run-of-the-mill" means common, ordinary, or average. "The food at our school isn't bad, but it isn't great, either; it's run-of-the-mill cafeteria food."

**shipshape**  "Shipshape" means very neat and tidy, the way that sailors must keep a ship. "His mother warned him that he couldn't go out until his room was shipshape."

**sit on the fence**  When you "sit on the fence," you refuse to take sides in some argument. "You can't sit on the fence forever.

Sooner or later you'll have to make a choice."

**sour grapes**  When you want something and don't get it and then pretend that what you wanted was no good, you are like the fox who called the grapes sour when he couldn't reach them in Aesop's fable "The Fox and the Grapes." "When Eric said that running was a silly sport after he lost the race, it was just sour grapes."

**steal someone's thunder**  When someone is planning to do something impressive and you do it first, you are "stealing that person's thunder." "Dad was planning to tell us about the vacation plans at dinner, but Mom was so excited that she told us first and stole his thunder."

**take the bull by the horns**  When you "take the bull by the horns," you face up to a difficult situation. "You can't always run away from your problems; sometimes you just have to take the bull by the horns."

**tempest in a teapot**  A "tempest in a teapot" is a big fuss that is made over something unimportant. "Herman is throwing a fit because he can't go to the movies tonight. It's just a tempest in a teapot."

**tenderfoot**  A "tenderfoot" is a beginner. "Chris may have made a few mistakes on the job, but he's only a tenderfoot."

**through thick and thin**  When you stay with someone "through thick and thin," you stay loyal to that person no matter what happens. "She stood beside her friend through thick and thin."

**till the cows come home**  If you do something "till the cows come home," you do it for a long time. "Mr. Rowland said that as far as he was concerned, the students could stay there washing blackboards till the cows came home." The idiom originally meant until the early morning hours, when the cows would come to the gate to be milked.

**Timbuktu**  Timbuktu, a city in Africa, is sometimes used to mean a faraway place. "Mr. Carver wants to stay in this area, but he's afraid that his company will send him to Timbuktu."

**tit for tat**  When you give "tit for tat," you are giving back exactly what you receive. "If you support me I'll support you; it's tit for tat."

**Tom, Dick, and Harry**  "Tom, Dick, and Harry" means everyone or just anyone. "I asked you to keep my plans secret, but you've told them to every Tom, Dick, and Harry."

**touch and go**  A "touch and go" situation is dangerous or uncertain. "The hockey season is almost over, but the outcome is still touch and go."

**turn over a new leaf**  Someone who begins anew or changes his or her ways is said to "turn over a new leaf." "Since he was grounded, Larry has turned over a new leaf and does his homework every night."

**wolf in sheep's clothing**  A "wolf in sheep's clothing" is a person who seems kind or friendly but is in fact the opposite. "Dan seems nice, but I think he's really a wolf in sheep's clothing." The reference is taken from one of AESOP'S FABLES, the story of a wolf who puts on a sheepskin in order to fool the sheep it wants to eat.

# English

In order to express and explain your ideas, you must be able to write good, clear English. Writing and speaking well involve knowing the rules of grammar, spelling, and punctuation. Only by following these rules can you communicate your ideas effectively. If you want to write well, you need to practice often and show your writing to other people for their advice. Here we explain some of the terms you should be familiar with in order to learn the rules of written English.

**abbreviation** An abbreviation is a shortened form of a word and is usually followed by a PERIOD. For instance, *Mr.* is the abbreviation of *Mister*; *Jan.* is the abbreviation of *January*.

**adjective** An adjective is a PART OF SPEECH that modifies (acts upon or describes) a NOUN or PRONOUN. In these PHRASES, the words in italics are adjectives: the *red* raincoat; a *shy* boy; the *next* street; *those* apples.

**adverb** An adverb is a PART OF SPEECH that modifies (acts upon) a VERB, an ADJECTIVE, or another adverb and often ends in *ly*. In these examples, the words in italics are adverbs:

Sam works *quickly*.
(*Quickly* modifies the verb *works*.)

My father drives *carefully*.
(*Carefully* modifies the verb *drives*.)

The trees look *very* old.
(*Very* modifies the adjective *old*.)

Please speak *more softly*.
(*More* modifies the adverb *softly*, and *softly* modifies the verb *speak*.)

**agreement** In every SENTENCE, the SUBJECT must agree with (or match up with) the VERB. A SINGULAR subject takes a singular verb, and a PLURAL subject takes a plural verb. For instance, the following sentence is wrong because the verb and subject do not agree:

My grandparents *is* coming to visit us.

It should read:

My grandparents *are* coming to visit us.

In addition, a PRONOUN must always agree with the NOUN it refers to. A singular noun takes a singular pronoun, and a plural noun takes a plural pronoun. For instance, the example that follows is wrong because the noun and pronoun do not agree:

Each boy will have to buy *their* own uniform.

It should read:

Each boy will have to buy *his* own uniform.

A pronoun must also agree with its function as a SUBJECT or OBJECT in a sentence:

*They* (subject) praised *them* (object) for singing.

**alliteration** (uh-lit-uh-RAY-shuhn) Alliteration is the repetition of the same sound, usually at the beginning of words. "Peter Piper picked a peck of pickled peppers" is an example of alliteration.

**antonyms** Antonyms are words of opposite meaning. For example, *cold* and *hot* are antonyms. *Compare* SYNONYMS.

**apostrophe** An apostrophe is a PUNCTUATION MARK ['] used with a NOUN and some PRONOUNS to indicate possession:

Sarah's book
my mother's car
anyone's guess

An apostrophe is also used to indicate missing letters in a CONTRACTION, as in these examples:

Paul can't come to the phone right now.
I'm getting impatient with you.

*See also* POSSESSIVE.

**article** The words *the, a,* and *an* are called articles. *The* is the *definite article* because it refers to specific (or definite) items:

Look at *the* boats.
*The* apples look good.

*A* and *an* are *indefinite articles* because they refer to any one of a general group of items:

My father wants to buy *a* boat.
Give me *an* apple. (*An* is used before a VOWEL.)

**auxiliary verb** When a PHRASE has more than one VERB, one is the main verb and the others are auxiliary, or helping, verbs. In the examples that follow, the auxiliary verbs are in italics:

The show *will* start in ten minutes.
Gail *should have* won that race.

**bibliography** A bibliography is a list of books and articles on a particular subject. For instance, if you wanted to read about the CIVIL WAR, you would find titles of works on the subject listed in a bibliography on the Civil War.

**capital letter** A capital letter indicates the beginning of a SENTENCE or a PROPER NOUN. In the examples that follow, the capital letters are in italics:

*S*tudents should not throw food in the cafeteria.
*M*artin *F*isher moved here from *T*oledo.

Capital letters are also called uppercase letters. *Compare* LOWERCASE LETTER.

**clause** A clause is a group of words that contains a SUBJECT and a PREDICATE. A SENTENCE may contain one or more clauses. Some clauses can stand alone as sentences: *Alfred caught the biggest fish.* Other clauses cannot stand alone: *Because he caught the biggest fish,* Alfred won the trophy. A clause that can stand alone as a sentence is called an *independent clause.* A clause that cannot stand alone as a sentence is called a *dependent clause.*

**colon** A colon is a PUNCTUATION MARK [:] used to introduce a list, a description, or an example:

She wanted only one present for her birthday: a new bicycle.
Before the camping trip, I had to buy several things: a backpack, a pocketknife, a canteen, and some boots.

**comma** A comma is a PUNCTUATION MARK [,] that separates the parts of a SENTENCE and indicates where to pause when reading a sentence:

First we'll go to the zoo, and then the bus will take us to the museum.

Commas are also used in dates and place names:

July 4, 1776, is the official birthday of the United States.
Paris, France, is known for the Eiffel Tower.

**conjunction** A conjunction is a word that joins words or groups of words, such as *and, but, or,* and *because.*

**consonants** The alphabet contains two kinds of letters, VOWELS and consonants. The letters that follow are vowels:

*a, e, i, o, u*

These letters are consonants:

*b, c, d, f, g, h, j, k, l, m, n, p, q, r, s, t, v, w, x, z*

The letter *y* is sometimes a vowel, as in *goodbye,* and sometimes a consonant, as in *yo-yo.*

**contraction** A contraction is one word made up of two words that have been shortened. For instance, *I'm* is a contraction of *I am; shouldn't* is a contraction of *should not.* An APOSTROPHE shows where letters or sounds have been left out.

**declarative sentence** A declarative sentence makes a statement or declares something. The sentences that follow are declarative:

He loves ice cream.
That is the new train station.
My mother will be coming home soon.

*Compare* IMPERATIVE SENTENCE; INTERROGATIVE SENTENCE.

**definite article** *See* ARTICLE.

**dependent clause** *See* CLAUSE.

**direct object** The NOUN that directly receives the action of a VERB in a sentence is called the direct object. In the sentences that follow, the direct objects are in italics:

Roger is eating *lunch.*
Karen threw the *ball* to Joe.

*Compare* INDIRECT OBJECT.

**exclamation** An exclamation is a word or SENTENCE that expresses excitement or gives a command:

Hey!
Help!
Let's go!
Get away from the fire!

**exclamation point** An exclamation point is the PUNCTUATION MARK [!] that comes at the end of an EXCLAMATION.

**grammar** Grammar is the study of the structure of language. It also refers to the rules of correct writing and speaking.

**helping verb** *See* AUXILIARY VERB.

**homonyms** (HOM-uh-nimz) Homonyms are words that sound alike, and may even be spelled alike, but have different meanings. *Trunk* (of an elephant) and *trunk* (a storage chest) are homonyms. *Deer* (a hoofed animal) and *dear* (a sweet person) are also homonyms.

**imperative sentence** An imperative sentence requests or commands someone to do something. The following sentences are imperative:

Come to the blackboard.
Please turn off the light.

*Compare* DECLARATIVE SENTENCE; INTERROGATIVE SENTENCE.

**indefinite article** *See* ARTICLE.

**independent clause** *See* CLAUSE; SEMICOLON.

**indirect object** When a VERB has more than one OBJECT, the NOUN that *directly* receives the action of the verb is called the DIRECT OBJECT. The NOUN that *indirectly* receives the action is called the indirect object. In the following sentences, the direct object is in italics and the indirect object is in boldface:

Throw the *ball* to **him.**
Throw **him** the *ball.*
He gave **Jennifer** the *ticket.*

**interjection** An interjection is a brief EX-CLAMATION, often containing only one word. Ouch! Hey! and Gosh! are interjections.

**interrogative sentence** An interrogative sentence asks a question:

Can Janet come along?
Have you read that book?

*Compare* DECLARATIVE SENTENCE; IMPERATIVE SENTENCE.

**irregular verb** In English, verbs that add *ed* in the past tense are called REGULAR VERBS. For instance, *walk* is a regular verb because it becomes *walked* in the past tense. Verbs that do not add *ed* in the past tense are called irregular verbs. Below are some irregular verbs, listed first in the present and then in the past tense:

swim    swam
teach    taught
fly    flew
feel    felt

**italics** Italics are a special kind of type used to set off a particular word or group of words. *Italics look like this.* The titles of books, magazines, and newspapers are often printed in italics.

**linking verb** A linking verb is a verb that connects or identifies the SUBJECT of a sentence with the PREDICATE. *Are* and *seem* are linking verbs in the following sentences:

The students *are* busy.
You *seem* tired.

**lowercase letter** A lowercase letter is a small (not capital) letter. For instance, all the letters in this sentence except the first letter ("F") are lowercase. *Compare* CAPITAL LETTER.

**modifier** A modifier is a word that acts upon, or tells about, another word. ADJECTIVES and ADVERBS are modifiers.

**nominative case** The nominative case in GRAMMAR indicates that a NOUN or PRONOUN is the SUBJECT of a VERB. In the sentences *The children played softball* and *I visited them last Friday*, the words *children* and *I* are in the nominative case.

**noun** A noun is a PART OF SPEECH that names a person, place, thing, or idea, such as cat, child, river, knife, friendship. *See also* PROPER NOUN.

**object** The NOUN, PRONOUN, or group of words that receives the action of a VERB is called the object of the verb. *See also* DIRECT OBJECT; INDIRECT OBJECT.

**objective case** The objective case in GRAMMAR indicates that a NOUN or PRONOUN is the OBJECT of a VERB in a SENTENCE or CLAUSE or that it is the object of a PREPOSITION. In the sentences *The children played softball* and *I visited them at home last Friday*, the words *softball, them,* and *home* are in the objective case.

**onomatopoeia** (ON-uh-mat-uh-PEE-uh) Onomatopoeia is the use of words that sound like what they describe, as in the *buzz* of a bee or the *hiss* of a snake.

**paragraph** A paragraph is a group of SENTENCES organized around a main idea. Most writing is broken up into paragraphs. The first line of a paragraph is usually indented (moved to the right) to indicate that a new paragraph has started.

**parentheses** Parentheses are PUNCTUATION MARKS ( ) that set off certain words inside a SENTENCE. They may contain helpful information: "Aunt Sarah (my mother's sister) will visit us over the holidays."

**parts of speech** In GRAMMAR, a part of speech is a class of words that have the same grammatical function: NOUNS, VERBS, ADJECTIVES, ADVERBS, PRONOUNS, ARTICLES, PREPOSITIONS, CONJUNCTIONS, and INTERJECTIONS.

**period** A period is a PUNCTUATION MARK [.] that comes at the end of an ABBREVIATION or a SENTENCE.

**person** Every PERSONAL PRONOUN is in the first, the second, or the third person. The first-person pronouns (*I, me, we,* and *us*) refer to the person or persons who are speaking. The second-person pronoun (*you*) refers to the person who is being spoken to. The third-person pronouns (*he, him, she, her, it, they,* and *them*) refer to the persons or things being discussed.

**personal pronoun** Personal pronouns represent a PERSON or persons in a sentence. They are: *I, me, we, us, you, he, him, she, her, it, they,* and *them. See also* PERSON.

**phrase** A phrase is a group of related words that cannot stand alone as a SENTENCE, such as: a flock of birds; Mr. Hayakawa's class; crossing the street; on top of the refrigerator. Unlike a CLAUSE, a phrase does not have both a SUBJECT and a PREDICATE.

**plural** NOUNS, PRONOUNS, and VERBS have both SINGULAR and plural forms. The singular form refers to only one thing, while the plural form refers to more than one thing. *See also* AGREEMENT.

**possessive** The possessive form of a NOUN or PRONOUN shows who owns (or possesses) something. SINGULAR nouns become possessive when they add an apostrophe followed by an *s*:

She borrowed her friend's tennis racket.

Plural nouns that already end in *s* become possessive by adding an apostrophe:

Those are the students' books.

**predicate** Every SENTENCE contains a SUBJECT and a predicate. The subject is a NOUN or a group of words that tells what the sentence is about. The predicate contains a VERB and sometimes a group of words related to the verb. It describes something about the subject. In the following sentences, the sub-ject is in italics and the predicate is in bold-face:

*The bell* **rang.**
*Pigs* **are intelligent.**
*My father* **couldn't find a parking place.**

**prefix** A prefix is one or more letters added to the beginning of a word to change its meaning. In the following words, the prefixes are in italics: *un*happy, *dis*qualify, *pre*school, *mis*understood, *over*eat, *post*script, *sub*terranean, *ultra*modern. *Compare* SUFFIX.

**preposition** A preposition is a PART OF SPEECH that shows how a particular word is related to other words in a SENTENCE. Common prepositions include: *at, in, into, on, by, from, for, to,* and *with.*

**prepositional phrase** A prepositional phrase is a PHRASE that includes a PREPOSITION and its OBJECT. In the sentence *The book was written by her, by her* is a prepositional phrase, where *by* is the preposition and *her* is its object.

**pronoun** A pronoun is the PART OF SPEECH that can take the place of a NOUN in a SENTENCE. The following words are all pronouns: *he, you, ours, herself, what, that, who,* and *which. See also* PERSONAL PRONOUN.

**proper noun** A proper noun is the name of a unique person, place, or thing. Proper nouns are capitalized, as in *Abraham Lincoln, Los Angeles,* and *World War I.*

**punctuation marks** Punctuation marks are standard signs used in writing to clarify the meaning. The most important punctuation marks are the PERIOD, the COMMA, QUOTATION MARKS, the COLON, the SEMICOLON, the QUESTION MARK, and the EXCLAMATION POINT.

**question mark** A question mark is a PUNCTUATION MARK [?] used at the end of a question.

**quotation marks** Quotation marks are double PUNCTUATION MARKS (" ") that set off dialogue, material quoted from another source, titles of short works such as poems, and definitions within a sentence. When something is quoted within a quotation, single quotation marks are used: "Mother said, 'Did you remember to brush your teeth?'"

**regular verb** A regular verb is a verb whose past tense is formed by adding *ed* to the present tense. For example, the verb *walk* becomes *walked* in the past tense, and the verb *open* becomes *opened*. Most verbs in English are regular verbs. *Compare* IRREGULAR VERB.

**semicolon** A semicolon is a PUNCTUATION MARK [;] that is used to join two independent CLAUSES: *Jim likes to run; Martha prefers swimming.*

**sentence** A sentence is a group of words that expresses a complete thought. Every sentence contains at least one SUBJECT and PREDICATE. *See also* DECLARATIVE SENTENCE; IMPERATIVE SENTENCE; INTERROGATIVE SENTENCE.

**singular** NOUNS, PRONOUNS, and VERBS have both singular and PLURAL forms. The singular form refers to only one thing, while the plural form refers to more than one thing. *See also* AGREEMENT.

**style** Style, when applied to writing, means the characteristic manner of the writing. Long or short SENTENCES, plain or fancy words, and serious or comic tones are some of the traits that define a writer's style.

**subject** Every SENTENCE contains a subject and a PREDICATE. The subject consists of the main NOUN (or a group of words acting like the main noun) and tells what the sentence is about. In the following sentences, the subject is in italics:

*My sister and her friends* joined the Girl Scouts.
*The river* looks too wide to swim across.

*Squirrels* are afraid of cats.
*Running* is good exercise.

**suffix** A suffix is one or more letters added to the end of a word to change its meaning. In the following words, the suffixes are in italics: disappoint*ment*, kind*ness*, machin*ist*, port*able*. *Compare* PREFIX.

**syllable** A syllable is the most basic part of a spoken word. It contains only one VOWEL sound. For example, the word *basic* is made up of two syllables: *ba-sic.*

**synonyms** Synonyms are words of similar meaning. For instance, *small* is a synonym of *little. Compare* ANTONYMS.

**tense** Tense is the form of a VERB that expresses when the action of the verb takes place. For example, in the sentence "He *runs,*" the verb is in the present tense. In the sentence "He *ran,*" the verb is in the past tense. In the sentence "He *will run,*" the verb is in the future tense.

**topic sentence** The most important sentence in a PARAGRAPH is the topic sentence because it states the main idea of the paragraph.

**uppercase letter** *See* CAPITAL LETTER.

**verb** A verb is a word that expresses action or a state of being. *Walk, fly, read, catch, turn, complain, grow, hold, smile, notice, play, decide, rattle, get,* and *release* are all action verbs. The verb *to be* expresses states of being; it tells what something *is* rather than what it *does.* Every sentence must contain (or imply) at least one verb. *See also* AUXILIARY VERB; LINKING VERB; IRREGULAR VERB; REGULAR VERB.

**vowels** The alphabet contains two kinds of letters, vowels and CONSONANTS. The letters *a, e, i, o,* and *u* are vowels. The letter *y* is sometimes a vowel, as in *try,* and sometimes a consonant, as in *your.* All the other letters in the alphabet are consonants.

# Literature

Literature is a category of writing that includes such works as novels, poems, and plays. The names of different literary works as well as terms that apply to them are listed and explained here.

Some of the works listed were written by well-known authors. Others, especially the stories we call folk tales, fairy tales, and fables and the children's poems known as nursery rhymes, have been handed down from generation to generation for so long that the original writer has been forgotten. All of these works have one thing in common, however: they have been read and remembered over many years for the stories they tell, the experiences they describe, and the wisdom they contain.

Included here are the literary works that people often refer to in writing and conversation. There is no substitute for reading literature in its original form or in a good translation. Many of the works mentioned below are useful and enjoyable to everyone.

**act** An act is a major division or part of a dramatic presentation, such as a PLAY or an OPERA. An act in a play can have many SCENES.

**Aesop's fables** (EE-sops, EE-suhps) Aesop's fables are stories thought to have been written by Aesop, a Greek storyteller who may have been a slave in the sixth century B.C. In many of the fables, animals are the main characters. They act like people, and their actions are used to teach a lesson, or moral, about human life. Two of Aesop's best-known fables are "THE FOX AND THE GRAPES" and "THE HARE AND THE TORTOISE."

**Aladdin's Lamp** Aladdin's Lamp is a magical lamp that appears in one of the stories of the ARABIAN NIGHTS. When Aladdin rubs the lamp, a magic spirit called a genie appears and offers to do anything that Aladdin asks. The genie makes Aladdin rich and powerful.

**Alcott, Louisa May** Louisa May Alcott was a popular American author of the 1800s who wrote novels for children, including LITTLE WOMEN and *Little Men*.

**Alger, Horatio** (hoh-RAY-shee-oh AL-jer) Horatio Alger was a nineteenth-century American author of more than 100 popular NOVELS. Most of his books were "rags-toriches stories" in which poor boys become wealthy through bravery and hard work.

**Ali Baba**  Ali Baba is a character in one of the stories of the ARABIAN NIGHTS. Ali is a poor man. One day he overhears a band of robbers enter a secret cave by saying, "Open, Sesame." When the robbers leave, Ali Baba repeats the magic words and enters the cave. He becomes rich by taking the treasure left by the thieves.

**Alice in Wonderland**  Alice appears in two books by LEWIS CARROLL. In the first book, *Alice's Adventures in Wonderland*, Alice falls down a rabbit hole and finds herself in Wonderland, where she meets the White Rabbit, the CHESHIRE CAT, the Mad Hatter, and the Queen of Hearts. In the second book, *Through the Looking-Glass*, Alice climbs through a looking glass, or mirror, to see what is on the other side. There she meets HUMPTY DUMPTY, the twins TWEEDLEDUM AND TWEEDLEDEE, and other characters.

**"All the world's a stage"**  A speech in the PLAY *As You Like It*, by WILLIAM SHAKE-SPEARE, begins, "All the world's a stage, and all the men and women merely players. . . ." This speech says that life is like a play—it lasts for only a short time, and people must try to play their parts well.

**Andersen, Hans Christian**  Hans Christian Andersen was a Danish author of the 1800s. He wrote many FAIRY TALES, such as "THE UGLY DUCKLING," "THE EMPEROR'S NEW CLOTHES," and "THE PRINCESS AND THE PEA."

**Androcles and the Lion**  (AN-druh-kleez) According to legend, Androcles, a Greek slave, escaped from his cruel master, but as he was running away, he stopped to remove a thorn from the paw of a lion. Some time later Androcles was caught and, as punishment, was sent into an arena before the emperor, to be attacked by a wild beast. The animal turned out to be the very lion he had helped, and it greeted him joyously.

**Angelou, Maya**  Maya Angelou is a modern writer known for her AUTOBIOGRAPHY, *I Know Why the Caged Bird Sings*, which recounts her experiences as a black girl growing up in the rural South.

***Animal Farm***  (1945) *Animal Farm* is a novel by the British writer George Orwell. It tells the story of farm animals who rebel against their tyrannical human masters, only to find that their new leaders, the pigs, are even more tyrannical. It includes the famous line "All animals are equal, but some animals are more equal than others."

***Arabian Nights***  The *Arabian Nights*, also known as *The Thousand and One Nights*, is a collection of old stories from India and the Middle East. According to legend, the stories were first told by Scheherezade (shuh-hair-uh-ZAHD), a sultan's wife. Some of the most familiar stories are about ALI BABA, ALADDIN'S LAMP, and SINBAD THE SAILOR.

**Arthur**  *See* KING ARTHUR.

**Austen, Jane**  Jane Austen was a British author of the late eighteenth and early nineteenth centuries. Her best-known works are the witty NOVELS *Pride and Prejudice, Sense and Sensibility*, and *Emma*. (*See* image, next page.)

**autobiography**  An autobiography is a book that tells the story of the author's own life. Some important autobiographies are *The Autobiography of Benjamin Franklin; The Story of My Life*, by HELEN KELLER; and *I Know Why the Caged Bird Sings*, by MAYA ANGELOU. *Compare* BIOGRAPHY.

**"Baa, Baa, Black Sheep"**  "Baa, Baa, Black Sheep" is a NURSERY RHYME:

Baa, baa, black sheep,
Have you any wool?
Yes, sir, yes, sir,
Three bags full;
One for my master,

**Jane Austen**

And one for my dame,
And one for the little boy
Who lives down the lane.

**Babar** Babar is an elephant in a series of children's books by the twentieth-century French writers and illustrators Jean de Brunhoff and his son, Laurent de Brunhoff.

**Baldwin, James** James Baldwin was an African-American writer of the twentieth century. His writings, mostly about the black experience in the United States, include the novel *Go Tell It on the Mountain*.

**"Beauty and the Beast"** "Beauty and the Beast" is a FAIRY TALE. Beauty is a young woman who is taken to live with the Beast, an ugly monster, in return for a favor he did for her father. Because the Beast is kind to her, Beauty eventually falls in love with him. Her love frees him from an evil spell.

He turns into a handsome prince, and they are married.

**Big Bad Wolf** The Big Bad Wolf is a character in the FAIRY TALE "THE THREE LITTLE PIGS." He threatens the little pigs by saying, "I'll huff, and I'll puff, and I'll blow your house down."

**biography** A biography is a book that tells the story of a person's life. Some good biographies are *Traitor: The Case of Benedict Arnold*, by Jean Fritz, and *Laura Ingalls Wilder: Growing Up in the Little House*, by Patricia Riley Giff. *Compare* AUTOBIOGRAPHY.

**"The Blind Men and the Elephant"** "The Blind Men and the Elephant" is a FABLE in which six blind men describe an elephant. Each one touches a different part of the elephant and says what he finds. But all they do is argue and argue, because no one will listen to the others. Each foolishly believes that his idea about the elephant is the only correct one.

**"The Boy Who Cried Wolf"** The boy who cried wolf is a character in one of AESOP'S FABLES. He is a shepherd boy who often tricked the people of his village by pretending that a wolf was attacking his sheep. The villagers came to help him chase away the wolf, only to find that he was lying. One day a wolf really did come. The boy ran to the village for help, but he had cried "Wolf!" so many times that nobody believed him, and the wolf ate his sheep.

**Brer Rabbit** Brer Rabbit is a character in the UNCLE REMUS stories by Joel Chandler Harris. He is a wily rabbit who outsmarts his rival, Brer Fox. (*Brer* means "brother.")

**Brontë, Charlotte and Emily** (BRON-tay) Charlotte and Emily Brontë were nineteenth-century British authors known for their dramatic NOVELS. Charlotte wrote *Jane Eyre*. Her sister, Emily, wrote *Wuthering Heights*.

**Brer Rabbit.** Brer Fox and Brer Rabbit.
Drawing by A. B. Frost.

**Camelot** Camelot was the place where KING ARTHUR and his KNIGHTS OF THE ROUND TABLE gathered.

**Captain Hook** In the story of PETER PAN, Captain Hook is an evil pirate whose hand has been bitten off by a crocodile and replaced by a hook.

**Carroll, Lewis** Lewis Carroll was the PEN NAME of a British writer of the late 1800s, Charles Lutwidge Dodgson. He is known for his books about ALICE IN WONDERLAND.

**"Casey at the Bat"** A poem by Ernest Lawrence Thayer. *See* "THERE IS NO JOY IN MUDVILLE."

***The Catcher in the Rye*** (1951) The NOVEL *The Catcher in the Rye* was written by American author J. D. Salinger. It tells the story of Holden Caulfield, a sensitive and re-

bellious teenager who runs away from his boarding school.

**Cervantes, Miguel de** (ser-VAHN-tayz) Miguel de Cervantes was a Spanish writer of the late 1500s and early 1600s. After serving in the military and following various other pursuits, he wrote his masterpiece, DON QUIXOTE.

**character** A character is any person, animal, or imaginary being who appears in works of FICTION (made-up, or imaginary, stories), such as NOVELS, POEMS, PLAYS, movies, cartoons and comic books, and television shows.

***Charlotte's Web*** (1952) The hugely popular children's NOVEL *Charlotte's Web* was written by American author E. B. White. Its SETTING is a barnyard in MAINE. It tells the story of a friendship between Charlotte, a clever spider, and Wilbur, a young pig.

**Cheshire Cat** (CHESH-uhr) The Cheshire Cat is one of the characters that Alice meets in Wonderland. He can make himself slowly disappear until all that can be seen is his big grin. *See also* ALICE IN WONDERLAND.

**Chicken Little** Chicken Little is a character in a children's story. One day she is hit on the head by an acorn that falls from a tree. She then tells the other animals that the sky is falling. The foolish animals set off to tell the king, but on the way they meet a clever fox, who catches them for his dinner.

***A Child's Garden of Verses*** (1885) *A Child's Garden of Verses* is a collection of poems by ROBERT LOUIS STEVENSON. It includes such popular rhymes as "Bed in Summer" and "My Shadow."

***A Christmas Carol*** (1843) *A Christmas Carol* is a book by CHARLES DICKENS that tells the story of Ebenezer SCROOGE, a mean old miser. Whenever someone wishes him a Merry Christmas, he says, "Bah, humbug." On Christmas Eve, Scrooge is haunted by three spirits who show him what an empty life he has led. Scrooge awakens on Christmas Day and becomes a generous and friendly man.

**"Cinderella"** "Cinderella" is a FAIRY TALE about a young girl who is badly treated by her stepmother and stepsisters. On the day of a ball (dance), Cinderella helps her stepsisters get ready but must stay at home herself. Later, Cinderella's fairy godmother appears and sends her to the ball, warning her that she must leave before midnight. That night, the prince falls in love with Cinderella, but at the first stroke of midnight she leaves, dropping one of her glass slippers in her haste. Soon after, the prince finds Cinderella, for hers is the only foot that will fit the slipper, and they are married.

**comedy** A comedy is a type of FICTION, whether a PLAY, story, or movie, that ends happily for the main CHARACTER and contains at least some humor.

**couplet** A couplet consists of two successive (one after the other) lines of VERSE that RHYME.

**Crane, Ichabod** Ichabod Crane is the tall, skinny schoolteacher in the story "THE LEGEND OF SLEEPY HOLLOW," by Washington Irving. *See also* HEADLESS HORSEMAN.

**Cullen, Countee** Countee Cullen was an African-American writer of the early 1900s and a prominent member of the HARLEM RENAISSANCE. His collections of verse include *Color* and *Copper Sun.*

***David Copperfield*** (1849–1850) *David Copperfield* is a novel by CHARLES DICKENS about David's life as a boy and young man. Many of the incidents in the book are based on Dickens's own life, especially his boyhood, when he had to go to work in a factory.

**Dickens, Charles** Charles Dickens was a British author of the 1800s who wrote many popular NOVELS and stories, including OLIVER TWIST, DAVID COPPERFIELD, *A Tale of Two Cities,* and A CHRISTMAS CAROL. His novels often deal with the problems of working-class people at the time of the INDUSTRIAL REVOLUTION.

**Dickinson, Emily** Emily Dickinson was an American poet of the 1800s whose verse is known for its short, simple lines, such as "I'm nobody! Who are you? / Are you nobody too?"

**Dr. Jekyll and Mr. Hyde** In a book called *The Strange Case of Dr. Jekyll and Mr. Hyde,* by ROBERT LOUIS STEVENSON, Dr. Jekyll is a kind doctor who develops a drug that changes him into an evil man called Mr. Hyde. A person who is sometimes kind and sometimes nasty may be said to have a Jekyll-and-Hyde personality.

***Don Quixote*** (kee-HOH-tay) *Don Quixote* is a novel by MIGUEL DE CERVANTES. Its hero, Don Quixote, has read so many stories about knights and their adventures that he begins to think he must travel about the world to fight evil and injustice. In his madness, he attacks a windmill, thinking it is a giant. He

**Emily Dickinson**

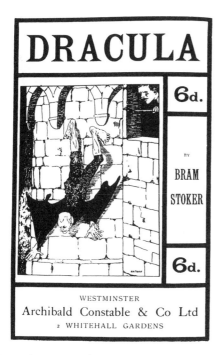

**Dracula.** A 1901 book jacket that shows Dracula climbing down his castle.

has many other comic adventures with his servant, SANCHO PANZA.

**Dracula**  Count Dracula is a vampire in a famous horror story by the nineteenth-century English author Bram Stoker. (A vampire is a dead person who comes out at night in search of human blood.) The vampire can be killed only by a wooden stake driven through its heart.

**Dunbar, Paul Laurence**  Paul Laurence Dunbar was a prominent nineteenth-century African-American poet. The title of MAYA ANGELOU's famous book, *I Know Why the Caged Bird Sings,* comes from one of his POEMS.

**elf**  An elf is a tiny, often mischievous creature, thought to have magical powers. Elves appear in many FAIRY TALES.

**Emerson, Ralph Waldo**  Ralph Waldo Emerson was an American thinker and writer of the 1800s. In his poem about the first battle of the REVOLUTIONARY WAR, "Concord Hymn," is the famous phrase "the shot heard round the world."

**"The Emperor's New Clothes"**  "The Emperor's New Clothes" is a story by HANS CHRISTIAN ANDERSEN about an emperor who loves to wear fine new clothes. Two swindlers tell him that they can make clothes out of a very unusual cloth that can be seen only by people who are very intelligent or very good at their jobs. The swindlers only pretend to make this cloth, so when the emperor puts on his new clothes and walks down the street, he is actually naked. Everyone acts as though he has on a fine new outfit until a child speaks up and says, "But he hasn't got any clothes on!"

**epic**  An epic is a long POEM that describes heroic deeds and adventures, such as the ILIAD and the ODYSSEY. HOMER, who wrote these epics, is called an epic poet.

**essay**  An essay is a short piece of writing, usually on one subject, that often presents the author's point of view. RALPH WALDO EMERSON wrote numerous essays.

**Excalibur**  (ek-SKAL-h-buhr) Excalibur is the name of KING ARTHUR's magic sword. According to one legend, the young knight Arthur proved he was worthy to be king when he pulled Excalibur out of a stone. According to another version of the story, Arthur received Excalibur from the LADY OF THE LAKE and returned it to her just before his death.

**fable**  A fable is a brief story that ends with a moral (a short message about how people should behave). *See also* AESOP'S FABLES.

**fairy**  A fairy is a tiny imaginary being in human form. Fairies are thought to have magical powers, as the fairy godmother does in "CINDERELLA."

**fairy tale**   A fairy tale is a story in which the HERO or HEROINE triumphs over adversity, often with the aid of a FAIRY or other supernatural creature. "CINDERELLA" is a fairy tale.

**Faulkner, William**   William Faulkner was an American author of the 1900s who wrote mostly about the American SOUTH. Two of his NOVELS are *The Sound and the Fury* and *As I Lay Dying*.

**fiction**   Fiction is a term that refers to imaginary stories about events that did not really happen as described. It can take the form of NOVELS, PLAYS, POETRY, or SHORT STORIES. *Compare* NONFICTION.

**folk tale**   A folk tale is a story that has been told by many generations of people before it is written down. Often the names of the people who made up the folk tales are not known. Many FAIRY TALES, such as "JACK AND THE BEANSTALK," are folk tales.

**"The Fox and the Grapes"**   "The Fox and the Grapes" is one of AESOP'S FABLES. A fox sees some grapes hanging from a vine, but he cannot reach them. He gives up, saying, "They were sour, anyway." This fable has given us the expression *sour grapes*, which refers to anything we criticize because it is something we want but cannot get.

***Frankenstein***   (1818) *Frankenstein* is a novel by the British author Mary Shelley about a scientist named Dr. Victor Frankenstein, who creates a monster that looks like a gigantic, hideous human being. The monster has human feelings and thoughts, but because he is so deformed he terrifies everyone who sees him. Today, people often use the name *Frankenstein* when they really mean *Frankenstein's monster*.

**free verse**   Free verse is POETRY that does not have a regular METER or RHYME SCHEME. WALT WHITMAN used free verse in poems such as "Song of Myself."

"The Fox and the Grapes"

**frog prince**   The frog prince is a CHARACTER in FAIRY TALES. In these stories, a frog is really a handsome prince who has been put under a spell. To break the spell, a beautiful lady must be kind to the frog or give it a kiss.

**Frost, Robert**   Robert Frost was an American poet of the 1900s who is best known for his verse about rural NEW ENGLAND. Two of his POEMS are "The Road Not Taken" and "Stopping by Woods on a Snowy Evening."

**Galahad, Sir**   Sir Galahad was the finest and most noble of KING ARTHUR'S knights. He was the only one who succeeded in the quest for the Holy Grail.

**"Georgie Porgie"**   "Georgie Porgie" is a NURSERY RHYME:

> Georgie Porgie, pudding and pie,
> Kissed the girls and made them cry;
> When the boys came out to play,
> Georgie Porgie ran away.

**Globe Theater** The Globe was a theater in LONDON, ENGLAND, during the early 1600s. WILLIAM SHAKESPEARE acted there, and many of his most famous plays were first presented on the theater's stage. In the late twentieth century, a copy of the theater was built near its original site.

**"God bless us, every one!"** "God bless us, every one!" is a line from CHARLES DICKENS's book *A CHRISTMAS CAROL*. The words are spoken at Christmas dinner by a young boy, Tiny Tim.

**"Goldilocks and the Three Bears"** "Goldilocks and the Three Bears" is a story about a little girl who visits the bears' house while they are out. She enjoys the little bear's porridge and eventually falls asleep in his bed. When the bears come home, the little bear sees Goldilocks asleep in his bed and says, "Somebody has been lying in my bed and here she is!" Goldilocks wakes up and runs all the way home.

***Gone with the Wind*** (1936) The NOVEL *Gone with the Wind* was written by American author Margaret Mitchell. Its SETTING is GEORGIA during the CIVIL WAR. It tells of the three marriages of Scarlett O'Hara, a southern belle, and of the destruction caused by the war. The film version (1939), starring Clark Gable and Vivien Leigh, is one of the most popular movies ever made.

**"The Goose That Laid the Golden Eggs"** "The Goose That Laid the Golden Eggs" is a FABLE. A man discovers that his goose lays a golden egg every morning. He grows rich, but he also grows greedy. He decides to cut open the goose so that he can take all the golden eggs at once. But when he cuts the goose open, he finds that it is empty, and he is left with no gold and no goose. When we say, "Don't kill the goose that lays the golden eggs," it means that we shouldn't lose what we have by trying to get more.

**Grimm Brothers** Jacob and Wilhelm Grimm were two brothers who lived in Germany in the early 1800s. They heard many stories from peasants and wrote them down, making a large, eventually famous collection called *Grimm's Fairy Tales*. "HANSEL AND GRETEL" and "SNOW WHITE AND THE SEVEN DWARFS" are two of the FAIRY TALES from that book.

**Grinch** The Grinch is a nasty creature in the children's story *How the Grinch Stole Christmas*, by the American writer DR. SEUSS. The Grinch is so mean that he does not want anyone else to enjoy Christmas, so he spends Christmas Eve stealing everyone's presents, decorations, and holiday food. But on Christmas morning he hears everyone singing and celebrating in spite of their losses. He realizes that the spirit of Christmas is something within each person that cannot be stolen, and he becomes a happier and wiser creature.

**Guinevere** (GWIN-uh-veer) Guinevere is the wife of KING ARTHUR. In some versions of the Arthurian stories, Guinevere and SIR LANCELOT fall in love, thus bringing about the conflict that led to the end of CAMELOT.

***Gulliver's Travels*** (1726) *Gulliver's Travels* is a book by the Irish author Jonathan Swift, who lived during the late 1600s and early 1700s. It describes the adventures of Lemuel Gulliver, who makes several sea journeys to strange lands. In the first he is washed ashore in LILLIPUT, where the people are six inches tall. The second voyage is to Brobdingnag, a land of giants. The third takes him to a flying island peopled by odd scientists and thinkers. In his final voyage, he arrives at a land where talking horses are superior beings. The story is a fantasy, but it is also meant to expose the faults and stupidities of humankind. (*See* image, next page.)

***Hamlet*** *Hamlet* is a TRAGEDY by WILLIAM SHAKESPEARE. The main character, Hamlet,

**Gulliver's Travels.** Gulliver in Lilliput.

is a Danish prince whose father, the king, has been murdered. The king's ghost appears and says that he was murdered by his own brother, Hamlet's uncle Claudius. The ghost demands that Hamlet kill Claudius, who has already married Hamlet's mother and become king. Much of the play is about Hamlet's thoughts as he prepares to avenge his father's death. Many familiar speeches and phrases come from this play, such as: "To be or not to be, that is the question" and "Neither a borrower, nor a lender be."

**"Hansel and Gretel"** "Hansel and Gretel" is a FAIRY TALE in the collection of the GRIMM BROTHERS about a brother and sister who are abandoned in the forest when their family has no more food. They come upon a cottage made of gingerbread and sugar candy and begin to eat it until an old woman comes out. She invites them in and gives them food. But she is really a wicked witch who plans to fatten them up and cook them in the oven. Gretel tricks her, however, pushing her into the oven instead. The witch

burns to death, and Hansel and Gretel escape and find their way home.

**"The Hare and the Tortoise"** "The Hare and the Tortoise," one of AESOP'S FABLES, tells about a race between the two animals. The hare runs so fast that he is sure he will win, so he takes a nap halfway through the race. The tortoise keeps plodding along until he is ahead of the hare. By the time the hare wakes up, the tortoise is almost at the finish line. He wins because he kept going even though he was slow. From this fable we get the expression "Slow and steady wins the race."

**Harlem Renaissance** The Harlem Renaissance was an African-American cultural movement of the 1920s based in the Harlem district of NEW YORK CITY. Its members celebrated black traditions and the black experience. The writers COUNTEE CULLEN, LANGSTON HUGHES, ZORA NEALE HURSTON, and

**The Hare and the Tortoise**

JAMES WELDON JOHNSON were all associated with the movement.

**Harry Potter**   Harry Potter, a boy wizard, is the hero of a hugely popular series of fantasy NOVELS by British author J. K. Rowling. The books tell of Harry's adventures at the Hogwarts School of Witchcraft and Wizardry.

Harry Potter. Author J. K. Rowling signs a copy of her new novel for a fan.

**Hawthorne, Nathaniel**   Nathaniel Hawthorne was an American author of the 1800s who wrote SHORT STORIES and NOVELS, among them *The Scarlet Letter.* Two of his books for children retell some of the best-known Greek myths.

**Headless Horseman**   The Headless Horseman is a legendary ghost rider who appears in the story "THE LEGEND OF SLEEPY HOLLOW," by Washington Irving. *See also* CRANE, ICHABOD.

**Hemingway, Ernest**   Ernest Hemingway was an American author of the 1900s who wrote NOVELS and SHORT STORIES about war, hunting, fishing, and bullfighting. Two of his novels are *The Sun Also Rises* and *The Old Man and the Sea.*

**hero**   A hero is the main male figure in a PLAY or story, such as a NOVEL, myth, or legend. In legendary tales, the hero is usually especially strong and able.

**heroine**   A heroine is the main female figure in a PLAY or story. In legendary tales, the heroine is usually beautiful and clever.

**"Hey Diddle Diddle"**   "Hey Diddle Diddle" is a NURSERY RHYME:

> Hey diddle diddle,
> The cat and the fiddle,
> The cow jumped over the moon;
> The little dog laughed
> To see such sport,
> And the dish ran away with the spoon.

**Hiawatha**   (HEYE-uh-woth-uh)   Hiawatha was an American Indian chief of the 1500s. A poem by HENRY WADSWORTH LONGFELLOW, "The Song of Hiawatha," tells some of the legends that have been passed down about Hiawatha's life.

**"Hickory, Dickory, Dock"**   "Hickory, Dickory, Dock" is a NURSERY RHYME:

> Hickory, dickory, dock,
> The mouse ran up the clock.
> The clock struck one,
> The mouse ran down,
> Hickory, dickory, dock.

**Homer**   Homer was a great poet of ancient GREECE who wrote two EPICS, or long POEMS: the ILIAD, about the TROJAN WAR, and the ODYSSEY, about the adventures of the Greek hero Odysseus. Homer is said to have been blind.

**"Hot Cross Buns"**   "Hot Cross Buns" is a NURSERY RHYME. The first verse is:

> Hot cross buns! Hot cross buns!
> One a penny, two a penny,
> Hot cross buns!

**"The House That Jack Built"**   "The House That Jack Built" is a nursery tale. It begins with the single line "This is the house that

Jack built," and a new line is added to make each verse:

> This is the malt
> That lay in the house that Jack built.
>
> This is the rat,
> That ate the malt
> That lay in the house that Jack built.
>
> This is the cat,
> That killed the rat,
> That ate the malt
> That lay in the house that Jack built.

The story continues until there are eleven lines in the final verse.

**Huckleberry Finn, The Adventures of** (1884) *The Adventures of Huckleberry Finn* is a NOVEL by MARK TWAIN. Huck Finn escapes from his cruel father and travels down the MISSISSIPPI RIVER on a raft with an escaped slave, Jim, and together they have many adventures.

**Hughes, Langston**   Langston Hughes was an African-American writer of the twentieth century who often wrote poems about the black experience in the United States. He was a leading figure in the HARLEM RENAISSANCE.

**"Humpty Dumpty"**   "Humpty Dumpty" is a NURSERY RHYME:

> Humpty Dumpty sat on a wall,
> Humpty Dumpty had a great fall.
> All the king's horses,
> And all the king's men,
> Couldn't put Humpty together again.

This rhyme is also a riddle. If you are asked, "What is Humpty Dumpty?" the answer is "an egg," because no one can put an egg back together once it is broken. In the second ALICE IN WONDERLAND book, *Through the Looking-Glass*, Alice meets Humpty Dumpty, a character who actually is a large egg.

**The Hunchback of Notre Dame** (1831)   *The Hunchback of Notre Dame* is a NOVEL by

**Humpty Dumpty**

Victor Hugo, a French writer. It tells the story of Quasimodo, a physically deformed man who works as a bell ringer in the great CATHEDRAL of NOTRE DAME in PARIS.

**Hurston, Zora Neale**   Zora Neale Hurston was an African-American writer and anthropologist of the twentieth century. Known for her collections of black folklore, she was a leading figure in the HARLEM RENAISSANCE.

**"I think I can, I think I can"**   *See* "THE LITTLE ENGINE THAT COULD."

**Iliad** (IL-ee-uhd, IL-ee-ad)   The *Iliad* is an EPIC by the ancient Greek poet HOMER that tells the story of the TROJAN WAR.

**imagery**   The mental pictures created by a piece of writing are called imagery. In the Harry Potter books, the imagery of Hogwarts School—a great castle with endless halls, floating candles, and moving staircases—shows that it is a magical and mysterious place.

**Invisible Man** (1952)   *Invisible Man* is a NOVEL by African-American author Ralph Ellison. It tells of a black man in the 1930s who wants the world to see him as the unique person that he is. In a prejudiced society, however, he often feels invisible.

*Ivanhoe* (1819) *Ivanhoe* is a NOVEL written by Sir Walter Scott. Set in medieval ENGLAND, it is a classic tale of love and CHIVALRY (bravery, honesty, and courtesy). It tells of the adventures of the crusader Ivanhoe. *See* CRUSADES.

**"Jabberwocky"** "Jabberwocky" is a POEM in *Through the Looking-Glass*, one of the ALICE IN WONDERLAND books by LEWIS CARROLL. It tells the story of the dragon Jabberwock and uses many words that Carroll made up, such as *chortle*, from a combination of the words *chuckle* and *snort*.

**"Jack and Jill"** "Jack and Jill" is a NURSERY RHYME:

> Jack and Jill went up the hill,
> To fetch a pail of water;
> Jack fell down and broke his crown,
> And Jill came tumbling after.

(*Crown* means "head.")

**"Jack and the Beanstalk"** "Jack and the Beanstalk" is a FAIRY TALE about a boy who finds a huge magic beanstalk in his garden. He climbs it until he comes to a strange land in the sky. There he finds the castle of a giant, who cries, "Fee fie fo fum, I smell the blood of an Englishman!" The giant chases Jack down the beanstalk, but Jack gets to the bottom first and chops it down. The giant falls from the sky and is killed.

**"Jack Be Nimble"** "Jack Be Nimble" is a NURSERY RHYME:

> Jack be nimble,
> Jack be quick,
> Jack jump over
> The candlestick.

**"Jack Sprat"** "Jack Sprat" is a NURSERY RHYME:

> Jack Sprat could eat no fat,
> His wife could eat no lean,
> And so betwixt them both,
> They licked the platter clean.

**Jekyll and Hyde** *See* DR. JEKYLL AND MR. HYDE.

**Johnson, James Weldon** James Weldon Johnson was an African-American writer and CIVIL RIGHTS leader of the early 1900s. He was a prominent member of the HARLEM RENAISSANCE and wrote the verse "Lift Ev'ry Voice and Sing," which was later set to music.

***Julius Caesar*** *Julius Caesar* is a play by WILLIAM SHAKESPEARE that tells the story of a group of men who killed Caesar, the Roman ruler, and took over the empire. Caesar's famous last line, "Et tu, Brute?" ("Even you, Brutus?"), is spoken when he discovers his friend Brutus among the assassins.

**King Arthur** King Arthur is the legendary HERO of a group of stories about ancient ENGLAND. He proved that he was truly a king by being the only knight to be able to pull EXCALIBUR, a magical sword, from a stone.

**King Arthur**

The leader of the KNIGHTS OF THE ROUND TABLE, he was known as a just ruler who fought many battles and had many wonderful adventures. *See also* GALAHAD; GUINEVERE; LADY OF THE LAKE; LANCELOT; MERLIN.

**Kipling, Rudyard**   Rudyard Kipling was a British author of the late 1800s and early 1900s who is known for his stories, POEMS, and several children's books, such as *The Jungle Book* and *Just So Stories.*

**Knights of the Round Table**   The Knights of the Round Table were the knights of KING ARTHUR'S court.

**Lady of the Lake**   In the stories about KING ARTHUR, the Lady of the Lake is a mysterious supernatural creature who lived in the middle of a lake and bewitched the magician MERLIN.

**"Ladybug, Ladybug, Fly Away Home"**   "Ladybug, Ladybug, Fly Away Home" is a NURSERY RHYME. It has many versions, but it is often recited as follows:

> Ladybug, ladybug,
> Fly away home,
> Your house is on fire,
> Your children all gone.

**Lancelot**   Sir Lancelot is the bravest and most famous of KING ARTHUR'S knights. He falls in love with the king's wife, GUINEVERE.

**"The Legend of Sleepy Hollow"**   "The Legend of Sleepy Hollow" is a SHORT STORY written by the American author Washington Irving. The story is about a village schoolteacher, ICHABOD CRANE, who wants to marry a pretty farm girl. One night he meets a terrifying ghost called the HEADLESS HORSEMAN, who chases him through the woods of Sleepy Hollow. Crane disappears and is never seen again. Some people think he has been carried off by the ghost, but others know that the Headless Horseman was really another man who wanted to marry the young farm girl himself.

**Lilliput**   Lilliput is a land of tiny people that is one of the places Lemuel Gulliver visits in the book *GULLIVER'S TRAVELS* by Jonathan Swift.

**limerick**   A limerick is a humorous POEM with five lines. One familiar limerick is:

> A fly and a flea in a flue
> Were imprisoned, so what could they do?
> Said the fly, "Let us flee!"
> Said the flea, "Let us fly."
> So they flew through a flaw in the flue.

**"Little Bo-peep"**   "Little Bo-peep" is a NURSERY RHYME that begins:

> Little Bo-peep has lost her sheep,
> And can't tell where to find them:
> Let them alone, and they'll come home,
> Wagging their tails behind them.

**"Little Boy Blue"**   "Little Boy Blue" is a NURSERY RHYME that begins:

> Little boy blue, come blow your horn,
> The sheep's in the meadow, the cow's in
>   the corn.

**"The Little Engine That Could"**   "The Little Engine That Could" is a children's story by Watty Piper. The Little Engine is a train engine that tries to pull a load of toys over the top of the mountain. Even though it is not very powerful, it keeps saying, "I think I can, I think I can," as it struggles up the mountain. It finally succeeds where other engines had refused even to try.

**"Little Jack Horner"**   "Little Jack Horner" is a NURSERY RHYME:

> Little Jack Horner sat in the corner,
> Eating a Christmas pie;
> He put in his thumb, and pulled out a
>   plum,
> And said, "What a good boy am I!"

**"Little Miss Muffet"**   "Little Miss Muffet" is a NURSERY RHYME:

> Little Miss Muffet
> Sat on a tuffet,

Eating her curds and whey;
Along came a spider,
Who sat down beside her
And frightened Miss Muffet away.

(A *tuffet* is a low seat.)

**Little Red Hen**   The Little Red Hen is a character in a FOLK TALE. She works hard to plant, hoe, and harvest wheat, and then grinds it into flour and bakes it into bread. At every stage she asks, "Who will help me?" but her animal companions always reply, "Not I." When the bread is baked, the hen asks, "Who will help me eat the bread?" and the others call out, "I will!" But the hen says that she has done each step alone, and she will eat the bread alone.

**"Little Red Riding Hood"**   "Little Red Riding Hood" is a FAIRY TALE. A little girl named Red Riding Hood sets off for her grandmother's house. In the woods, she meets a wolf and tells him where she is going. The wolf gets to the house first and eats up the grandmother. He then puts on her clothes and gets into her bed. When Little Red Riding Hood comes in, the wolf pretends to be the grandmother. The little girl is fooled and is soon eaten by the wolf. But a huntsman passing by runs in and chops the wolf open. Out step Red Riding Hood and her grandmother, alive and well.

***Little Women*** (1868–1869)   *Little Women* is a novel by LOUISA MAY ALCOTT about the four March sisters, Jo, Meg, Beth, and Amy, in a NEW ENGLAND family of the 1800s. One of the most popular children's stories, *Little Women* is mostly AUTOBIOGRAPHICAL; that is, it tells about many things that happened to the author and her family.

**Longfellow, Henry Wadsworth**   Henry Wadsworth Longfellow was a well-known American poet of the 1800s. Among his works are "The Song of HIAWATHA," about a real Indian hero, and "PAUL REVERE'S RIDE."

**Little Red Riding Hood.** Red Riding Hood with the wolf disguised as Grandmother.

***Lord of the Flies*** (1954)   *Lord of the Flies* is a NOVEL by British writer William Golding. It tells the story of a group of boys who are stranded on a desert island and form a cruel and unfair society, showing that even children have evil elements in them.

***Macbeth***   *Macbeth* is a TRAGEDY by WILLIAM SHAKESPEARE. The nobleman Macbeth is told by three witches that he will become the king of SCOTLAND. His wife persuades him to murder the king and take the throne himself. In order to stay in power, he must keep killing the people who oppose him. Finally, Macbeth himself is killed in battle.

**magic carpet**   A magic carpet is a rug that can carry people wherever they wish to go. Magic carpets appear in MIDDLE EASTERN stories, such as those in the *ARABIAN NIGHTS*.

**"Mary Had a Little Lamb"**   "Mary Had a Little Lamb" is a NURSERY RHYME that begins:

Mary had a little lamb,
Its fleece was white as snow,
And everywhere that Mary went,
The lamb was sure to go.

**"Mary, Mary, Quite Contrary"**   "Mary, Mary, Quite Contrary" is a NURSERY RHYME:

Mary, Mary, quite contrary,
How does your garden grow?
With silver bells, and cockle shells,
And pretty maids all in a row.

**Melville, Herman** Herman Melville was an American author of the 1800s who wrote SHORT STORIES and NOVELS, among them *MOBY DICK*.

**Merlin** In the stories about KING ARTHUR, Merlin is a magician and the king's chief adviser.

**metaphor** A metaphor is a way of describing something by comparing it to something else but without using the words *like* or *as*. For example, Christina Rossetti, a British writer of the late 1800s, uses metaphors to describe the clouds and the sky in the poem "Clouds":

White sheep, white sheep,
On a blue hill,
When the wind stops
You all stand still.

If Rossetti had written, "The clouds are *like* white sheep," she would have been using a SIMILE.

**meter** Meter is the arrangement of stressed and unstressed words or SYLLABLES in a line of POETRY. In the following lines by Gelett Burgess, the stressed words or syllables are in bold type:

I **nev**er **saw** a **pur**ple **cow**, I **nev**er **hope** to **see** one.

**Millay, Edna St. Vincent** Edna St. Vincent Millay was an American poet of the early twentieth century. Among her popular POEMS is "Afternoon on a Hill," in which she says, "I will be the gladdest thing / Under the sun!" Millay also wrote PLAYS in FREE VERSE.

**"Mirror, mirror, on the wall"** In the FAIRY TALE about Snow White, Snow White's stepmother, the wicked queen, says these words to her mirror: "Mirror, mirror, on the wall, who is the fairest of us all?"

**_Moby Dick_** (1851) In HERMAN MELVILLE'S NOVEL *Moby Dick*, Moby Dick is a huge white whale, so fierce that he can sink the boats of the sailors who try to hunt and kill him.

**moral** The moral is the lesson that a story or a FABLE is meant to teach. *See also* AESOP'S FABLES.

**Morrison, Toni** Toni Morrison is a modern African-American author of NOVELS and ESSAYS. Among her best-known novels are *The Bluest Eye* and *Beloved*. In 1993 she won the Nobel Prize for literature.

**Mother Goose** Mother Goose is the name used in English for the make-believe person who is supposed to have first told many familiar NURSERY RHYMES to children. They are often called Mother Goose rhymes, but in fact several people collected and told these songs and POEMS. Many nursery rhymes have been repeated by so many generations of people that we no longer know who first made them up. Among the best-known rhymes are "JACK AND JILL" and "LITTLE MISS MUFFET."

**_Narrative of the Life of Frederick Douglass_** (1845) The AUTOBIOGRAPHY of the ABOLITIONIST leader FREDERICK DOUGLASS is called *Narrative of the Life of Frederick Douglass*. It is one of the most important works by an African American in the nineteenth century.

**narrator** In a work of FICTION, the narrator is the person who tells the story.

**Never-Never Land** Never-Never Land is where PETER PAN'S adventures take place.

**night before Christmas, 'Twas the** (1823) These are the first words of a favorite Christmas POEM by Clement C. Moore, a nineteenth-century American scholar and writer. It begins:

'Twas the night before Christmas, when
   all through the house
Not a creature was stirring, not even a
   mouse;
The stockings were hung by the chimney
   with care,
In hopes that St. Nicholas soon would be
   there.

**nonfiction**   Nonfiction is a term for writing that is factually true, or tries to be. Types of nonfiction include BIOGRAPHIES, ESSAYS, and historical accounts. *Compare* FICTION.

**novel**   A novel is a long story, written in PROSE. *THE ADVENTURES OF HUCKLEBERRY FINN, LITTLE WOMEN, Harry Potter and the Sorcerer's Stone,* and *DAVID COPPERFIELD* are all novels. A person who writes novels is called a novelist.

**"Now I Lay Me Down to Sleep"**   "Now I Lay Me Down to Sleep" is a child's PRAYER:

Now I lay me down to sleep,
I pray the Lord my soul to keep;
If I should die before I wake,
I pray the Lord my soul to take.

**nursery rhyme**   A nursery rhyme is a short POEM for young children, like "One, two, buckle my shoe." Many nursery rhymes are so old that no one knows who composed them or who first set them down in writing.

**Odyssey** (OD-i-see)   The *Odyssey* is an EPIC by the ancient Greek poet HOMER. It tells of the adventures of the Greek hero ODYSSEUS as he journeys back to his kingdom after the TROJAN WAR. *See also* ODYSSEUS *under "Mythology."*

**"Old King Cole"**   "Old King Cole" is a NURSERY RHYME that begins:

Old King Cole was a merry old soul,
And a merry old soul was he;
He called for his pipe, and he called for
   his bowl,
And he called for his fiddlers three.

**"Old Mother Hubbard"**   "Old Mother Hubbard" is a NURSERY RHYME that begins:

Old Mother Hubbard
Went to the cupboard,
To fetch her poor dog a bone;
But when she got there
The cupboard was bare,
And so the poor dog had none.

**Oliver Twist.** Undated woodcut by
J. Mahoney, circa 1870.

**Oliver Twist** (1838)   *Oliver Twist* is a NOVEL by CHARLES DICKENS. Oliver is a boy who does not know who his parents are. He runs away from a workhouse where he is badly treated. To survive, he has to join a gang of thieves. Oliver finally discovers his real family and escapes a life of crime.

**"One, Two, Buckle My Shoe"**   "One, Two, Buckle My Shoe" is a NURSERY RHYME that begins:

One, two, buckle my shoe;
Three, four, shut the door;
Five, six, pick up sticks;
Seven, eight, lay them straight;
Nine, ten, a big fat hen.

**One if by land, and two if by sea**   *See* "PAUL REVERE'S RIDE."

**"Open, Sesame"** "Open, Sesame" is the magic expression used in one of the tales of the *ARABIAN NIGHTS*. ALI BABA says, "Open, Sesame," to get into a secret cave where thieves have stored their treasure.

***Othello*** *Othello* is a TRAGEDY by WILLIAM SHAKESPEARE. Othello is a Moor (a MUSLIM from North AFRICA) who is tricked by an evil soldier, Iago, into thinking that his wife has been unfaithful to him. He kills her in a jealous rage. When Othello realizes that his wife was innocent, he kills himself in his grief.

**"The Owl and the Pussycat"** "The Owl and the Pussycat" is a POEM for children by the nineteenth-century British writer Edward Lear. It begins:

> The Owl and the Pussycat went to sea
> In a beautiful pea-green boat.
> They took some honey, and plenty of
>     money,
> Wrapped up in a five-pound note.

**"Paul Revere's Ride"** "Paul Revere's Ride," by HENRY WADSWORTH LONGFELLOW, is a POEM based on a patriot of the REVOLUTIONARY WAR. PAUL REVERE rode to warn the villages of Lexington and Concord, near BOSTON, MASSACHUSETTS, that British troops were coming. The poem begins:

> Listen, my children, and you shall hear,
> Of the midnight ride of Paul Revere.

The poem goes on to tell how Revere waited for a friend to hang one or two lamps in a church steeple to signal how the British were traveling: "One if by land, and two if by sea." When he saw two lamps, Revere began his ride.

**Pecos Bill** Pecos Bill is a giant cowboy known for his daring exploits in many TALL TALES of the American SOUTHWEST.

**pen name** A pen name is a fictitious name, or pseudonym (SOOH-doh-nim), used by a writer. It may be completely made up or may come from the writer's middle name or someone else's name. MARK TWAIN was the pen name of Samuel Langhorne Clemens; DR. SEUSS was the pen name of Theodore Seuss Geisel.

**personification** Personification is the use of human forms or qualities to describe non-human things. Examples of personification include *the trees whispered* and *jealousy has green eyes.*

***Peter Pan*** (1904) *Peter Pan* is a favorite children's PLAY by J. M. Barrie, a Scottish author of the late 1800s and early 1900s. Peter Pan is a young boy in NEVER-NEVER LAND who never wants to grow up. He lives with the FAIRY TINKER BELL, who teaches him to fly and protects him and his friends from danger. His enemy is the evil CAPTAIN HOOK, the leader of a band of pirates.

***Peter Rabbit, The Tale of*** (1901) *The Tale of Peter Rabbit* is by the British illustrator and writer Beatrix Potter, who lived in the late 1800s and early 1900s. It is a favorite children's story about a mischievous little rabbit who gets into a farmer's garden and is almost caught.

**"The Pied Piper of Hamelin"** "The Pied Piper of Hamelin" is an old FOLK TALE about a man who gets rid of all the rats in the town of Hamelin. He plays enchanting music on his pipe (a kind of flute), and the rats all follow him down to the river, where they drown. When the townspeople refuse to pay the Pied Piper, he uses his pipe to lure the children away from the town, and they are never seen again. Many people know this story from a long POEM of the same name written by the British poet Robert Browning in the 1800s.

**Pinocchio** *The Adventures of Pinocchio* is a book by the nineteenth-century Italian writer C. Collodi. Pinocchio is a wooden puppet who wants to be a real boy. He is watched over by a good FAIRY, but he has many adventures before he proves himself worthy of becoming a real child. Whenever Pinocchio tells a lie, his nose grows longer, and everyone can see that he has been lying.

**play** A play is a story that is performed by actors and actresses on a stage. It may consist only of dialogue (spoken words) or may include music and dance (*see* MUSICAL *under "Music, Art, and Architecture"*). Plays are often presented in a building called a theater, but they can also be staged outdoors or in television programs. *See also* TRAGEDY.

**playwright** A playwright is a person who writes PLAYS. WILLIAM SHAKESPEARE is one of the most famous playwrights in English literature.

**plot** The plot is the series of events in a story. Almost every story has a plot, whether it is a NOVEL, SHORT STORY, PLAY, movie, or television show.

**Poe, Edgar Allan** Edgar Allan Poe was an American author of the 1800s who wrote POEMS, horror stories, and detective stories. He is well known for his poem "THE RAVEN" and the story "The Tell-Tale Heart."

**poem** A poem is a work of literature that is written in lines, like a song. Poems often have a particular rhythm, or repeated beat. Sometimes the word at the end of one line RHYMES with the word at the end of another line. Poems that have no rhyme or regular rhythm are called FREE VERSE. A person who writes poems is called a poet. *See also* COUPLET; EPIC; METER; STANZA.

**poetry** Poetry refers to POEMS or the language they contain. It can also mean the poems of an individual poet, as in *the poetry of Emily Dickinson.*

***Pollyanna*** (1913) *Pollyanna,* by the American author Eleanor Porter, is a book about a young girl who always looks on the bright side of things.

**"The Princess and the Pea"** "The Princess and the Pea," by HANS CHRISTIAN AN-DERSEN, is a story about a prince who is searching for a true princess to marry. A young, bedraggled woman comes to his door and claims to be a true princess. To see whether she is telling the truth, the prince's mother covers a pea with many mattresses and offers this bed to the young woman. The next morning, the young woman says she couldn't sleep because there was something very hard in her bed. The queen then knows that the young woman is telling the truth, for only a true princess could be so sensitive.

**prose** Prose is nonpoetic language, as opposed to POETRY. NOVELS, ESSAYS, and SHORT STORIES are usually written in prose.

**Pulitzer Prizes** (PYOOH-lit-suhr) Pulitzer Prizes are awarded every year for outstanding work in American journalism, literature, drama, and music. They are named for newspaper publisher Joseph Pulitzer.

**"Puss-in-Boots"** "Puss-in-Boots" is a FAIRY TALE about a clever cat who brings good fortune to its master.

**"Rain, Rain, Go Away"** "Rain, Rain, Go Away" is a RHYME chanted by children when it rains:

Rain, rain, go away,
Come again another day.

**"Rapunzel"** "Rapunzel" is a FAIRY TALE about a girl who has long, beautiful hair. She is locked in a high tower, and the only way anyone can get into the tower is by calling, "Rapunzel, Rapunzel, let down your hair." (*See* image, next page.)

**"The Raven"** "The Raven" is a POEM by EDGAR ALLAN POE. A mysterious black bird visits the poet, who is mourning the loss of his beloved, and repeats, "Nevermore."

**rhyme** When a word or the last part of a word sounds like another word or the last part of another word, those words are said to rhyme; for example, *part* rhymes with *heart*, *rougher* rhymes with *tougher*, and *believ-*

**Rapunzel.** Drawing by Walter Crane.

*able* rhymes with *inconceivable*. *See also* RHYME SCHEME.

**rhyme scheme**    A rhyme scheme shows the arrangement or pattern of rhymes in a POEM. For example, in this poem by the nineteenth-century British writer and artist Edward Lear, the rhyme scheme is A A B B A (the rhyming words are in italic):

> A: There was an old person of *Ware*
> A: Who rode on the back of a *bear;*
> B: When they asked does it *trot*
> B: He said, "Certainly *not!*
> A: He's a Moppsikon Floppsikon *bear!*"

**"Rip Van Winkle"**    "Rip Van Winkle" is a SHORT STORY by the American author Washington Irving about a man who goes hunting in the mountains one day and falls asleep for twenty years.

**Robin Hood**    Robin Hood is a legendary English outlaw who stole from the rich to give to the poor. He and his band of men, in-cluding Friar Tuck and Little John, lived in SHERWOOD FOREST.

***Robinson Crusoe*** (1719)    *Robinson Crusoe* is a NOVEL by the English author Daniel Defoe. It tells how Robinson Crusoe, an English sailor, is shipwrecked on a desert island and lives there alone for many years. He survives with the help of his man, Friday, by making, finding, or growing everything he needs.

**"Rock-a-Bye Baby"**    "Rock-a-Bye Baby" is a NURSERY RHYME and lullaby:

> Rock-a-bye, baby, on the tree top;
> When the wind blows, the cradle will
>    rock;
> When the bough breaks, the cradle will
>    fall,
> And down will come baby, cradle and all!

***Romeo and Juliet***    *Romeo and Juliet* is a TRAGEDY by WILLIAM SHAKESPEARE. Two young lovers, Romeo and Juliet, are kept apart by their families, who hate each other. When Romeo kills a cousin of Juliet's for killing one of his friends, he is forced to leave the city. Juliet's family tries to make her marry another man, but she drinks a potion to make it look as if she were dead. Romeo hears that she is dead and believes it. He goes to her tomb and kills himself by drinking poison. When Juliet awakens to find her lover dead beside her, she stabs herself.

**Roses are red**    "Roses are red" are the first words of a Valentine's Day poem. The poem has many forms, but in the United States it is often recited as follows:

> Roses are red, violets are blue,
> Sugar is sweet, and so are you.

**"Rub-a-Dub-Dub"**    "Rub-a-Dub-Dub" is a NURSERY RHYME:

> Rub-a-dub-dub,
> Three men in a tub;
> And who do you think they be?
> The butcher, the baker,

The candlestick maker;
Turn them out, knaves all three!

**"Rumpelstiltskin"** "Rumpelstiltskin" is a FAIRY TALE from the collection of the GRIMM BROTHERS. A little man named Rumpelstiltskin helps the beautiful young wife of a prince to spin straw into gold thread in exchange for her firstborn child. In order to keep her baby, she has to guess his name. When she discovers it, the dwarf destroys himself in a rage.

**Sancho Panza** Sancho Panza is the companion of the title CHARACTER in *DON QUIXOTE* and is his opposite in every way. He is short and fat while Don Quixote is tall and thin. He is uneducated while Quixote is well read, and he is practical and has common sense while Quixote is an idealist and a dreamer. Still, he agrees to be Don Quixote's squire (the assistant to a KNIGHT) and follows him on his adventures.

**Sandburg, Carl** Carl Sandburg was a twentieth-century American author of POEMS and BIOGRAPHIES. He is best known for his poems about American cities, especially CHICAGO, which he describes as "Stormy, husky, brawling / City of the big shoulders."

**scene** A scene is a section of a PLAY, movie, or television program that happens in a single place at a single time.

**Scrooge** Scrooge is the stingy old man in CHARLES DICKENS's *A CHRISTMAS CAROL* whose life is changed when he meets a series of ghosts on Christmas Eve. The term *scrooge*, meaning someone who is miserly, has become very common in English.

**The Secret Garden** (1912) *The Secret Garden*, a book written by the American writer Frances Hodgson Burnett, tells the story of Mary Lennox, a miserable girl who is sent to England to live with her uncle after the death of her parents in India. Mary discovers a garden on her uncle's property that has been locked up for years. She and her friends secretly restore the garden and become happy and healthy.

**setting** The setting of a work of literature is the place and time in which the action occurs. For example, the setting of the NOVEL *Holes*, by Louis Sachar, is a juvenile detention center in Texas in the 1990s.

**Seuss, Dr.** Dr. Seuss was the PEN NAME of the twentieth-century American writer Theodore Seuss Geisel. His picture books (for example, *The Cat in the Hat* and *How the Grinch Stole Christmas*) include fantastical characters and are written in humorous verse.

**Seven Dwarfs** The Seven Dwarfs are the CHARACTERS who take care of Snow White when she comes into their house. In the WALT DISNEY cartoon film of the story, the Seven Dwarfs are given the names Happy, Sleepy, Doc, Bashful, Sneezy, Grumpy, and Dopey.

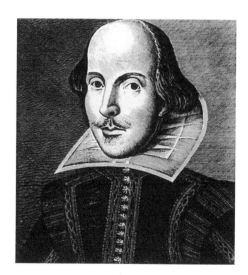

**William Shakespeare**

**Shakespeare, William** William Shakespeare was a great English writer of the late 1500s and early 1600s. His PLAYS and POEMS are considered to be among the best literary works ever written. Some of his most familiar plays are HAMLET, ROMEO AND JULIET, MACBETH, OTHELLO, JULIUS CAESAR, and *A Midsummer Night's Dream.*

**Sherlock Holmes**   Sherlock Holmes is a famous fictional detective who appears in a series of NOVELS and stories by the British writer Sir Arthur Conan Doyle, who lived during the late 1800s and early 1900s. When investigating a crime, Holmes finds clues that other people have not noticed or understood. He always amazes the other people in the stories by cleverly getting to the bottom of any mystery.

**Sherwood Forest**   Sherwood Forest was where ROBIN HOOD and his men lived.

**short story**   A short story is a work of FICTION in PROSE that is shorter than a NOVEL. Often, a number of short stories are brought together to make a book.

**Silverstein, Shel**   Shel Silverstein was a twentieth-century author and illustrator of humorous POEMS for children. His best-known collections are *A Light in the Attic* and *Where the Sidewalk Ends.*

**simile**   A simile describes something by comparing it to something else. Many common expressions are similes, such as, "He is as strong as an ox" and "He eats like a pig." Similes usually use the word *like* or *as.* In the poem "My Bed Is a Boat," by ROBERT LOUIS STEVENSON, the first line contains a simile: "My bed is like a little boat." *Compare* METAPHOR.

**"Simple Simon"**   "Simple Simon" is a NURSERY RHYME. The first verse goes:

> Simple Simon met a pieman
> Going to the fair;
> Says Simple Simon to the pieman,
> "Let me taste your ware."

**Sinbad the Sailor**   Sinbad the Sailor is a merchant in one of the stories of the ARA-BIAN NIGHTS. He sails around the world and has many fantastic adventures.

**"Sing a Song of Sixpence"**   "Sing a Song of Sixpence" is a NURSERY RHYME. The first verses go:

> Sing a song of sixpence,
> A pocket full of rye;
> Four and twenty blackbirds
> Baked in a pie.
>
> When the pie was opened,
> The birds began to sing;
> Wasn't that a dainty dish
> To set before the king?

**"Sleeping Beauty"**   "Sleeping Beauty" is a FAIRY TALE about a beautiful princess who is put under a curse that makes her sleep for one hundred years. When a handsome prince finds her and falls in love with her, his kiss releases her from the evil spell, and she awakens.

**"Snow White and the Seven Dwarfs"**   "Snow White and the Seven Dwarfs" is a FAIRY TALE in the collection of the GRIMM BROTHERS. Snow White is a beautiful girl with a wicked stepmother. The stepmother owns a magic mirror, and every day she asks it, "Mirror, mirror, on the wall, who is the fairest of us all?" At first the mirror always answers, "You are, my queen," but when Snow White grows to be a young woman, the mirror says that Snow White is the fairest. Enraged, the queen sends Snow White into the woods to be killed. Instead, the queen's servant lets the girl go. In the woods, Snow White finds the home of the SEVEN DWARFS and hides in their tiny cottage. The queen finds her, however, and tricks her into eating a poisoned apple, which makes the girl fall into a deep sleep. Finally Snow White is rescued by a prince, awakens, and becomes his wife.

**stanza**   A stanza is a unit of lines in a POEM usually arranged in a recurring pattern of RHYME or rhythm.

**"Star Light, Star Bright"** "Star Light, Star Bright" is a NURSERY RHYME:

Star light, star bright,
First star I see tonight,
I wish I may, I wish I might,
Have the wish I wish tonight.

**Stevenson, Robert Louis** Robert Louis Stevenson was a Scottish-born writer of the late 1800s. His works include *The Strange Case of Dr. Jekyll and Mr. Hyde*, TREASURE ISLAND, *Kidnapped*, and *A CHILD'S GARDEN OF VERSES*.

**Superman** Superman is a comic book hero who has also appeared in television shows and movies. He can fly, run faster than a speeding bullet, and leap tall buildings in a single bound. He uses these superhuman powers to protect people from evil and injustice.

**tall tale** A tall tale is a FOLK TALE usually set on the American frontier in which the main CHARACTER, such as PAUL BUNYAN or PECOS BILL, has superhuman characteristics and performs daring exploits.

**Tarzan** Tarzan is a CHARACTER created by Edgar Rice Burroughs in the early 1900s. He has appeared in many books, comic books, and movies. As a baby, Tarzan is abandoned in the African jungle and raised by a family of apes. He grows up to become a strong hero.

**There is no joy in Mudville** "There is no joy in Mudville" is a line from a poem by Ernest Lawrence Thayer, "Casey at the Bat," which tells the story of a baseball player on the team from Mudville. Casey comes to bat in the ninth inning with his team behind. He confidently lets two strikes go by before he swings mightily at the third pitch. The poem ends: "But there is no joy in Mudville—mighty Casey has struck out."

**There was a little girl** These are the first words of a POEM by HENRY WADSWORTH LONGFELLOW. It begins:

There was a little girl
Who had a little curl
Right in the middle of her forehead;
And when she was good
She was very, very good,
But when she was bad she was horrid.

**"There Was an Old Woman Who Lived in a Shoe"** "There Was an Old Woman Who Lived in a Shoe" is a NURSERY RHYME:

There was an old woman who lived in a
   shoe,
She had so many children she didn't
   know what to do;
She gave them some broth without any
   bread;
And spanked them all soundly and put
   them to bed.

**"Thirty Days Hath September"** "Thirty Days Hath September" is a RHYME that helps us remember how many days there are in each month:

Thirty days hath September,
April, June, and November;
All the rest have thirty-one,
Excepting February alone,
And that has twenty-eight days clear
And twenty-nine in each leap year.

**This little piggy went to market** These words are the first line of a toe-counting game. It is often recited as follows:

This little piggy went to market,
This little piggy stayed home,
This little piggy had roast beef,
This little piggy had none,
And this little piggy cried, "Wee-wee-
   wee-wee,"
All the way home.

**Thoreau, Henry David** Henry David Thoreau was an American writer of the 1800s. In his book *Walden*, he tells about living in a cabin that he built in the woods on Walden Pond, in Concord, MASSACHUSETTS. He also wrote a well-known essay, "Civil Disobedience," in which he says that people should follow their own conscience. If that means they must break the laws of their government, he says, they should be prepared to take the punishment given to them.

**"The Three Bears"**  See "GOLDILOCKS AND THE THREE BEARS."

**"Three Blind Mice"**  "Three Blind Mice" is a NURSERY RHYME:

> Three blind mice, see how they run!
> They all ran after the farmer's wife,
> She cut off their tails with a carving
>    knife,
> Did you ever see such a sight in your life,
> As three blind mice?

**"Three Little Kittens"**  "Three Little Kittens" is a NURSERY RHYME. The first verse is:

> Three little kittens
> They lost their mittens
> And they began to cry
> "Oh mother dear
> We sadly fear
> That we have lost our mittens."

**"The Three Little Pigs"**  "The Three Little Pigs" is a children's story about three pigs who leave home to make their own way in the world. The first one builds a house of straw, the second a house of twigs, and the third a house of bricks. A wolf comes along and is able to blow the first two houses down, but the third is too strong, so the third little pig lives happily ever after. *See also* BIG BAD WOLF.

**Tinker Bell**  In the story PETER PAN, Tinker Bell is a FAIRY who teaches Peter to fly and helps him and his friends.

**Tolkien, J.R.R.**  J.R.R. Tolkien was a British scholar of the middle 1900s. In *The Hobbit* and a series of three novels, *The Lord of the Rings*, he wrote about the adventures of small creatures called Hobbits. Movie versions of all three *Lord of the Rings* books were released in 2001–2003.

**Tom Sawyer, The Adventures of** (1876) *The Adventures of Tom Sawyer* is a novel by MARK TWAIN. Tom is a clever boy with a strong imagination and a desire for adventure. In one famous scene, he tricks his friends into painting a fence that he was supposed to paint by himself.

**Tom Thumb**  Tom Thumb is the tiny hero of a FAIRY TALE. When he is born, he is no bigger than his father's thumb, and he never grows any bigger.

**"The Tortoise and the Hare"**  See "THE HARE AND THE TORTOISE."

**tragedy**  A tragedy is a serious PLAY in which the main CHARACTER (usually an important, heroic person) meets with disaster, either because of a personal fault or through events that cannot be prevented.

**Treasure Island** (1883)  *Treasure Island* is an adventure story about a boy who finds a treasure map. Two men hire a ship to search for the treasure on an island. Among the ship's crew are the pirate Long John Silver and his men, who try to get the treasure for themselves. The story was written by ROBERT LOUIS STEVENSON.

**Twain, Mark**  Mark Twain was the PEN NAME of an American writer of the 1800s whose real name was Samuel Langhorne Clemens. *See also* HUCKLEBERRY FINN, THE ADVENTURES OF; TOM SAWYER, THE ADVENTURES OF.

**Tweedledum and Tweedledee**  Tweedledum and Tweedledee are two identical twins whom Alice meets in the story *Through the Looking-Glass*. *See also* ALICE IN WONDERLAND.

**Mark Twain**

**"Twinkle, Twinkle, Little Star"** "Twinkle, Twinkle, Little Star" is a POEM for children that is often sung. The first part goes:

Twinkle, twinkle, little star,
How I wonder what you are!
Up above the world so high,
Like a diamond in the sky.

**"The Ugly Duckling"** "The Ugly Duckling," by HANS CHRISTIAN ANDERSEN, is a story about a baby bird who is hatched into a family of ducks. He is bigger and uglier than the rest of the ducklings, and the other barnyard creatures mock him. He leaves, but everywhere he goes he is threatened or laughed at. When spring comes, however, he finds he has grown up to be a beautiful swan.

**Uncle Remus** Uncle Remus is a CHARACTER in a series of stories by the nineteenth-century American writer Joel Chandler Harris. Uncle Remus is an old black man who tells stories to a young white boy. Some of the stories about animals, such as the wily

BRER RABBIT and his enemy, Brer Fox, are well known. Many of the Uncle Remus stories were originally African-American FOLK TALES.

**Uncle Tom's Cabin** (1852) *Uncle Tom's Cabin,* by the American writer Harriet Beecher Stowe, was a famous NOVEL of the 1800s that exposed the evils of SLAVERY.

**verse** Verse can be used to mean POETRY in general or to refer to a STANZA of a POEM or song. See also FREE VERSE.

**"The Village Blacksmith"** "The Village Blacksmith" is a POEM about a strong and hardworking man. It was written in the 1800s by HENRY WADSWORTH LONGFELLOW. The first lines of the poem are well known: "Under the spreading chestnut tree / The village smithy stands." (A *smithy* is where a blacksmith works.)

**Virgil** (VUHR-jil) Virgil was a poet of ancient ROME. He wrote the *Aeneid* (i-NEE-id), an EPIC about the adventures of the hero Aeneas (i-NEE-is) after the TROJAN WAR.

**Alice Walker**

**Walker, Alice** Alice Walker is a modern African-American author of NOVELS and ESSAYS.

Her writing often focuses on black women's friendships and families. Her novel *The Color Purple* won a PULITZER PRIZE.

**Welty, Eudora** (yoo-DOH-rah) Eudora Welty was a twentieth-century American author of NOVELS and SHORT STORIES. The SETTING of her work is usually the rural SOUTH. Her novel *The Optimist's Daughter* won a PULITZER PRIZE.

**Laura Ingalls Wilder**

**Phillis Wheatley**

**Wheatley, Phillis** Phillis Wheatley was an African-American poet of the eighteenth century. Born in AFRICA, she was brought to America and became the household slave of a BOSTON merchant, whose family encouraged her education and writing. She produced the earliest-published important black works in America.

**Whitman, Walt** Walt Whitman was a nineteenth-century American poet. His POEM "I Hear America Singing" celebrates strong, proud American workers. "O Captain, My Captain!" honors ABRAHAM LINCOLN. Both are from his book *Leaves of Grass.*

**Wilder, Laura Ingalls** Laura Ingalls Wilder was an American writer who was born in the pioneer days of the 1800s. In *The Little House in the Big Woods, The Little House on the Prairie,* and seven other books, she gives many details about the everyday activities and adventures of the settlers.

**William Tell** William Tell is a legendary hero of Switzerland who was able to shoot an apple off his son's head with an arrow.

***The Wind in the Willows*** (1908) *The Wind in the Willows* is a book written by the English author Kenneth Grahame. It describes the adventures of three animals, Mr. Toad, Mole, and Rat, and their friend Badger.

**Winnie-the-Pooh** Winnie-the-Pooh is a toy bear who is the main character in several books for children published in the early 1900s by the British writer A. A. Milne. The author's son, Christopher Robin, is also a character in the books.

**Wizard of Oz, The Wonderful** (1900) *The Wonderful Wizard of Oz*, by the American writer L. Frank Baum, who lived during the late 1800s and early 1900s, tells about the adventure of a little girl, Dorothy. Dorothy and her dog, Toto, are carried by a tornado from KANSAS to the land of Oz. There she meets many strange characters, including a scarecrow who wants a brain, a cowardly lion who wants courage, and a tin woodman who wants a heart. Many people know the story from the 1939 movie *The Wizard of Oz*, starring Judy Garland.

**Wordsworth, William** William Wordsworth was a nineteenth-century British poet. His POEMS express deep feelings and a love of nature. One of his best-loved poems is "Daffodils," which begins: "I wandered lonely as a cloud."

**Wright, Richard** Richard Wright was an African-American novelist of the 1900s whose best-known book is *Native Son*.

# Mythology

Myths are traditional stories about gods, goddesses, and mortals with special powers, and they were an important part of the religious belief of many ancient peoples. Although we do not believe that the events in these stories actually took place as they are described, myths are still an important part of our culture. They often speak about the beginning of the world, about the forces of nature, about good and evil, and about universal human qualities and emotions. Every culture has some form of myths. The ones we are most familiar with are those of classical mythology (from the ancient Greek and Roman civilizations) and, to some extent, those of the Norse (Scandinavian and North German) peoples as well.

Many of the gods and goddesses listed here have two names, a Greek name and a Roman name. When the Greek civilization declined and the Romans conquered much of Europe and parts of Asia, they took over many of the Greek myths and gave the gods and goddesses new names in their own language, Latin. When two names are given together in the following entries, the *Greek* name is given first and the *Roman* name follows it in parentheses.

**Achilles** (uh-KIL-eez) Achilles was the greatest Greek warrior in the TROJAN WAR. The only way to kill him was to attack his one weak spot, his heel. Today we use the term *Achilles' heel* to describe the one weakness in a person's character.

**Adonis** (uh-DON-is) Adonis was a Greek youth who was so handsome that even APHRODITE, the goddess of love, fell in love with him. Today we call any young man who is extremely handsome an Adonis.

**Agamemnon** (ag-uh-MEM-non) Agamemnon was the king who led the Greek forces in the TROJAN WAR.

**Amazons** In Greek mythology, the Amazons were a tribe of female warriors who were known for their great size, strength, and fierceness.

**Aphrodite** (af-ruh-DEYE-tee) (VENUS) Aphrodite was the beautiful goddess of love and beauty. In some versions of the myth, she was said to have been born from the sea

**Adonis.** Detail of *Venus and Adonis* by Titian. National Gallery of Art, Washington; Widener Collection.

foam. A famous fifteenth-century painting shows her rising from the water on a seashell.

**Apollo** (uh-POL-oh)  Apollo was the god of prophecy, music, POETRY, medicine, and light. He was a very important god for both the Greeks and the Romans, because he controlled many of the activities necessary for civilized life. People often visited his oracle, or shrine, in the city of Delphi to ask him questions through a priestess. *See also* DELPHIC ORACLE.

**Ares** (AIR-eez) (MARS)  Ares was the god of war.

**Artemis** (AHR-tuh-muhs) (DIANA)  Artemis was the goddess of the hunt. She is often pictured with a deer.

**Asgard** (AS-gahrd, AHZ-gahrd)  In Norse mythology, Asgard was the domain of the gods and heroes killed in battle. Asgard was situated at the center of the universe and could be reached only by crossing a rainbow bridge.

**Athena** (MINERVA)  Athena was the goddess of wisdom as well as the protector of ATHENS and other cities. Her birth was unusual: she sprang fully grown and in full armor from the head of ZEUS. The PARTHENON, a beautiful temple overlooking the city of Athens, was dedicated to her.

**Atlas**  Atlas was a TITAN who rebelled against the gods. He was punished by being forced to hold up the earth and sky on his shoulders for eternity. Today, a person who is very strong is sometimes called an Atlas.

**Bacchus** (BAK-uhs)  Bacchus is the Roman name for DIONYSUS, the god of wine.

**Balder**  Balder was the Norse god of light. According to one legend, his mother, FRIGG, commanded all things to do him no harm. She forgot to include the mistletoe, however, and Balder was killed by a rival who wielded a sprig of mistletoe.

**Batman**  The comic strip character Batman first appeared in 1939. With his loyal sidekick, Robin, Batman fights crime in Gotham

**Athena**

**Centaur**

City. His adventures have also appeared on television and in movies.

**Bunyan, Paul** Paul Bunyan, a giant lumberjack, is a hero in TALL TALES about the forests of the American North and Northwest. His pet is a huge blue ox named Babe.

**centaurs** In Greek mythology, centaurs were creatures that had the upper body of a man and the lower body of a horse.

**Cerberus** (SUR-buh-ruhs) Cerberus was the three-headed dog that guarded the gates of the underworld, HADES. He allowed all dead souls to enter but none to leave.

**Ceres** (SEER-eez) Ceres is the Roman name for DEMETER, the goddess of grain and farming. The word *cereal* comes from her name because cereal is made of grain.

**chimera** (keye-MEER-uh) The chimera was a monster with the head of a lion, the body of a goat, and the tail of a dragon or serpent.

**Cupid** Cupid was the Roman god of love. When he shot his arrows into people's hearts, they fell in love. Cupid is now often pictured on Valentine's Day cards as a baby dressed in red or pink and carrying a bow and arrows. *See also* EROS.

**Cyclops** (SEYE-klops) The Cyclopes (seye-KLOH-peez) were giants with only one eye, set in the middle of the forehead. The best-known Cyclops imprisoned the Greek hero ODYSSEUS and his men, but Odysseus finally escaped by tricking the giant and putting out his eye.

**Daedalus** (DED-l-uhs) Daedalus was a mythical Greek inventor who built the LABYRINTH, a great maze from which no one could escape. He was the father of ICARUS. *See also* MINOTAUR.

**Daphne** (DAF-nee) Daphne was a NYMPH who was loved by APOLLO. To escape him, she asked the gods to turn her into a laurel, or bay tree. Thereafter, Apollo adopted the bay leaf as his symbol.

**Delphic oracle** The Delphic oracle was a temple at the city of Delphi, in GREECE, where people tried to find guidance and ad-

**Cupid**

vice about the future. A priestess, who was also called an oracle, sat in the temple and uttered puzzling messages from the god APOLLO. These messages, also called oracles, prophesied (or predicted) the future. Priests heard the oracles and explained them.

**Demeter** (di-MEE-tuhr) (CERES) Demeter was the goddess of grain and of farming. When her daughter PERSEPHONE was kidnapped and taken to the underworld by HADES, she caused all the crops to wither and die as she searched the earth for her daughter. Finally, ZEUS allowed Persephone to join Demeter for eight months each year. Every year, when Demeter finds her daughter, her happiness brings the spring. But when she loses her again, the four months of winter begin.

**Diana** Diana is the Roman name for ARTEMIS, the goddess of the hunt.

**Dionysus** (deye-oh-NEYE-suhs) (BACCHUS) Dionysus was the god of wine. Because he showed people how to turn grapes into wine, he was often pictured with a wreath of grape leaves on his head. The religious groups, or cults, that worshiped him performed ceremonies in his honor.

**Dragon** A mythical beast often shown as a large, dangerous, lizardlike animal that blows fire. Dragons appear in the Bible and in the stories of many peoples. They usually represent something evil and destructive and must be killed by a hero. The Chinese believe that dragons are not evil and that they bring good luck.

**Echo** Echo was a NYMPH who loved NARCISSUS. When he rejected her love, she became so sad that she wasted away until only her voice remained. Our word *echo*, for a repeated sound, comes from her name.

**Eros** (AIR-os, EER-os) (CUPID) Eros was the god of love and is often identified as the son of APHRODITE.

Diana

**Eurydice** (yoo-RID-i-see) Eurydice was the wife of ORPHEUS. When she died, her husband followed her to the underworld and charmed HADES with his music to secure her release. On the way to the upper world, Orpheus disobeyed Hades' instructions and turned back to see if Eurydice was following, thus losing her forever.

**Fates** The Fates were three old women who decided how long everybody would live and what would happen during their lifetimes. Every person's life was represented by a thread. One Fate spun the thread of life, one measured it, and one cut it at death.

**Freya** (FRAY-uh) Freya was the goddess of love and beauty in some Norse legends. She is often identified with FRIGG. (*See* image, next page.)

**Frigg** Frigg was the supreme Norse goddess, wife of ODIN. She is identified in some legends with FREYA. Friday is named after Frigg.

**Freya** Riding Chariot Driven by Cats

**Furies**  The Furies were horribly ugly goddesses of revenge who had snakes for hair. They pursued people who were guilty of terrible crimes and drove them mad.

**Golden Fleece**  The Golden Fleece was the gold wool coat that had been taken from a magical, winged ram. It was the prize sought by the hero Jason in one of the quests, or journeys, of Greek mythology. *See also* JASON AND THE GOLDEN FLEECE.

**Gordian knot**  The Gordian knot was a very complicated knot tied by a Greek king. According to legend, whoever untied the knot would rule all of Asia. One story has it that ALEXANDER THE GREAT undid the knot by cutting through it with his sword.

**Hades** (HAY-deez) (PLUTO)  Hades was the god of the underworld. Hades is also the Greek name for the underworld, the gray and gloomy kingdom where the dead lived.

**Hector**  Hector was the noblest of the Trojan warriors and the leader of the Trojan army. He was slain by ACHILLES, who dragged his body around the walls of TROY. *See also* TROJAN WAR.

**Hel**  Hel was the Norse goddess of the dead. She presided over the underworld, which was also called Hel. The Norse underworld was the abode of the spirits of those who had not died in battle.

**Helen of Troy**  Helen was the most beautiful woman in the world. Even though she was Greek by birth, she was called Helen of TROY because Paris, a prince of Troy, kidnapped her and made her his princess. The TROJAN WAR began when the Greeks sent a huge fleet of ships to attack Troy and win her back.

**Hephaestus** (hi-FES-tuhs, hi-FEE-stuhs) (VULCAN)  Hephaestus was the god of fire. He was also the blacksmith of the gods and used fire to make their tools and weapons.

**Hera** (HEER-uh) (JUNO)  Hera was the wife of ZEUS and the queen of the Greek gods and goddesses. She was also the goddess of marriage.

**Hercules** (HUR-kyuh-leez)  Hercules was the strongest man in the world and one of the greatest Greek heroes. He proved his strength by performing a series of supposedly impossible tasks called the Twelve Labors of Hercules.

**Hermes** (HUR-meez) (MERCURY)  Hermes was the messenger of the gods. He wore winged sandals and a winged cap, which allowed him to travel very fast, and he carried a magic wand.

**Icarus** (IK-uh-ruhs)  Icarus was the son of DAEDALUS, the great inventor. Daedalus made wings of wax that he and Icarus used to escape from the island where they were imprisoned. Daedalus warned his son not to fly too close to the sun, but Icarus ignored his warning. The heat of the sun melted the wings, and Icarus fell into the sea and drowned.

**Jason and the Golden Fleece**  Jason was one of the first great heroes of Greek mythology. In order to claim his rightful throne, he had to sail off in search of the GOLDEN FLEECE, the coat of a magical ram. This task was

**Hercules.** One of his Twelve Labors was to kill the Nemean lion. From its skin Hercules fashioned a garment that made him invulnerable. Courtesy Museum of Fine Arts, Boston.

thought to be impossible because the fleece was far away and guarded by a terrible snake. Jason sailed in his ship, the *Argo*, with other Greek heroes, called the Argonauts. He survived many perilous adventures and recovered the fleece.

**Juno** (JOOH-noh)  Juno is the Roman name for HERA, the wife of JUPITER and therefore queen of the gods and goddesses and the goddess of marriage. The month of June is named after her.

**Jupiter**  Jupiter is the Roman name for ZEUS, the king of all the gods and goddesses. The largest planet in our solar system is named Jupiter.

**Labyrinth** (LAB-uh-rinth)  The Labyrinth was a large maze (a building full of confusing hallways and dead ends). It was designed by the inventor DAEDALUS for King Minos of Crete. Those who entered the Labyrinth would get lost in the endless passages and could never escape. A monster, the MINO-TAUR, was kept in the center of the Labyrinth.

**leprechaun**  In the folklore of Ireland, leprechauns are little men who look like elves. It is said that they will reveal (to anyone who catches them) a buried treasure, usually a crock of gold at the end of the rainbow.

**Loch Ness Monster** (lokh nes)  The Loch Ness monster is a gigantic, humped, dragonlike creature that is rumored to live in Loch Ness, a lake in SCOTLAND.

**Loki**  Loki was the Norse god of strife and spirit of evil. According to one legend, he was finally sentenced to be chained to a rock, where he would remain until the Twilight of the Gods, the day of doom, when a final battle between the forces of good and the forces of evil would cause the destruction of the universe.

**Mars**  Mars is the Roman name for ARES, the god of war. The planet Mars is named for him, possibly because it is red, the color of blood. The month of March is also named for Mars.

**Medusa**  Medusa was a Gorgon, a horrible monster with snakes for hair. Whoever looked directly at her was turned to stone. A hero, Perseus, was able to kill her by looking at her reflection in a polished shield as he aimed his sword.

**Mercury**  Mercury is the Roman name for HERMES, the messenger of the gods. The planet closest to the sun is named Mercury because it moves swiftly in its orbit.

**Midas** (MEYE-duhs)  Midas was a greedy king who wished that everything he touched would turn to gold. The gods granted his wish, but he soon found that he could not eat, because his food turned to gold as soon as he touched it. Midas asked the gods to take away his power so that he would not starve, and he was allowed to live a normal life again.

**Minerva** Minerva is the Roman name for ATHENA, the goddess of wisdom.

**Minotaur** (MIN-uh-tawr) The Minotaur was a terrible monster, half man and half bull, who was kept by King Minos in the LABYRINTH to kill anyone who entered. He was finally destroyed by the hero Theseus.

**Narcissus** Narcissus was a beautiful youth who gazed into a pool and fell in love with his own reflection. He wasted away staring into the pool, and the gods turned him into the flower now called the narcissus.

**Neptune** Neptune is the Roman name for POSEIDON, the god of the sea. The large planet that is eighth in order from the sun is named Neptune.

**nymph** In Greek mythology, a nymph was a female spirit who lived in forests, bodies of water, and other outdoor places.

**Odin** (OH-din) In Norse mythology, Odin was the ruler of the gods as well as the god of wisdom, POETRY, farming, and war. Wednesday is named after Odin, using a form of his name that begins with *W*.

**Odysseus** (oh-DIS-yoohs, oh-DIS-ee-uhs) (ULYSSES) Odysseus was a Greek hero who fought in the TROJAN WAR. Making his way home to Ithaca, he encountered many adventures and was imprisoned several times. His journey, or odyssey, took ten years, but he was finally reunited with his wife, PENELOPE, and his son. The story of this journey is told in the ODYSSEY, an epic by the Greek poet HOMER. *See also* SIRENS.

**Oedipus** (ED-uh-puhs) Oedipus was a great but tragic king. He saved the city of Thebes by solving the riddle of the SPHINX. However, the DELPHIC ORACLE predicted that he would kill his father and marry his mother. Because Oedipus had been abandoned as a child, he did not know his true parents. He argued with an old man on the road to Thebes and killed him; the man was his father. After he saved the city of Thebes, he married its queen, his mother. When he found out that the prophecy had come true, Oedipus blinded himself.

**Olympus** Olympus is the legendary home of the Greek gods. It is an actual mountain in GREECE, the highest in the country. The ancient Olympic games were a celebration held every four years on the plain of Olympus in honor of ZEUS. Our modern Olympic games are modeled after them.

**Orpheus** (AWR-fyoos, AWR-fee-uhs) Orpheus was the husband of EURYDICE and an outstanding musician who could play and sing nearly as well as the gods.

**Pan** Pan was the Greek god of shepherds and their flocks. He was half man and half goat, and he often played tunes on his musical pipes.

**Pandora's box** (pan-DOHR-uh) Pandora's box was a box that ZEUS gave to Pandora, the first woman. Zeus warned her never to open it, but her curiosity was too strong. When she opened the box, all the evils and miseries of the world, such as sorrow, disease, and hatred, flew out, and they have made us suffer ever since. At the bottom of the box, however, was one good thing: hope.

**Paris** Paris was the prince of TROY who kidnapped HELEN and thus started the TROJAN WAR. Paris killed ACHILLES by piercing his heel with an arrow.

**Pegasus** (PEG-uh-suhs) In Greek mythology, Pegasus was a magnificent winged horse that could fly above the earth.

**Penelope** (puh-NEL-uh-pee) Penelope was the wife of ODYSSEUS. Many men tried to convince her to marry them while Odysseus

**Pegasus.** Drawing by Peter Paul Rubens.

was making his ten-year journey home. But Penelope had faith that he would return and remained true to him.

**Persephone** (pur-SEF-uh-nee) (PROSERPINA) Persephone was the goddess of spring and the daughter of DEMETER. When she was kidnapped by HADES, she became queen of the underworld.

**phoenix** (FEE-niks) In Greek mythology, the phoenix was a bird that burned itself to death and arose from its ashes as a new phoenix.

**Pluto** Pluto is the Roman name for HADES, the king of the underworld. The cold, dark planet that is farthest from the sun is named Pluto.

**Poseidon** (puh-SEYED-n) (NEPTUNE) Poseidon was the god of the sea, one of the most powerful gods, after ZEUS. He is often pictured as a bearded giant who has a fish's tail and is holding a trident (a three-pronged spear).

**Prometheus** (pruh-MEETH-yoohs, pruh-MEE-thee-uhs) Prometheus was a TITAN who stole fire from the gods and gave it to humans. He was punished for his theft by ZEUS, who had him chained to a rock while a great eagle gnawed at his liver. The giant was later rescued by HERCULES.

**Proserpina** (proh-SUR-peen-nuh) Proserpina, the daughter of CERES, is the Roman name for PERSEPHONE, the goddess of spring.

**Psyche** (SEYE-kee) Psyche was a beautiful maiden who loved CUPID. After a long series of trials imposed by Cupid's jealous mother, the goddess VENUS, Psyche became immortal and was allowed to marry Cupid.

**Pygmalion** (pig-MAYL-yuhn, pig-MAY-lee-uhn) Pygmalion was a sculptor and a king of ancient Cyprus. He fell in love with a statue he had carved and begged the goddess APHRODITE to find him a perfect woman. Aphrodite brought the statue to life so that Pygmalion and his beloved could be together.

**Romulus and Remus** (ROM-yuh-luhs; REE-muhs) Romulus and Remus were twin brothers who were taken from their mother and abandoned when they were babies. A she-wolf found them and cared for them until they were taken in by a shepherd. Romulus later founded the city that was named for him, ROME, the capital of the ROMAN EMPIRE.

**Saturn** Saturn is the Roman name for the king of the TITANS. He was the father of JUPITER. The second largest planet in the solar system is named Saturn.

**Sirens** The Sirens were evil creatures that lived on a rocky island. Their beautiful singing lured many passing sailors to their deaths. The wanderer ODYSSEUS wanted to hear the Sirens' song, so before he sailed past them he plugged his sailors' ears with wax and had them tie him to the mast of his ship.

**Sphinx** (SFINKS)   The Sphinx was a terrible monster with the body of a winged lion and the head of a woman. She devoured anyone who could not answer this riddle: "What goes on four feet in the morning, on two at noon, and on three in the evening?" The answer is "man," because human beings crawl when they are babies, stand up and walk when they are grown, and walk with a cane (the third foot) when they are old. When OEDIPUS solved the riddle, the Sphinx killed herself. The most famous statue of a sphinx is the huge Great Sphinx of Egypt, near the PYRAMIDS.

**Styx** (STIKS)   The Styx was the river that dead souls crossed to get to the underworld. *See also* HADES.

**Tell, William**   William Tell is a legendary archery hero of SWITZERLAND. He shot an apple off his son's head with an arrow.

**Thor**   In Norse mythology, Thor was the god of thunder. His weapon was a hammer, which made the sound of thunder. Thursday is named after him.

**Titans** (TEYE-tunz)   The Titans were a race of immensely strong giants who ruled the universe until ZEUS and the other Greek gods overthrew them.

**Trojan horse**   The Trojan horse was a gigantic wooden horse left by the Greek army outside the walls of TROY during the TROJAN WAR. Inside the horse were hidden the Greeks' best soldiers. Another Greek soldier, pretending to have deserted his comrades, tricked the Trojans into bringing the horse inside the city walls. That night the Greeks crept out of the horse and conquered Troy.

**Trojan War**   The Trojan War was fought by the Greek cities against the walled city of TROY. It began when PARIS, a Trojan prince, kidnapped HELEN, a beautiful woman who

was supposed to marry one of the Greek rulers. The Greeks sent a fleet of one thousand ships full of soldiers to attack Troy. After ten years, the Greeks still had not taken the city. ODYSSEUS, a Greek leader, finally made up a plan to trick the Trojans. He and his best soldiers hid inside the TROJAN HORSE, surprised the Trojan army, and set fire to the city. After fierce fighting, Troy was conquered and destroyed. The story of the Trojan War is told in the ILIAD of HOMER.

**troll**   In Norse mythology, trolls were horrible dwarfs who lived in caves or other hidden places. They were very nasty and often hoarded treasure.

**Troy**   Troy was a powerful city in ancient TURKEY. It sat on a hill overlooking the sea and was protected by high walls. Its people were called Trojans. *See also* TROJAN WAR.

**Ulysses** (yoo-LIS-eez)   Ulysses is the Roman name for ODYSSEUS.

**Trojan horse.** An engraving showing the Greek army emerging from the Trojan Horse.

**Zodiac.** Surrounding the sun is a round calendar showing the seasons and the symbols of the zodiac.

**unicorn**  The unicorn is a mythical animal that looks like a small white horse with a long, straight, pointed horn growing from its forehead.

**Valhalla**  In Norse mythology, Valhalla was the great hall in ASGARD that was reserved for the souls of those who died heroic deaths.

**Venus**  Venus is the Roman name for APHRODITE, the goddess of love and beauty. The brightest planet in the sky is named Venus.

**Vulcan**  Vulcan is the Roman name for HEPHAESTUS, the god of fire.

**Zeus** (ZOOHS) (JUPITER)  Zeus was the supreme ruler of the gods and goddesses of ancient Greece. He controlled the thunder and lightning and often used thunderbolts as weapons. He was more powerful than all the other gods and goddesses. *See also* JUPITER.

**zodiac**  The zodiac is an imaginary band across the sky about 30 degrees wide through which the SUN, our MOON, and the PLANETS appear to move. It is divided into twelve parts, with each part named for a nearby CONSTELLATION (Aquarius, Pisces, and so on). The constellations are the familiar signs of the zodiac used in astrology.

# Music, Art, and Architecture

Many well-known songs, monuments, buildings, paintings, and artists are listed here. There are also a number of terms that will help you learn about the arts of music, painting, drawing, sculpture, and architecture. Some of the entries are the lyrics (words) of familiar songs. It is hard to appreciate them fully without their tunes, but the words themselves are an important part of American culture.

**abstract art**   Abstract art is a kind of PAINTING, DRAWING, and SCULPTURE that flourished in the twentieth century. It does not present objects as they appear to the eye, but rather is an arrangement of colors and forms as imagined by the artist. PABLO PICASSO, Alexander Calder, and Henry Moore all created this form of art.

**Acropolis**   The Acropolis is a hill that overlooks the city of ATHENS, GREECE. The ruins of ancient buildings, including the PARTHENON, are on top of this hill. *Acropolis* means "summit of the city" in Greek.

**Alhambra** (al-HAM-bruh)   The Alhambra is a magnificent palace in Granada, in southern SPAIN. It was built in the thirteenth and fourteenth centuries by the Moors, Muslims from North AFRICA.

**alto**   Alto is a female singing voice that is lower than SOPRANO. It is sometimes called contralto.

**"Amazing Grace"**   "Amazing Grace" is a popular hymn that begins:

> Amazing Grace! How sweet the sound
> That saved a wretch like me!

> I once was lost, but now am found,
> Was blind, but now I see.

**"America"**   "America" is a patriotic song:

> My country, 'tis of thee,
> Sweet land of liberty,
> Of thee I sing:
> Land where my fathers died,
> Land of the pilgrims' pride,
> From every mountainside
> Let freedom ring.

**"America the Beautiful"**   "America the Beautiful" is a patriotic song by Katherine Lee Bates that begins:

> O beautiful for spacious skies,
> For amber waves of grain,
> For purple mountain's majesty
> Above the fruited plain!
> America! America!
> God shed his grace on thee
> And crown thy good with brotherhood
> From sea to shining sea!

***American Gothic***   *American Gothic* is a painting by the twentieth-century American artist Grant Wood. It depicts a stern-faced couple in front of a prairie farmhouse; the man is holding a pitchfork.

**American Gothic**

**aqueduct** An aqueduct is a structure similar to a bridge that supports a pipe or channel, usually one carrying water from a distant source. The ancient Romans built many impressive stone aqueducts, especially in SPAIN and FRANCE.

**arch** An arch is a curved, sometimes pointed, opening. It can be part of a building's doorway or window or it can stand by itself, like the Gateway Arch in ST. LOUIS, MISSOURI, or the ARCH OF TRIUMPH in PARIS, FRANCE.

**architecture** Architecture is the art of designing buildings and other structures, including fortresses and walls (the BASTILLE and the GREAT WALL OF CHINA), and towers (the EIFFEL TOWER and SKYSCRAPERS). The person who practices this art is called an architect.

**Armstrong, Louis** Louis Armstrong was a twentieth-century African-American JAZZ trumpet player. He was known for his trum-

pet solos and for the gravelly voice in which he sang songs such as "Hello, Dolly" and "It's a Wonderful World."

**"Auld Lang Syne"** "Auld Lang Syne" is a traditional Scottish song that is sung on New Year's Eve to mark the passing of the old year:

> Should auld acquaintance be forgot,
> And never brought to min'?
> Should auld acquaintance be forgot,
> And days of auld lang syne?

> For auld lang syne, my dear,
> For auld lang syne,
> We'll tak a cup o' kindness yet,
> For auld lang syne!

The words, passed down orally, were recorded by the poet Robert Burns. (*Auld lang syne* is Scottish for "long ago." *Tak* means "take.")

**Bach, Johann Sebastian** Johann Sebastian Bach was a German composer, organist, and choirmaster of the 1700s. He composed a large number of instrumental and choral (singing) works, including "Jesu, Joy of Man's Desiring" and the *Brandenburg Concertos*.

**ballad** A ballad is a simple song or POEM that tells a story, such as "CLEMENTINE" or "CASEY JONES."

**ballet** A ballet is an elaborate dance presented on a stage set to instrumental music. It usually tells a story or sets a mood and is performed by a group of highly trained dancers, both male and female. The nineteenth-century Russian composer PETER TCHAIKOVSKY wrote three ballets that are still performed today, *The Nutcracker* (frequently presented during the Christmas season), *Sleeping Beauty*, and *Swan Lake*.

**baroque** (buh-ROHK) The word *baroque* is used to describe a dramatic and often fancy style of art, ARCHITECTURE, and music that was popular in EUROPE and LATIN AMERICA

**Baroque.** St. Paul's Cathedral in London features elaborate Baroque architecture.

**The Beatles,** circa 1964.

from about 1600 to 1750. JOHANN SEBASTIAN BACH and Antonio Vivaldi were famous baroque composers. Latin America is known for its richly decorated baroque churches.

**bass** A bass voice is the lowest male singing voice.

**"The Battle Hymn of the Republic"** "The Battle Hymn of the Republic" is a patriotic hymn from the CIVIL WAR written by Julia Ward Howe:

> Mine eyes have seen the glory of the
> coming of the Lord;
> He is trampling out the vintage where
> the grapes of wrath are stored;
> He hath loosed the fateful lightning of
> his terrible swift sword;
> His truth is marching on.

**beat** In music, the beat is one of the units used to mark the METER of a song or other musical work. When you count the beat, it is just like counting time.

**The Beatles** The Beatles were a British ROCK 'N' ROLL group of the mid- to late

1960s. The four Beatles were John Lennon, Paul McCartney, George Harrison, and Ringo Starr. Among their many hit songs were "Hard Day's Night" and "Yellow Submarine."

**Beethoven, Ludwig van** Ludwig van Beethoven was a German musician of the 1700s

**Ludwig van Beethoven.** Composing the *Missa Solemnis.*

and 1800s who is considered one of the greatest composers of all time. The *Moonlight Sonata* and the "Ode to Joy" from the Ninth Symphony are two of his more familiar works. Although he began to grow deaf midway in his career, he continued to compose music.

**Big Ben** Big Ben is the nickname for the bell in the clock tower of the Houses of Parliament in London, England.

**bluegrass** Bluegrass is a style of music that developed in the South in the 1940s. It uses guitar, violin, banjo, and other string instruments. Bluegrass often has a quick tempo and may include three or four voices singing together. *See also* folk songs.

**blues** The blues is a kind of sad, slow music, usually with words, that developed among blacks in the southern United States. Major blues artists of the twentieth century include Bessie Smith and Billie Holiday.

**brass** The brass are a family of musical instruments that are often made of brass. Each instrument has a mouthpiece that the player blows through and a horn that produces the sound. The brass instruments are trumpets, trombones, tubas, bugles, cornets, and French horns.

**Brooklyn Bridge** The Brooklyn Bridge spans the East River between Manhattan and Brooklyn in New York City. When it was built in the late 1800s, it was one of the longest bridges in the world.

**Calypso** Calypso is a type of music that originated in the West Indies. It has a distinctive rhythm and often includes improvised lyrics about humorous or current-day topics.

**"Camptown Races"** "Camptown Races" is a folk song by the nineteenth-century American composer Stephen Foster. It begins:

**Big Ben**

The Camptown ladies sing this song,
Doo-da, doo-da,
The Camptown racetrack's five miles
    long,
Oh, doo-da day.

**carol** A carol is a folk song that expresses happiness or joy and is often sung on festive holidays, such as Christmas. "Silent Night," "O Come, All Ye Faithful," and "Deck the Halls" are Christmas carols.

**"Casey Jones"** "Casey Jones" is a popular American folk song about a railroad engineer who died in a train crash. It starts:

Come all you rounders, for I want you to
    hear
The story of a brave engineer.
Casey Jones was the rounder's name,
On a big eight-wheeler of a mighty fame.

**cathedral** A cathedral is a Christian church that is usually the home church of a bishop. Cathedrals are often large, impressive buildings with high arches, domed ceilings, and stained-glass windows.

**cave paintings**  Paintings on cave walls are some of the earliest known works of art. The oldest, in AUSTRALIA, may be 50,000 years old. Some in SPAIN and FRANCE may be 30,000 years old. The most famous are in a cave in Lascaux (la-SKOH), FRANCE, where running horses, deer, and other animals are painted in bright colors across the walls. *See also* LASCAUX CAVE PAINTINGS.

**Chaplin, Charlie**  Charlie Chaplin was a comedian and movie star of the early 1900s. His most famous character was the Little Tramp, a man with a small mustache who wore a bowler hat, fancy gloves, a ragged suit, and shoes that were too big.

**Chopin, Frédéric**  (SHOH-pan) Frédéric Chopin was a nineteenth-century Polish composer who worked mostly in FRANCE. Almost all of his musical compositions were written for the piano.

**classical music**  Classical music is complex music written for an ORCHESTRA or for smaller groups of instruments. Some of the most notable composers of classical music are BACH, BEETHOVEN, Brahms, HAYDN, MOZART, and TCHAIKOVSKY.

**"Clementine"**  "Clementine" is an American FOLK SONG that begins:

> In a cavern, in a canyon,
> Excavating for a mine,
> Dwelt a miner, forty-niner,
> And his daughter, Clementine.
> Oh, my darling, oh, my darling,
> Oh, my darling Clementine,
> You are lost and gone forever,
> Dreadful sorry, Clementine.

(A forty-niner is someone who took part in the California GOLD RUSH OF 1849.)

**Colosseum**  The Colosseum was a large stadium where competitions were held in ancient ROME. Its ruins are still standing. To-day, sports arenas called coliseums are named after this building.

**concerto**  A concerto is a piece of instrumental music usually written for an ORCHESTRA and a solo performer. For instance, a piano concerto uses an orchestra and a piano.

**conductor**  A conductor directs a group of musicians to make sure that they are playing at the right speed and volume.

**Copland, Aaron**  Aaron Copland was an American composer of the twentieth century who was noted for his works with a regional setting, such as the music for the BALLETS *Appalachian Spring* and *Rodeo*.

**country and western music**  Songs about love and everyday life that have a regular beat and usually rhymed lyrics are examples of country and western music. It is especially popular in the southeast United States. Well-known modern country and western singers include Johnny Cash, Loretta Lynn, and Garth Brooks.

**cubism**  (KYOOB-iz-uhm) Cubism was a movement in modern art that emphasized the geometrical forms of natural images. PABLO PICASSO produced many notable cubist works in the early 1900s.

**Disney, Walt**  Walt Disney, who created the cartoon characters Mickey Mouse and Donald Duck, was the first person to make full-length animated cartoons, early in the 1900s. Disneyland, in CALIFORNIA, and Walt Disney World and EPCOT Center, in FLORIDA, are amusement parks based on his ideas.

**"Dixie"**  "Dixie" is a battle song that was sung by Confederate soldiers during the CIVIL WAR. It begins:

> I wish I was in the land of cotton,
> Old times there are not forgotten.
> Look away, look away,
> Look away, Dixie land.

The word *Dixie* has been used as a nickname for the SOUTH since the Civil War.

**dome**   A dome is a roof that is shaped like an upside-down bowl. The CAPITOL in WASHINGTON, D.C., has a dome.

**"Down by the Riverside"**   "Down by the Riverside" is an American SPIRITUAL:

Gonna lay down my burden,
Down by the riverside,
Down by the riverside.
Down by the riverside,
Gonna lay down my burden,
Down by the riverside,
Going to study war no more.

**"Down in the Valley"**   "Down in the Valley" is an American FOLK SONG:

Down in the valley, the valley so low,
Hang your head over, hear the wind blow.
Hear the wind blow, dear, hear the wind
   blow,
Hang your head over, hear the wind blow.

**drawing**   Drawing is the creation of an image by producing lines on a surface, usually with pencils, pens, or crayons. In drawing, the outline of a figure is marked by a noticeable line, whereas in PAINTING, lines are usually blended. Cartoons are examples of drawings.

**Eiffel Tower** (EYE-fuhl)   The Eiffel Tower is a tall structure that is probably the most familiar landmark in PARIS, FRANCE. It is made of steel girders that curve from the ground upward into a long thin tower.

**Ellington, Duke**   Duke Ellington was an African-American composer and bandleader of the twentieth century. He is remembered especially for his JAZZ compositions.

**Empire State Building**   The Empire State Building is an office building in NEW YORK CITY that was built in the 1930s. It was the tallest building in the world for many years.

**Eiffel Tower**

**expressionism**   Expressionism was an artistic style that flourished in the late nineteenth and early twentieth centuries. The expressionist artists, such as VINCENT VAN GOGH, emphasized feelings and experiences, often distorting rather than directly representing visual images.

**"The Farmer in the Dell"**   "The Farmer in the Dell" is a NURSERY RHYME and circle game. Players join hands and sing around the farmer, who then chooses a wife; the wife then chooses a child, and so on. In the last of the ten verses, "the cheese stands alone."

**filmmaking**   Filmmaking is the art of making movies. American filmmakers include animator WALT DISNEY, Steven Spielberg, and Francis Ford Coppola.

Ella Fitzgerald

**Fitzgerald, Ella**   Ella Fitzgerald was a twentieth-century African-American singer. She brought her clear voice and playful style to many JAZZ and popular songs, such as "Anything Goes," by Cole Porter, and "Love You Madly," by DUKE ELLINGTON.

**folk dance**   A folk dance is a traditional dance of a region. There are many types of folk dances, including the SQUARE DANCE. Some of these dances date back many years.

**folk song**   A folk song is a simple song, like a BALLAD, that is passed down from generation to generation by word of mouth. More recent songs, composed in this century by Pete Seeger and Woody Guthrie, for example, are called folk songs because they were inspired by the older tradition.

**"For He's a Jolly Good Fellow"**   "For He's a Jolly Good Fellow" is a favorite American FOLK SONG from the nineteenth century. The first verse is:

> For he's a jolly good fellow
> For he's a jolly good fellow

For he's a jolly good fellow
Which nobody can deny.

**"Frère Jacques"** (frair zhahk) "Frère Jacques" ("Brother John") is an old French lullaby. Here is the first verse, in English:

> Are you sleeping, are you sleeping
> Brother John? Brother John?
> Morning bells are ringing,
> Morning bells are ringing:
> Ding, ding, dong. Ding, ding, dong.

**fresco**   A fresco is a PAINTING done on wet plaster so that the colors become a permanent part of the plaster. A fresco is often a large MURAL, such as *The Last Supper* by LEONARDO DA VINCI.

**fugue**   A fugue is a musical composition in which one or more melodies are played against each other rather than together.

**gargoyle**   A gargoyle is a spout or decorative sculpture in the shape of an ugly or strange-looking human or animal form. Mouths of gargoyles were often used as spouts on the roofs of medieval buildings and churches to carry off rainwater.

**Gershwin, George**   George Gershwin was a twentieth-century American composer who combined JAZZ and CLASSICAL MUSIC. His works include *Rhapsody in Blue* and the music for the OPERA *Porgy and Bess*. With his brother, Ira Gershwin, he wrote many popular MUSICAL COMEDIES.

**"God Bless America"**   "God Bless America" is a patriotic American song that begins: "God bless America, / Land that I love."

**Golden Gate Bridge**   The Golden Gate Bridge, in SAN FRANCISCO, CALIFORNIA, is noted for its graceful design and is one of the longest suspension bridges in the world.

**gospel music**   Gospel music is strong and rhythmic religious music that is especially popular in the southern United States.

**Gothic architecture**   Gothic architecture was the main style of European ARCHITEC-

**Golden Gate Bridge**

**Gothic.** The Cathedral of Notre-Dame, Rheims, has the narrow towers and pointed arches common to Gothic architecture.

TURE during the twelfth through fifteenth centuries. It used narrow towers, pointed arches, soaring ceilings, and flying buttresses. Many great churches were built in this style.

**Great Wall of China**  The Great Wall of China is an ancient stone wall that runs for 1,500 miles along the northern border of CHINA.

**"Greensleeves"**  "Greensleeves" is a famous song written during the period between 1400 and 1600. The refrain goes:

> Greensleeves was all my joy,
> Greensleeves was my delight,
> Greensleeves was my heart of gold,
> And who but my lady Greensleeves.

**Gregorian chant**  (gre-GOHR-ee-an)  Gregorian chant is traditional music that is sung during worship in the ROMAN CATHOLIC CHURCH. It is sung in Latin and without musical instruments. Gregorian chant is also called "plainsong."

**Hagia Sophia**  (HAH-gee-uh soh-FEE-uh)  Hagia Sophia is a magnificent church in ISTANBUL, TURKEY. It was built in the 530s. For nearly 1,000 years, it was the most important church for the EASTERN ORTHODOX faith. It is now a MUSEUM.

**Handel, George Frederick**  George Frederick Handel was a German-born composer of the eighteenth century. He spent most of his life in ENGLAND and is best remembered for his *Messiah,* a musical composition for singers and an ORCHESTRA.

**harmony**  Harmony is the pleasing sound that results when different musical notes are played or sung together.

**Haydn, Franz Josef**  (HEYED-n)  Franz Josef Haydn was an eighteenth-century Austrian composer. Of his more than one hundred SYMPHONIES, *Surprise Symphony* and *Clock Symphony* are especially well known. Haydn is given credit for establishing the symphony as a musical form.

**"Here We Go 'Round the Mulberry Bush"**
"Here We Go 'Round the Mulberry Bush" is a children's singing game:

> Here we go 'round the mulberry bush,
> The mulberry bush, the mulberry bush;
> Here we go 'round the mulberry bush,
> So early in the morning.

**"He's Got the Whole World in His Hands"**
"He's Got the Whole World in His Hands" is a traditional American FOLK SONG. It was especially popular in the 1960s.

**hip-hop**   Hip-hop is a style of music, dance, and fashion created by young people in cities in the late twentieth century. Music videos helped to make RAP music one of the most familiar forms of hip-hop style.

**"Home on the Range"**   "Home on the Range" is a cowboy song about life in the old American West:

> Oh, give me a home where the buffalo
>     roam,
> Where the deer and the antelope play,
> Where seldom is heard a discouraging
>     word
> And the skies are not cloudy all day.

**Homer, Winslow**   Winslow Homer was an American painter of the late 1800s and early 1900s. He is best known for his PAINTINGS of fishermen and the changing effects of the sea and wind.

**horizon**   The horizon in a PAINTING, DRAWING, or other artwork is the line along which the earth and sky appear to meet.

**Hush, little baby**   "Hush, little baby" are the first words of a well-known lullaby (a song used to soothe a baby to sleep). The first part goes:

> Hush, little baby, don't say a word,
> Papa's going to buy you a mocking bird.
> If that mocking bird won't sing,
> Papa's going to buy you a diamond ring.

**hymn**   A hymn is a song that is sung usu-ally as part of a religious service. "God of Our Fathers," "A Mighty Fortress Is Our God" (by MARTIN LUTHER), "For All the Saints," and "Praise to the Lord, the Almighty" are favorite hymns. They are collected in books called hymnals.

**igloo**   An igloo is a domed house built of ice or hard snow that is built by some INUIT. (An Inuit is a native of the far northern regions of NORTH AMERICA.)

**Impressionism.** *The Japanese Footbridge,*
by Claude Monet, circa 1899.

**impressionism**   Impressionism is a style of art mainly associated with French painters of the late nineteenth century. It seeks to recreate the artist's or viewer's impression of a scene, rather than actual reality.

**"I've Been Working on the Railroad"**   "I've Been Working on the Railroad" is an American FOLK SONG:

> I've been working on the railroad
> All the livelong day,
> I've been working on the railroad
> Just to pass the time away.
> Don't you hear the whistle blowing?
> Rise up so early in the morn.
> Don't you hear the captain shouting,
> "Dinah blow your horn."

**jazz** Jazz is a form of American music invented by black musicians in NEW ORLEANS, LOUISIANA, early in the twentieth century. It is America's most important contribution to the world of music. Prominent jazz musicians include LOUIS ARMSTRONG, DUKE ELLINGTON, Benny Goodman, and ELLA FITZGERALD.

**"John Brown's Body"** "John Brown's Body" is a song written during the CIVIL WAR in honor of JOHN BROWN, who fought against SLAVERY. It begins: "John Brown's body lies a-moldering in the grave." "THE BATTLE HYMN OF THE REPUBLIC" was written to this tune.

**"John Henry"** "John Henry" is an American FOLK SONG about a race to build a railroad between a machine and a strong black man with a hammer. John Henry tried to build more track than the machine and died from his heroic effort. One verse goes:

> John Henry told his captain,
> Says, "A man ain't nothin' but a man,
> And before I'd let your steam drill beat
>    me down,
> I'd die with the hammer in my hand."

**Joplin, Scott** Scott Joplin was an African-American pianist and composer of the late nineteenth and early twentieth centuries. His "Maple Leaf Rag" and "The Entertainer" are two famous works written in ragtime, a musical JAZZ style characterized by jaunty rhythms.

**"Joshua Fit the Battle of Jericho"** "Joshua Fit the Battle of Jericho" is an American SPIRITUAL based on the biblical story of Joshua:

> Joshua fit the battle of Jericho,
> Jericho, Jericho,
> Joshua fit the battle of Jericho,
> And the walls come tumbling down.

(*Fit* means "fought.") *See also* JERICHO, BATTLE OF *under "Religion and Philosophy."*

**Key, Francis Scott** Francis Scott Key was a lawyer and poet of the late 1700s and early 1800s. He wrote the words to "THE STAR-SPANGLED BANNER" when he saw the United States flag still flying over Fort McHenry in Maryland after a heavy bombardment by the British during the WAR OF 1812.

**Lascaux cave paintings** (las-KOH) The Lascaux CAVE PAINTINGS were discovered in a cave in southern FRANCE in 1940. They date from prehistoric times (perhaps as early as 14,000 B.C.) and depict lively scenes of animals and hunters.

**Leaning Tower of Pisa** The Leaning Tower of Pisa is a tall, round building in Pisa, ITALY, that was constructed during the RENAISSANCE. Soon after it was built, its foundation sank, causing it to lean.

**Leonardo da Vinci** Leonardo da Vinci was a great Italian artist, scientist, and inventor

**Leaning Tower of Pisa**

who lived during the RENAISSANCE. He painted such works as *The Last Supper* and the *MONA LISA*, perhaps the most famous painting in the world. Leonardo also kept notebooks of his sketches, including designs for flying machines and other technological inventions.

**Lincoln Memorial** The Lincoln Memorial is a large monument in WASHINGTON, D.C., built in memory of ABRAHAM LINCOLN, the president of the United States during the CIVIL WAR. The memorial contains a statue of Lincoln and the texts of his Second Inaugural Address and GETTYSBURG ADDRESS engraved in stone.

**"London Bridge Is Falling Down"** "London Bridge Is Falling Down" is a children's singing game:

> London Bridge is falling down,
> Falling down, falling down,
> London Bridge is falling down,
> My fair lady.

**lyrics** Lyrics are words that are set to music.

**Matisse, Henri** (ma-TEES) Henri Matisse was a French sculptor and painter of the late nineteenth and early twentieth centuries. He was known for using brilliant colors and bold, simple shapes in paintings such as *The Dance.* He had a major influence on the course of modern art.

**measure** In music, a measure is the music between two vertical bars on a STAFF. It contains a definite number of BEATS (equal units of time) that recur in a composition. The first beat of a measure is often accented. *See* METER.

**melody** A melody is a recognizable tune.

**meter** In music, the meter is the pattern of BEATS in a MEASURE.

**Michelangelo** Michelangelo was an Italian painter and sculptor of the RENAISSANCE. Considered one of the greatest artists of all

**Lincoln Memorial**

time, he is best known for his SISTINE CHAPEL FRESCOES and for his sculptures *David* (the boy who slew the giant Goliath in the OLD TESTAMENT) and the *Pietà* (a pietà is the figure of MARY, the mother of JESUS, holding Jesus' dead body).

**mobile** A mobile is a SCULPTURE made up of suspended parts that move in the wind. Alexander Calder, an American sculptor of the twentieth century, created many lively and playful mobiles.

***Mona Lisa*** The *Mona Lisa* is a painting by LEONARDO DA VINCI that portrays a woman sitting with her hands crossed and with a mysterious half-smile on her face. Probably the most famous painting in the world, it hangs in the Louvre art MUSEUM in PARIS, FRANCE.

**Monticello** (mon-tuh-CHEL-oh) Monticello, in central VIRGINIA, was the home of President THOMAS JEFFERSON. Jefferson designed the brick mansion himself. Monticello appears on the back ("tails" side) of the nickel.

**mosaic** A mosaic is a picture or design made from small pieces of colored tile, glass, or stone that are cemented together on a sur-

***Mona Lisa.*** Painting by Leonardo da Vinci

face. Mosaics are often found in early Christian churches.

**Mozart, Wolfgang Amadeus**  Wolfgang Amadeus Mozart was an Austrian musician of the 1700s who began composing music when he was only five years old. Among the great variety of choral and ORCHESTRAL music he wrote, two OPERAS, *The Magic Flute* and *The Marriage of Figaro*, are especially well known.

**mural**  A mural is a PAINTING, usually a very large one, made on a wall or ceiling. Many modern murals are found on the sides of buildings.

**museum**  A museum is a building that displays objects considered to be of lasting interest and value in a particular subject, such as art, history, science, and sports. There are museums in almost every city. Some with especially notable PAINTINGS, DRAWINGS, and SCULPTURE are the Metropolitan Museum of Art, in NEW YORK CITY; the Louvre, in PARIS, FRANCE; the British Museum, in LONDON, ENGLAND; and the Hermitage, in St. Petersburg, RUSSIA. The National Air and Space Museum, part of the Smithsonian Institution in WASHINGTON, D.C., displays aircraft, old and new. The National Baseball Hall of Fame, in Cooperstown, NEW YORK, is devoted to the history of baseball.

**musical**  A musical is a play or film that includes song and dance as major elements. *The Sound of Music, West Side Story, Annie,* and *Cats* are all musicals.

**musical instruments**  Musical instruments are the devices used to make music. They are divided into four main groups, often called families: BRASS, PERCUSSION, STRINGS, and WOODWINDS.

**musical notation**  The standard way of writing music so that it can be played or sung is called musical notation. *See also* STAFF.

**My country, 'tis of thee**  These words are the first line of the patriotic song "AMERICA."

**national anthem**  A national anthem is the official song of a country. The national anthem of the United States is "THE STAR-SPANGLED BANNER." It is sometimes called "The National Anthem." Two other familiar national anthems are those of Canada, "O Canada," and France, "La Marseillaise."

**"Nobody Knows the Trouble I've Seen"**  "Nobody Knows the Trouble I've Seen" is an American SPIRITUAL. It begins: "Nobody knows the trouble I've seen, / Nobody knows but Jesus."

**Notre Dame**  (noh-truh DAHM) Notre Dame is a CATHEDRAL built during the MIDDLE AGES on an island in the Seine River in PARIS, FRANCE. It is one of the best-known examples of medieval ARCHITECTURE and has notable windows made of colored, or stained, glass.

**The Nutcracker**   The Nutcracker is a BAL-LET set to music by PETER TCHAIKOVSKY. It tells the story of a girl named Clara and her toy nutcracker, which is shaped like a soldier. One night the nutcracker comes to life and takes Clara to a land where toys and fairies dance. The Nutcracker is often enjoyed at Christmas.

**O beautiful for spacious skies**   These words are the first line of the patriotic song "AMER-ICA THE BEAUTIFUL."

**"O Susanna"**   "O Susanna" is an American FOLK SONG. The refrain is:

O, Susanna! O, don't you cry for me,
I've come from Alabama, with my banjo
on my knee.

**octave**   In music, an octave is the difference in PITCH between two tones when one is exactly twice as high in pitch as the other. Tones that are an octave apart have the same name. For instance, the middle tone "A" is 440 vibrations per second, and the "A" an octave above it is 880 vibrations per second. The word *octave* comes from the Latin word *octavus,* meaning eighth, because in some musical systems the octave is divided into eight tones.

**O'Keeffe, Georgia**   Georgia O'Keeffe was an American artist of the twentieth century. She is known for her paintings of flowers, shells, and desert scenes from the American SOUTHWEST.

**"On Top of Old Smoky"**   "On Top of Old Smoky" is an American FOLK SONG:

On top of old Smoky
All covered with snow,
I lost my true lover
By courtin' too slow.

**opera**   An opera is a PLAY set to music in which the lines are all sung instead of spoken. It is performed by an ORCHESTRA, singers, and sometimes dancers. Operas usually have many CHARACTERS, dramatic action, and elaborate costumes and stage sets. *Don Giovanni, Madame Butterfly,* and *Aïda* are all operas.

**orchestra**   An orchestra is a large group of musicians who play STRING, WOODWIND, BRASS, and PERCUSSION instruments. The musicians are led by a CONDUCTOR.

**organ**   The organ is a keyboard instrument that produces sound through large pipes. Large organs are found in churches and SYNA-GOGUES. Smaller, electronic organs can be played at home.

**painting**   A painting is an artwork that is created by the application of paint to a surface. There are different types of paintings. A portrait is a painting of a person, for example, the MONA LISA. A landscape represents scenery. A still life shows inanimate objects (things that do not move), such as a bowl of fruit on a table. There are also many different styles within painting, including AB-STRACT ART, BAROQUE art, CUBISM, and IM-PRESSIONISM.

**The Pantheon**   The Pantheon was built in A.D. 118 in ROME, ITALY, as a TEMPLE to all the gods. At the top of its enormous dome, a window in the shape of a perfect circle is open to the sky. Its floor is made of marble in beautiful colors and patterns. This temple replaced an earlier one built on the same site.

**Parthenon**   The Parthenon was a beautiful TEMPLE overlooking the city of ATHENS, GREECE. It is now in ruins, but its white marble columns are often visited by tourists. *See also* ACROPOLIS.

**"Pat-a-Cake, Pat-a-Cake"**   "Pat-a-Cake, Pat-a-Cake" is a hand-clapping song enjoyed by young children:

Pat-a-cake, pat-a-cake, baker's man,
Bake me a cake as fast as you can;
Pat it and prick it, and mark it with B,
Put it in the oven for baby and me.

Parthenon

Elvis Presley

**percussion** Percussion describes the family of musical instruments that are played by being struck. They include all kinds of drums, such as snare, bass, and kettledrums (also called timpani), as well as triangles, tambourines, woodblocks, and xylophones. Pianos are also considered percussion instruments, because the keys control hammers that hit strings.

**perspective** Perspective is a way of portraying three dimensions on a flat surface, as in a DRAWING or PAINTING. Realistic perspective shows a scene as it would appear from a single point of view in the real world, with close objects larger and more distant ones smaller. An artist may also play with perspective, for example, by making a scene appear more flat than it is in real life. *See also* VANISHING POINT.

***Peter and the Wolf*** *Peter and the Wolf* is a piece of music for an ORCHESTRA by the twentieth-century Russian composer Sergei Prokofiev. Through the music, it tells the story of a disobedient boy's encounter with a wolf.

**Picasso, Pablo** Pablo Picasso was a Spanish painter of the twentieth century and one of the most influential contemporary artists.

**pitch** In music, pitch refers to the high or low quality of a musical sound. The pitch is determined by the number of vibrations per second.

**Presley, Elvis** Twentieth-century American singer Elvis Presley was one of the first stars of ROCK 'N' ROLL. His many hit songs include "Hound Dog" and "Blue Suede Shoes." Presley died in 1977 while in his early forties.

**primary colors** Red, yellow, and blue are the primary colors. Primary colors cannot be made from any other colors, but all other colors are made from them. For example, red and yellow make orange; red and blue make purple; and yellow and blue make green.

**printmaking** Printmaking is an art form in which a design is created on a surface, then covered with ink or dye and stamped or pressed on a piece of paper, thus printing a copy of the design on the paper. Many copies of the original design can be made in this fashion. Posters are often made this way.

**proportion** Proportion in PAINTINGS and other artworks is the pleasing or balanced arrangement of the parts of the whole, as in a still life painting of fruits or vegetables.

**Pyramids** The Pyramids are huge stone structures shaped like four triangles that rise to a point; they were built as tombs for the rulers of ancient EGYPT. Three of the greatest Pyramids are still standing at Giza, near CAIRO, Egypt.

**quartet** In music, a quartet is a group of four singers or four musicians. It is also a piece of music written for four people or instruments.

**rap** Rap music combines LYRICS spoken in RHYME with music that has a strong BEAT. Its RHYTHMS and wordplay grew out of African-American traditions. Queen Latifah and the group De La Soul have been rap stars since the 1980s. *See also* HIP-HOP.

**reggae** (REG-ay) Reggae is a kind of pop music that began in JAMAICA. It combines elements of CALYPSO and BLUES. Bob Marley was one of the first reggae musicians to become well known outside of Jamaica.

**Rembrandt** Rembrandt was a Dutch painter of the seventeenth century and is considered one of the greatest European painters. He is especially known for his fine portraits.

**rest** In music, a rest tells the singers or musicians when to pause for a certain length of time.

**rhythm** Rhythm is the pattern of stressed and unstressed notes in music and poetry. The *down beat* is the name for the main stress in rhythm.

**"Ring Around the Rosies"** "Ring Around the Rosies" is a children's singing game:

> Ring around the rosies,
> A pocket full of posies,
> Ashes, ashes,
> We all fall down.

**Pyramids**

There are many ways of singing this song. Sometimes it begins: "Ring-a-ring o' roses."

**rock 'n' roll** Rock 'n' roll is a form of popular music that grew out of GOSPEL MUSIC and COUNTRY AND WESTERN MUSIC in the 1950s. ELVIS PRESLEY, the Supremes, and THE BEATLES were early rock 'n' roll stars.

**round** A round is a song that is begun at different times by different voices and results in harmonious singing. Two rounds are "ROW, ROW, ROW YOUR BOAT" and "FRÈRE JACQUES."

**"Row, Row, Row Your Boat"** "Row, Row, Row Your Boat" is a popular ROUND:

> Row, row, row your boat,
> Gently down the stream,
> Merrily, merrily, merrily, merrily,
> Life is but a dream.

**Saint Peter's Basilica** Saint Peter's is one of the largest ROMAN CATHOLIC churches in the world. It is located in the VATICAN. The home of the POPE is connected to it, and it is used for many of his speeches and ceremonies. MICHELANGELO contributed to its design.

**scale** In music, a scale is the series of principal tones in an OCTAVE. One well-known scale is sung "do, re, mi, fa, sol, la, ti, do." These same tones are also named c, d, e, f, g, a, b, c.

**sculpture** Sculpture is the art of creating three-dimensional figures or designs out of

**Saint Peter's Basilica**

wood, stone, clay, or metal. Two common types of sculpture are statues and busts. A statue usually represents a person, such as the STATUE OF LIBERTY or MICHELANGELO'S *David.* A bust portrays just the head and shoulders of a person. Modern sculpture sometimes represents only a shape rather than people or things.

**Sesame Street** The children's television program *Sesame Street* began in 1969. Although the series uses actors and animated characters, its true stars are the "Muppet" puppets, which include Cookie Monster, Oscar the Grouch, Kermit the Frog, and Bert and Ernie.

**Sistine Chapel** The Sistine Chapel is a chapel adjoining ST. PETER'S BASILICA in the VATICAN. It includes notable FRESCOES by MICHELANGELO on its walls and ceilings.

**skyscraper** Skyscrapers are extremely tall buildings. Two cities known for their skyscrapers are NEW YORK CITY (the EMPIRE STATE BUILDING, the Chrysler Building) and CHICAGO (the Sears Tower, the John Hancock Building).

**soprano** A soprano voice is the highest female singing voice.

**Sousa, John Philip** (SOOH-zuh) John Philip Sousa, known as "the March King," was a

bandleader and composer of the late 1800s and early 1900s. His many compositions include "Stars and Stripes Forever."

**spiritual** A spiritual is a religious FOLK SONG, such as "SWING LOW, SWEET CHARIOT" and "WHEN THE SAINTS GO MARCHING IN." Many spirituals were first composed and sung by African slaves in America.

**square dance** A square dance is a FOLK DANCE in which groups of people move in patterns, such as squares, circles, and straight lines, following the direction of a caller.

**staff** A staff is a way of showing MUSICAL NOTATION. It includes five lines, the spaces between the lines, and all the notes needed to play a piece of music.

**"The Star-Spangled Banner"** "The Star-Spangled Banner," which was written by FRANCIS SCOTT KEY during the WAR OF 1812, is the NATIONAL ANTHEM of the United States:

> Oh, say, can you see by the dawn's early light,
> What so proudly we hailed at the twilight's last gleaming?
> Whose broad stripes and bright stars, through the perilous fight,
> O'er the ramparts we watched were so gallantly streaming?
> And the rockets' red glare, the bombs bursting in air,
> Gave proof through the night that our flag was still there.
> Oh, say, does that star-spangled banner yet wave
> O'er the land of the free and the home of the brave?

**Star Wars** *Star Wars* is a series of science fiction movies created by American director George Lucas. The first movie, *Star Wars,* was released in 1977. The films combine classic good-versus-evil stories with the latest special effects.

The Statue of Liberty

**Statue of Liberty** The Statue of Liberty is the large statue of a woman holding a torch in one hand and a book in the other at the entrance to New York Harbor. The statue, which represents Liberty, was given to the United States by FRANCE in the late 1800s. The base of the Statue of Liberty is inscribed with a poem by Emma Lazarus that includes the lines: "Give me your tired, your poor, / Your huddled masses yearning to breathe free."

**strings** The strings are the family of musical instruments that use strings to produce sound. Some are played by drawing a bow over their strings, such as violins, cellos, violas, and double basses. Others are plucked with the fingers or a pick; these include harps, guitars, banjos, and mandolins.

**"Swing Low, Sweet Chariot"** "Swing Low, Sweet Chariot" is an American SPIRITUAL:

I looked over Jordan, and what did I see,
Coming for to carry me home?
A band of angels coming after me,
Coming for to carry me home.
Swing low, sweet chariot,
Coming for to carry me home.

**symphony** A symphony is a long piece of music usually with four parts, called movements, that is played by an ORCHESTRA. HAYDN, MOZART, BEETHOVEN, and Brahms composed some of the greatest symphonies.

**symphony orchestra** A symphony orchestra is a full-size ORCHESTRA usually devoted to playing CLASSICAL MUSIC.

**Taj Mahal** (TAHJ muh-HAHL) The Taj Mahal is a marble building in INDIA built by an Indian ruler in memory of his wife. It is one of the world's most beautiful buildings and a popular tourist attraction.

**"Take Me Out to the Ball Game"** "Take Me Out to the Ball Game" is a popular song about baseball. It begins:

Take me out to the ball game,
Take me out with the crowd.
Buy me some peanuts and Cracker Jack,
I don't care if I never come back.

Taj Mahal

**Tepee.** Chief Old Bull's tepee (foreground) at Standing Rock Reservation, North Dakota. Photographed circa 1900.

**tap dance**   A person doing a tap dance wears special shoes with metal attachments that "click" against a hard surface. Tap dancing derives from a number of sources and places, including AFRICA. Gregory Hines was one of America's best-known tap dancers.

**taps**   Taps is a short piece of music that is usually played on a bugle or drums. It is played in the military at night as a signal to put out the lights. It is also played at military funerals and memorial services.

**Tchaikovsky, Peter Ilyich** (cheye-KAWF-skee)   Peter Tchaikovsky was a nineteenth-century Russian composer. He wrote the music for three famous BALLETS that are still being performed: *THE NUTCRACKER, Swan Lake,* and *Sleeping Beauty.*

**tempo**   In music, the tempo is how fast or slow a song or other musical work is sung or played.

**tenor**   A tenor is an adult male singing voice that is higher than BASS.

**tepee**   A tepee is a tent shaped like a cone that is made of skins or bark. It was used by North American Indians of the GREAT PLAINS.

**"This Land Is Your Land"**   "This Land Is Your Land" is an American modern FOLK SONG by Woody Guthrie. It begins: "This land is your land, this land is my land."

**van Gogh, Vincent** (van GOH)   Vincent van Gogh was a nineteenth-century painter from THE NETHERLANDS. He is known for using

*Venus de Milo*

tury by King Louis XIV near Paris, France. It has ornately decorated rooms, including the Hall of Mirrors, and lavish gardens and fountains.

**The Vietnam Veterans Memorial**   The Vietnam Veterans Memorial is a monument in Washington, D.C., that honors Americans who died in the Vietnam War. The memorial is a large black marble wall that is engraved with the names of the dead. Asian-American architect Maya Lin designed it.

**Washington Monument**   The Washington Monument is a narrow, tall shaft of white stone in Washington, D.C. It was built to honor George Washington, the first President of the United States.

**"We Shall Overcome"**   The song "We Shall Overcome" began as a field song among slaves and was later adapted for a nineteenth-century hymn. It first became popular among labor unions in the 1940s, and the civil rights movement made it famous in the 1960s.

thick swirls of brilliantly colored paint in such paintings as *Starry Night* and *Sunflowers*.

**vanishing point**   A vanishing point is the point in a painting, drawing, or other artwork at which parallel lines drawn in perspective meet or seem to meet in the distance. An example would be a depiction of railroad tracks that are far apart in the near distance and gradually come closer together until they meet in the far distance at the vanishing point.

***Venus de Milo***   *Venus de Milo* is a Greek statue of Venus that is known for its beauty. It is in the Louvre art museum in Paris, France.

**Versailles** (ver-SEYE)   Versailles is a large royal residence built in the seventeenth cen-

**The Washington Monument**

**Frank Lloyd Wright.** The Guggenheim Museum, New York City.

**"When Johnny Comes Marching Home"**
"When Johnny Comes Marching Home" is a song from the CIVIL WAR:

> When Johnny comes marching home
>    again,
> Hurrah! hurrah!
> We'll give him a hearty welcome then,
> Hurrah! hurrah!
> The men will cheer, the boys will shout,
> The ladies, they will all turn out,
> And we'll all feel gay
> When Johnny comes marching home.

**"When the Saints Go Marching In"** "When the Saints Go Marching In" is an American SPIRITUAL about entering heaven that was played by NEW ORLEANS JAZZ musicians:

> Oh, when the saints go marching in,
> Oh, when the saints go marching in,

> Lord, I want to be in that number,
> When the saints go marching in.

**woodwinds** Woodwinds are the family of long, thin musical instruments that make a softer sound than the BRASS instruments. (All woodwinds used to be made of wood, but now many are made of metal.) Many woodwinds use reeds, which are thin pieces of wood that vibrate when a musician blows air through them. The woodwinds include piccolos, flutes, clarinets, oboes, English horns, saxophones, recorders, fifes, and bassoons.

**Wright, Frank Lloyd** Frank Lloyd Wright was an American architect of the late 1800s and early 1900s known for his highly original methods of uniting structures with their surroundings. He designed both houses and public buildings, such as Fallingwater, in

Bear Run, PENNSYLVANIA, and the Guggenheim Museum, in NEW YORK CITY.

**Wyeth, Andrew** Andrew Wyeth is an American painter of the twentieth century who is known for his realistic paintings. His best-known work is *Christina's World*.

**"Yankee Doodle"** "Yankee Doodle" is an American song sung during the REVOLUTIONARY WAR. The British soldiers first sang it to make fun of the Americans, but the American soldiers liked it and began to sing it too.

Yankee Doodle came to town
Riding on a pony,
He stuck a feather in his hat
And called it macaroni.
Yankee Doodle, keep it up,
Yankee Doodle dandy,
Mind the music and the step,
And with the girls be handy.

(The early settlers of New York were Dutch, and the Dutch name for Johnny is *Janke*, pronounced "Yankee." In the 1600s *doodle* meant "a simple, foolish person.")

# The Bible

The Bible is the holy book of the Jewish and Christian religions. It is really two sets of books, one, the Old Testament, stemming from an earlier period of history than the other, the New Testament. For Christians, both sets are the basis of their beliefs. For Jews, only the earlier set is valid, and they use the terms *old* and *new* as a matter of convenience. The Old Testament, principally written in Hebrew, tells the story of the ancient Israelites and their special relationship with God. The later set was originally written in Greek and is the story of the life and teachings of Jesus and the early Christian church.

The Bible is by far the best-known book in our culture. Hundreds of its sayings have become part of our everyday speech. Biblical stories are frequently referred to in books, newspapers, and magazines, and on television. Many paintings and other works of art portray people or scenes from the Bible. Furthermore, the Bible is the basis of some of our most important ideas about law and government. Because it is such a basic part of our culture, it is important for you to know something about the Bible, regardless of your individual religious belief.

**Abraham and Isaac** According to the OLD TESTAMENT, Abraham was the first of the ISRAELITES. Once GOD decided to test Abraham's faith and ordered him to kill his son Isaac and offer him to God as a sacrifice. Though Abraham loved Isaac very much, he started to obey God's command, but an angel appeared and told him not to hurt Isaac. The angel said that Abraham already proved his faith in God when he was willing to give up the son he loved.

**Adam and Eve** According to the OLD TESTAMENT, Adam and Eve were the first man and the first woman in the world. After GOD created Adam, he made Eve out of one of Adam's ribs. He placed Adam and Eve in a beautiful garden, called EDEN, where all kinds of fruit grew on the trees. God warned Adam not to eat the fruit on one particular tree. One day a serpent came up to Eve and told her that if she ate the forbidden fruit, she would know good and evil. Eve ate some

## Books of the Bible

### Hebrew Scriptures

| | | | |
|---|---|---|---|
| Genesis | II Kings | Nahum | Ruth |
| Exodus | Isaiah | Habakkuk | Lamentations |
| Leviticus | Jeremiah | Zephaniah | Ecclesiastes |
| Numbers | Ezekiel | Haggai | Esther |
| Deuteronomy | Hosea | Zechariah | Daniel |
| Joshua | Joel | Malachi | Ezra |
| Judges | Amos | Psalms | Nehemiah |
| I Samuel | Obadiah | Proverbs | I Chronicles |
| II Samuel | Jonah | Job | II Chronicles |
| I Kings | Micah | Song of Songs | |

### Old Testament

| Jerusalem Version | King James Version | Jerusalem Version | King James Version |
|---|---|---|---|
| Genesis | Genesis | Song of Solomon | Song of Solomon |
| Exodus | Exodus | Wisdom | |
| Leviticus | Leviticus | Ecclesiasticus | |
| Numbers | Numbers | Isaiah | Isaiah |
| Deuteronomy | Deuteronomy | Jeremia | Jeremia |
| Joshua | Joshua | Lamentation | Lamentation |
| Judges | Judges | Baruch | |
| Ruth | Ruth | Ezekiel | Ezekiel |
| I Samuel | I Samuel | Daniel | Daniel |
| II Samuel | II Samuel | Hosea | Hosea |
| I Kings | I Kings | Joel | Joel |
| II Kings | II Kings | Amos | Amos |
| I Chronicles | I Chronicles | Obadia | Obadia |
| II Chronicles | II Chronicles | Jonah | Jonah |
| Ezra | Ezra | Micah | Micah |
| Nehemiah | Nehemiah | Nahu | Nahu |
| Tobit | | Habakkuk | Habakkuk |
| Judith | | Zephaniah | Zephaniah |
| Esther | Esther | Haggai | Haggai |
| Job | Job | Zechariah | Zechariah |
| Psalms | Psalms | Malachi | Malachi |
| Proverbs | Proverbs | I Maccabees | |
| Ecclesiastes | Ecclesiastes | II Maccabees | |

### New Testament

| | | | |
|---|---|---|---|
| Matthew | II Corinthians | I Timothy | II Peter |
| Mark | Galatians | II Timothy | I John |
| Luke | Ephesians | Titus | II John |
| John | Philippians | Philemon | III John |
| Acts | Colossians | Hebrews | Jude |
| Romans | I-Thessalonians | James | Revelation |
| I Corinthians | II-Thessalonians | I Peter | |

Copyright © 1996 by Houghton Mifflin Company

**Adam and Eve.** Albrecht Dürer's engraving *The Fall of Man.* Courtesy, Museum of Fine Arts, Boston.

of the fruit and then gave some to Adam. When God learned that Adam and Eve had disobeyed him, he punished them by forcing them to leave Eden.

**apostles** In the NEW TESTAMENT, JESUS had twelve main followers who traveled with him as he spread his religious beliefs. They have become known as the apostles. Sometimes the apostles are referred to as Jesus' disciples. Four of the apostles, Matthew, Mark, Luke, and John, are said to have written the GOSPELS, the first four books of the New Testament.

**Babel, Tower of** The building of the Tower of Babel is described in the OLD TESTAMENT. The people who built it tried to make it so tall that it would reach up to heaven, but GOD punished them for their pride by making each of them speak a different language. Since they could not understand each other, they could not work together, and the tower was never finished.

**beginning, In the**   The first words in the Bible are: "In the beginning God created the heaven and the earth." *See also* CREATION.

**Bethlehem**   The NEW TESTAMENT says that JESUS was born in the town of Bethlehem. *See also* NATIVITY.

**brother's keeper**   In an OLD TESTAMENT story, Cain killed his brother Abel. When GOD asked Cain where Abel was, Cain said, "I know not: Am I my brother's keeper?" (in other words, "Am I supposed to look after my brother?"). *See* CAIN AND ABEL.

**Cain and Abel**   According to the OLD TESTAMENT, Cain and Abel were sons of ADAM AND EVE. Once, when they both offered gifts to GOD, God liked Abel's gift but not Cain's. Cain was so jealous and angry that he killed Abel, committing the first murder. God punished Cain by sending him to a distant land.

**Calvary**   According to the NEW TESTAMENT, JESUS was crucified on a hill named Calvary. *See also* CRUCIFIXION.

**chosen people**   The OLD TESTAMENT says that GOD chose the Israelites as his special people. He promised that they would possess a land of their own and grow into a great nation. *See also* HOLY LAND; ISRAELITES.

**coat of many colors**   In an OLD TESTAMENT story, Joseph was a young man whose father gave him a beautiful coat of many colors. This coat made Joseph's brothers so envious that they decided to sell him as a slave. *See also* JOSEPH AND HIS BROTHERS.

**Creation**   The OLD TESTAMENT says that GOD created the world in seven days. Because God rested on the seventh day, Jews and Christians take the seventh day of each week as a day of prayer and rest. For Jews it is Saturday, and for Christians, Sunday. *See also* SABBATH.

**crown of thorns**   The NEW TESTAMENT says that before JESUS was crucified, he was handed over to some soldiers who laughed at him, saying that he wanted to be king of the Jews. They made a king's crown out of some thorny branches and forced Jesus to wear this crown of thorns. *See also* CRUCIFIXION.

**Crucifixion**   The Crucifixion is the name for the death of JESUS, as described in the NEW TESTAMENT. After being sentenced to death, Jesus was beaten and mocked. Then he was forced to carry his own cross to the place where people were crucified, a hill called CALVARY. Christians believe that Jesus died to make up for the sins of all people. The cross on which he died has become a symbol of the Christian faith.

**Daniel in the lions' den**   Daniel was an ISRAELITE who, according to the OLD TESTAMENT, was captured and taken to a foreign country. The king of that land made it illegal to pray to anyone but the king himself. But Daniel prayed only to GOD. One day he was caught saying his prayers, and he was punished by being thrown into a den of lions. God sent an angel to keep the lions from attacking him. When the king saw that Daniel was unharmed, he let him go free. (*See* image, next page.)

**David and Goliath**   In an OLD TESTAMENT story, the ISRAELITES were at war. Their enemies had a great fighter, a giant named Goliath, who stood almost ten feet tall. All of the Israelites were afraid of him except a boy named David. David went out to fight Goliath armed with only a slingshot and some stones. Because GOD was on his side, David was able to kill the giant. Later, David became one of the greatest kings of the Israelites. Many of the PSALMS are thought to have been written by him.

Daniel in the lions' den

**Day of Judgment** According to the NEW TESTAMENT, on the last day of the world, the Day of Judgment, JESUS will return to judge all the living and the dead. The good will be sent to HEAVEN and the wicked to HELL.

**Dead Sea Scrolls** The Dead Sea Scrolls are a large collection of scrolls (rolls of paper for writing) that contain much of the OLD TESTAMENT and other Jewish writings. They were found in caves near the DEAD SEA in the late 1940s and the 1950s. The scrolls give important information about JUDAISM during the centuries before the birth of JESUS.

**Eden** According to the OLD TESTAMENT, the Garden of Eden was a beautiful place where ADAM AND EVE lived until they disobeyed GOD by eating the forbidden fruit. Eden has come to mean a place where life is perfect.

**Exodus** The OLD TESTAMENT describes how MOSES led the ISRAELITES out of EGYPT, where they were being kept in slavery, across the RED SEA to their new home in the PROMISED LAND. This journey is called the Exodus, which means "going out."

**Genesis** Genesis is the first book of the Bible. The word *genesis* means "beginning" or "origin."

**Gethsemane** (geth-SEM-uh-nee) Gethsemane is a garden near JERUSALEM. In the GOSPELS, it is the place where JESUS was betrayed.

**golden calf** According to the OLD TESTAMENT, MOSES went up to the top of a mountain to receive the TEN COMMANDMENTS from GOD. While he was gone, the ISRAELITES made a golden statue in the shape of a calf and began to worship it. When Moses came down from the mountain, he was very angry. He destroyed the statue and scolded

**Dead Sea Scrolls.** On display at the House of the Book, Jerusalem.

the people for abandoning their God for an idol.

**Good Samaritan**   JESUS tells the story of the Good Samaritan in the NEW TESTAMENT. Once a man traveling along a road was attacked by robbers, who beat him up and left him to die. Other people passed on the same road, but they ignored the injured man. Then a man from another country, a Samaritan, came along. He took care of the injured man, bandaging his wounds and helping him to an inn. Jesus then tells his followers that they should act like this good Samaritan.

**Gospel**   The four books that tell about the life and teachings of Jesus—Matthew, Mark, Luke, and John—are called the Gospels. They are named after the four APOSTLES who are traditionally considered to have written these books.

**Holy Land**   Most of the events described in the Bible happened in a region in the MIDDLE EAST called the Holy Land. It is bordered on the west by the MEDITERRANEAN SEA, on the east by the JORDAN RIVER, on the north by LEBANON, and on the south by the Sinai Peninsula. This area has also been known as the PROMISED LAND, since, according to the OLD TESTAMENT, GOD promised it to the ISRAELITES.

**Israelites**   The OLD TESTAMENT is the story of the Israelites, or the Hebrews, a people who lived in the HOLY LAND in ancient times and were considered God's CHOSEN PEOPLE. Later, they became known as the Jews.

**Jehovah**   In English translations of the OLD TESTAMENT, *Jehovah* is another name for GOD.

**Jericho, Battle of**   In an OLD TESTAMENT story, the ISRAELITES were trying to capture the city of Jericho when GOD told Joshua, their leader, that he should order his priests to blow their trumpets and his soldiers to give a great shout. At the noise, the walls of the city fell, and Joshua's soldiers were triumphant.

**Jerusalem**   Jerusalem, a city in the HOLY LAND, is a spiritual center of JUDAISM and the capital of modern ISRAEL. The OLD TESTAMENT describes how SOLOMON built a great TEMPLE in Jerusalem. According to the NEW TESTAMENT, JESUS was crucified in Jerusalem.

**Jesus**   The main figure in the NEW TESTAMENT, Jesus of Nazareth, is worshiped by Christians as Jesus Christ, the Son of GOD. According to the GOSPELS, Jesus was born and brought up in the HOLY LAND. His mother, MARY, was the wife of a carpenter named JOSEPH. When Jesus was a grown man, he was baptized by JOHN THE BAPTIST. Afterward, he traveled across the Holy Land, teaching about the coming kingdom of God. The most important teachings of Jesus are given in the SERMON ON THE MOUNT. In his travels, Jesus healed the sick and performed miracles. Soon many people became his followers. However, some powerful people thought that he was stirring up trouble among the people and breaking religious laws. Finally, his enemies had him arrested and sentenced to death. On a hill called CALVARY, Jesus was crucified (nailed to a cross and left to die). The New Testament says that, after lying in his tomb for three days, Jesus arose and appeared to his followers. Christians often refer to Jesus as Jesus Christ or simply Christ. In fact, *Christ* is a title, not a name, and means "the anointed one," that is, the one chosen by God. *See also* APOSTLES; CRUCIFIXION; JUDAS ISCARIOT; LAST SUPPER; LOAVES AND FISHES; NATIVITY; PILATE, PONTIUS; RESURRECTION; *and* JESUS CHRIST *under "Religion and Philosophy."*

**Job** (JOHB)   Job is the central figure in the OLD TESTAMENT Book of Job, which tells the story of a man whose faith in GOD is tested by great suffering. A person who suffers for a long time without complaining is sometimes said to be as patient as Job.

**John the Baptist**  John the Baptist was a religious teacher who lived at the time of JESUS. According to the NEW TESTAMENT, he was sent by GOD to prepare for Jesus' coming. After he baptized Jesus, he was arrested and beheaded for speaking out against the country's leaders.

**Jonah** (JOH-nah)  According to the OLD TESTAMENT, GOD commanded Jonah to preach to foreigners. Jonah tried to escape God's will by going on a voyage. God then raised a great storm, which nearly sank Jonah's ship. The sailors, knowing that his disobedience had caused the storm, threw Jonah into the sea, where he was swallowed by a "great fish" (often thought of as a whale). After staying in the fish's belly for three days, he prayed to God for forgiveness. God then pardoned Jonah, and the fish coughed him up onto dry land.

**Joseph**  In the NEW TESTAMENT, Joseph was the husband of MARY, the mother of JESUS. Some Christians refer to him as Saint Joseph.

**Joseph and his brothers**  The OLD TESTAMENT tells the story of Joseph, whose brothers envied him because he was their father's favorite son. One day, his brothers sold Joseph into slavery in EGYPT. Joseph became a servant of the PHARAOH, who suffered from strange and frightening dreams he did not understand. Joseph was the only one who could explain the dreams; he showed the king how they predicted the future. To reward Joseph, the king made him rich and powerful. Years later, a famine broke out in Joseph's own country. When Joseph's brothers came to Egypt to ask for food, Joseph was the official who heard their request. At first, they did not recognize their brother, but in time Joseph revealed his identity. He forgave his brothers, and they had a joyous reunion. *See also* COAT OF MANY COLORS.

**Jonah.** Being swallowed by a "great fish."

**Joshua**  *See* Jericho, Battle of.

**Judas Iscariot** (JOOH-duhs i-SKAR-ee-uht)  Judas Iscariot was one of the APOSTLES, the twelve closest followers of JESUS, in the NEW TESTAMENT. In a famous betrayal, Judas used a kiss to identify Jesus to his enemies, who arrested and crucified him. Judas felt so much guilt that he hanged himself.

**Judge not, that ye be not judged**  In the SERMON ON THE MOUNT in the NEW TESTAMENT, JESUS says, "Judge not, that ye be not judged," thus warning his followers that all humans have weaknesses and shortcomings.

**land flowing with milk and honey**  In the OLD TESTAMENT, God calls the PROMISED LAND "the land flowing with milk and honey."

***The Last Supper.*** Leonardo da Vinci's fresco, in the refectory of Santa Maria delle Grazie in Milan.

**Last Supper** The night before JESUS was crucified, according to the NEW TESTAMENT, he ate a meal with the APOSTLES that has become known as the Last Supper. During the meal, he announced that one of his followers would betray him. His prediction came true when JUDAS ISCARIOT identified him to his enemies by a kiss.

**Lazarus** (LAZ-uhr-uhs) Lazarus was a man who was dead for four days before JESUS brought him back to life. His story is told in the GOSPEL of John.

**Let there be light** According to the OLD TESTAMENT story of the CREATION, the world was completely dark until GOD said, "Let there be light."

**loaves and fishes** The NEW TESTAMENT describes the miracle of the loaves and fishes. One day five thousand people gathered to see JESUS heal the sick. At dinnertime there were only five loaves of bread and two fishes to feed the huge crowd. After Jesus blessed the loaves and fishes, they multiplied until there was plenty of food for everyone.

**Lord's Prayer** The Lord's Prayer, in the NEW TESTAMENT, is the most important Christian prayer:

> "Our Father, which art in heaven, hallowed be thy name; thy kingdom come; thy will be done, on earth as it is in heaven. Give us this day our daily bread. And forgive us our debts as we forgive our debtors. And lead us not into temptation, but deliver us from evil."

Some versions of the Bible add words of praise at the end: "For thine is the kingdom, and the power, and the glory, forever. Amen." JESUS taught his followers this prayer in the SERMON ON THE MOUNT.

**Lot's wife** In the OLD TESTAMENT story, there was once a city so full of wicked people that GOD decided to destroy it, but he wanted to save one good man, named Lot. God told Lot and his family to leave their home, but he warned them not to look back at the city. Lot's wife looked back, and God punished her by changing her into a pillar of salt.

**Mary.** *The Small Cowper Madonna* by Raphael. National Gallery of Art, Washington; Widener Collection.

**Magi** (MAY-jeye)  The Magi, or Wise Men, visited the infant JESUS in BETHLEHEM. According to the GOSPELS, they followed a star and arrived on the twelfth day after his birth, which is now called the feast of Epiphany. They brought three gifts: gold, frankincense, and myrrh.

**Mary**  The mother of JESUS was named Mary. According to the NEW TESTAMENT, she gave birth to Jesus while she was still a virgin.

**Mary Magdalene** (MAG-duh-luhn)  Mary Magdalene was one of the first followers of JESUS. In the GOSPELS, she is said to have been present at the CRUCIFIXION, at the burial of Jesus, and when the empty tomb was discovered.

**Moses**  Moses was the greatest leader of the ancient ISRAELITES. As told in the OLD TES-TAMENT, he was born in EGYPT, where the Israelites were living as slaves. When he was still a baby, the Egyptian ruler, the PHARAOH, ordered his soldiers to kill all the male children of the Israelites. Moses' mother saved his life by placing him in a marsh, where he was found by the daughter of the pharaoh and raised as if he were her own son. When Moses was grown, GOD spoke to him out of a burning bush and commanded him to lead the Israelites out of Egypt. When the pharaoh refused to free the Israelites from slavery, Moses appealed to God, who sent a series of disasters, or plagues, to persuade the Egyptians. Eventually the pharaoh gave in, and the Israelites began their long journey, known as the EXODUS. It was during this journey that God gave Moses the TEN COMMANDMENTS, the laws God expected the Israelites to follow. Moses and his people wandered in the wilderness for forty years. Just as they came within sight of the PROMISED LAND, Moses died. *See also* PLAGUES OF EGYPT; RED SEA, PARTING OF THE.

**Moses**

**Nativity** The birth of JESUS, described in the NEW TESTAMENT, is also called the Nativity. Jesus was born in BETHLEHEM, where his parents, MARY and JOSEPH, were visiting. Because there was no room for them in the inn, the couple spent the night in a stable, and it was there that Jesus was born. Mary had no cradle for the infant, so she placed him in a manger (a box that holds food for animals). While Jesus and his parents were still in the stable, they were visited by three wise men from the East, also called MAGI, who brought valuable gifts for the child.

**New Testament** The New Testament, originally written in Greek, is the second part of the Christian Bible. It tells the story of JESUS' life and presents the main ideas of CHRISTIANITY. *See also* OLD TESTAMENT.

**Noah and the Flood** The OLD TESTAMENT describes a time when people everywhere were living in evil ways. This made GOD so angry that he decided to send a great flood to destroy the world. Noah, however, had always lived a good life. God told Noah to build a great ship, or ark, so that he and his family would survive the flood, and to take into the ark a pair of every kind of animal on earth. Then God made it rain for forty days and forty nights, until the whole world was flooded. Every living creature on earth drowned except the people and animals in the ark, which eventually came to rest on the top of a mountain. When the rain ended, Noah sent out a dove from the ark. The bird returned with an olive branch in its mouth, so Noah knew that the water was disappearing from the land and he could begin a new life on earth. God promised that he would never again destroy the world by flood, and as a sign, he placed a rainbow in the sky.

**Old Testament** The Old Testament is the name commonly used to refer to the first part of the Bible, which was written principally in Hebrew. For Jews, the books of the Old Testament are the whole Bible. They

**Noah.** Detail from a French Book of Hours, circa 1470.

tell the stories of the ancient ISRAELITES, including such figures as NOAH, MOSES, Joshua, Deborah, RUTH, and SAMSON. *See also* NEW TESTAMENT.

**Paul** Paul, known also as the Apostle Paul and as Saint Paul, was an influential religious leader who converted to CHRISTIANITY and helped spread the new religion through his activities as a missionary. He wrote some of the books of the NEW TESTAMENT in the form of letters to the churches he helped found.

**Peter** Peter was one of the twelve APOSTLES of JESUS. He was originally a fisherman named Simon. Jesus gave him the name *Peter* (which means "rock") and said that Peter would be the rock on which he would build

**Plagues of Egypt.** The plague of flies.

his church. On the night before the CRUCIFIXION, the NEW TESTAMENT says, Jesus predicted that before the cock crowed, Peter would deny three times that he was one of Jesus' followers. That night, after Jesus' arrest, Peter did as Jesus had said because he was afraid of being arrested. Nevertheless, Peter went on to become the greatest leader of the early Christians. Some Christians call him Saint Peter.

**Pilate, Pontius** (PAHN-shuhs PEYE-lit)  As told in the NEW TESTAMENT, Pontius Pilate was the Roman official who sentenced JESUS to death. Before delivering the sentence, Pilate washed his hands and said that he was not responsible for Jesus' death.

**plagues of Egypt**  The OLD TESTAMENT says that in the time of MOSES, GOD was angry with the Egyptians because they were keeping the ISRAELITES in slavery. So he punished them by inflicting ten disasters, or plagues, on their land. He turned the waters of the rivers into blood; he sent swarms of insects to destroy the crops; he covered the Egyp-

tians' bodies with painful sores. Eventually he sent the most terrible plague of all: he killed the oldest child in each family. After this plague, the Israelites were permitted to leave Egypt. *See also* PASSOVER *under "Religion and Philosophy."*

**prodigal son**  In the NEW TESTAMENT, JESUS tells the story of a father who divided all he had between his two sons. One of the sons left home and went to a foreign country, where he lived in a wild and foolish way, thinking only of his own enjoyment. Soon he had wasted all his father's money. Poor and hungry, he returned to his father and begged his forgiveness. The father was so pleased to see his son that he forgave him and joyfully ordered a feast to celebrate his return.

**Promised Land**  GOD promised the ancient ISRAELITES, in the OLD TESTAMENT, that they would rule a great and beautiful country. When MOSES led them out of EGYPT, they began their search for this Promised Land. After forty years, they found it in the region occupied today by ISRAEL. *See also* HOLY LAND.

**psalms** (SAHMS)   The psalms are songs and PRAYERS that have been part of Jewish and Christian worship services for thousands of years. These songs are collected in the OLD TESTAMENT in the Book of Psalms. *See also* TWENTY-THIRD PSALM.

**Red Sea, parting of the**   According to the OLD TESTAMENT, when MOSES led the Israelites out of EGYPT, they were chased by an Egyptian army. When they reached the RED SEA, GOD parted the waves, making a path of dry land. When the Egyptians tried to follow, God sent back the water to stop them.

**Resurrection**   Christians believe in the Resurrection (or rising) of JESUS. The NEW TESTAMENT says that after he was crucified, he lay in his tomb for three days. On the third day he rose from the dead and appeared again to his followers.

**Ruth**   According to the book named for her in the OLD TESTAMENT, Ruth was a Moabite who married an ISRAELITE who had come to her country. When he died, she returned to his land with her mother-in-law, Naomi. Ruth then married Boaz, a relative of her husband's, and became known for her kindness and faithfulness. She was the great-grandmother of King David.

**Sabbath**   In JUDAISM and CHRISTIANITY, the Sabbath is a holy day, one day each week that is set aside for rest and worship. For Jews, it falls on Saturday, and for Christians, on Sunday. *See also* CREATION.

**Samson**   The OLD TESTAMENT tells the story of Samson, a leader of the ISRAELITES and the strongest man in the world. The secret of his strength lay in his long hair, which had never been cut. The enemies of the Israelites paid Delilah to cut off Samson's hair and make him helpless. Then they captured Samson, forcing him into slavery. Eventually, though, Samson's hair grew back, and his strength returned. He took his

revenge on his enemies by pulling down the pillars that held up their largest TEMPLE. When the building collapsed, Samson was killed along with great numbers of the Israelites' enemies.

**Satan**   In the NEW TESTAMENT, Satan is another name for the DEVIL, the spirit of evil. Satan always tries to work against GOD's plan.

**Sermon on the Mount**   The most important sermon that JESUS preached is known as the Sermon on the Mount, in the NEW TESTAMENT. It contains the LORD's PRAYER and many other well-known teachings, such as: "Blessed are the meek, for they shall inherit the earth" and "Whosoever shall smite thee on the right cheek, turn to him the other also."

**Solomon**   One of the greatest kings of the ISRAELITES in the OLD TESTAMENT, Solomon built a great TEMPLE in JERUSALEM. He was famous for the wisdom with which he ruled his people.

**Ten Commandments**   The Ten Commandments are the ten most important laws, or rules, that Jews and Christians are supposed to follow. According to the OLD TESTAMENT, GOD gave the commandments to MOSES on tablets of stone. Among the commandments are: "Thou shalt not kill" and "Thou shalt not steal."

**Twenty-third Psalm**   The Twenty-third Psalm is the most familiar song in the OLD TESTAMENT:

> The Lord is my shepherd; I shall not
> want.
> He maketh me to lie down in green pas-
> tures;
> He leadeth me beside the still waters.
> He restoreth my soul;
> He leadeth me in the paths of righteous-
> ness for his name's sake.
> Yea, though I walk through the valley of
> the shadow of death,

I will fear no evil;
For thou art with me;
Thy rod and thy staff, they comfort me.
Thou preparest a table for me in the
    presence of mine enemies;
Thou anointest my head with oil; my
    cup runneth over.

Surely goodness and mercy will follow
    me all the days of my life:
And I will dwell in the house of the Lord
    forever.

*See also* PSALMS.

# Religion and Philosophy

Some of the important words, names, and ideas that will help you begin to understand religion and philosophy are explained below. A *religion* is a set of beliefs about a supernatural power that created the universe, about why we are here on earth, and about how we should conduct our lives.

*Philosophy*, which means "love of wisdom," answers questions about the nature of reality and about how to lead a good life. Philosophy is more concerned with the nature of the world than with religious beliefs about God. People who write about and study philosophy are called philosophers.

**Allah**   In the religion of ISLAM, Allah is the name for GOD, the Supreme Being.

**Amish**   The Amish are a PROTESTANT group that follow a traditional lifestyle. They drive horse-drawn buggies instead of cars and do not have electricity. Because of their plain clothing, they are sometimes called "Plain People." The Amish first came to the United States from EUROPE in the early 1700s. The largest Amish communities today are in OHIO, PENNSYLVANIA, INDIANA, and IOWA.

**Aristotle**   (AR-uh-stot-uhl)   Aristotle was a great PHILOSOPHER of ancient GREECE. He was a student of PLATO and studied and wrote about many subjects, including politics, science, and literature. He placed particular importance on the direct observation of the natural and political world.

**asceticism**   (uh-SET-uh-siz-uhm)   Asceticism is a way of life that opposes fancy clothes, expensive possessions, fine food and

**Amish.** An Amish family in a horse-drawn buggy.

drink, and physical pleasures. It favors a simple, thoughtful way of life devoted to moral and religious purposes and helping other people.

**Ash Wednesday** The seventh Wednesday before EASTER is Ash Wednesday. For most Christians, it marks the beginning of LENT.

**baptism** Baptism is a religious ceremony practiced by Christians. The person being baptized is sprinkled with water, though some churches immerse the person completely. The water represents GOD's power to cleanse a person's soul. A person being baptized as a Christian is being accepted into the Christian faith and is thought to be united with God and JESUS CHRIST. *See also* CHRISTIANITY.

**bar mitzvah** (bahr MITS-vuh)  A bar mitzvah, a Jewish religious ceremony for thirteen-year-old boys, marks the point at which boys take on adult religious and social responsibilities. *See also* BAT MITZVAH; JUDAISM. *Compare* CONFIRMATION.

**bat mitzvah** (baht, bahs MITS-vuh)  A bat mitzvah, a religious ceremony for girls twelve to fourteen, is performed by some Reform Jews to mark the time when girls take on adult religious and social responsibilities. *See also* BAR MITZVAH; JUDAISM. *Compare* CONFIRMATION.

**Bible**  The Bible is the sacred book of JUDAISM and CHRISTIANITY. *See also the section called "The Bible."*

**bishop**  A bishop is a high church official who directs the activities of other religious officials. The ROMAN CATHOLIC CHURCH, the EASTERN ORTHODOX CHURCHES, and some PROTESTANT CHURCHES have bishops.

**Buddha** (BOOH-duh)  The Buddha was a holy man in ancient INDIA. His teachings form the basis of BUDDHISM.

**Buddhism** (BOOH-diz-uhm)  Buddhism is a major religion of ASIA based on the teachings of the BUDDHA. Buddhists seek wisdom, meaning, inner peace, and freedom from desire through physical and spiritual discipline. Meditation, a way of thinking deeply and calmly that takes many years to learn, is one Buddhist discipline.

**Calvin, John**  John Calvin was a French religious reformer of the sixteenth century. During the REFORMATION, he founded a religion called Calvinism, which stressed that people are saved through GOD's grace rather than their own merits.

**Catholicism**  *See* ROMAN CATHOLIC CHURCH.

**Chanukah**  *See* HANUKKAH.

**charity**  Charity in the NEW TESTAMENT means love of others and is considered one of the greatest virtues. It has also come to mean helping people in need.

**Christianity**  Christianity is a religion based on the life and teachings of JESUS

**Buddha.** Statue of the Great Buddha in Kamakura, Japan.

CHRIST. Its main ethical belief is love of others. There are many different Christian churches and forms of worship, but all Christians believe that Jesus Christ is the son of GOD and that he was sent by God to redeem, or save, humankind. Christianity is the major religion of EUROPE and of NORTH and SOUTH AMERICA. *See also* EASTERN ORTHODOX CHURCHES; PROTESTANT CHURCHES; ROMAN CATHOLIC CHURCH.

**Christmas** Christmas is the holiday on which Christians celebrate the birth of JESUS CHRIST. For most Christians, it falls on December 25. In the countries where CHRISTIANITY is the dominant faith, such as the United States, it is a national holiday as well.

**Communion** Communion is a part of the religious service practiced by many Christians. It is also called the Eucharist. A priest or minister gives bread to the church members. Some churches also use wine in the ceremony. When the worshipers eat the bread and drink the wine, they are celebrating their union with JESUS CHRIST. *See also* CHRISTIANITY; MINISTER; PRIEST.

**confession** Confession is a religious ceremony that is especially important in the ROMAN CATHOLIC CHURCH. A person speaks privately to a PRIEST, admits (confesses) to having done wrong in some way, and asks to be forgiven.

**confirmation** Confirmation is the ceremony in Christian churches that marks the point at which a person becomes a full member of the church after receiving religious education. Some Reform Jewish temples also confirm fifteen- or sixteen-year-olds when they have completed their religious study. *Compare* BAR MITZVAH; BAT MITZVAH.

**Confucianism** (kuhn-FYOOH-shuh-niz-uhm) Confucianism is an important reli-

Confucius

gion in CHINA and JAPAN based on the teachings of CONFUCIUS.

**Confucius** Confucius was an ancient Chinese teacher known for his wisdom. He developed a system of ETHICS that is still influential in CHINA and other parts of ASIA.

**Day of Atonement** *See* YOM KIPPUR.

**Descartes, René** René Descartes was a seventeenth-century French philosopher. He is known for his statement "I think; therefore I am."

**devil** In CHRISTIANITY and other religions, the devil is the source of evil in the universe, for he tries to lead people away from GOD and goodness. Also called Satan, he is often pictured with horns on his head, a tail, and hooves like a goat's. Some religions believe in lesser devils or demons as well.

**Easter** Easter is the holiday on which Christians celebrate the return to life, or RESURRECTION, of JESUS CHRIST. According to the NEW TESTAMENT, Jesus was crucified (nailed to a wooden cross), died, and was buried, but after three days he rose from the dead. The Easter holiday is observed every spring. *See also* LENT.

**Eastern Orthodox churches** The Eastern Orthodox churches, which include the Greek, Russian, and Syrian Orthodox churches, among others, form one of the three main branches of CHRISTIANITY. (The others are the ROMAN CATHOLIC CHURCH and the PROTESTANT CHURCHES.) The buildings used by Orthodox Christians are usually square, with domes, and have likenesses of holy people, called icons, on their walls. Eastern Orthodoxy is the dominant form of Christianity in much of Eastern Europe and in GREECE. There are also many Orthodox Christians in the United States.

**ethics** Ethics is a set of beliefs about what is right and wrong in people's actions. Ethical rules sometimes come from religion, for example, from the TEN COMMANDMENTS and the SERMON ON THE MOUNT, and sometimes from social traditions.

**Eucharist** *See* COMMUNION.

**fasting** Fasting means going without food or certain foods for a period of time. In many religions, it is used to help cleanse the soul of sin and guilt.

**Friends, Religious Society of** *See* QUAKER.

**God** God is the name for the Supreme Being worshiped by Jews, Christians, MUSLIMS, and followers of other religions. In the BIBLE, God created the universe and all humankind. Muslims call God by the name ALLAH. *See also* CHRISTIANITY; ISLAM; JUDAISM.

**gods** Gods are the supernatural beings or spirits worshiped in religions whose followers believe in many gods rather than one.

**Good Friday** Good Friday is the Friday before EASTER Sunday, when Christians remember the CRUCIFIXION of JESUS CHRIST. It is called *good* because Jesus' death led to the RESURRECTION, or return to life, which is celebrated on Easter.

**Hanukkah** (HAN-nuh-kuh, KHAN-nuh-kuh) Hanukkah is a Jewish festival that occurs each December. It lasts eight days and commemorates the victory of the Jews over the Syrians in the second century B.C. and the rededication of the TEMPLE in JERUSALEM. Observers of Hanukkah light one candle each night for eight nights in a candleholder called a MENORAH, in memory of a legend that after the temple was rededicated, its lamp burned miraculously for a week on only a day's supply of oil. The word *Hanukkah* is also spelled Chanukah.

**heaven** In many religions, heaven is the happy and peaceful place where good people will go to live with GOD after death. It is often thought to be above the clouds and is depicted as a place where angels play harps.

**hell** In many religions, hell is the place of damnation where bad people will go to be punished after death. It is often thought to be below the earth and is depicted as a place with flames and devils.

**Hinduism** (HIN-dooh-iz-uhm) Hinduism is the ancient religion of INDIA and is practiced by people called Hindus. Hindus believe that the soul is reborn into a new body after death through a process called REINCARNATION. The major religious goal of the Hindus is to escape the cycle of death and rebirth so that the soul may be released into eternity. Some Hindus worship one god or goddess, while others worship many gods and goddesses. *See also* GODS; REINCARNATION.

**Islam** Islam is the religion based on the teachings communicated by MUHAMMAD, an Arabian prophet, in the KORAN. People who practice Islam, called MUSLIMS, believe in obeying the will of GOD, or ALLAH. Religious observances such as PRAYER, FASTING, and giving gifts to the poor are central to the Muslim faith. Congregational prayer takes place on Fridays. Once in their lives, Muslims try to make a PILGRIMAGE to MECCA, the city where Muhammad was born. Islam is the major religion of Arab countries, central ASIA, and INDONESIA.

**Jesus Christ** Jesus was a religious leader from PALESTINE, in what is now called the MIDDLE EAST. His life and teachings are the basis of CHRISTIANITY. Jesus became known as Christ, which means "the anointed one," the one who is chosen by God. The important events of Jesus' life are marked by major Christian holidays. CHRISTMAS celebrates his birth and EASTER, his RESURRECTION, or return to life. *See* JESUS *under "The Bible."*

**jihad** (ji-HAHD) In ISLAM, *jihad* means "struggle." The most important meaning of *jihad* is the struggle to become a better person. *Jihad* can also mean a physical struggle for justice or a struggle to defend Islam.

**Judaism** (JOOH-dee-IZ-uhm) Judaism is a religion based on the teachings of the Jewish Bible, or OLD TESTAMENT, especially the TORAH, which consists of the first five books of the BIBLE. It has three main branches: Orthodox, Conservative, and Reform. People who follow Judaism are called Jews and believe in one GOD. Many of their laws and ideas, such as "Remember the sabbath day, to keep it holy," are shared with CHRISTIANITY, which grew out of Judaism. Judaism is the dominant religion in ISRAEL, a nation in the MIDDLE EAST. There are also many Jews in the United States as well as in EUROPE and parts of ASIA. *See also* TALMUD.

**King James Bible** The King James Bible is an important English translation of the BIBLE that is famous for its noble language. (The Bible was first written in the ancient languages of Hebrew in the OLD TESTAMENT

***Jesus Healing the Sick.*** From an engraving by Gustave Doré.

and Greek in the NEW TESTAMENT.) It is named after James I, a king of ENGLAND in the 1600s, who commissioned this particular translation. Many familiar biblical quotations come from this translation.

**Koran** (kuh-RAN, kuh-RAHN) The Koran is the sacred book of ISLAM and contains the rules and ideals that MUSLIMS follow. Muslims believe that GOD (or ALLAH) revealed the Koran to the prophet MUHAMMAD and that it is the direct word of God. Koran is also spelled Qur'an.

**kosher** The term *kosher* is used in JUDAISM to describe food and other objects that are ritually pure according to its laws. The kosher laws are contained in the TORAH and forbid, for example, the eating of pork.

**Kwanzaa** (KWAHN-zuh) Kwanzaa is a winter festival that celebrates African-American history and culture. It is observed from December 26 to January 1. Although Kwanzaa was first celebrated in the United States in the 1960s, it honors old African traditions.

**Martin Luther**

**Lent** In CHRISTIANITY, Lent is the solemn period of FASTING and repentance that begins on ASH WEDNESDAY and ends on EASTER.

**Locke, John** John Locke was an English PHILOSOPHER of the seventeenth century. Locke argued against the belief that human beings are born with certain ideas already in their minds; rather, he said, the mind is like a blank slate until experience begins to "write" on it. Locke also argued against the doctrine that kings and queens have a God-given right to rule and must be obeyed; he declared that all governments depend on the consent of the governed. *See also* EN-LIGHTENMENT *under "World History Since 1600."*

**logic** Logic is the science concerned with the rules of reasoning. An important logical principle is the syllogism (SIL-uh-jiz-uhm), the most famous example of which is: All men are mortal. SOCRATES is a man. There-fore, Socrates is mortal.

**Luther, Martin** Martin Luther was a German religious leader of the 1500s. He founded Protestantism after protesting against the policies of the ROMAN CATHOLIC CHURCH that he felt were wrong. *See also* PROTESTANT CHURCHES.

**Madonna** The Madonna, which is Italian for "my lady," is a Christian title for the VIR-GIN MARY, the mother of JESUS CHRIST. Paintings or statues of Mary holding the baby Jesus are called Madonnas.

**Magen David** *See* STAR OF DAVID.

**Mardi Gras** (MAHR-dee gras) Mardi Gras is the day before ASH WEDNESDAY, which marks the beginning of LENT. In French, "mardi gras" means Fat Tuesday. It is the last day to indulge in rich foods before the fast of Lent begins. NEW ORLEANS, LOUISI-ANA, is famous for its Mardi Gras parades and parties.

**Mary, Virgin** *See* VIRGIN MARY. *See also* MARY *under "The Bible."*

**mass** The mass is the public celebration of COMMUNION in the Roman Catholic faith. *See also* ROMAN CATHOLIC CHURCH.

**Mecca** Mecca, in modern SAUDI ARABIA, is the birthplace of the prophet MUHAMMAD

**Mecca**

and thus the holy city of ISLAM. All MUSLIMS try to make a PILGRIMAGE to Mecca at least once in their lives. The word *mecca* is often used to mean a destination that attracts many people.

**Menorah**

**menorah**   A menorah is the nine-pronged candleholder used during the Jewish festival of HANUKKAH.

**minister**   A minister is the leader of the congregation of worshipers in a Protestant church. Ministers preach, celebrate COMMUNION, BAPTISMS, and marriages, and advise the members of their churches. *See also* PROTESTANT CHURCHES.

**monk**   A monk is a man who devotes himself to a holy life of study, PRAYER, and good works. Most monks live in buildings called monasteries. *See also* NUN.

**mosque**   A mosque is a Muslim house of worship. It usually has a dome. *See also* ISLAM.

**Muhammad**   Muhammad was the founder of ISLAM. He was born in MECCA in the sixth century. MUSLIMS believe that an angel sent from GOD told Muhammad the words of the KORAN.

**Muslims**   A Muslim is a person who believes in ISLAM.

**New Age**   Since the 1970s, the term *New Age* has been used for a variety of spiritual beliefs and practices. Followers of the New Age movement may be interested in crystals, REINCARNATION, health food, ECOLOGY, or American Indian religions. New Age music often has a dreamy quality and may include sounds from nature.

**nun**   A nun is a woman who devotes herself to a life of study, PRAYER, and good works. Nuns often live in buildings called convents. *See also* MONK.

**Orthodox churches**   *See* EASTERN ORTHODOX CHURCHES.

**Palm Sunday**   Palm Sunday is the Sunday before EASTER, when Christians remember the day JESUS entered JERUSALEM. The people of the city welcomed him by spreading palm leaves in his path. Today some churches hand out palm leaves during Palm Sunday services.

**Paradise**   Paradise is a place where everything is perfect and everyone is happy. *See also* EDEN *under "The Bible";* HEAVEN.

**Passover**   Passover is the Jewish festival that celebrates the EXODUS, the escape of the ancient ISRAELITES from slavery in EGYPT. The eight-day holiday is observed in the spring. During Passover, unleavened bread, called matzo, is eaten. *See also* SEDER.

**philosopher**   A philosopher is a person who thinks and writes about basic questions, such as What is Truth? What is the Good? How should we act?

**pilgrimage**   A pilgrimage is a journey to a holy place. *See also* MECCA.

**Plato**   Plato was an ancient Greek PHILOSOPHER who was a student of SOCRATES and the teacher of ARISTOTLE. In his writings, he searches for answers to basic questions about human life, such as, What is the Good? and What is Truth? His best-known book is *The Republic,* which describes an ideal government.

**Pope John Paul II**

**pope**   The pope is the leader and ultimate authority of the ROMAN CATHOLIC CHURCH. He lives and works in a tiny nation within ROME, ITALY, called the VATICAN. The first pope was PETER, whom Catholics believe was appointed by JESUS CHRIST. Other popes were then chosen to succeed Saint Peter, and his authority was passed on to them.

**prayer**   Prayers are thoughts or words addressed to GOD, a GOD, or another object of worship. Sometimes they are spoken by several people using the same words, sometimes by individuals out loud or silently. Most often, prayers give thanks or ask for help.

**prayer rug**   A prayer rug is a mat on which a MUSLIM says prayers. It is often woven in beautiful, detailed patterns. Because a devoted Muslim prays five times a day, a prayer rug must be easy to roll up and carry.

**priest**   A priest is the person who leads worshipers in ROMAN CATHOLIC, EASTERN ORTHODOX, and Episcopalian churches. All Roman Catholic and Orthodox priests are men; some Episcopal priests are women. *See also* EASTERN ORTHODOX CHURCHES; ROMAN CATHOLIC CHURCH; SACRAMENT.

**Protestant churches**   Protestant churches as a group make up one of the three main branches of CHRISTIANITY. (The others are the ROMAN CATHOLIC CHURCH and the EASTERN ORTHODOX CHURCHES.) Protestants believe that the ultimate religious authority is the BIBLE rather than PRIESTS or the church. Protestantism originated in GERMANY in the 1500s, when MARTIN LUTHER "protested" against certain practices of the Roman Catholic Church. Protestantism is a major religion in Western Europe as well as the United States, where the Protestant churches with the largest memberships are Baptist, Episcopal, Lutheran, Methodist, Pentecostal, and Presbyterian.

**Purim**   Purim is a Jewish holiday that occurs in the spring, before PASSOVER. It cele-

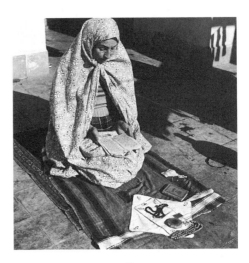

**Prayer rug.** A Muslim woman prays.

brates how Queen Esther of Persia used her wits and courage to save the Jews from being murdered by Haman. *See also* JUDAISM.

**Quaker**   A Quaker is a member of the Religious Society of Friends, a Christian faith that believes in simplicity of life and worship. Services, called meetings, consist mainly of silent meditation.

**Qur'an**   *See* KORAN.

**rabbi**   A rabbi is a Jewish religious teacher and spiritual guide, similar to a PRIEST or MINISTER. Rabbis study the TORAH and TALMUD in order to pass on their teachings to others. *See also* JUDAISM.

**Ramadan**   (RAM-uh-dahn)   Ramadan is the holy month in ISLAM. In order to purify themselves, MUSLIMS FAST (eat no food) from sunrise to sunset throughout the month.

**reincarnation**   Reincarnation is the belief that the soul lives on after death and returns to existence in another body. Hindus and some Buddhists believe in reincarnation. *See also* HINDUISM.

**Roman Catholic Church**   The Roman Catholic Church, or Roman Catholicism, is one of the three main branches of CHRISTIANITY. (The other two are the EASTERN ORTHODOX CHURCHES and the PROTESTANT CHURCHES.) The POPE is the leader of the Roman Catholic Church. Many Catholics look to his judgments and teachings on religious matters, which are passed on to them by their BISHOPS and PRIESTS (in contrast to Protestants, who rely more directly on the BIBLE). Catholicism is the major religion of southern EUROPE, IRELAND, and LATIN AMERICA. There are also many Catholics in the United States.

**Rosh Hashanah**   (rosh-huh-SHAH-nuh; rosh-huh-SHOH-nuh)   Rosh Hashanah marks the beginning of the Jewish New Year. The first ten days of the year are special days of penitence, which end on YOM KIPPUR. The

holiday usually falls in September or early October. *See also* JUDAISM.

**sacrament**   A sacrament is a very holy religious ceremony. For many Christians, BAPTISM, COMMUNION, and marriage are considered sacraments.

**sacred**   Something that is sacred is worshiped or has to do with religious and spiritual life.

**saint**   In some Christian churches and in other religions, saints are very holy people who have died and gone to heaven and who may be called upon to ask GOD for help. A person who lives a holy life is sometimes called saintly.

**Saint.** *St. George and the Dragon* by Carlo Crivelli, an artist of the fifteenth century.

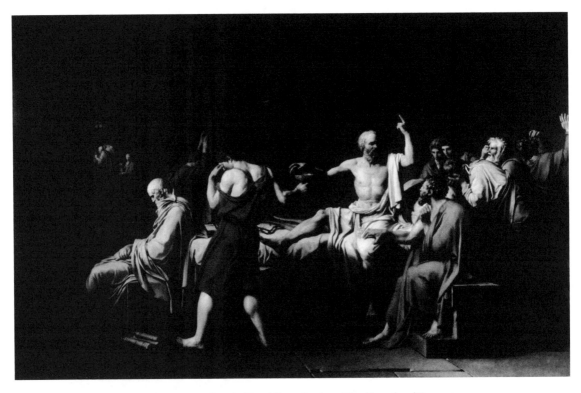

**Socrates.** Jacques-Louis David's painting *The Death of Socrates.*

**salvation** In religion, salvation means being saved from sin and the penalties of sin. In CHRISTIANITY, JESUS CHRIST promised salvation to his faithful followers.

**seder** (SAY-duhr) The seder is the ceremonial dinner held at the beginning and, for some observers, the end of the Jewish feast of PASSOVER. The story of the Jews' EXODUS from EGYPT is read during the meal.

**sermon** A sermon is a prepared talk, often based on stories from the BIBLE, given by the leaders of many religions to a group of worshipers. It is part of the service in many churches and SYNAGOGUES.

**Shinto** Shinto is an ancient Japanese religion that today has been influenced by CONFUCIANISM and BUDDHISM. Its followers take PILGRIMAGES and show special reverence for their ancestors.

**Socrates** (SOK-ruh-teez) Socrates was a great Greek PHILOSOPHER and teacher who taught his students by asking them questions rather than by telling them what to think. In this way, his students learned to find and correct their own errors. This type of teaching is called the Socratic method. *See also* PHILOSOPHER; PLATO.

**Star of David** The Star of David is a symbol of JUDAISM. It is a six-pointed star formed by

**Star of David**

placing two triangles together, one inverted over the other. It is also called a Magen David.

**synagogue** (SIN-uh-gog) A synagogue is a Jewish house of worship and study. It is also called a TEMPLE. *See also* JUDAISM.

**Talmud** (TAHL-mood, TAL-muhd) The Talmud is the collection of writings that contain the religious laws and traditions of JUDAISM. It includes centuries of interpretation of Jewish ideas.

**Taoism** (DOU-iz-uhm) Taoism is an important religion of CHINA based on the writings of the sixth-century B.C. philosopher Lao-Tzu. It stresses meditation and serenity in the face of life's troubles.

**temple** A temple is a building used for religious worship. The followers of many religions, such as JUDAISM, HINDUISM, and BUDDHISM, call their houses of worship temples. *See also* SYNAGOGUE.

**Torah** (TOH-ruh; TAWR-uh) The Torah is the group of religious writings sacred to JUDAISM. It consists of the five books of MOSES,

**Totem poles**

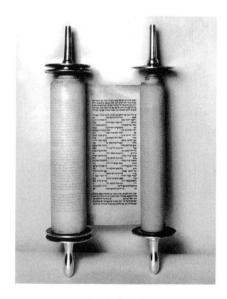

**Torah Scroll**

which are the first five books of the Jewish Bible (called the OLD TESTAMENT by Christians). The word *torah* also refers in a general way to the sacred laws and teachings of Judaism. *See also* TALMUD.

**totem pole** A totem pole is a large wooden pole made by the Indians of the Pacific Northwest that often has the heads of animals, gods, and people carved on it. These carvings express a family's kinship with nonhuman creatures.

**Trinity** Many Christians think of GOD as a trinity, or a being made up of three parts, or persons: the Father, the Son, and the Holy

Ghost (also called the Holy Spirit). Together, these three persons, making one God, are known as the Trinity. *See also* CHRISTIANITY.

**Vatican**   The Vatican is the headquarters of the ROMAN CATHOLIC CHURCH and the home of the POPE. It is an independent state within the city of ROME, ITALY.

**Virgin Mary**   The Virgin Mary was the mother of JESUS CHRIST. She is especially honored by Roman Catholic and Orthodox Christians. *See also* MARY *under "The Bible."*

**Wailing Wall**   *See* WESTERN WALL.

**Western Wall**   The Western Wall is a wall in JERUSALEM, where the ancient TEMPLE of the Jews once stood. The area in front of the wall is the holiest place in JUDAISM, where Jewish people go to pray. Some people call it the Wailing Wall because it reminds them of the past sorrows of the Jews. *See also* JUDAISM.

**Western Wall.** Men praying at the Western Wall in Jerusalem. Men and women pray separately at the wall.

**Yom Kippur**   (YOHM ki-POOR; YOM KIP-uhr)   Yom Kippur, also called the Day of Atonement, is the most important Jewish holiday. On this day Jews atone, or make amends, for their sins through PRAYER and FASTING. *See also* JUDAISM; ROSH HASHANAH.

# United States History to 1865

This section covers the period of United States history up to and including the Civil War. The entries below are about soldiers and battles, ideas and speeches, Indian peoples, and presidents and patriots who were an important part of the first centuries of United States history.

When Columbus sailed to America in 1492 and returned to Spain to announce his discovery, Indian peoples were already well established in North America. The first British settlers did not arrive in North America until the early 1600s, and as more and more British and other Europeans settled in America, they found themselves struggling with the Indians over the land.

In 1776, the colonists, who came mainly from Britain and were living under British rule, declared their independence. After the Revolutionary War against Britain, the Constitution became the foundation of the government.

From the earliest days of the colonies, soon after the first Europeans established their settlements, slaves had been brought to America from Africa. The United States gradually began to divide, North against South, over the issue of slavery, resulting in the Civil War. It ended in victory for the North, which wanted to free the slaves, and the nation was reunited.

**1492**   In 1492, the Italian explorer CHRISTOPHER COLUMBUS voyaged to the American continents. He was the first modern European to do so.

**1776**   The American colonies declared their independence from ENGLAND in 1776. *See also* REVOLUTIONARY WAR.

**1861–1865**   The CIVIL WAR was fought from 1861 to 1865.

**abolition**   Abolition was a movement to end, or abolish, slavery. People who spoke out against slavery were called abolitionists. Some well-known abolitionists were FREDERICK DOUGLASS, SOJOURNER TRUTH, and

HARRIET TUBMAN. Abolition was an important movement leading to the CIVIL WAR.

**Adams, Abigail** Abigail Adams was the wife of President JOHN ADAMS. The many letters she wrote to her husband are famous. They show that she was his trusted adviser in politics and in business. She also advised her son, President JOHN QUINCY ADAMS.

**Adams, John** John Adams was one of the FOUNDING FATHERS who helped draft the DECLARATION OF INDEPENDENCE. He was the first vice president and the second president of the United States.

**Adams, John Quincy** John Quincy Adams was president of the United States from 1825 to 1829. At other times he served as a senator, congressman, and secretary of state. He was the son of President JOHN ADAMS.

**Alamo** (AL-uh-moh) The Alamo was a building in what is now San Antonio, TEXAS. A famous battle was fought there in the early 1800s, when Texas belonged to MEXICO. A group of Americans, wanting to gain independence for Texas, held off a much larger Mexican army until the Americans, including DAVY CROCKETT, were all killed. *See also* REMEMBER THE ALAMO!

**Algonquins** The Algonquins are an American Indian people living in eastern CANADA. During colonial times, the Algonquins were allies of the French government in a war against ENGLAND and its Indian allies, the Iroquois.

**all men are created equal** These words, from the DECLARATION OF INDEPENDENCE, express a basic belief held by the founders of the United States. The Declaration states: "We hold these truths to be self-evident: That all men are created equal; that they are endowed by their Creator with certain unalienable rights; that among these are life, liberty, and the pursuit of happiness." ABRAHAM LINCOLN also used the phrase "all men

are created equal" in his GETTYSBURG ADDRESS.

**American Revolution** *See* REVOLUTIONARY WAR.

**Apaches** (uh-PACH-eez) The Apaches are an American Indian people who live in the southwest United States. Many Apaches fought the United States army in the late 1800s rather than move onto RESERVATIONS.

**Appleseed, Johnny** Johnny Appleseed was the nickname of an American pioneer and folk hero of the early 1800s. He traveled through frontier America planting apple trees and starting orchards. His real name was John Chapman.

**Appomattox Court House** (ap-uh-MAT-uhks) Appomattox Court House is a village in central VIRGINIA where the CIVIL WAR came to an end in 1865. The Southern general, ROBERT E. LEE, surrendered to the Northern general, ULYSSES S. GRANT.

**Arapahos** (uh-RAP-uh-hohs) The Arapahos are an American Indian people of the western GREAT PLAINS. Arapahos were formerly buffalo hunters who followed the traditional PLAINS INDIAN way of life.

**Arnold, Benedict** Benedict Arnold was an American general of the REVOLUTIONARY WAR and a famous traitor. In 1780 he was given command of an American fort, which he planned to give over to the British. The plot was discovered, but Benedict Arnold escaped. He spent the rest of his life in disgrace living in exile in ENGLAND and CANADA.

**Articles of Confederation** A confederation is a coming together of different groups for some special purpose. When the THIRTEEN COLONIES declared their independence from ENGLAND, the Articles of Confederation formed the basis of the national government. This document proved to be too weak to govern the United States, and it was replaced soon after by the CONSTITUTION.

**Attucks, Crispus** Crispus Attucks was a black sailor and one of five colonists who were killed by the British in the BOSTON MASSACRE.

**Banneker, Benjamin** Benjamin Banneker was a black mathematician and scientist of the late eighteenth and early nineteenth centuries. He taught himself advanced mathematics in order to make astronomical calculations for his almanacs. ABOLITIONISTS cited his achievements as proof of the intellectual equality of blacks.

Clara Barton

**Barton, Clara** Clara Barton founded the American Red Cross in 1881. She is also known for her work as a nurse and an organizer of relief efforts during the CIVIL WAR.

**Bill of Rights** The Bill of Rights is the name for the first ten amendments to the CONSTITUTION. These amendments were added soon after the Constitution was adopted because the original document did not offer enough protection for individual rights. *See also* BILL OF RIGHTS *under "Politics and Economics."*

**Blackfeet** The Blackfeet are an American Indian people of the northern GREAT PLAINS. The Blackfeet were formerly buffalo hunters who followed the traditional PLAINS INDIAN way of life.

**Boone, Daniel** Daniel Boone was a pioneer of the late 1700s and early 1800s who explored and settled KENTUCKY.

**Booth, John Wilkes** John Wilkes Booth assassinated President ABRAHAM LINCOLN in 1865. Booth, a well-known actor, supported SLAVERY and the CONFEDERACY.

**Boston Massacre** The Boston Massacre occurred in 1770. British troops fired into a crowd that was taunting them, killing five people, including CRISPUS ATTUCKS. The killings increased the tensions between the British and the colonists leading up to the REVOLUTIONARY WAR.

**Boston Massacre.** A lithograph by W. Champney. Crispus Attucks (center) was one of five killed at the scene.

**Boston Tea Party**  The Boston Tea Party was one of the events that led to the REVO-LUTIONARY WAR. In 1773, a group of Ameri-cans wanted to protest English laws that im-posed taxes on goods such as tea. They boarded three British ships in Boston Harbor and dumped more than three hundred chests of tea overboard.

**Brown, John**  John Brown was an ABOLI-TIONIST of the nineteenth century. He wanted to seize part of VIRGINIA to create a new state where enslaved people could find freedom. In 1859, he and twenty-one follow-ers took over a federal arsenal (weapon stor-age) in Harpers Ferry, VIRGINIA. Brown was captured by the militia, tried for treason, and hanged.

**Bunker Hill, Battle of**  The Battle of Bunker Hill, in June 1775, was one of the first battles of the REVOLUTIONARY WAR. American sol-diers defended a hill near BOSTON, MASSA-CHUSETTS, against two British attacks. The British took the hill on the third attack, when the Americans ran out of ammunition, but the battle proved that the Americans could fight effectively against the British.

**California Gold Rush**  *See* GOLD RUSH OF 1849.

**Cherokees** (CHER-uh-keez)  The Cherokees are an American Indian people who origi-nally farmed and hunted in the mountains of the southeast United States. In the 1830s, the American government forced the Chero-kees to move west to OKLAHOMA. The route they traveled is now called the TRAIL OF TEARS.

**Cheyennes** (SHEYE-en)  The Cheyennes are an American Indian people of the western and northern GREAT PLAINS who formerly followed the PLAINS INDIAN way of life. Cheyenne warriors fought alongside the SIOUX in the Battle of the Little Bighorn, also known as CUSTER'S LAST STAND.

**Civil War**  The American Civil War was fought between the Northern (Union) and Southern (Confederate) states from 1861 to 1865. The war had many causes, but the main issue dividing the country was SLAV-ERY. The Southern states wanted slavery to be permitted in the new territories of the western United States. The Northern states opposed the spread of slavery to these ter-ritories. The Southern states decided to se-cede (separate) from the United States and form a new nation, which was called the CONFEDERACY. After four years of bloody fighting, the South surrendered to the North at APPOMATTOX COURT HOUSE. *See also* FORT SUMTER; GETTYSBURG, BATTLE OF; GRANT, ULYSSES S.; LEE, ROBERT E.; LINCOLN, ABRA-HAM.

**Confederacy**  The Confederacy was the group of states that seceded (separated) from the United States in 1860 and 1861 to form a new nation. SOUTH CAROLINA was the first to secede, followed by MISSISSIPPI, FLORIDA, ALABAMA, GEORGIA, LOUISIANA, TEXAS, VIR-GINIA, ARKANSAS, NORTH CAROLINA, and TENNESSEE. Jefferson Davis was president of the Confederacy. *See also* CIVIL WAR; SECES-SION.

**Constitution**  The Constitution is the docu-ment that established the national govern-ment of the United States. It was written and adopted after the REVOLUTIONARY WAR and set forth the basic laws of the new na-tion. *See also* ARTICLES OF CONFEDERATION; BILL OF RIGHTS; FOUNDING FATHERS. *See also* CONSTITUTION *under "Politics and Econ-omics."*

**Constitutional Convention**  The Constitu-tional Convention of 1787 was a gathering of delegates from twelve of the thirteen origi-nal states. It took place in PHILADELPHIA and resulted in the drafting of the CONSTITUTION of the United States.

**Continental Army**  The Continental Army was the military force led by GEORGE WASHINGTON that defeated the British in the REVOLUTIONARY WAR.

**Continental Congress**  The First Continental Congress met in 1774 to organize a BOYCOTT of British goods and to ask each colony to gather its own military forces. The First Congress was made up of representatives from all the colonies except GEORGIA.

The Second Continental Congress met for the first time in 1775, after the start of the REVOLUTIONARY WAR. It was made up of representatives from all THIRTEEN COLONIES. JOHN HANCOCK served as the group's president. The Second Congress organized an American army, with GEORGE WASHINGTON as its commander, and passed the DECLARATION OF INDEPENDENCE. It governed the country during the war and under the ARTICLES OF CONFEDERATION.

**Cornwallis, Charles**  (kawrn-WAH-lis) Charles Cornwallis was the British general who commanded the British forces in the REVOLUTIONARY WAR. The Revolutionary War ended when Lord Cornwallis surrendered to GEORGE WASHINGTON at Yorktown in 1781.

**Creeks**  The Creeks are an American Indian people who originally lived as farmers and hunters in the southeast United States. In the 1830s, the American government forced most of the Creeks to move west to OKLAHOMA so that white settlers could have their lands.

**Crockett, Davy**  Born in TENNESSEE, Davy Crockett was a frontier settler, politician, and folk hero of the early 1800s. He was known for his shooting ability and died defending the ALAMO.

**Dakota**  Dakota is another name for the SIOUX people.

**Dare, Virginia**  Virginia Dare was the first child born in America of English parents. She was born in 1587, but she disappeared with the other members of the LOST COLONY of Roanoke Island.

**Davis, Jefferson**  Jefferson Davis was the president of the CONFEDERACY during the CIVIL WAR.

**Declaration of Independence**  The Declaration of Independence was written in 1776, largely by THOMAS JEFFERSON. It declared that the American colonies were an independent nation, no longer ruled by the British king, and proclaimed that all people have the right to "life, liberty, and the pursuit of happiness." The Declaration was adopted on July 4, 1776, the day henceforth celebrated as the nation's birthday.

**Delawares**  The Delawares are an American Indian people who originally lived in the northeast United States. The Delawares lived peacefully with the Dutch and English settlers. After they sold their lands in the 1600s, the Delawares were forced to move

**The Declaration of Independence**

west to new lands in OKLAHOMA, WISCONSIN, and CANADA.

**Douglass, Frederick** Frederick Douglass escaped from SLAVERY before the CIVIL WAR and became an eloquent speaker and writer for the ABOLITIONIST cause.

**Dred Scott decision** The Dred Scott decision was a ruling made by the SUPREME COURT in 1857, shortly before the CIVIL WAR. Dred Scott was a slave who sued for his freedom. For several years, Scott had lived with his owner in states where the MISSOURI COMPROMISE had forbidden slavery. When Scott returned to Missouri, he claimed that because he had lived in free states, he should be a free citizen. The court ruled that a slave was not a citizen at all, but instead the property of his or her owner. It also ruled that the Missouri Compromise was unconstitutional (went against the CONSTITUTION).

**Emancipation Proclamation** (i-man-suh-PAY-shuhn) To *emancipate* means to set free. The Emancipation Proclamation was the document issued during the CIVIL WAR in which President ABRAHAM LINCOLN declared that all the slaves held in the Confederate states should be freed. However, SLAVERY was not actually abolished until the war was over. *See also* CONFEDERACY.

**father of his country** GEORGE WASHINGTON is often called the father of his country because he was the head of the American armies during the REVOLUTIONARY WAR and the first president of the United States.

**flag** *See* ROSS, BETSY; STARS AND STRIPES.

**Fort McHenry** Fort McHenry, a military post in Baltimore Harbor, was bombarded by a British fleet on the night of September 13, 1814, during the WAR OF 1812. The American defense of the fort inspired FRANCIS SCOTT KEY to write "THE STAR-SPANGLED BANNER."

Frederick Douglass

**Fort Sumter** Fort Sumter, at the entrance to the harbor of CHARLESTON, SOUTH CAROLINA, was the site of the first military engagement of the CIVIL WAR. In 1860 South Carolina seceded from the UNION and demanded the surrender of Fort Sumter. When the commander of the fort refused to surrender, the South Carolinians opened fire.

**forty-niners** The forty-niners were the thousands of people who flocked to CALIFORNIA in 1849 in search of gold, which had been discovered there in 1848. *See also* GOLD RUSH OF 1849.

**Founding Fathers** The Founding Fathers were the men who signed the DECLARATION OF INDEPENDENCE and helped write the CONSTITUTION of the United States. The most famous ones are BENJAMIN FRANKLIN, THOMAS JEFFERSON, GEORGE WASHINGTON, JAMES MADISON, ALEXANDER HAMILTON, JOHN HANCOCK, and John Jay.

**Fourscore and seven years ago** These words begin ABRAHAM LINCOLN'S GETTYSBURG ADDRESS. A score equals twenty. Fourscore and seven equals eighty-seven. The country was founded in 1776, eighty-seven years before Lincoln's address, which was delivered in 1863.

**Fourth of July** The Fourth of July is the national holiday that celebrates the founding of the United States. On July 4, 1776, the DECLARATION OF INDEPENDENCE was adopted by the THIRTEEN COLONIES.

**Franklin, Benjamin** Benjamin Franklin, one of the FOUNDING FATHERS of the United States, was one of the most talented men in American history. He wrote a book of sayings called *Poor Richard's Almanack* and an autobiography that became famous. Many of his sayings, such as "Early to bed and early to rise / Makes a man healthy, wealthy, and wise," are still quoted. In addition to being a printer, patriot, statesman, and author, Franklin was a scientist and inventor. In his most famous experiment, he flew a kite in a thunderstorm to prove that lightning was electricity.

**Freedmen's Bureau** The Freedmen's Bureau was founded by CONGRESS at the end of the CIVIL WAR. It helped freed slaves to get housing, food, employment, and education. The bureau was active for only a few years. However, in that time it started more than 3,000 schools.

**Gettysburg, Battle of** The Battle of Gettysburg was the most important battle of the CIVIL WAR. The Northern troops defeated the Southern troops, thus preventing the Confederate army from moving farther into Union territory. The battle was fought near the small town of Gettysburg, in southeast PENNSYLVANIA, and is often called the turning point of the war. *See also* CONFEDERACY.

**Benjamin Franklin.** Testing his theory that lightning is electricity.

**Gettysburg Address** The Gettysburg Address was a short speech, about three minutes long, given by President ABRAHAM LINCOLN on the battlefield at Gettysburg, PENNSYLVANIA, four months after the battle. In the speech, Lincoln honored the men who died at Gettysburg and stated the ideals for which they fought. The speech begins: "FOURSCORE AND SEVEN YEARS AGO our fathers brought forth on this continent a new nation, conceived in liberty and dedicated to the proposition that all men are created equal." It ends with these words: "government of the people, by the people, for the people shall not perish from the earth."

**Give me liberty, or give me death!** These words were spoken by Patrick Henry, a VIRGINIA patriot, in an address urging Americans to revolt against ENGLAND. *See also* REVOLUTIONARY WAR.

**Gold Rush of 1849**  In 1849, after gold was discovered in CALIFORNIA, thousands of people, who came to be known as FORTY-NINERS, moved west to try to make their fortunes.

**Grant, Ulysses S.**  Ulysses S. Grant was the leader of the UNION armies at the end of the CIVIL WAR. He later became the eighteenth president of the United States.

**Hamilton, Alexander**  Alexander Hamilton was one of the FOUNDING FATHERS who helped draft the CONSTITUTION. He served under GEORGE WASHINGTON first as a soldier and adviser during the REVOLUTIONARY WAR and later as first secretary of the treasury in the new government.

**Hancock, John**  John Hancock is best known as the first person to sign the DECLARATION OF INDEPENDENCE. He was also president of the Second CONTINENTAL CONGRESS and the first governor of the state of MASSACHUSETTS. A "John Hancock" is a signature.

**Hemings, Sally**  Sally Hemings was a slave who was owned by President THOMAS JEFFERSON. Based on GENETIC evidence, many scholars believe that Hemings and Jefferson had at least one child together.

**Honest Abe**  Abraham Lincoln was called Honest Abe because he was well known for his great sincerity, integrity, and strength of character.

**Hopis** (HOH-peez)  The Hopis are an American Indian people living in northeast ARIZONA. Hopi villages are usually built on high, flat hills called mesas. The Hopis are one of the PUEBLO peoples.

**Hutchinson, Anne**  Anne Hutchinson was a PURITAN religious leader who was banished from MASSACHUSETTS for her religious beliefs.

**I only regret that I have but one life to lose for my country**  These words are said to be the last spoken by Nathan Hale, an American REVOLUTIONARY WAR soldier who volun-

teered to spy on the British. He was captured and executed by British troops.

**Independence Day**  *See* FOURTH OF JULY.

**Indian removal policy**  During the early 1800s the United States government forced many Indian tribes to give up their traditional homelands and move west so that white settlers could have their land. The CHEROKEES, CREEKS, SEMINOLES, and other southeast peoples were among the first to be removed. A few of these people refused to go, but today most of the southeast Indians live in OKLAHOMA, along with many Indian peoples from other parts of the country.

**Inuit**  The Inuit are native peoples of the ARCTIC CIRCLE region. There are large Inuit communities in GREENLAND, ALASKA, and northern CANADA, especially NUNAVUT. Traditionally, the Inuit are hunters of seals, whales, and walruses.

**Iroquois League** (IR-uh-kwoi; IR-uh-kwoiz)  The Iroquois were an alliance of five (eventually six) American Indian peoples living in northern NEW YORK State. The Iroquois were farmers and hunters who were important allies of the English during their colonial wars against FRANCE.

**Jackson, Andrew**  Andrew Jackson, who was nicknamed "Old Hickory," was a military hero and the seventh president of the United States.

**Jackson, Thomas J. "Stonewall"**  "Stonewall" Jackson was a Confederate general in the CIVIL WAR. He earned his nickname in 1861, during the First Battle of Bull Run, when he stood "like a stone wall" against the Union attack. He was accidentally shot and killed by his own troops in 1863.

**Jamestown**  Jamestown, VIRGINIA, became the first permanent English settlement in America when English colonists arrived there early in the 1600s.

**Stonewall Jackson**

**Jefferson, Thomas** Thomas Jefferson was the principal author of the DECLARATION OF INDEPENDENCE and the third president of the United States. While he was president, he arranged with FRANCE for the Louisiana Purchase, a treaty that gave the United States an immense territory that stretched from the MISSISSIPPI RIVER to the ROCKY MOUNTAINS, doubling its size. Jefferson was a talented architect, scientist, and inventor and a strong defender of religious and political freedom. *See also* LEWIS AND CLARK EXPEDITION.

**Lafayette, Marquis de** (lah-fee-ET) The Marquis de Lafayette was a French nobleman who served as a general in the American army during the REVOLUTIONARY WAR. When he returned to FRANCE he also served in the FRENCH REVOLUTION.

**Lee, Robert E.** Robert E. Lee was the brilliant general who commanded the Confeder-

ate armies during the CIVIL WAR. He won several important victories but ultimately had to surrender to General ULYSSES S. GRANT at APPOMATTOX COURT HOUSE, ending the war.

**Lewis and Clark Expedition** In the early 1800s, Meriwether Lewis and William Clark were sent by President THOMAS JEFFERSON to explore the land acquired in the Louisiana Purchase. They led a group of men through the new territories west of the MISSISSIPPI RIVER, reached the ROCKY MOUNTAINS, and continued on through OREGON to the PACIFIC. They drew maps and claimed the Oregon Territory for the United States. Their expedition encouraged the further settlement of the West.

**Lexington and Concord, Battle of** (KONG-kuhrd) The Battle of Lexington and Concord was the first battle of the REVOLUTIONARY WAR. It was fought in MASSACHUSETTS on April 19, 1775. Thousands of MINUTEMEN forced British troops into retreat.

**Liberty Bell** The Liberty Bell is a symbol of American independence and freedom because it was one of the bells rung on July 4, 1776, to proclaim the signing of the DECLARATION OF INDEPENDENCE. The bell, which is on display in Independence Hall in PHILADELPHIA, PENNSYLVANIA, is easily recognized by the large crack in it.

**life, liberty, and the pursuit of happiness** These words from the DECLARATION OF INDEPENDENCE describe the rights proclaimed for all Americans.

**Lincoln, Abraham** Abraham Lincoln was president during the CIVIL WAR and one of the greatest American leaders. Born in a log cabin in KENTUCKY, he educated himself and became a politician and lawyer in ILLINOIS who was respected for his sincerity and character. As president, he opposed the extension of SLAVERY and fought to preserve the UNION. During the Civil War, he issued the EMANCI-

**Abraham Lincoln**

PATION PROCLAMATION, which led to the end of slavery in America. His GETTYSBURG ADDRESS and his Second Inaugural Address, in which he urged the nation to reunite in a spirit of forgiveness, are among the finest speeches in American history. After the war, he was assassinated by JOHN WILKES BOOTH.

**Lost Colony** The Lost Colony of Roanoke was an English settlement on Roanoke Island off the coast of NORTH CAROLINA. Settlers had come to the island in 1587, but when supply ships returned in 1591 all the settlers had disappeared.

**Louisiana Purchase** *See* JEFFERSON, THOMAS.

**Madison, Dolley** First Lady Dolley Madison was the wife of President JAMES MADISON. She was known for having saved the original DECLARATION OF INDEPENDENCE and other important items from the WHITE HOUSE after the British set it on fire during the WAR OF 1812.

**Madison, James** James Madison is known as the father of the CONSTITUTION because of his ideas about organizing the United States government. He became the fourth president of the United States.

**manifest destiny** "Manifest destiny" was a popular slogan in the 1840s. It refers to the belief held by many people that the United States was destined, some said by GOD, to expand across NORTH AMERICA all the way to the PACIFIC OCEAN. The idea of manifest destiny was used to justify the acquisition of large parts of the West and SOUTHWEST. *See also* MEXICAN WAR.

**Mann, Horace** Horace Mann was a legislator and reformer of the nineteenth century who worked to improve the public schools in his home state of MASSACHUSETTS. He has been called the father of the American public school.

**Mason-Dixon line** The Mason-Dixon line, which runs between PENNSYLVANIA and MARYLAND, is the traditional boundary between the North and the South. Before the CIVIL WAR, it was said to divide free states from slave states, and today "below the Mason-Dixon line" still refers to the South, although Maryland is also considered a Middle Atlantic state.

**Massachusetts** The Massachusetts were an American Indian people living in the northeast United States near where the PILGRIMS first settled. Most of the Massachusetts died in the early 1600s from the new diseases that came with the white settlers.

**Massachusetts Bay Colony** The Massachusetts Bay Colony was one of the first settlements in NEW ENGLAND. It was established in the early 1600s by the PURITANS. Their main settlement became the city of BOSTON, MASSACHUSETTS.

*Mayflower* The *Mayflower* was the ship that carried the PILGRIMS from ENGLAND to America in the early 1600s and landed in

**Mayflower.** A detail from *Mayflower in Plymouth Harbor,* circa 1880, by William Formby Halsall.

what is now MASSACHUSETTS. *See also* PLYMOUTH COLONY.

**Mayflower Compact** The Mayflower Compact was an agreement signed by the PILGRIMS on the ship the *MAYFLOWER* in 1620 just before they landed at PLYMOUTH ROCK. It served as the law of PLYMOUTH COLONY until the colony was absorbed into MASSACHUSETTS in the late 1600s.

**Mexican War** The Mexican War was fought between the United States and MEXICO from 1846 to 1848 and resulted in the United States's gaining territory in the SOUTHWEST, including the present states of CALIFORNIA, NEVADA, and UTAH. *See also* ALAMO.

**minutemen** Minutemen were volunteer soldiers in the years before the REVOLUTIONARY WAR. Volunteers were organized and trained to be ready to fight "at a minute's notice." *See also* LEXINGTON AND CONCORD, BATTLE OF.

**Missouri Compromise** The Missouri Compromise of 1820 aimed to decide whether new states would allow SLAVERY. It made MISSOURI a slave state and MAINE a free state. It also made slavery illegal in land of the LOUISIANA PURCHASE that lay north of the 36°30'9 line of LATITUDE. The SUPREME COURT ruled the Missouri Compromise unconstitutional (against the CONSTITUTION) in the Dred Scott decision. *See also* DRED SCOTT DECISION.

**Monroe Doctrine** The Monroe Doctrine was a foreign policy statement issued by President James Monroe in 1823. It declared that the United States would not tolerate the intervention of European nations in the affairs of countries in either NORTH or SOUTH AMERICA.

**Mormons** The Mormons are members of the Church of Jesus Christ of Latter-Day Saints, or LDS church. They are an American religious group that was founded by Joseph Smith. The Mormons settled UTAH under the leadership of Brigham Young and founded SALT LAKE CITY in the 1800s.

**Mott, Lucretia** Lucretia Mott was an ABOLITIONIST and reformer. With ELIZABETH CADY STANTON, she organized the first convention for women's rights, held at Seneca Falls, NEW YORK, in 1848. *See also* SENECA FALLS CONVENTION.

**Navajos** (NAV-uh-hohz) The Navajos are an American Indian people of the southwest

**Navajos**

United States. Shortly after the CIVIL WAR, they were forced by the United States government to move onto a RESERVATION. The Navajos are farmers and sheepherders who are known for their fine jewelry and crafts.

**no taxation without representation** In the mid-1700s BRITAIN tried to impose certain taxes on the American colonists. This angered the colonists, who felt that Britain did not have the right to tax them since they were not represented in the British Parliament and had no say in such decisions. The issue of taxation without representation was one of the causes of the REVOLUTIONARY WAR.

**Old Ironsides** Old Ironsides is the nickname of the *Constitution*, a famous American warship of the eighteenth century.

**Oregon Trail** The Oregon Trail was the route by which settlers in the 1840s and 1850s reached OREGON. It passed through what is now MISSOURI, KANSAS, NEBRASKA, WYOMING, and IDAHO and crossed the CONTINENTAL DIVIDE.

**Paine, Thomas** Thomas Paine was a patriot and leader in the REVOLUTIONARY WAR who wrote the pamphlet *Common Sense*, in which he argued for American independence from Britain.

**Penn, William** William Penn was a colonist of the late seventeenth and early eighteenth centuries and the founder of PENNSYLVANIA. The colony he established there was a refuge for many QUAKERS who had been persecuted in ENGLAND.

**Pilgrims** The Pilgrims were the settlers who came to America in the early 1600s because their Separatist religion had been outlawed in ENGLAND. The Separatists, like the PURITANS, were Protestants who found the Church of England corrupt. Where the Puritans sought to purify the doctrine and practice of the established church, the Separatists sought complete separation by founding their own religious community. The first group of Pilgrims came to America on the *MAYFLOWER* and founded the PLYMOUTH COLONY, which became MASSACHUSETTS. The original meaning of *pilgrim* is "someone who goes on a pilgrimage," which is a journey in search of a sacred goal.

**Pitcher, Molly** Molly Pitcher was the nickname of Mary Ludwig Hays McCauley, a REVOLUTIONARY WAR heroine who carried water to the soldiers during a battle.

**Plains Indians** The Plains Indians are a large group of American Indian peoples who lived by hunting buffalo on the GREAT PLAINS. Most Plains Indians lived in tepees, rode horses, and moved their villages from place to place at different times of the year. The SIOUX, BLACKFEET, ARAPAHOS, and CHEYENNES are all Plains Indians.

**Plymouth Colony** (PLIM-uhth) The Plymouth Colony was the settlement started by the PILGRIMS in the early 1600s in what is now eastern MASSACHUSETTS.

**Plymouth Rock** Plymouth Rock is a large boulder in Plymouth, MASSACHUSETTS. The PILGRIMS landed near this spot at the end of their voyage from ENGLAND.

**Pocahontas** (poh-kuh-HON-tuhs) Pocahontas, the daughter of the Indian chief POWHATAN, lived in VIRGINIA in the early 1600s. According to the English explorer Captain JOHN SMITH, Pocahontas prevented her father from taking Smith's life.

**Pony Express** The Pony Express was a method of delivering mail through the western territories. Riders on fast horses carried the mail in pouches and switched to a fresh horse about every ten miles. The Pony Express came to an end in the mid-1800s when the telegraph began to be used to send important messages and when regular mail could be taken by stagecoach without danger of Indian attack.

**Powhatan** (pow-HAT-n) Powhatan was the chief of an American Indian people living in VIRGINIA during the time when JAMESTOWN was founded. Powhatan made peace with the English colonists and agreed to let his daughter POCAHONTAS marry John Rolfe, one of the settlers.

**Pueblos** (PWEB-lohz) The Pueblos are a group of American Indian peoples living in permanent villages in the southwest United States. Pueblo villages are usually made up of large adobe buildings centered around a public square. The Pueblos are known for their skill at farming and for their crafts, such as pottery and basketry.

**Puritans** The Puritans were English Protestants who settled the MASSACHUSETTS BAY COLONY in NEW ENGLAND. *See also* PILGRIMS.

**Quakers** (KWAY-kuhrs) The Quakers were an English religious group that came to America and settled in what is now PENNSYLVANIA in the 1600s. *See also* QUAKER *under "Religion and Philosophy."*

**Raleigh, Sir Walter** (RAW-lee) Sir Walter Raleigh was an English explorer. In the late sixteenth century, he organized several expeditions to what is now VIRGINIA. His efforts led the way for the founding of the THIRTEEN COLONIES. Raleigh, NORTH CAROLINA, is named for him.

**Redcoat** Redcoat was the name given to a British soldier fighting in the REVOLUTIONARY WAR.

**Remember the Alamo!** (AL-uh-moh) "Remember the Alamo!" was the battle cry used by the Texans in their war to win independence from MEXICO in the early 1800s. *See also* ALAMO; MEXICAN WAR.

**reservation** A reservation is an area of land set aside by the United States government as a home for certain American Indian peoples.

**Revere, Paul** Paul Revere was a REVOLUTIONARY WAR patriot. He is famous for his midnight ride from BOSTON to Lexington, MASSACHUSETTS, to warn the colonists that the British troops were coming. *See also* "PAUL REVERE'S RIDE" *under "Literature."*

**Revolutionary War** The Revolutionary War was the war for independence fought in the late 1700s by the American colonies against GREAT BRITAIN. The colonists opposed the British control of American trade and resented having to pay taxes to Britain. The fighting began in 1775, with "THE SHOT HEARD ROUND THE WORLD" at the BATTLE OF LEXINGTON AND CONCORD. It lasted until 1781, when GEORGE WASHINGTON and the CONTINENTAL ARMY triumphed over the British general CHARLES CORNWALLIS at the BATTLE OF YORKTOWN. *See also* BOSTON TEA PARTY; BUNKER HILL, BATTLE OF; DECLARATION OF INDEPENDENCE; NO TAXATION WITHOUT REPRESENTATION; THIRTEEN COLONIES; VALLEY FORGE.

**Ross, Betsy** Betsy Ross was a PHILADELPHIA seamstress during the REVOLUTIONARY WAR who, it is said, made the first official American flag in the form of the STARS AND STRIPES.

**Sacajawea** (sak-uh-juh-WEE-uh) Sacajawea was a young SHOSHONE Indian woman who

**Sacajawea.** Guiding Lewis and Clark on their expedition, by Alfred Russell.

served as a guide and interpreter on the LEWIS AND CLARK EXPEDITION. Her knowledge of the land and of the Indians who lived there helped make the expedition a success.

**Salem witch trials**   In the late 1600s, many people believed in witchcraft. In 1692, twenty people in Salem, MASSACHUSETTS, were accused of being witches and were tried, convicted, and hanged.

**secession**   Secession refers to the withdrawal from the United States of eleven Southern states in 1860 and 1861. The seceding states formed a government, the CONFEDERACY, in early 1861. The war that broke out between the Confederacy and the remaining United States, the UNION, is called the CIVIL WAR. The Civil War is sometimes also called the War of Secession.

**Seminoles**   (SEM-uh-nohlz)   The Seminoles are an American Indian people from FLORIDA. The U.S. government forced most of them to move west in the early 1800s, but some kept their lands in the EVERGLADES, a large swamp in southern Florida.

**Seneca Falls Convention**   The Seneca Falls Convention was the first convention in America devoted to women's rights. It met in Seneca Falls, NEW YORK, in 1848, and passed several resolutions, including a demand that women be given the right to vote. LUCRETIA MOTT and ELIZABETH CADY STANTON were among its organizers. *See also* WOMEN'S MOVEMENT *under "United States History Since 1865."*

**Sequoya**   (si-KWOY-uh)   Sequoya was a CHEROKEE scholar who developed a written alphabet for the Cherokee language. Sequoya's alphabet made it possible for his people to learn to read and write in their own language.

**Shawnees**   (shaw-NEEZ)   The Shawnees are an American Indian people who originally inhabited parts of what is now the MIDWEST of the United States. They fought several wars against the white settlers.

**Shoshones**   (shoh-SHOH-neez)   The Shoshones are an American Indian people living in the northern ROCKY MOUNTAINS. The LEWIS AND CLARK EXPEDITION passed through Shoshone lands on its way across the mountains to the PACIFIC OCEAN.

**the shot heard round the world**   The phrase "the shot heard round the world" refers to the first shot fired in the REVOLUTIONARY WAR at the BATTLE OF LEXINGTON AND CONCORD in MASSACHUSETTS. The words come from a POEM by RALPH WALDO EMERSON commemorating the event.

**Sioux**   (SOOH)   The Sioux are an American Indian people on the GREAT PLAINS of the American MIDWEST. They fought many battles against the white settlers and government troops until they were finally defeated and moved to RESERVATIONS in the late 1800s. The Sioux were the people who fought against Lieutenant Colonel George A. Custer at CUSTER'S LAST STAND. Two famous Sioux chiefs were SITTING BULL and CRAZY HORSE.

**slavery**   Slavery is a system in which human beings are treated as personal property and forced to work without pay. In the United States, slavery was abolished after the CIVIL WAR. *See also* ABOLITION; DRED SCOTT DECISION; EMANCIPATION PROCLAMATION; UNDERGROUND RAILROAD.

**Smith, Captain John**   Captain John Smith was an English soldier and explorer who helped to found the settlement at JAMESTOWN, VIRGINIA, in the early 1600s. *See also* POCAHONTAS.

**Sojourner Truth**   Sojourner Truth was an escaped slave of the nineteenth century who became an ABOLITIONIST and a FEMINIST leader. She was about six feet tall and gave powerful speeches. At a women's rights convention in 1851, the audience questioned

**Slavery.** The scars from a whipping.

whether she was actually a woman. Truth bared her chest and said, "Ain't I a woman?"

**Stanton, Elizabeth Cady** Elizabeth Cady Stanton was a reformer of the 1800s and early 1900s. In 1848, she helped organize the SENECA FALLS CONVENTION, the first women's rights convention. As a writer, lecturer, and organizer, Elizabeth Cady Stanton worked tirelessly for legal and political equality for women.

**Stars and Stripes** The Stars and Stripes is a nickname for the official flag of the United States. The design of white stars on a blue field (one star for each state) and thirteen alternating red and white stripes (for the thirteen original colonies) was adopted during the REVOLUTIONARY WAR.

**Thanksgiving** The Thanksgiving holiday is celebrated in the United States on the fourth Thursday in November. It honors an autumn harvest feast that was shared by American Indians and PILGRIMS in the PLYMOUTH COLONY in 1621. President ABRAHAM LINCOLN declared Thanksgiving to be an official national holiday in 1863.

**thirteen colonies** Before the REVOLUTIONARY WAR, the English-speaking people on the east coast of NORTH AMERICA were organized into thirteen colonies governed by ENGLAND. On July 4, 1776, they became the original United States of America. They were CONNECTICUT, DELAWARE, GEORGIA, MARYLAND, MASSACHUSETTS, NEW HAMPSHIRE, NEW JERSEY, NEW YORK, NORTH CAROLINA, PENNSYLVANIA, RHODE ISLAND, SOUTH CAROLINA, and VIRGINIA. (*See* map, next page.)

**three-fifths compromise** Delegates at the CONSTITUTIONAL CONVENTION of 1787 had to decide whether to count slaves in a state's population. The issue was important because the number of a state's representatives in CONGRESS is based on that state's population. The decision made is known as the "three-fifths compromise." It said that three-fifths of the total number of slaves in a state would be counted in its population.

**Trail of Tears** The Trail of Tears is the route along which the CHEROKEES were forced to move from their traditional homelands in the southeast United States to new lands west of the MISSISSIPPI RIVER. Those on the march suffered greatly from sickness and hunger, and many died along the way.

**transcontinental railroad** The transcontinental railroad connected the eastern part of the United States with the PACIFIC OCEAN. Before 1865 railroad lines had been laid down in the eastern part of the country. Then, in 1865, construction began in NEBRASKA and CALIFORNIA, and after years of hard labor the two lines met in UTAH in 1869.

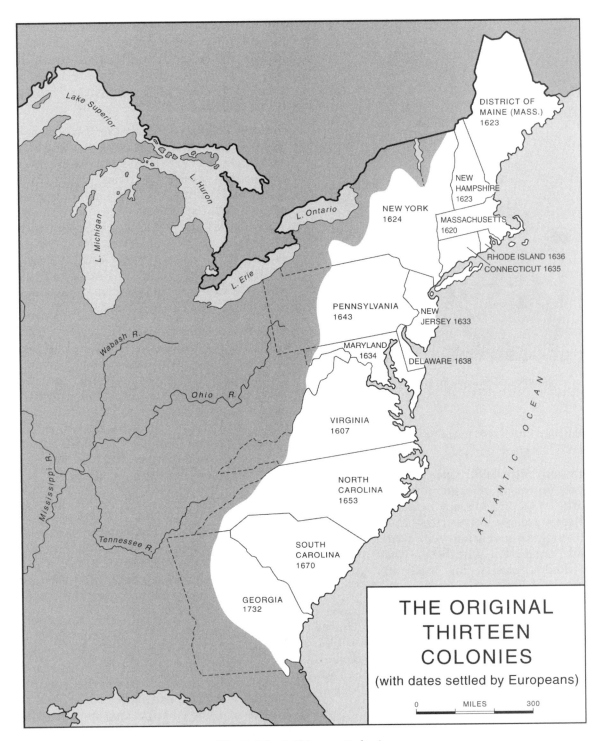

Lake Superior

L. Huron

L. Michigan

L. Ontario

L. Erie

Wabash R.

Ohio R.

Mississippi R.

Tennessee R.

DISTRICT OF
MAINE (MASS.)
1623

NEW
HAMPSHIRE
1623

NEW YORK
1624

MASSACHUSETTS
1620

RHODE ISLAND 1636

CONNECTICUT 1635

PENNSYLVANIA
1643

NEW
JERSEY 1633

MARYLAND
1634

DELAWARE 1638

VIRGINIA
1607

NORTH
CAROLINA
1653

SOUTH
CAROLINA
1670

GEORGIA
1732

ATLANTIC OCEAN

**THE ORIGINAL
THIRTEEN
COLONIES**

(with dates settled by Europeans)

0    MILES    300

**The Original Thirteen Colonies**

**Harriet Tubman.** Harriet Tubman (far left) with former slaves.

**Truth, Sojourner**  *See* SOJOURNER TRUTH.

**Tubman, Harriet**  Harriet Tubman, an ABOLITIONIST of the 1800s, was an escaped slave who helped hundreds of other slaves gain their freedom through the UNDERGROUND RAILROAD. During the CIVIL WAR, she served as a nurse, scout, and spy for the UNION army. *See also* ABOLITION.

**Turner, Nat**  Nat Turner was a slave in the early 1800s who led a slave revolt in VIRGINIA. Later, he was captured and hanged.

**Uncle Tom**  Uncle Tom is a CHARACTER in a famous NOVEL written by Harriet Beecher Stowe before the CIVIL WAR, *UNCLE TOM'S CABIN*, which exposed the terrible conditions of SLAVERY. Uncle Tom was a kind and religious slave who lived under a cruel master. A black person who accepts white domination is sometimes called an Uncle Tom.

**Underground Railroad**  The Underground Railroad was a network of houses and other buildings used to help slaves escape to freedom in the Northern states or CANADA. It operated for many years before and during the CIVIL WAR. *See also* ABOLITION; SLAVERY; TUBMAN, HARRIET.

**Union**  The Union was the group of Northern states that fought against the Southern states (the CONFEDERACY) in the CIVIL WAR. "The Union" is also used in a general sense to refer to the entire United States.

**Valley Forge**  GEORGE WASHINGTON and the American army camped at Valley Forge, PENNSYLVANIA, near PHILADELPHIA, during one winter early in the REVOLUTIONARY

**George Washington.** Emanuel Leutze's painting *Washington Crossing the Delaware.*

WAR. It was a harsh season, and there was not enough food or clothing. Many of the men deserted, but Washington inspired the remaining soldiers to continue the fight and shaped them into a skilled army.

**War of 1812**   The War of 1812 was fought between Britain and the United States. During the war, the British attacked WASHINGTON, D.C., and burned the WHITE HOUSE and the CAPITOL. The war ended with the signing of the Treaty of Ghent in 1814, by which both Britain and the United States gave back the territories they had captured. In the end, Americans viewed it as a victory because British attacks on the U.S. had failed.

**Washington, George**   George Washington, the leader of the American armies during the REVOLUTIONARY WAR, became the first president of the United States. One of the most honored men in American history, he is called the FATHER OF HIS COUNTRY. The nation's capital, WASHINGTON, D.C., is named after him, and his picture is on the one-dollar bill. *See also* FOUNDING FATHERS; VALLEY FORGE.

**Washington, Martha**   Martha Washington was the wife of President GEORGE WASHINGTON. She was the first First Lady of the United States. She was also the first American woman to appear on a postage stamp.

**Williams, Roger**   Roger Williams was a PURITAN religious leader who was banished from MASSACHUSETTS for his religious beliefs. He founded the colony of RHODE ISLAND as a place of religious toleration.

**Winthrop, John**   John Winthrop was a PURITAN political leader of the seventeenth century and founder of the MASSACHUSETTS BAY COLONY. He played a leading role in banishing ANNE HUTCHINSON from the colony.

**Yorktown, Battle of**   The Battle of Yorktown was the last battle of the REVOLUTIONARY WAR. It was fought in 1781 at Yorktown on the coast of VIRGINIA. There the British general CHARLES CORNWALLIS surrendered his army to General GEORGE WASHINGTON.

# United States History Since 1865

This section covers the period of United States history after the Civil War, when the United States, and the world in general, changed faster than during any other time in human history. During this period the United States fought in several wars and became a world power. Americans of African ancestry struggled against racial prejudice to secure their civil rights, which were not fully recognized until the 1960s, one hundred years after the Civil War brought slavery to an end. Americans invented the telephone, phonograph, tractor, and hand-held camera, flew the first airplane, and put a man on the moon. This section of the dictionary lists leaders and important events. It lists outlaws and marshals of the Wild West, Indian chiefs, inventors, athletes, entertainers, and astronauts. It also lists persons and events that have become important since the first version of this dictionary was published in 1989.

**9-11**  *See* SEPTEMBER 11 ATTACKS.

**Addams, Jane**  Jane Addams was a reformer of the late nineteenth and early twentieth centuries. She founded a SETTLEMENT HOUSE, Hull House, in CHICAGO, and she also worked for peace and for women's rights.

**Ali, Muhammad** (MOO-ham-id al-EE)  Muhammad Ali was a heavyweight boxing champion during the 1960s and 1970s known for his clever fighting style. He often boasted, "I am the greatest," and he proved it in the ring.

**Anthony, Susan B.**  Susan B. Anthony was a reformer of the 1800s and early 1900s and an advocate of women's right to vote. Before the

**Susan B. Anthony**

CIVIL WAR, she was an ABOLITIONIST. *See also* WOMEN'S MOVEMENT.

**Armstrong, Neil** In 1969, Neil Armstrong became the first man to walk on the moon. As he stepped from the spacecraft onto the moon's surface, he said, "That's one small step for man, one giant leap for mankind."

**Ashe, Arthur** Arthur Ashe was a twentieth-century American tennis player who won many championships, including the U.S. Open and Wimbledon. He was the first African American to rise to fame in tennis.

**Ask not what your country can do for you** In his inaugural address, President JOHN F. KENNEDY told Americans, "Ask not what your country can do for you; ask what you can do for your country."

**atomic bomb** An atomic bomb is a powerful explosive weapon. At the start of WORLD WAR II American scientists began working in secret to develop such a bomb. To end the war, President HARRY S. TRUMAN ordered an atomic bomb, or A-bomb, dropped on HIROSHIMA, JAPAN, on August 6, 1945. A second bomb was dropped on NAGASAKI, Japan, on August 9, and Japan surrendered shortly after, on August 14. *See also* MANHATTAN PROJECT.

**Barnum, P. T.** P. T. Barnum was a showman of the 1800s. He started the Barnum and Bailey Circus and was a skillful advertiser and promoter who claimed, "There's a sucker born every minute."

**Bell, Alexander Graham** Alexander Graham Bell invented the telephone in the late 1800s.

**Billy the Kid** Billy the Kid was an outlaw, a killer, and a cattle thief who lived in NEW MEXICO in the WILD WEST of the 1870s and 1880s. His real name was William Bonney.

**Black Power** Black Power was a movement that grew out of the CIVIL RIGHTS MOVEMENT in the 1960s. It called for political and eco-

nomic empowerment of black Americans and emphasized pride in black culture. MALCOLM X was a leader in the Black Power movement.

**Bloomer, Amelia** Amelia Bloomer was a reformer and women's rights advocate of the nineteenth century. She wore a shortened skirt over long loose trousers gathered at the ankles. These trousers came to be called "bloomers."

**boycott** A boycott is a refusal to communicate or carry on trade, usually as a form of protest. From December 1955 to December 1956, blacks in Montgomery, ALABAMA, boycotted the city's public buses in order to protest against SEGREGATION laws. *See also* MONTGOMERY BUS BOYCOTT.

***Brown* versus *Board of Education*** *Brown* versus *Board of Education of Topeka, Kansas,* is a famous and very important case that was decided by the SUPREME COURT in 1954. The case concerned SEGREGATION, or the separation of black children and white children into different public schools. The Court ruled that segregation in schools was not allowed by the CONSTITUTION. THURGOOD MARSHALL led the legal team that won this case.

**Buffalo Bill** Buffalo Bill was a buffalo hunter, Indian fighter, and scout in the western United States in the 1860s and 1870s. He later became a circus performer known for his shooting skill. His real name was William Cody.

**Bush, George H. W.** George Bush became president of the United States in 1988, after serving as vice president under RONALD REAGAN. Bush was a TEXAS oilman before he turned to politics. He was president during the PERSIAN GULF WAR. He is the father of GEORGE W. BUSH.

**Bush, George W.** George W. Bush was elected president in 2000. He had served as governor of TEXAS since 1995. He is the son of President GEORGE H. W. BUSH. During his presidency, he sent U.S. troops to AFGHANISTAN and IRAQ.

**Carnegie, Andrew** Andrew Carnegie was a wealthy industrialist whose steel company became one of the largest in the world. He used his enormous wealth to benefit humanity by building libraries and supporting universities and the arts.

**carpetbagger** Carpetbaggers were Northerners who went to the South after the CIVIL WAR to make money. Resentful Southerners called them carpetbaggers because they carried their belongings in suitcases made of carpeting.

**Carter, Jimmy** President from 1977 to 1981, Jimmy Carter had been a naval officer and peanut farmer before he became governor of GEORGIA and then ran for the presidency. After leaving the presidency, he visited several nations as a peacemaker. He also participated in projects to build housing for the poor.

**Carver, George Washington** George Washington Carver, the child of slaves, was a scientist and agricultural researcher of the late 1800s and early 1900s. He improved farming methods in the South and discovered many uses for peanuts, which increased the demand for this important southern crop.

**Chavez, Cesar** Cesar Chavez was an American-born labor leader who organized migrant farm workers in the 1960s and 1970s. He worked tirelessly for many years to raise the salaries of farm workers and improve their working conditions.

**Chief Joseph** Chief Joseph was a leader of an American Indian people of the northwest United States. When white settlers made life difficult for his people, Chief Joseph led them on a long march in hopes of reaching safety in CANADA, but he surrendered to the United States Army before he could get there. Chief Joseph is remembered for the moving speech he gave when he surrendered.

**Civil Rights Act of 1964** The Civil Rights Act of 1964 was a law that made racial discrimination and public SEGREGATION illegal. The passing of this law was an important victory for the CIVIL RIGHTS MOVEMENT.

**civil rights movement** The civil rights movement was a national effort, especially during the 1950s and 1960s, to achieve equal rights for blacks. Civil rights workers used NONVIOLENCE as a method to protest against SEGREGATION. The MARCH ON WASHINGTON and the MONTGOMERY BUS BOYCOTT are two of the best-known events of the civil rights movement. One of the principal leaders of the movement was the Reverend MARTIN LUTHER KING, JR. *See also BROWN VERSUS BOARD OF EDUCATION*; CIVIL RIGHTS ACT OF 1964; FREEDOM RIDERS; VOTING RIGHTS ACT OF 1965. (*See* image, next page.)

**Clinton, William Jefferson** Bill Clinton was governor of ARKANSAS and the forty-second president, serving from 1992 until 2000. During his second term, he was impeached after being accused of perjury (lying under oath). However, he was later acquitted by the SENATE. *See also* IMPEACHMENT *under "Politics and Economics."*

**Cold War** The Cold War refers to the tension between the United States and the SOVIET UNION between WORLD WAR II and the late 1980s. After the end of the "hot" war against GERMANY, the Soviet Union kept control of East Germany and much of Eastern Europe, and the United States became the leader of the free countries of Western Europe. The resulting disputes, which did not lead to open warfare between the United States and the Soviet Union, were considered to be a "cold" conflict. *See also* COLD WAR *under "World History Since 1600."*

**Civil rights movement.** Civil rights supporters marching from Selma, Alabama, to the state capital in Montgomery in 1965.

**crash of 1929**  The crash of 1929 was a deep and sudden drop in STOCK market prices. It marked the start of the GREAT DEPRESSION.

**Crazy Horse**  Crazy Horse was a SIOUX chief who joined SITTING BULL in defeating the United States Army in the Battle of the Little Bighorn, also known as CUSTER'S LAST STAND.

**Cuban missile crisis**  The Cuban missile crisis was a confrontation between the United States and the SOVIET UNION that occurred in 1962 during the COLD WAR. The leader of the Soviet Union, Nikita Khrushchev, had placed missiles in CUBA that could be used to attack the United States. President JOHN F. KENNEDY set up a naval blockade of Cuba and insisted that Khrushchev remove the missiles, which he did.

**Custer's Last Stand**  Custer's Last Stand is the nickname of the Battle of the Little Bighorn, which was fought in the Dakota Territory in the late 1800s. When United States troops led by Lieutenant Colonel George Custer were attacked by the SIOUX, Custer and all his men were killed. *See also* CRAZY HORSE; SITTING BULL.

**D-Day**  D-Day was June 6, 1944, the day that British and American troops invaded German-occupied FRANCE during WORLD WAR II. The forces were led by the American general DWIGHT D. EISENHOWER. This invasion marked the beginning of victory for the ALLIES. *See also* WORLD WAR II.

**Depression**  *See* GREAT DEPRESSION.

**Du Bois, W.E.B.** (dooh-BOYS)  W.E.B. Du Bois was a black author and teacher of the late nineteenth and early twentieth centuries. He helped found the National Association for the Advancement of Colored People (NAACP).

**Dust Bowl**   During the 1930s, the western and southern GREAT PLAINS became known as the Dust Bowl. A severe drought turned the region's rich soil into dust. John Steinbeck's NOVEL *The Grapes of Wrath* tells the story of the many migrant farmers who had to flee their homes as a result of the drought.

**Earhart, Amelia** (AIR-hahrt)  Amelia Earhart was a famous aviator of the early twentieth century. Earhart was the first woman to pilot an airplane across the ATLANTIC OCEAN. She disappeared in a flight over the PACIFIC in 1937.

**Earp, Wyatt** (URP)  Wyatt Earp was a United States marshal and a gunfighter in the WILD WEST.

**Dust Bowl refugee family.** Crossing Texas in 1936.

**Amelia Earhart.** Before the 1937 flight around the world from which she did not return.

**Eisenhower, Dwight D.** (EYE-zuhn-how-uhr) Dwight D. Eisenhower, nicknamed "Ike," was an American general and the commander of the Allied forces in EUROPE in WORLD WAR II. He was the president of the United States from 1953 to 1961.

**Ellis Island** Ellis Island is a small island in New York Harbor, near the STATUE OF LIBERTY. In the early 1900s, people moving to the United States from other countries had to stop first at Ellis Island to register before they could enter the country. The island is now the site of the Ellis Island Immigration Museum.

**FDR** *See* ROOSEVELT, FRANKLIN D.

**flapper** "Flapper" is a nickname for the stylish young woman of the 1920s who took off her corset, cut her hair, and wore short skirts. Close-fitting hats, drop-waist dresses,

**Flapper.** Photograph circa 1925.

and long bead necklaces were popular parts of the flapper look.

**Ford, Henry** Henry Ford was an American business leader of the late nineteenth and early twentieth centuries. He was a champion of the ASSEMBLY LINE method of factory work. His factory produced many early automobiles, including more than 15 million Model T Fords.

**Freedom Riders** The Freedom Riders were people, both black and white, who traveled through the southern states in the 1960s to protest against SEGREGATION and racial injustice. They were an important part of the CIVIL RIGHTS MOVEMENT.

**Friedan, Betty** (fri-DAN) Betty Friedan is a modern author who has worked for women's rights. Her book *The Feminine Mystique* helped revive the WOMEN'S MOVEMENT in the 1960s.

**Garvey, Marcus** Marcus Garvey was a black Jamaican-born leader of the late nineteenth and early twentieth centuries who advocated black self-help and separation of the races. He encouraged blacks in the United States and the CARIBBEAN to move to AFRICA.

**Gehrig, Lou** (GER-ig) Lou Gehrig was an American baseball player of the early twentieth century. He set a major-league record, not broken until 1999, by playing in more than two thousand games in a row. While in his thirties, Gehrig died from a rare disease of the MUSCLES and NERVES, which has become known as "Lou Gehrig's disease."

**Geronimo** (juh-RON-uh-moh) Geronimo was an APACHE leader who was one of the last Indian warriors to fight against whites.

**Glenn, John** In 1962, John Glenn was the first American astronaut to orbit EARTH.

**Great Depression** The Great Depression was the worst economic period in American history. It began when the STOCK market col-

Lou Gehrig

lapsed, or crashed, in 1929. Businesses, banks, and factories had to close, leaving many people unemployed. The Depression lasted for more than ten years. *See also* NEW DEAL.

**Great Society**  In the 1960s, President LYNDON JOHNSON challenged the federal government to create a "great society" in America by establishing programs for improving social justice and the quality of life in the United States. Some Great Society goals included ensuring clean air and water, increasing educational opportunities, and decreasing poverty and disease.

**Hickok, Wild Bill** (HIK-ok)  James "Wild Bill" Hickok was a United States marshal in the WILD WEST who was famous for his gunfights with outlaws.

**Hoover, J. Edgar**  J. Edgar Hoover was the head of the FEDERAL BUREAU OF INVESTIGATION (FBI) from the 1920s to the early 1970s.

**I have a dream**  These words are from a speech given by the Reverend MARTIN LUTHER KING, JR., at the MARCH ON WASHINGTON during the struggle for civil rights in the 1960s. The speech described his dream, which was to see peace and equality among blacks and whites. *See also* CIVIL RIGHTS MOVEMENT.

**Great Depression.** Men standing in line for a free meal from a soup kitchen.

**integration**   Integration is the act of bringing people, especially of different races, together in schools, neighborhoods, and public places such as restaurants and bus stations that were once segregated. The integration of blacks and whites was one of the goals of the CIVIL RIGHTS MOVEMENT. *Compare* SEGREGATION.

**Iwo Jima** (EE-wuh JEE-muh)   Iwo Jima is an island in the PACIFIC OCEAN. It was taken from the Japanese by United States Marines near the end of WORLD WAR II after a battle in which many lives were lost. The battle has been immortalized by a famous photograph and a sculpture based on the photograph of half a dozen Marines raising the American flag on Iwo Jima.

**James, Jesse**   Jesse James was the leader of a gang of outlaws in the WILD WEST. The gang became legendary for its daring robberies of banks and trains.

**JFK**   *See* KENNEDY, JOHN F.

**Jim Crow laws**   Jim Crow laws were enacted in the late 1800s in the southern states to legalize SEGREGATION, or separation of the races. The laws barred black people from many public places. They were not abolished until the middle of the twentieth century.

**Johnson, Andrew**   Andrew Johnson was a political leader of the nineteenth century. He was elected vice president in 1864 and became president when ABRAHAM LINCOLN was assassinated the following year. Andrew Johnson was the first president to have been impeached. The HOUSE OF REPRESENTATIVES charged him with illegally dismissing a government official. The SENATE tried him, and he missed being convicted by a single vote. *See also* IMPEACHMENT *under "Politics and Economics."*

**Johnson, Lyndon B. (LBJ)**   Lyndon B. Johnson became president of the United States in 1963, after JOHN F. KENNEDY was assassinated, and served until 1969. He started the

**Michael Jordan**

WAR ON POVERTY and increased American participation in the VIETNAM WAR. *See also* GREAT SOCIETY.

**Jordan, Michael**   Michael Jordan is a twentieth-century basketball superstar. He played mainly with the Chicago Bulls. Many people believe he is the best basketball player of all time.

**Keller, Helen**   Helen Keller, who was blind and deaf as a child, learned to read and write and use sign language. She graduated from college in the early 1900s and inspired many people by overcoming her handicaps. The play and the movie *The Miracle Worker* are about Helen Keller and her teacher, Anne Sullivan, who taught her sign language.

**John F. Kennedy**

**Kentucky Derby.** The one-hundred-twenty-ninth running of the Derby on May 3, 2003.

**Kennedy, John F.** John F. Kennedy, also known as JFK, was the president of the United States for only two years. He is remembered for his youth, good looks, and impressive speaking style. He was the first Roman Catholic president and the youngest man ever elected to that office. He encouraged the development of the space program and promised that one day an American would walk on the moon. Kennedy was assassinated in 1963 in DALLAS, TEXAS. *See also* ASK NOT WHAT YOUR COUNTRY CAN DO FOR YOU; CUBAN MISSILE CRISIS.

**Kentucky Derby** The Kentucky Derby is the most famous American horse race. It is held each spring at Churchill Downs racetrack in Louisville, KENTUCKY.

**King, Martin Luther, Jr.** Martin Luther King, Jr., was a clergyman who led the CIVIL RIGHTS MOVEMENT in the SOUTH in the 1960s. He organized marches to protest SEGREGATION and racial injustice and delivered one of the most powerful speeches in American history, in which he told the nation, "I HAVE A DREAM" of peace and racial equality.

**Martin Luther King, Jr.** Delivering his "I have a dream" speech in Washington, D.C., on August 28, 1963.

He urged his followers to use nonviolent means, known as "passive resistance," to call attention to the wrongs suffered by blacks. During various protest activities, civil rights workers were often attacked by the police or angry whites, but the civil rights workers did not fight back. Their courage eventually won support for their cause from many people. King was assassinated in Memphis, Tennessee, in 1968.

**Korean War** (kuh-REE-uhn) The Korean War was fought between NORTH KOREA and SOUTH KOREA in the early 1950s. North Korea was supported by the SOVIET UNION and the People's Republic of CHINA. South Korea was supported by the UNITED NATIONS, but most of the troops were United States soldiers. A truce, or end to the fighting, was declared, but there is still great tension between the two Koreas.

**Ku Klux Klan** The Ku Klux Klan was a group of white people in the South who committed acts of terror and violence against blacks after the CIVIL WAR. They wore white sheets and white, pointed hoods to disguise themselves and frighten their victims. Other racist groups calling themselves the Ku Klux Klan were formed in the 1920s. In the 1960s, similar groups opposed the CIVIL RIGHTS MOVEMENT.

**Labor Day** Labor Day is an American holiday honoring workers and is celebrated on the first Monday in September.

**Lindbergh, Charles A.** (LIND-burg) Charles Lindbergh was a famous aviator of the twentieth century. In 1927 he flew alone from LONG ISLAND to PARIS across the ATLANTIC OCEAN, traveling nonstop in his plane, THE SPIRIT OF ST. LOUIS. His was the first nonstop flight across the Atlantic. His wife, Anne Morrow Lindberg, was a poet and essayist.

**Malcolm X** Malcolm X was a black political leader of the twentieth century. He converted to ISLAM while he was in prison and went on to become a MUSLIM minister and a powerful speaker on the subject of BLACK POWER. He was assassinated in 1965 while giving a speech.

**Manhattan Project** The Manhattan Project was the code name for the development of the ATOMIC BOMB in the United States during WORLD WAR II. The project was carried out with great secrecy. After a test explosion in July 1945, the United States dropped atomic bombs on the Japanese cities of HIROSHIMA and NAGASAKI, killing hundreds of thousands of people.

**March on Washington** In August 1963 black leaders, including A. PHILIP RANDOLPH, organized a March on WASHINGTON, D.C., in order to gather support for the CIVIL RIGHTS ACT. The march was an enormous success. More than a quarter of a million people attended. Addressing the marchers from the steps of the LINCOLN MEMORIAL, the Reverend MARTIN LUTHER KING, JR., gave his famous "I HAVE A DREAM" speech.

**Marshall, Thurgood** In 1967 Thurgood Marshall became the first black judge appointed to the SUPREME COURT. As a lawyer before his appointment to the Court, he had argued before the Court against SEGREGATION in the case of BROWN VERSUS BOARD OF EDUCATION. As a Supreme Court justice he was known for his LIBERAL record and for advocating the rights of women and minorities.

**Marshall Plan** The Marshall Plan, also called the European Recovery Program, was a program in which the United States made donations to countries in EUROPE to help rebuild their ruined economies after WORLD WAR II. The plan, which was a great success, was named after General George C. Marshall, who was secretary of state when he proposed the plan in 1947.

**Memorial Day** Memorial Day is the holiday observed on the last Monday in May in honor of American soldiers killed in wartime.

**Montgomery bus boycott** In December 1955, blacks in Montgomery, ALABAMA, organized a BOYCOTT of public buses in order to protest the city's SEGREGATION laws. The boycott was sparked when ROSA PARKS refused to give up her seat on a city bus to a white man. The boycott ended a year later when public transportation was desegregated.

**Morgan, J. P.** John Pierpont Morgan was an American banker who became fantastically wealthy in the late nineteenth century. He was involved in the growth of railroads and in businesses such as General Electric and U.S. Steel. Some called him a ROBBER BARON.

**Nixon, Richard** Richard Nixon was the president of the United States from 1969 to 1974. He was elected to a second term by a large margin, but because of the WATERGATE scandal he became the first president ever to resign from office.

**nonviolence** Nonviolence, or nonviolent resistance, is a method of protest that was used by members of the CIVIL RIGHTS MOVEMENT in the 1950s and 1960s. To protest against SEGREGATION in public areas such as buses and restaurants, blacks would sit in places meant for whites, and whites would sit in places meant for blacks. Even when they were taunted or beaten by people who wanted to maintain segregation, the protesters would not fight back. Some of them were seriously injured in these demonstrations, but their methods succeeded in gaining sympathy for the civil rights movement. Nonviolent methods of protest have also been used to further other political and social causes.

**Oakley, Annie** Annie Oakley was a theatrical performer and sharpshooter of the late nineteenth and early twentieth centuries. She starred with BUFFALO BILL in his Wild West Show.

**Onassis, Jacqueline Kennedy** Jacqueline Kennedy Onassis was the wife of President JOHN F. KENNEDY. She was famous for her style and charm. Five years after President Kennedy was killed, she married wealthy businessman Aristotle Onassis.

**the only thing we have to fear is fear itself** These words were spoken by President FRANKLIN D. ROOSEVELT during the GREAT DEPRESSION. He was trying to encourage Americans not to panic during this trying economic crisis.

**Parks, Rosa** Rosa Parks is a civil rights activist. Her refusal in December 1955 to give up her seat on a bus to a white man in Montgomery, ALABAMA, led to the MONTGOMERY BUS BOYCOTT.

**Pearl Harbor** Pearl Harbor is a large American naval base in HAWAII. Early in WORLD WAR II, on December 7, 1941, Japanese planes made a surprise attack on the base, killing many people and destroying ships and planes. President FRANKLIN D. ROOSE-

**Pearl Harbor.** Wreckage of the superdreadnought U.S.S. *Arizona* in Pearl Harbor.

VELT called the day of the attack "a day which will live in infamy" and declared that the United States was at war with JAPAN.

**Peary, Robert E.** (PEER-ee) Explorer Robert Peary is said to be the first person to reach the NORTH POLE, in 1909. However, records show that Peary's expedition missed the Pole by about 20 miles. With him were Matthew Henson, an African American, and four INUIT men.

**Powell, Colin** Colin Powell is a modern military leader and statesman. As an army general, he played a key role in the PERSIAN GULF WAR. In 2001 he became the first African American to serve as secretary of state.

**Prohibition** (proh-uh-BISH-uhn) Prohibition is the common name for the law passed in the 1920s to prevent, or prohibit, alcoholic drinks such as beer, wine, and liquor from being made or sold. Because alcoholic drinks were made and sold widely despite the law, Prohibition was hard to enforce. As a result, the law was repealed in the 1930s, making alcohol legal again.

**Randolph, A. Philip** Asa Philip Randolph was a black labor and civil rights leader of the nineteenth and twentieth centuries. In the 1920s he was president of the Brotherhood of Sleeping Car Porters, the first black LABOR UNION. He also helped to plan and direct the 1963 MARCH ON WASHINGTON.

**Reagan, Ronald** Ronald Reagan, a former movie actor and governor of CALIFORNIA, was the president of the United States from 1981 to 1989. In 1984, at age seventy-three, he became the oldest person ever to be elected president.

**Reconstruction** Reconstruction is the name for the ten years after the CIVIL WAR when the defeated Southern states were reorganized and admitted back into the UNION.

**Prohibition.** A federal agent smashes beer barrels.

**Roaring Twenties** The Roaring Twenties refers to the period from 1921 until the beginning of the GREAT DEPRESSION in 1929. The same time period is sometimes referred to as the Jazz Age. Many people ignored PROHIBITION, adopted new styles of dressing and dancing, and rejected many traditional moral standards. *See also* FLAPPER.

**robber barons** Robber barons were wealthy and powerful leaders in American business in the late nineteenth century. Oil executive JOHN D. ROCKEFELLER and banker J. P. MORGAN were called "robber barons." The term suggested that such men grew rich through dishonesty, like robbers, and acted as if they ruled other people, like barons.

**Robinson, Jackie** Jackie Robinson was the first black man to play major league baseball in the twentieth century. Before he joined the Brooklyn Dodgers, no major league team since the late 1800s had hired black players. Robinson came to represent the struggle of blacks to achieve social equality with whites. When his baseball career ended, he became a businessman and a spokesman for the CIVIL RIGHTS MOVEMENT.

**Rockefeller, John D.** In the late nineteenth century, businessman John D. Rockefeller controlled much of the American oil industry. Many called him a ROBBER BARON. Toward the end of his life, he gave hundreds of millions of dollars to charity.

**Roosevelt, Eleanor** (ROH-zuh-velt) Eleanor Roosevelt, the wife of President FRANKLIN D. ROOSEVELT, was a humanitarian, social reformer, political activist, and writer.

**Roosevelt, Franklin D.** (ROH-zuh-velt) Franklin Delano Roosevelt, also known as FDR, was the president of the United States during the GREAT DEPRESSION and WORLD WAR II. His social and economic policies, known as the New Deal, helped to end the Depression. A calm and encouraging leader, he often spoke to the American people over the radio in what became known as fireside chats. He was the only president to be elected to four terms of office. *See also* WORLD WAR II.

**Roosevelt, Theodore R.** (ROH-zuh-velt) Theodore Roosevelt was the president of the United States in the early 1900s. He was sickly as a child but overcame his ailments to become a robust and physically active rancher, big-game hunter, and outdoorsman. During the SPANISH-AMERICAN WAR, he led a troop of volunteer cavalry soldiers called the Rough Riders. As president, he conducted an aggressive foreign policy, particularly in LATIN AMERICA. He summed up his policy by saying, "Speak softly, and carry a big stick."

**Ruth, Babe** George Herman "Babe" Ruth was a baseball player for the New York Yan-

Franklin D. Roosevelt

kees in the 1920s and 1930s. Before that, he was a pitcher for the Boston Red Sox. He was the first great home run hitter and is considered by many fans to be the greatest player of all time.

**segregation** Segregation is the practice of keeping people separated, especially on the basis of race. A segregated school is a school that admits students of only one race. A segregated neighborhood is one where people of only one race live. Segregation is illegal in the United States. *Compare* INTEGRATION.

**September 11 attacks** The most destructive attacks ever launched on the U.S. mainland occurred on September 11, 2001. A group of terrorists who were believed to be part of the AL QAEDA network hijacked four jet airplanes. They crashed two into the Twin Towers of the WORLD TRADE CENTER in NEW YORK CITY and one into the PENTAGON in Arlington, VIRGINIA. The fourth crashed in a field in PENNSYLVANIA. More than three thousand people were killed.

**settlement house** Settlement houses were social and cultural centers established by reformers in slum areas of American cities during the 1890s and the early 1900s. A famous settlement house, Hull House, was founded in CHICAGO by JANE ADDAMS in 1889.

**sharecropping**   Sharecropping was a system of farming that developed in the South after the CIVIL WAR. The system divided farmland into three shares—one for the landowner, one for the worker, and one for whoever provided seeds and equipment. The crops were also shared three ways.

**sit-in**   A sit-in is a form of nonviolent protest that was used in the 1960s in the CIVIL RIGHTS MOVEMENT and later in the movement against the VIETNAM WAR. In a sit-in, demonstrators occupy a place open to the public, such as a racially segregated lunch counter or bus station, and then refuse to leave. People who participate in a sit-in are usually arrested, which brings attention to their cause. *See also* SEGREGATION.

**Sitting Bull**   Sitting Bull was the SIOUX chief of the late 1800s who led his warriors at the Battle of the Little Bighorn, also known as CUSTER'S LAST STAND.

**Spanish-American War**   The Spanish-American War was a brief war between SPAIN and the United States that was fought in CUBA and in the PHILIPPINES at the end of the 1800s. The American victory gave the United States control over PUERTO RICO, GUAM, HAWAII, and the PHILIPPINES.

***The Spirit of St. Louis***   *The Spirit of St. Louis* is the name of the plane that CHARLES LINDBERGH flew from LONG ISLAND to PARIS in 1927. It was the first solo nonstop flight across the ATLANTIC OCEAN.

**Steinem, Gloria**   Gloria Steinem is a modern writer and leader in the WOMEN'S MOVE-MENT. She also helped found several groups that fight discrimination against women.

**Super Bowl**   The Super Bowl is the championship game of the National Football League. It is held each year in January.

**Thorpe, Jim**   Jim Thorpe, an athlete in the early 1900s, is considered one of the finest all-around athletes of all time. An American Indian by ancestry, he played college and professional football and professional baseball, and he won a number of Olympic events in track and field.

**Truman, Harry S.**   Harry S. Truman became the president of the United States when FRANKLIN D. ROOSEVELT died at the end of WORLD WAR II, and he served until 1953.

**Sitting Bull**

President Truman made the decision to drop ATOMIC BOMBS on the Japanese cities of HIROSHIMA and NAGASAKI in 1945. After World War II, he supported programs to aid European and Japanese recovery.

**Vietnam War** (vee-et-NAHM)  The Vietnam War was fought in SOUTHEAST ASIA between South Vietnam and communist North Vietnam in the 1960s and 1970s. The United States became seriously involved in the war in the early 1960s, hoping to prevent communists from taking over Southeast Asia. From the beginning, some Americans objected to United States participation in the war, and antiwar sentiment grew stronger and more widespread during the 1960s. Conflicts in the United States between supporters and protesters of the war became extremely bitter and sometimes violent. The war ended when North Vietnam conquered South Vietnam in 1975. American soldiers who died during the war are honored at the VIETNAM VETERANS MEMORIAL in WASHINGTON, D.C.

**Voting Rights Act of 1965**  The Voting Rights Act of 1965 was a law that was passed during the CIVIL RIGHTS MOVEMENT. Its purpose was to eliminate various devices, such as literacy tests, that had traditionally been used to restrict voting by black people. It authorized the enrollment of voters by federal registrars in states where fewer than 50 percent of the eligible voters were registered or voted. All such states were in the South.

**War on Poverty**  The War on Poverty is the name given to the social and economic programs of the 1960s, started by President LYNDON B. JOHNSON, that were designed to end poverty in the United States.

**Washington, Booker T.**  Booker T. Washington was a black educator and leader who attempted to improve the situation of black people in the 1800s and early 1900s. He founded the Tuskegee Institute, a college dedicated to educating blacks.

**Watergate**  Watergate, the worst political scandal in American history, occurred in the early 1970s during the reelection campaign of President RICHARD NIXON. Its name comes from the Watergate Hotel in Washington, D.C., where five men were caught breaking into the headquarters of the DEMOCRATIC PARTY. It was later discovered that the men were operating under orders from high officials in Nixon's administration, and the president himself was found to be involved in an effort to cover up the crime. Many people believed that Nixon should be impeached, or formally charged with committing crimes while in office, but he resigned from office before he could be brought to trial. He became the first president to resign from the presidency.

**Wild West**  The Wild West is a name given to the states and territories west of the MISSISSIPPI RIVER during the late 1800s. The outlaws, gunfighters, sheriffs, and cowboys of the time are depicted in many movies and books. *See* JAMES, JESSE; HICKOK, WILD BILL.

**Wilson, Woodrow**  Woodrow Wilson was the president of the United States early in the 1900s, when the country entered WORLD WAR I. After the war, he helped found the League of Nations, a peace-keeping organization that the United States did not join. The league proved important as a forerunner of the UNITED NATIONS. *See also* WORLD WAR I. (*See* image, next page.)

**women's movement**  The women's movement is an effort to secure legal, economic, and social equality for women. It is also called the feminist movement. The women's movement began in the nineteenth century, when reformers sought, among other things, to secure property rights and voting rights for women. The early leaders of the move-

Woodrow Wilson

Tiger Woods

ment included SUSAN B. ANTHONY, ELIZABETH CADY STANTON, and LUCRETIA MOTT. They were called suffragists because they worked for women's suffrage, the right to vote, which was finally won in 1920. The modern women's movement began in the 1960s in an effort to secure greater educational and professional opportunities for women as well as political and economic power. Leaders of this movement include BETTY FRIEDAN and GLORIA STEINEM.

**Woods, Eldrick "Tiger"** American golf superstar Tiger Woods has won many tournaments. He became the first golfer to win all four majors—the Masters, the British Open, the U.S. Open, and the PGA Championship.

**World Series** The World Series is a series of baseball games between the champions of the two major baseball leagues, the American League and the National League. It is held each year in October.

**World Trade Center** The World Trade Center was a complex of commercial buildings

**World Trade Center.** The Twin Towers defined the New York City skyline until their destruction by terrorists in September 2001.

**Wright Brothers.** The first flight at Kitty Hawk, North Carolina. Orville is at the controls while Wilbur remains on the ground.

in MANHATTAN. Its Twin Towers, which stood more than one hundred stories high, were destroyed in the SEPTEMBER 11 ATTACKS, with more than three thousand lives lost.

**World War I**  World War I began in Europe in 1914. GERMANY and its allies fought against other countries, led by BRITAIN and FRANCE. The United States at first tried to stay neutral; that is, it tried not to take sides. In 1917, however, the United States entered the war on the side of Britain and France. The war ended in 1918 when Germany surrendered. *See also* WORLD WAR I *under "World History Since 1600."*

**World War II**  World War II began in 1939 with the German invasion of POLAND. The United States entered the war formally in 1941, after the Japanese attack on PEARL HARBOR. During the war, American workers

produced an astonishing number of planes, ships, weapons, and ammunition to support the Allied forces in EUROPE, led by BRITAIN, FRANCE, and the SOVIET UNION. The war also required Americans to work long hours and conserve essential supplies, such as gasoline. In Europe, Allied troops under the American general DWIGHT D. EISENHOWER landed in France on June 6, 1944, which is known as D-DAY. During the next year the Allies pushed through France, liberated PARIS, entered Germany, and raced toward BERLIN. Germany surrendered in May 1945. The war against JAPAN ended when American planes dropped ATOMIC BOMBS on the Japanese cities of HIROSHIMA and NAGASAKI. *See also* WORLD WAR II *under "World History Since 1600."*

**Wounded Knee**  Wounded Knee is a creek in SOUTH DAKOTA where in 1890 soldiers of the

United States Army, alarmed by a rifle shot, killed some 150 unarmed American Indians, including many women and children. The Wounded Knee massacre was the last major conflict in the wars between the United States government and the PLAINS INDIANS during the late 1800s.

**Wright brothers**   Orville and Wilbur Wright invented the airplane when they flew the first motor-driven, heavier-than-air flying machine at Kitty Hawk, NORTH CAROLINA, in the early 1900s.

# Politics and Economics

*Politics* concerns the way a society is organized and governed. It pertains both to national governments and to smaller groups, such as states, cities, and even clubs and businesses. There are a number of different political systems, including democracies, monarchies, and dictatorships. There are also different ideas about how a government should operate. Here we focus especially on the American political system.

*Economics* is the study of how people earn and spend money and make and sell goods. An economic system is a particular way of producing, distributing, and consuming the goods and services of society so that members of that society can prosper. Just as there are different political systems, so, too, there are different economic systems. Two of the most important ones are capitalism and socialism.

**amendment**  An amendment is a change made in a law. The first ten amendments to the CONSTITUTION are called the BILL OF RIGHTS.

**Bill of Rights**  The first ten amendments to the CONSTITUTION, called the Bill of Rights, define the rights and freedoms of American citizens in relation to their government. They concern: (1) freedom of religion, speech, press, assembly, and petition; (2) the right to bear arms; (3) the right not to quarter soldiers; (4) protection from unreasonable searches and seizures; (5) the rights of those accused of crimes; (6) the right to a jury trial in criminal cases; (7) civil suits; (8) protection from unreasonable bail and cruel punishment; (9) other rights not specifically discussed in the Constitution; and (10) powers not enumerated in the Constitution and kept by the states or the people.

**branches of government**  *See* CHECKS AND BALANCES; EXECUTIVE BRANCH; JUDICIAL BRANCH; LEGISLATIVE BRANCH.

**budget**  A budget is a plan for spending money. The national budget in the United States is the yearly plan for how much money the government will spend on different programs.

**capitalism**  Capitalism is the economic system under which most economic decisions are made and ownership is retained by individuals rather than the government. For instance, an individual owner of a business can decide whether to make a certain product and how much to charge. Capitalism is

**Capitol Hill**

sometimes called FREE ENTERPRISE. It is often considered the opposite of SOCIALISM.

**Capitol**  The Capitol is the white, domed building on Capitol Hill, in WASHINGTON, D.C., where the United States CONGRESS meets.

**checks and balances**  Checks and balances are a fundamental principle of American government guaranteed by the CONSTITUTION, which gives each branch of government some power or influence over the other branches. Checks and balances prevent any one branch from accumulating too much power and encourage cooperation between branches. For example, in order to enact a law, the CONGRESS, comprising the SENATE and the HOUSE OF REPRESENTATIVES, must vote on it. If it passes in both houses of Congress, it goes to the PRESIDENT, who can approve the law by signing it or reject the law by vetoing it. Even if the president vetoes the law, the Congress can vote again and, by a two-thirds majority, override the presi-

dent's veto. *See also* EXECUTIVE BRANCH; JUDICIAL BRANCH; LEGISLATIVE BRANCH; VETO.

**CIA**  The CIA, or Central Intelligence Agency, is a government agency that keeps track of information, or "intelligence," regarding other nations. Some people who work for the CIA are spies.

**civil rights**  In the United States, people have the right to be treated the same regardless of their race, sex, or religion. These rights, which are guaranteed by law, are often called civil rights.

**communism**  Communism is an economic and political movement started in the 1800s by KARL MARX. Marx called for a form of SOCIALISM in which all property is owned by the community. Communists believe that workers should take power and control all aspects of social and economic life.

**Congress**  *Legislative* means "lawmaking." In the United States, the part of the FEDERAL GOVERNMENT that makes the laws, the legislative branch, is called Congress. It consists of two groups, or houses: the SENATE and the HOUSE OF REPRESENTATIVES. Members of both houses are elected by the people.

**conservative**  A conservative is a person who believes that the main purpose of government is to maintain or gradually change the established order and tradition. Conservatives often oppose the viewpoints of LIBERALS.

**Constitution**  The Constitution is the document that established the United States government and its system of laws. It describes the different branches of the government and defines the rights to which all Americans are entitled. The Preamble to the Constitution reads:

> We, the people of the United States, in order to form a more perfect Union, establish justice, insure domestic tranquillity, provide for the common defense, promote the general welfare, and secure the blessings of liberty to ourselves and our posterity, do ordain and establish this Constitution for the United States of America.

**consumer**  A consumer buys goods or uses services. Things that people use up and wear out, such as food and clothing, are called consumer goods.

**corporation**  A corporation is a business owned by a group of people, called shareholders, each of whom has bought shares of the business. *See also* STOCK.

**credit**  A person who buys something now and agrees to pay for it later is buying it on credit.

**debt**  A debt is a sum of money that one person owes another. To be in debt is to owe money.

**Declaration of Independence**  The Declaration of Independence, written mainly by THOMAS JEFFERSON, is the document that de-

clared the United States to be an independent nation. It begins:

> When, in the course of human events, it becomes necessary for one people to dissolve the political bands which have connected them with another and to assume, among the powers of the earth, the separate and equal station to which the laws of nature and nature's God entitle them, a decent respect to the opinions of mankind requires that they should declare the causes which impel them to the separation.
>
> We hold these truths to be self-evident; That all men are created equal; that they are endowed by their Creator with certain unalienable rights; that among these are life, liberty, and the pursuit of happiness.

**democracy**  Democracy is the form of government in which power is held by the people and granted to their freely elected representatives for the purpose of running the government.

**Democratic party**  A party is a group of people with similar views who work to get their members elected to office. The Democratic party is one of the two main parties in American politics. Members of the Democratic party are called Democrats. The other main party in the United States is the REPUBLICAN PARTY.

**dictatorship**  A government in which all the power is held by one person or a small group of people is called a dictatorship.

**discount**  A discount is the lowering, or reduction, of a price. If something usually costs $5 but a merchant is now selling it for $4, the buyer benefits from a discount of $1.

**down payment**  When you buy something for a large amount of money, you sometimes pay only part of the price right away and agree to pay the rest later. The part you pay right away is called a down payment.

**Dictatorship.** Mussolini (second from right) walking beside Adolf Hitler.

**e pluribus unum** (EE PLOOR-uh-buhs YOOH-nuhm) *E pluribus unum* is a Latin phrase meaning "Out of many, one." It is a motto, or special saying, of the United States because we are one nation made up of many states.

**election**   An election is the process of voting through which we choose a person for an elective position. In a national election, we choose a PRESIDENT.

*E pluribus unum.* The Great Seal of the United States.

**Equal Rights Amendment**   The Equal Rights Amendment, also known as the ERA, was an amendment to the CONSTITUTION that was passed by Congress in 1972 but never approved by the number of states required. The amendment guaranteed equal rights for women and men. It was an important issue for the WOMEN'S MOVEMENT.

**ERA**   *See* EQUAL RIGHTS AMENDMENT.

**executive branch**   The executive branch is one of the three main parts, or branches, of the FEDERAL GOVERNMENT. It is made up of the PRESIDENT, the vice president, and other officials. Its function is to carry out laws passed by the LEGISLATIVE BRANCH, also known as CONGRESS. *See also* CHECKS AND BALANCES.

**export**   To export means to send goods out of the country. The goods themselves are called exports. *Compare* IMPORT.

**fascism** (FASH-iz-uhm)   Fascism is a system of government dominated by one strong leader, often called a dictator.

**FBI**   The FBI, or Federal Bureau of Investigation, is a national law enforcement group that gathers information and investigates the breaking of federal laws.

**federal government**   The United States has a national, or federal, government, which is based in WASHINGTON, D.C. It helps to govern the fifty states, each of which has its own STATE GOVERNMENT.

**feminism**   Feminism is a political movement that works to achieve equal rights for women and men. *See also* WOMEN'S MOVEMENT *under "United States History Since 1865."*

**Fifteenth Amendment**   Adopted in 1870, the Fifteenth Amendment to the U.S. CONSTITUTION guarantees all male inhabitants of the United States the right to vote, including former slaves. It was one of the three amendments that marked the end of the CIVIL WAR.

**Fifth Amendment** The Fifth Amendment to the U.S. CONSTITUTION protects the rights of U.S. citizens who are accused of crimes. It says that a person cannot be tried twice for the same crime and that a person cannot be forced to testify against himself. It also says that every person has a right to "due process of law"—that is, to fair legal procedures, such as a public trial. *See also* BILL OF RIGHTS.

**First Amendment** The First Amendment to the U.S. CONSTITUTION protects the rights of U.S. citizens to express themselves. These rights include FREEDOM OF RELIGION, FREEDOM OF SPEECH, FREEDOM OF THE PRESS, and freedom of assembly (people gathering together). *See also* BILL OF RIGHTS.

**free enterprise** Free enterprise is another name for CAPITALISM. In a free enterprise system, most economic decisions are made by individuals rather than by the government.

**freedom of the press** The United States CONSTITUTION grants freedom of the press, which means that all Americans may write what they please and make public what they think in books, magazines, newspapers, radio, and television. *See also* FIRST AMENDMENT.

**freedom of religion** The United States CONSTITUTION grants freedom of religion, which means that all Americans are allowed to practice whatever religion they choose without interference. *See also* FIRST AMENDMENT.

**freedom of speech** The United States CONSTITUTION grants freedom of speech, which means that all Americans may express their ideas even if they disagree with and criticize the government. *See also* FIRST AMENDMENT.

**governor** In the United States, the head of each of the fifty states is called the governor.

**House of Representatives** One of the two groups, or houses, in the United States CONGRESS is the House of Representatives. The number of representatives, each of whom is elected for a term of two years, is based on the number of people who live in each state. The chief officer of the House is called the Speaker of the House. *See also* SENATE.

**immigration** The United States is a country that was built by immigrants from other countries. Many came to escape religious persecution or poverty in their native lands. In the thirteen original colonies, the immigrants were mainly English, Welsh, and German. During the 1800s, the number of immigrants, mostly from northern EUROPE, then from eastern and southern Europe, increased dramatically. Immigration rates were kept low in the first half of the twentieth century by WORLD WAR I, the GREAT DEPRESSION, and WORLD WAR II. Following World War II, Europeans continued to make up the largest number of immigrants, but after 1965 a drastic shift occurred, and immigrants from ASIA and LATIN AMERICA began to outnumber those from Europe. Immigrants have continued to contribute enormously to the economic vigor and cultural richness of the United States.

**impeachment** Impeachment is a formal accusation of wrongdoing against a public official. According to the CONSTITUTION, the HOUSE OF REPRESENTATIVES can vote to impeach an official, but the SENATE actually tries the case. Two PRESIDENTS of the United States have been impeached: ANDREW JOHNSON and WILLIAM JEFFERSON CLINTON. Both were acquitted by the Senate. President RICHARD NIXON resigned from office as the House of Representatives prepared to begin the impeachment process.

**import** When one country brings in a product that was made in another country, it is said to import that product. The product itself is also called an import. *Compare* EXPORT.

**inflation** Inflation is an economic term that means prices are rising. One dollar buys less as a result of inflation.

**interest** Interest is an extra sum of money you must pay to someone who has lent you money when you pay back the loan. For instance, if you were charged 10% interest on a $500 loan, you would have to pay back $550, the extra $50, which is 10% of $500, being the interest.

**investment** An investment is something you pay money for in the hope that it will become more valuable over time. For instance, you could invest in piano lessons because you hope to earn money or gain enjoyment by playing well in the future.

**judge** A judge rules over a court of law and makes decisions about legal procedures.

**judicial branch** The judicial branch is one of the three main parts, or branches, of the FEDERAL GOVERNMENT. It is made up of the courts, which explain and apply the laws passed by the LEGISLATIVE BRANCH. The SUPREME COURT is the head of the judicial branch. *See also* CHECKS AND BALANCES; EXECUTIVE BRANCH.

**labor union** A labor union is an organization of workers formed to get its members better pay, better working conditions, and job security. The leaders of a labor union represent the workers' side in bargaining with employers.

**legislative branch** The legislative branch is one of the three main parts, or branches, of the FEDERAL GOVERNMENT. It is responsible for making the laws and is made up of the two houses of CONGRESS. *See also* CHECKS AND BALANCES; EXECUTIVE BRANCH; JUDICIAL BRANCH.

**liberal** A liberal is a person who believes that the main purpose of government is to increase freedom and equality. Liberals often oppose the viewpoints of CONSERVATIVES.

**Library of Congress** The Library of Congress, in WASHINGTON, D.C., is the largest library in the United States. It is run by the FEDERAL GOVERNMENT.

**loan** A loan is a sum of money that one person or institution gives another with the expectation of being repaid. *See also* INTEREST.

**local government** Local government usually means city or county government as distinct from STATE GOVERNMENT and FEDERAL GOVERNMENT. A mayor is part of local government.

**Marx, Karl** Karl Marx was a German writer in the 1800s who believed that CAPITALISM would be destroyed and the workers would come to power. Marxism formed the basis of COMMUNISM. With Friedrich Engels, Marx wrote two important books, *Das Kapital (Capital)* and *The Communist Manifesto.*

**monarchy** A government that is headed by a king or a queen is called a monarchy. Kings and queens are not elected by the people. Their power is inherited, that is, passed on to them through their families.

**NASA** NASA, or the National Aeronautics and Space Administration, is the United States government agency that runs the space program.

**nationalism** Nationalism is devotion to the interests and culture of one's nation. People who share a common language, history, and culture often identify themselves as a nation.

**Nineteenth Amendment** Adopted in 1920, the Nineteenth Amendment to the CONSTITUTION gives women the right to vote.

**Nobel Prizes** Nobel Prizes are awarded each year for worldwide leadership in PHYSICS, CHEMISTRY, literature, peace, economics, and medicine or physiology (the study of living ORGANISMS). The prizes were founded by Swedish engineer Alfred Nobel.

**Pentagon** The Pentagon is a large, five-sided building that is the headquarters of the United States armed forces. It is in Arlington, VIRGINIA, across the river from WASHINGTON, D.C. It was severely damaged in the SEPTEMBER 11 ATTACKS.

**Pledge of Allegiance** The Pledge of Allegiance is a formal promise of loyalty to the United States that is often recited at public events. It says: "I pledge allegiance to the flag of the United States of America and to the Republic for which it stands, one nation, under God, indivisible, with liberty and justice for all."

**president** The president is the chief executive of the United States and thus holds the highest elected position in the government. He is the head of the EXECUTIVE BRANCH of the FEDERAL GOVERNMENT and commander-in-chief of the armed forces. In the United States, a presidential election is held every four years. A president may serve no more than two four-year terms.

**propaganda** Propaganda is rhetoric, spoken, written, or visual, that seeks to persuade people to believe certain political ideas. Propaganda is often sly and dishonest.

**republic** A republic is a type of DEMOCRACY in which power is distributed to officials who are elected by the people.

**Pentagon.** An aerial view.

**Republican party** A party is a group of people with similar views who work to get their members elected to office. The Republican party is one of the two main parties in American politics. Members of the Republican party are called Republicans. The other main party is the DEMOCRATIC PARTY.

**Senate** One of the two groups, or houses, in the United States CONGRESS is the Senate. Each state is represented by two senators, each of whom is elected for a term of six years. The presiding officer of the Senate is the vice president. *See also* HOUSE OF REPRESENTATIVES.

**socialism** Under the economic system called socialism, the government runs the economy and tries to spread the wealth so that nobody will be poor. Natural resources are controlled by the government, which also owns the factories. Socialism is often opposed to CAPITALISM. *See also* COMMUNISM.

**social security** Social security is a system of monthly payments for retired workers after they reach the age of sixty-five. The money for social security pensions is raised through taxes on employers and employees. This important social program was established in 1935 during the presidency of FRANKLIN D. ROOSEVELT.

**state government** State government is controlled by the GOVERNOR. It is distinct from LOCAL GOVERNMENT and the FEDERAL GOVERNMENT.

**stock** Stock represents a share in the ownership of a corporation. People who own stock are called shareholders.

**strike** A strike occurs when a group of people stop working because they believe they are being treated unfairly. People may go on strike for higher wages or better working conditions.

**suffrage** (SUF-rij) Suffrage means the right to vote. In the United States, the word often brings to mind the early FEMINIST movement. Women in the nineteenth and early twentieth centuries who fought for voting rights were called suffragists (SUF-rij-ists). *See also* FIFTEENTH AMENDMENT; NINETEENTH AMENDMENT; VOTING RIGHTS ACT OF 1965.

**supply and demand, law of** The law of supply and demand is the idea that when there is a great demand for goods that are in limited supply, the price of those goods will go up. For example, when a lot of people want to buy gas but there is not a lot of gas available, the price of gas will go up.

**Supreme Court** The highest, or most powerful, court in the American judicial system is called the Supreme Court. It can overturn, or reject, the decisions of lower courts and has the final say on how our laws are applied. It is the head of the JUDICIAL BRANCH. The Supreme Court meets in WASHINGTON, D.C.

**Uncle Sam** Uncle Sam is a symbol of the United States and is shown as a tall old man with a white beard, dressed in clothes that

**Uncle Sam.** A World War I army poster.

look like parts of the American flag. Uncle Sam's initials, U.S., are the same as those of the United States. He is often seen on posters and in newspaper cartoons.

**union** *See* LABOR UNION.

**The White House**

**veto** A veto is a vote that blocks a decision. In the UNITED NATIONS, for example, each of the five permanent members of the Security Council has the power of veto.

**Wall Street** Wall Street is a street in NEW YORK CITY where the New York Stock Exchange is located. The street's name is often used for the business that takes place there: "STOCK prices fell on Wall Street today."

**We, the people** These are the opening words of the CONSTITUTION of the United States.

**White House** The White House, in WASHINGTON, D.C., is both the home and the office of the PRESIDENT of the United States.

# World History to 1600

This section lists important people and events in world history from the earliest times through the 1500s. We include more about the cultures of Africa in this edition than in earlier ones. We also include important events that marked the rise of Islam, and we recognize the importance of persons and events that form the backgrounds of many in our country whose families have come from Central and South America. We pay particular attention to European history because Europe was historically so closely related to the United States. In fact, the cultures of Europe and the Americas, taken together, are often referred to as *Western* culture in contrast to the cultures of Asia, which are referred to as *Eastern* culture.

Western culture has its roots in the ancient civilizations of Israel, Greece, and Rome. The history and culture of ancient Israel are described in the Bible section. Here we focus on ancient Greece and Rome, which have given us many of our central ideas about politics, law, art, nature, and the meaning of human life. We also include two later periods of European history, the Middle Ages and the Renaissance. In the Middle Ages, Christianity was the major force in European life. The Renaissance (which means "rebirth") was an age when great artists and explorers flourished.

---

**A.D.** A.D. is an abbreviation used with a date to indicate a year after the birth of JESUS. It stands for *anno Domini*, a Latin phrase meaning "in the year of the Lord." Many writers now use the abbreviation C.E., which means "of the common era," instead of A.D. *Compare* B.C.

**Alexander the Great** Alexander the Great, one of the greatest military leaders of all time, was a king of ancient GREECE who conquered most of western ASIA. According to legend, he conquered the whole ancient world and then wept because he had no more worlds to conquer.

**Anglo-Saxons** The Anglo-Saxons were a group of Germanic-speaking peoples who invaded ENGLAND around 500 A.D. and who ruled most of the country until the NORMAN CONQUEST in 1066. The language of the Anglo-Saxons was the basis of modern English.

**Ashantis** The Ashantis are a people of western AFRICA who joined together to create a powerful kingdom from the 1600s to the early 1900s.

**Athens** Athens is the capital of GREECE. In ancient times, it was a city-state and the first DEMOCRACY. It was also the home of great artists, poets, playwrights, and philosophers.

**Augustus Caesar** Augustus Caesar was the first emperor of ROME. He was the adopted son of JULIUS CAESAR. While he was in power, from 44 B.C. to A.D. 14, Rome enjoyed peace and great achievements in the arts, especially in literature. The month of August is named for Augustus.

**Aztecs** The Aztecs were a Native American people who once ruled a great empire in MEXICO. In the 1500s, the Aztec empire was conquered by the Spanish. *See also* CONQUISTADORES; CORTÉS, HERNANDO; MONTEZUMA.

**Babylon** (BAB-uh-lon) Babylon was a city in the ancient MIDDLE EAST that was known for its great wealth.

**Balboa, Vasco Núñez de** (bal-BOH-uh) Vasco Núñez de Balboa was a Spanish explorer of the early sixteenth century. He traveled across PANAMA and became the first European to see the PACIFIC OCEAN. He claimed it for SPAIN.

**Bantus** The Bantus are a large group of African peoples who speak related languages. Many of the peoples of central, eastern, and southern AFRICA are Bantus.

**B.C.** Events that took place in ancient times often bear the abbreviation B.C., which

**Aztecs.** The Aztec Calendar Stone was used in ceremonies to honor the sun god Tonatiuh. Tonatiuh's face can be seen in the center of the calendar.

means "before Christ." Many writers now use the abbreviation B.C.E., which means "before the common era," instead. In these dates, the larger the number, the earlier the year. *Compare* A.D.

**Black Death** Black Death is a name for a deadly disease, also called bubonic plague, that killed as many as half the people in EUROPE in the late MIDDLE AGES. Many people in ASIA died as well. The Black Death was caused by bacteria spread by fleas that infested rats.

**Boleyn, Anne** (boo-LIN) Anne Boleyn was the second wife of King HENRY VIII of ENGLAND and the mother of Queen ELIZABETH I. Anne Boleyn was beheaded for allegedly being unfaithful to her husband.

**Bronze Age** The Bronze Age was the period of history, from about 4000 to about 2000 B.C., when people learned to use metal in making tools and weapons. The most important metal they used was bronze, a mixture of copper and tin. The Bronze Age was followed by the IRON AGE.

**Brutus** (BROOH-tuhs) Brutus was a political leader in ancient ROME who is remembered for betraying JULIUS CAESAR. Although Caesar had been a friend, Brutus helped to murder him. *See also* JULIUS CAESAR *under "Literature."*

**Byzantine Empire** The Byzantine Empire, centered at CONSTANTINOPLE, began as the eastern part of the ROMAN EMPIRE in the third century A.D. It included parts of EUROPE and western ASIA. After the FALL OF ROME, the Byzantine Empire continued many of the Roman customs and ideas until it was conquered by MUSLIM armies in the middle 1400s. *See also* CONSTANTINOPLE.

**Caesar, Augustus** *See* AUGUSTUS CAESAR.

**Caesar, Julius** (JOOHL-yuhs SEE-zuhr) Julius Caesar was a talented Roman general who became the ruler of ROME. He was killed by a group of Romans who were unhappy with his command. Among the murderers was Caesar's friend BRUTUS. Caesar's family continued to reign through the days of the ROMAN EMPIRE. The month of July was named after him. *See also* AUGUSTUS CAESAR; ROMAN EMPIRE.

**Carthage** CARTHAGE was a city in ancient North AFRICA. During the third and second centuries B.C., it was a commercial rival of ancient ROME. Carthage and Rome fought each other in three wars, which were known as the PUNIC WARS. Carthage was destroyed after the last Punic War.

**Cartier, Jacques** Jacques Cartier was a French navigator who explored the ST. LAWRENCE RIVER. He made three voyages to NORTH AMERICA in the early 1500s in search of the NORTHWEST PASSAGE. He established FRANCE's claim to lands that would later become part of French-speaking CANADA.

**Champlain, Samuel de** (sham-PLAYN) Samuel de Champlain was a French explorer who founded QUEBEC in the early 1600s. Though Quebec was later taken by the British and became part of CANADA, its main language today is still French.

**Charlemagne** (SHAR-luh-mayn) Charlemagne was the first emperor of the HOLY ROMAN EMPIRE. His name means "Charles the Great." He was king of FRANCE in the late eighth and early ninth centuries and was crowned emperor in the year 800.

**China** China, one of the principal civilizations of ASIA, has had a continuous history from ancient times to the present.

**chivalry** Chivalry was the code of behavior by which the KNIGHTS of the European MIDDLE AGES were expected to live. A chivalrous knight fought fairly and bravely in battle and treated women with special courtesy. The legends of KING ARTHUR and his knights portray the age of chivalry. The idea of behaving "like a gentleman" is based on the knights' code of conduct.

**civilization** A civilization is a large and complex culture with systems of transportation and communication. It is run by an organized government that makes and keeps the laws. A civilization often has its own written language, religion, literature, and art. Its people often construct large buildings, and at least some of them live in cities. (The word *civilization* is derived from the Latin word for "city.") Some of the world's first great civilizations were those of EGYPT, INDIA, and CHINA. The civilizations of ancient GREECE and ROME were especially important in the development of Western CULTURE.

**Cleopatra** (KLEE-uh-PAT-ruh) Cleopatra was a famous queen of ancient EGYPT who fell in love with the Roman general Marc Antony.

**Columbus, Christopher** Christopher Columbus was an Italian explorer who voyaged to America in 1492, when he was searching for a new route to the Indies. His three ships

**Christopher Columbus.** Presenting New World treasures to King Ferdinand and Queen Isabella of Spain.

were the *Niña,* the *Pinta,* and the *Santa María. See also* FERDINAND AND ISABELLA.

**conquistadors** (kong-kees-tuh-DAWRS) The conquistadors were the Spanish soldiers who defeated the AZTECS and MAYA in MEXICO and the INCAS in SOUTH AMERICA. HERNANDO CORTÉS and FRANCISCO PIZARRO are two of the most famous conquistadors. *Conquistador* is a Spanish word that means "conqueror."

**Constantine the Great** Constantine the Great was a Roman emperor who founded the city of CONSTANTINOPLE in the fourth century A.D. He was the first Roman emperor to allow Christians to practice their religion without being punished by the government.

**Constantinople** (kon-stan-tuh-NOH-puhl) Constantinople was the city founded by CONSTANTINE THE GREAT in the fourth century A.D. as the eastern capital of the ROMAN EMPIRE. Later it became the capital of the BYZANTINE EMPIRE. Constantinople is at the eastern end of the MEDITERRANEAN SEA in what is now the country of TURKEY. Its modern name is ISTANBUL.

**Coronado, Francisco de** Francisco de Coronado was a Spanish soldier who explored parts of MEXICO and the southwest United States in the middle 1500s. He spent several years searching for cities of gold that he had heard stories about, but he never found any treasure. His expedition made contact with several PUEBLO Indian peoples, and some of his men became the first Europeans to see the GRAND CANYON.

**Cortés, Hernando** (kawr-TEZ) Hernando Cortés was a Spanish explorer who conquered the AZTEC empire in the 1500s. *See also* MONTEZUMA.

**Crusades** During the European MIDDLE AGES, the HOLY LAND (the area that is now ISRAEL) was ruled by MUSLIMS. Many Christians in EUROPE believed that this region, where JESUS lived and died, should be governed by Christians. Christian armies from all over Europe tried to conquer the Holy Land but eventually had to withdraw. From the Crusades we now have the term "a crusade," meaning a strong effort for an idea or cause.

**culture** The culture of a particular group is its total way of life. It includes all the things the group as a whole thinks, believes, and does. To study a group's culture is to study its art, literature, religion, philosophy, sports, clothing, politics, customs, and habits. We may speak of the culture of a country (American culture), the culture of a region of the world (Southeast Asian culture), or the culture of a racial group (black culture). A culture that is especially large and complex is called a CIVILIZATION.

**De Soto, Hernando** Hernando De Soto was a Spanish soldier who explored parts of the southern United States in the middle 1500s in search of gold and treasure. He and his men were the first Europeans to see the MIS-

SISSIPPI RIVER. De Soto and many others died on the expedition without finding any treasure.

**Drake, Sir Francis**   Sir Francis Drake was an English admiral and explorer who made several voyages to the Americas in the late 1500s. He raided many Spanish cities in Central and SOUTH AMERICA, and he became the first Englishman to sail around the world. Drake also fought against the SPANISH ARMADA and helped to destroy it.

**Egypt**   Egypt, a country in northeast AFRICA, was the home of one of the world's oldest civilizations. The ancient Egyptians built great monuments, such as the PYRAMIDS and the SPHINX. Many preserved bodies of ancient Egyptians, called mummies, can still be seen in MUSEUMS. The Egyptians used a system of picture writing called HIEROGLYPHICS. *See also* PHARAOH.

**Eleanor of Aquitaine**   During the twelfth century, Eleanor of Aquitaine was the most powerful woman in all of EUROPE. She took part in the CRUSADES and helped to develop the British legal system. She married the French king Louis VII and, soon after that marriage was annulled, the English king Henry II. At age fifty, she was imprisoned for leading a rebellion against Henry II. She was set free fifteen years later by her son, King RICHARD THE LION-HEARTED.

**Elizabeth I**   Elizabeth I was a queen of ENGLAND in the 1500s. During her reign, WILLIAM SHAKESPEARE gained fame as a playwright and the SPANISH ARMADA was defeated. Her time on the throne is called the Elizabethan period.

**Ericson, Leif** (LEEF)   Leif Ericson was an Icelandic and Norwegian explorer who made several voyages in the northern ATLANTIC OCEAN around the year 1000. He probably landed in America five hundred years before COLUMBUS, but there is no way to know for certain.

**Fall of Rome**   The ROMAN EMPIRE lasted for some five hundred years, but it finally grew weak and was destroyed by groups of people from northern EUROPE in the fifth century A.D. After the Fall of Rome, the BYZANTINE EMPIRE continued for another thousand years.

**Ferdinand and Isabella** (IZ-uh-BEL-uh)   King Ferdinand and Queen Isabella were the rulers of SPAIN in the late 1400s who sponsored CHRISTOPHER COLUMBUS's voyage to America.

**feudalism** (FYOOHD-uhl-iz-uhm)   Feudalism was the political system of EUROPE during the MIDDLE AGES. Under this system, rulers granted land to certain people under their authority, called VASSALS. In return, the vassals promised to support their rulers in time of war. Those who owned land were called nobles. The poor people who lived and worked on the land were called SERFS.

**Fountain of Youth**   The Fountain of Youth is a legendary spring whose water was supposed to make people young again. The ex-

**Elizabeth I**

plorer PONCE DE LEÓN was said to be searching for it when he reached FLORIDA.

**Genghis Khan** (GENG-gis KAHN) Genghis Khan was a Mongol emperor who conquered a large part of northern CHINA and western ASIA around the year 1200. He was both a fierce warrior and a skilled ruler whose empire was admired for how well it was run.

**gladiators** Gladiators were men who fought to the death with swords or other weapons for the entertainment of crowds in ancient ROME. Gladiators fought against each other in large stadiums like the COLOSSEUM.

**Greece** Greece is a country in southeast EUROPE. One of the earliest civilizations appeared in ancient Greece and lasted from about 3000 to about 300 B.C. Its high point was in ATHENS from 700 to 300 B.C. The first great poets, artists, PLAYWRIGHTS, and PHILOSOPHERS of Europe lived in Greece during this period. Among them were poets like HOMER, playwrights like Sophocles, and philosophers like PLATO and ARISTOTLE. Ancient Greece was divided into city-states (cities that ruled themselves as if they were separate countries). The two most important city-states were Athens, the first DEMOCRACY, and SPARTA. Later, when the Romans conquered Greece, they took over much of Greek culture, including the myths described in the mythology section of this dictionary. The influence of ancient Greece can still be felt in the literature, art, philosophy, and political ideas of Europe and America.

**guild** A guild was an organization of workers during the MIDDLE AGES and RENAISSANCE in EUROPE. Each guild was made up of individuals who participated in the same craft, profession, or business. Guilds set standards of quality and tried to ensure that their members were paid a fair price for their work. Some of the important guilds in Europe in the 1400s were those for judges, bankers, doctors, wool and silk manufac-

turers, shoemakers, wood carvers, innkeepers, carpenters, armorers, and bakers.

**Hannibal** Hannibal was a general from the ancient city of CARTHAGE, in northern AFRICA. When Carthage went to war with ROME, Hannibal set off to invade ITALY. He led his army and a number of elephants across the ALPS, one of the most notable accomplishments in military history.

**Henry VIII** Henry VIII was a king of ENGLAND in the early 1500s. He declared himself to be the head of the Christian church in England instead of the POPE, and from that time on England has officially been a PROTESTANT nation instead of a ROMAN CATHOLIC one. Henry VIII married six times and was the father of ELIZABETH I.

**hieroglyphics** (HEYE-ruh-GLIF-iks) Hieroglyphics is a type of writing used in ancient EGYPT and elsewhere. This system uses designs rather than letters to stand for language. The word *hieroglyphics* comes from a Greek term meaning "holy writing," because the ancient Egyptians believed that Thoth, the god of learning, had invented writing.

**Holy Roman Empire** The Holy Roman Empire was a loosely organized political institution in EUROPE that lasted from the ninth century to the nineteenth century. It in-

**Hieroglyphics.** From the tomb of Hesire.

**Incas.** Ruins of Machu Picchu, near Cuzco, Peru.

cluded great amounts of territory in central and western Europe. Its first emperor was CHARLEMAGNE.

**Hudson, Henry**  Henry Hudson was an English explorer of the early 1600s. He traveled the HUDSON RIVER while sailing for the Dutch and HUDSON BAY while sailing for the English.

**The Hundred Years' War**  The Hundred Years' War was a series of conflicts that occurred between FRANCE and ENGLAND from 1337 to 1453. The kings of England invaded France, claiming that they should be kings of France as well. Toward the end of the war, JOAN OF ARC helped the French to drive out the English.

**Huns**  The Huns were a warlike people from ASIA who fought the Romans in the last days of the ROMAN EMPIRE.

**"I came, I saw, I conquered"**  JULIUS CAESAR was a general of ancient ROME. After one of his military victories, he told the Roman government, "I came, I saw, I conquered."

**Ibn Batuta** (IB-uhn bah-TOO-tah)  Ibn Batuta was an Arab traveler and writer during the late MIDDLE AGES. His book of travels described life in the MUSLIM world of SPAIN, North AFRICA, and the MIDDLE EAST, as well as the lands he visited in INDIA and CHINA.

**Ice Ages**  The Ice Ages describe the time when GLACIERS covered much of NORTH AMERICA and EUROPE. This period lasted until about 10,000 years ago.

**Incas**  The Incas were a group of Native American peoples who ruled an empire in western SOUTH AMERICA and built great cities high in the ANDES MOUNTAINS. They were conquered by the Spanish in the 1500s. *See also* CONQUISTADORS; PIZARRO, FRANCISCO.

**India** India, one of the chief civilizations of ASIA, has had a continuous history from ancient times to the present. The ancient Indian culture is often called the Indus Valley civilization because it flourished in the valley of the INDUS RIVER.

**Iron Age** The Iron Age was the period of history following the BRONZE AGE when iron was the most important metal used in tools, weapons, and machines. The Iron Age began around 2000 B.C. and has continued into modern times.

**Ivan the Great** Ivan the Great (Ivan III) was a Russian ruler of the late 1400s. It was during his rule that RUSSIA started to become a unified state. He was the grandfather of IVAN THE TERRIBLE.

**Ivan the Terrible** Ivan the Terrible (Ivan IV) was a Russian ruler of the middle 1500s. He was famous for his fits of rage and for his cruelty toward those he considered his enemies.

**Joan of Arc** Joan of Arc was a young French girl in the MIDDLE AGES who became one of the national heroines of FRANCE. She lived during a period when France and ENGLAND were at war and England occupied much of France. Joan heard voices that she believed were those of God and certain Christian saints; the voices inspired her to lead the French in battle during the HUNDRED YEARS' WAR. She was eventually captured by the English, tried for witchcraft, and burned at the stake. Later, she was named a saint of the ROMAN CATHOLIC CHURCH.

**knight** In the European MIDDLE AGES, a knight was a soldier of the noble class trained as a horseman. He sometimes wore armor, or metal protection, over his body. A knight pledged loyalty to a particular ruler,

Joan of Arc

who gave him land in return. Knights were expected to follow the ideals of CHIVALRY.

**Machu Picchu** (MAH-choo PEEK-choo, PEE-choo) Machu Picchu was a city built by the INCAS in a remote part of the ANDES MOUNTAINS in SOUTH AMERICA. It was probably built as a fortified city around 1500 but was later abandoned. Machu Picchu was rediscovered in 1911 and is now a popular place for tourists to visit.

**Magellan, Ferdinand** (muh-JEL-uhn) Ferdinand Magellan was a Portuguese explorer of the 1500s who led the first group of ships that sailed around the world. Magellan himself died on the voyage, but some of his sailors were able to complete the journey.

**Magna Carta** The Magna Carta was the great charter of CIVIL RIGHTS granted by the English king to his nobles in the MIDDLE AGES. It is one source of American ideals of liberty.

**Marathon, Battle of**   Marathon is the site of a famous battle in which the ancient Greeks defeated the Persian army during the PERSIAN WARS. The modern marathon, a long-distance race, is so named because according to legend, a messenger ran without stopping all twenty-six miles from Marathon to ATHENS with the news of the Greek victory, after which he collapsed and died.

**Maya** (MEYE-uh)   The Maya are a group of Native American people who in ancient times built a great civilization in MEXICO and CENTRAL AMERICA. They are known for their highly accurate calendar, their HIEROGLYPHIC writing, and their TEMPLES built on the top of PYRAMIDS. Mayan civilization began to decline around the year A.D. 900, and the Maya were later conquered by the Spanish CONQUISTADORS.

**Mesopotamia**   (mes-uh-puh-TAY-mee-uh) Mesopotamia is an area between the TIGRIS and EUPHRATES Rivers in western ASIA. It is known as the "cradle of civilization" because it was here that some of the world's first cities were built and that the practice of writing first developed.

**Middle Ages**   The period of European history between the FALL OF ROME and the RENAISSANCE, from about 500 to about 1500, is called the Middle Ages. During this time, the Christian church had an especially strong influence on all aspects of European life. FEUDALISM was the dominant political system. The first half of the Middle Ages is sometimes called the Dark Ages. *See also* ROMAN EMPIRE.

**Ming dynasty**   The Ming dynasty (a series of rulers in the same family) ruled CHINA from the mid-fourteenth to the mid-seventeenth century. During this time the Chinese brought trade goods to East AFRICA, the MIDDLE EAST, and SOUTHEAST ASIA. The Ming dynasty was also known for its beautiful porcelains and for its development of the NOVEL.

**Montezuma** (mon-tuh-ZOOH-muh)   Montezuma was a ruler of the AZTECS whose empire was conquered by HERNANDO CORTÉS in the early 1500s. Montezuma did not want to fight Cortés because he thought Cortés might be a god. Later Cortés took Montezuma prisoner, and when the Aztecs rebelled, Montezuma was stoned by his own subjects and died a few days later. *See also* CORTÉS, HERNANDO.

**Nero**   Nero was an emperor of ancient ROME who is famous for his cruelty. According to legend, which modern scholars reject, Nero set Rome on fire and played his fiddle while he watched it burn.

**Norman Conquest**   In 1066, England was conquered by an army of Normans (people from Normandy, in northern FRANCE) at the Battle of Hastings, in southern ENGLAND. After the Norman Conquest, French language and culture became a part of English life. *See also* WILLIAM THE CONQUEROR.

**Northwest Passage**   The Northwest Passage is a sea route around NORTH AMERICA be-

**Ming dynasty.** Detail from a screen from the Forbidden City of Beijing, China. The symbols in the design represent happiness.

tween the ATLANTIC and PACIFIC OCEANS. Many European explorers tried in vain to find a Northwest Passage so that trading ships would not have to make the long and dangerous journey around SOUTH AMERICA in order to reach the Far East. It is now known that such a passage does exist, but it is too far north to be of use, since most of the year it is closed by ice.

**Peloponnesian War** (pel-uh-puh-NEE-zhuhn) The Peloponnesian War was a long war that was fought between the ancient Greek city-states of ATHENS and SPARTA during the fifth century B.C. Sparta won the war.

**Persian Empire** The Persian Empire was an ancient empire in western ASIA, centered in what is now the country of IRAN. The Persian Empire challenged ancient GREECE in a series of battles known as the PERSIAN WARS. In the end Persia was defeated by the Greeks.

**Persian Wars** The Persian Wars were a series of battles between ancient GREECE and the PERSIAN EMPIRE. The most famous battle was at MARATHON, in which the Greeks defeated the Persians and saved their cities from invasion.

**pharaoh** (FAIR-oh) In ancient EGYPT, the ruler was called the pharaoh.

**Pizarro, Francisco** (puh-ZAHR-oh) Francisco Pizarro was a Spanish soldier who conquered the INCA Empire in the 1500s. Pizarro captured the ruler of the Inca, who offered to give Pizarro a roomful of gold if he would set him free. Pizarro accepted the gold, but instead of freeing the Inca ruler, he ordered him to be killed.

**Polo, Marco** Marco Polo was an Italian explorer during the MIDDLE AGES. He traveled as far as CHINA and later returned to tell the Europeans about his travels in ASIA. Marco Polo wrote about a number of things known to the people of Asia that Europeans had

never heard of, such as paper money, coal, and the fireproof material called asbestos.

**Pompeii** (pom-PAY) Pompeii was a city of the ROMAN EMPIRE. It lay on the southern coast of ITALY. In A.D. 79, it was destroyed, along with its neighbor, Herculaneum (hur-kyoo-LAY-nee-uhm), by an eruption of MOUNT VESUVIUS. The ruins of Pompeii were discovered in 1748.

**Ponce de León, Juan** Juan Ponce de León was a Spanish soldier who conquered the island of PUERTO RICO in the early 1500s. He also discovered and named FLORIDA, supposedly while searching for the legendary FOUNTAIN OF YOUTH.

**Ptolemy** (TOL-uh-mee) Ptolemy was an ancient Greek astronomer who believed that the PLANETS, along with the SUN and the STARS, revolved around EARTH. His belief was accepted for nearly 1,500 years, until the modern idea of the SOLAR SYSTEM, in which the planets revolve around the sun, developed from the ideas of COPERNICUS.

**Punic Wars** (PYOOH-nik) The three Punic Wars were fought between CARTHAGE and ROME during the third and second centuries B.C. The general HANNIBAL led the forces of Carthage during the second Punic War. Carthage was destroyed after the third Punic War.

**Pyramids** The Pyramids are huge stone monuments in EGYPT. Each one has four triangular sides, which come to a point at the top, and a square base. They were built in ancient times as tombs for the Egyptian PHARAOHS. Other civilizations, such as the MAYA, have also built pyramids for use as tombs or TEMPLES.

**Reformation** (ref-uhr-MAY-shun) In the 1500s, many Roman Catholics rebelled against the authority of the church and broke away to set up new churches, which became known as PROTESTANT CHURCHES.

This rebellion is called the Reformation because it began as an effort to reform Christianity. After the Reformation, much of northern EUROPE became Protestant while most of southern Europe remained Catholic.

**Renaissance** (REN-i-SANS) The period of European history from about 1400 to about 1600 is called the Renaissance and marks the end of the MIDDLE AGES. The Renaissance was a time of great achievements in art and literature when artists such as LEONARDO DA VINCI and MICHELANGELO and writers such as CERVANTES and SHAKESPEARE were active. The Renaissance was also the great age of exploration, when CHRISTOPHER COLUMBUS reached the New World.

**Richard the Lion-Hearted** Richard the Lion-Hearted was an English king of the late 1100s. He fought in the CRUSADES and was known for his bravery and chivalry in battle.

**Roman Empire** In ancient times, Rome (which today is the capital of ITALY) was the center of a great empire. At the height of its power, the Roman Empire included Italy, GREECE, FRANCE, BRITAIN, SPAIN, and parts of North AFRICA and the eastern Mediterranean. The Romans were remarkable soldiers, engineers, and lawmakers. Their empire was connected by a huge network of roads, many of which can still be seen in EUROPE. The Roman Empire also left its mark on the languages of Europe, for Italian, French, and Spanish all come from Latin, the language of the Romans. English, too, has many Latin words. The Roman Empire lasted from just before the birth of JESUS to about A.D. 500. *See also* AUGUSTUS CAESAR; CAESAR, JULIUS; ROMAN REPUBLIC.

**Roman Republic** The Roman Republic was the government that ruled ancient ROME for hundreds of years until the beginning of the ROMAN EMPIRE under AUGUSTUS CAESAR. The republic was ruled by a senate of noblemen who met to discuss important matters and make decisions about what to do. In contrast, the Roman Empire was ruled by a single person known as the emperor.

**Rome** *See* Roman Empire.

**Saladin** (SAL-uh-din) Saladin was a MUSLIM ruler of EGYPT and other regions of the MIDDLE EAST in the late 1100s. He recaptured the city of JERUSALEM during one of the CRUSADES and is considered a great hero of Muslim history.

**samurai** (SAM-uh-reye) The samurai were trained soldiers who belonged to the Japanese noble class during the time of the SHOGUNS. They followed a strict code of behavior that valued honor more than life.

**serf** Under the feudal system of the MIDDLE AGES, the land was farmed by poor people who were called serfs. The serfs were under the complete control of the nobles who owned the land. *See also* FEUDALISM.

**Samurai**

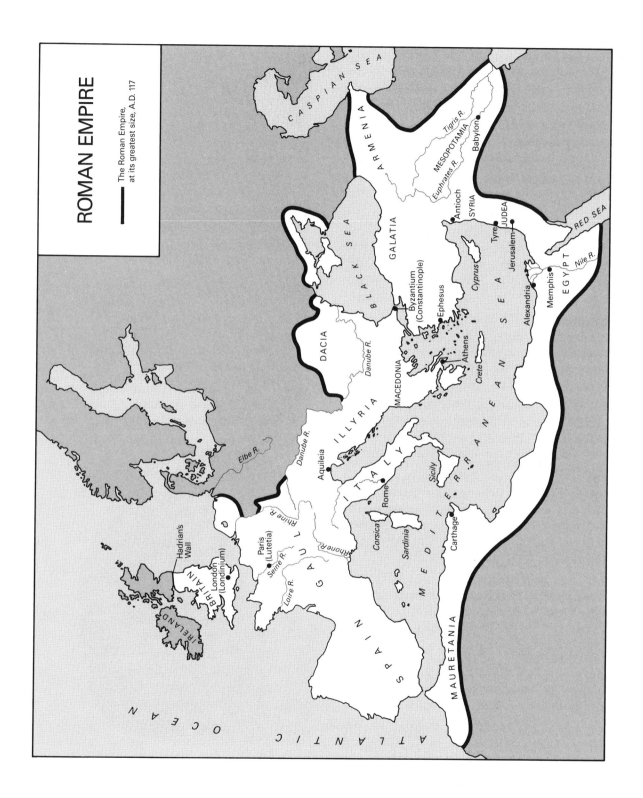

ROMAN EMPIRE

The Roman Empire,
at its greatest size, A.D. 117

CASPIAN SEA

ARMENIA

Tigris R.

MESOPOTAMIA

Babylon

Euphrates R.

Antioch

SYRIA

RED SEA

GALATIA

Tyre

JUDEA

Jerusalem

EGYPT

Nile R.

BLACK SEA

Byzantium
(Constantinople)

Ephesus

Cyprus

Memphis

Alexandria

DACIA

Danube R.

MACEDONIA

Athens

Crete

M E D I T E R R A N E A N   S E A

ILLYRIA

Elbe R.

Danube R.

Aquileia

ITALY

Sicily

Rome

Corsica

Sardinia

Carthage

GAUL

Rhine R.

Rhone R.

Paris
(Lutetia)

Seine R.

Loire R.

Hadrian's
Wall

London
(Londinium)

BRITAIN

IRELAND

SPAIN

MAURETANIA

A T L A N T I C   O C E A N

**shoguns** The shoguns were Japanese military leaders who ruled the country for hundreds of years. Modern Japanese history begins when the last shogun was overthrown in the middle 1900s.

**Spanish Armada** The Spanish Armada was a huge fleet of ships that the king of SPAIN sent to attack ENGLAND in the 1500s. The Armada was destroyed by the English ships. *See also* ELIZABETH I.

**Sparta** Sparta was one of the two most important city-states of ancient GREECE. The Spartans were known as a warlike, disciplined people. *See also* ATHENS; PELOPONNESIAN WAR.

**Sphinx** (SFINKS) The Sphinx is an enormous stone statue built by the ancient Egyptians. It has the head of a woman and the body of a lion. *See also* SPHINX *under "Mythology."*

**Stone Age** The Stone Age was the earliest period of human history. During this time, before people learned how to shape metal, all tools were made of stone. *See also* BRONZE AGE; IRON AGE.

**Stonehenge** Stonehenge is a circle of huge stones standing upright on an open plain in ENGLAND. The stones were set in place in ancient times, but no one knows who put them there or what precisely they were used for.

**Tang dynasty** A dynasty is a series of rulers who belong to the same family. The Tang dynasty ruled in CHINA during one of the greatest periods of its history. The dynasty lasted for three hundred years (618–907), during which time many important advances were made in the sciences, technology, and the arts.

**Tutankhamen** (tooht-ahng-KAH-muhn) Tutankhamen was an Egyptian PHARAOH who lived around 1400 B.C. His tomb remained

**Stonehenge**

undiscovered for more than three thousand years. When it was finally opened, in the 1920s, it was found to contain many treasures and objects that show how people lived in ancient EGYPT. Tutankhamen is also known as King Tut.

**vassal** In the feudal system, a KNIGHT who swore loyalty to a particular ruler became the vassal, or follower, of that ruler. *See also* FEUDALISM.

**Tutankhamen.** A gold mask of the pharaoh.

**Vikings**

**Vikings** The Vikings were seagoing warriors from SCANDINAVIA who were famous for their skill as sailors. During the MIDDLE AGES, they repeatedly raided the coasts of EUROPE, attacking and looting towns.

**William the Conqueror** William the Conqueror was the leader of the Normans, who conquered ENGLAND in 1066. *See also* NORMAN CONQUEST.

**Zulus** (ZOOH-loohz) The Zulus are an African people who speak a BANTU language and live in the country of SOUTH AFRICA. The Zulus fought many battles against the Europeans who came into their lands in the 1900s. Today many Zulus live in large cities or work on farms or mine gold, diamonds, and other minerals.

# World History Since 1600

Here we describe important people and events in the last four hundred years or so. This period has seen three world-shaking revolutions, when the American, French, and Russian peoples overthrew their governments. These years have also seen two world wars and the rise of dictators such as Hitler and Stalin. In this period, the expansion of science and technology has enabled people to live in increasing comfort, to conquer disease, and to venture as far as the moon. The spread of technology has brought problems, however, especially that of pollution. In the first part of this period, the nations of Europe were dominant. Today, the nations of Asia, Africa, and Latin America have gained their independence from European rule and are playing a growing role in shaping world events.

**Allies** The Allies were the victorious nations who fought together in WORLD WAR I and WORLD WAR II. They were called the Allies because they were allied, or united, in their effort. In World War I, the Allies included BRITAIN, FRANCE, ITALY, RUSSIA, and the United States. In World War II, the Allies included Britain, France, the SOVIET UNION, and the United States.

**Al Qaeda** (ahl-KAY-da) Al Qaeda is a terrorist network that is headed by OSAMA BIN LADEN. It is believed to have been responsible for the SEPTEMBER 11 ATTACKS (*under "United States History Since 1865"*). *See also* BIN LADEN, OSAMA.

**apartheid** (uh-PAHRT-heyet) In the nation of SOUTH AFRICA, for many years a white minority ruled over a black majority. The government enforced a policy of SEGREGATION of the races known as apartheid. This policy, which helped to keep blacks powerless, was condemned by most of the countries in the world. In the early 1990s, the acts that made apartheid legal were repealed, and whites voted to end their minority rule.

**Arab-Israeli conflict** The Arab-Israeli conflict is a conflict between Arabs and Israelis in the MIDDLE EAST. In the late 1940s, the UNITED NATIONS created the nation of ISRAEL in an area known as PALESTINE, where Arabs were living. Both the Arabs and the Israelis believe that land in Palestine should be theirs. As a result, war has broken out between them a number of times.

**Axis powers** During WORLD WAR II, the group of nations headed by GERMANY, ITALY, and JAPAN that fought against the ALLIES were known as the Axis powers.

**arms race**   The arms race refers to the competition between various countries after WORLD WAR II to have the most sophisticated and the greatest number of weapons, especially NUCLEAR WEAPONS. The majority of these weapons were controlled by the United States and the SOVIET UNION. Since the 1970s a number of treaties have been signed to limit nuclear weapons.

**Bastille** (ba-STEEL)   The Bastille was a large prison in PARIS, FRANCE. In 1789, at the beginning of the FRENCH REVOLUTION, it was attacked and taken over by the revolutionaries. The day of the attack, July 14, is now a national holiday in France called Bastille Day.

**Berlin Wall**   East Germany built the Berlin Wall in the 1960s to prevent citizens of East Berlin from escaping to West Berlin, a part of West Germany that was surrounded by East Germany. The wall was torn down in 1989 during the peaceful popular uprising that led to the 1990 reunification of GERMANY.

**bin Laden, Osama** (LAH-duhn)   Osama bin Laden is the head of the AL QAEDA network of terrorists. He was born to a wealthy family in SAUDI ARABIA and had military training in AFGHANISTAN. He is believed to have helped plan the SEPTEMBER 11 ATTACKS.

**Boer War** (BOHR)   The Boer War was fought from 1899 to 1902 between British and Dutch settlers in what is now SOUTH AFRICA. After a long struggle, the Dutch settlers, or Boers, were defeated by the British.

**Bolívar, Simón** (see-MOHN buh-LEE-vahr)   Simón Bolívar was a Venezuelan soldier and revolutionary leader who helped the South American colonies win independence from SPAIN in the early 1800s. He was known as "the Liberator," and the country of BOLIVIA is named in his honor.

**Berlin Wall.** Tearing down the Berlin Wall in 1989.

**bourgeoisie** (boor-zhwah-ZEE)   *Bourgeoisie* is the French word for middle class. The FRENCH REVOLUTION was brought about in part by the bourgeoisie, which sought more personal and economic freedom.

**Castro, Fidel**   Fidel Castro, a communist, is the political leader of CUBA.

**Catherine the Great**   Catherine the Great was an empress of RUSSIA in the late 1700s who greatly expanded the Russian Empire by military and diplomatic conquests. Like PETER THE GREAT before her, she is known for bringing European art and culture to RUSSIA.

**Chiang Kai-shek**   (CHANG KEYE-SHEK) Chiang Kai-shek was a Chinese military and political leader of the twentieth century. He was president of CHINA but was driven to the island of TAIWAN in 1949 by the communists. He established a government there and became president.

**Churchill, Winston**   Winston Churchill, as prime minister of GREAT BRITAIN during WORLD WAR II, inspired the ALLIES to organize against HITLER. When he became prime minister, he said, "I have nothing to offer but blood, toil, tears, and sweat."

**Cold War**   Between WORLD WAR II and the 1980s, a state of tension and military rivalry existed between the SOVIET UNION and the United States. This was called the Cold War, because there was no "hot" war, with actual fighting. But because each country believed that the other threatened its existence, both stockpiled thousands of nuclear weapons, a number that is now being reduced slowly through disarmament talks and treaties.

**colonialism**   A colony is a settlement established in a distant land that maintains social and economic ties with the country of origin. Usually the country of origin benefits from colonialism, not the colonized land and people. In unpopulated or sparsely populated areas, such as the Americas, colonized by the British, French, Spanish, and Portuguese in the 1500s and 1600s, colonies can lead to the creation of new nations. In more populated areas, such as the parts of ASIA and AFRICA colonized by the British, French, Belgians, Dutch, and Germans in the 1700s and 1800s, colonies are often absorbed or rejected by the local people, who establish or reestablish their own nations.

**concentration camp**   A concentration camp is a kind of prison used by governments to confine large groups of people for political reasons. During WORLD WAR II, millions of people died in concentration camps run by the NAZIS. *See also* HITLER, ADOLF; HOLOCAUST.

**Cook, Captain James**   Captain James Cook, an English explorer of the 1700s, was the

**Concentration camp.** Prisoners in the Buchenwald concentration camp.

first European to visit the HAWAIIAN ISLANDS.

**Cromwell, Oliver**   Oliver Cromwell was a British PURITAN political leader and general of the seventeenth century. During the English Civil War, he led an army to victory over King Charles I. Cromwell ruled ENGLAND, SCOTLAND, and IRELAND as lord protector from 1653 until his death in 1658. He was particularly harsh in his suppression of rebellion in IRELAND.

**czar** (ZAHR)   Czar was the name given to the Russian rulers or emperors before the RUSSIAN REVOLUTION.

**D-Day**   During WORLD WAR II, a huge army of American and British troops landed on the coast of NORMANDY in FRANCE to fight the Germans, who had taken control of most of EUROPE. This invasion was the turning point of the war and the beginning of Germany's defeat. The day of the landing, June 6, 1944, is known as D-Day.

**D-Day.** American troops landing on the northern coast of France, June 6, 1944.

**De Gaulle, Charles** (di-GOHL)   Charles De Gaulle was a French president in the mid-1900s. During WORLD WAR II, he led the French Resistance, those people who defied Germany's occupation of FRANCE.

**East India Company**   The East India Company was a business organization that was formed in the 1600s for the purpose of trading by sea between EUROPE and various countries of southern ASIA. There were actually several companies with this name, including the Dutch East India Company, which traded mainly with the islands of INDONESIA, and the British East India Company, which traded mainly with INDIA.

**The Enlightenment**   The Enlightenment was a movement in EUROPE in the seventeenth and eighteenth centuries that celebrated human reason. It was marked by an interest in science, the spread of religious tolerance, and a desire to build fair govern-

ments. JOHN LOCKE was an important PHILOSOPHER of the Enlightenment.

**Frank, Anne**   Anne Frank, a Dutch Jewish girl, spent two years hiding from the NAZIS in AMSTERDAM during WORLD WAR II. She was eventually captured and sent to a CONCENTRATION CAMP, where she died. Her diary from her time in Amsterdam was found and published and is now a famous book, *Anne Frank: The Diary of a Young Girl. See also* HOLOCAUST.

**French Revolution**   In 1789, the French people revolted against their government. The revolution began with the storming of the BASTILLE, a prison. The king was overthrown and executed and FRANCE was declared a republic, but the struggle for freedom lasted several years and included the period known as the REIGN OF TERROR. The revolutionary government was eventually overthrown by NAPOLEON, who made himself ruler of France. *See also* MARIE ANTOINETTE.

**Gandhi, Mahatma** (GAHN-dee)   Mahatma Gandhi was the greatest political and spiritual leader of modern INDIA. Using nonviolent methods, he led India to independence

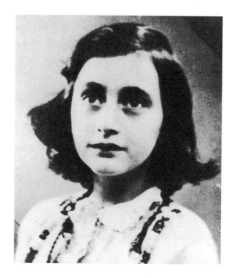

**Anne Frank**

**Mahatma Gandhi.** A photograph by Margaret Bourke-White.

from British rule in the mid-1900s. He was assassinated in 1948, just after India gained independence. The title *mahatma* means "great soul."

**George III** George III was the king of ENG-LAND during the American REVOLUTIONARY WAR.

**Hidalgo, Miguel** (hih-DAHL-goh) Miguel Hidalgo was a Mexican PRIEST who led an uprising against the Spanish government in the early 1800s. Though the uprising was unsuccessful, it inspired further rebellion, and MEXICO won its independence from SPAIN a few years later. Miguel Hidalgo is known as "the father of Mexican independence." September 16, when he proclaimed his revolt, is celebrated as Independence Day.

**Hiroshima** (heer-uh-SHEE-muh) During WORLD WAR II, American forces dropped an ATOMIC BOMB on the Japanese city of Hiroshima. This was the first time a nuclear device had been used as a weapon in wartime.

**Hitler, Adolf** Adolf Hitler was the leader of the Nazi movement. The NAZIS called him der Führer (the Leader). After he became dictator of GERMANY, Hitler started WORLD WAR II in 1939 by invading neighboring

countries, because he believed that Germany was destined to rule EUROPE. He hated the Jewish people and spread this hatred among his followers. Millions of Jews and other groups of people were murdered in CONCEN-TRATION CAMPS in a program of death and suffering that is known as the HOLOCAUST.

**Holocaust** During WORLD WAR II, the NA-ZIS murdered more than six million Jews and other people whom Hitler considered inferior. This mass murder has become known as the Holocaust. *See also* HITLER, ADOLF; NAZIS.

**Hussein, Saddam** (sah-DAHM HOOH-sayn) Saddam Hussein was president of IRAQ from 1979 until 2003, when U.S.-led forces removed him from power. He led brutal invasions of IRAN in 1980 and KUWAIT in 1990. *See also* PERSIAN GULF WAR.

**Industrial Revolution** Before the 1700s, most people in EUROPE lived and worked on farms. In the 1700s and 1800s, many new machines were invented, and they produced goods on a scale that had never been known before. Factories were built to house the machines. People moved from the country to find work in the factories, and industrial towns sprang up. Along with the machines came new methods of transportation, such

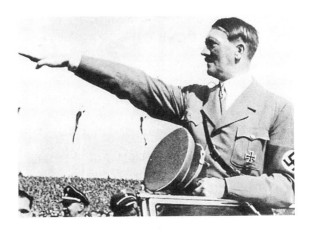

**Adolf Hitler**

as the railroad. Together, all these changes brought about by the rise of industry are called the Industrial Revolution. It had both good and bad effects on people's lives. More goods were available than ever before. Better means of transportation and communication were invented. On the other hand, most factory workers were poor, and factory towns were dirty and polluted.

**Iron Curtain**   The term "Iron Curtain," first used by the British prime minister WINSTON CHURCHILL, refers to an imaginary dividing line between the independent nations of Western Europe and the nations of Eastern Europe that came under the communist domination of the SOVIET UNION after WORLD WAR II. The Eastern European countries once said to be "behind the Iron Curtain" began to regain their autonomy in the 1980s. *See also* COMMUNISM.

**Jolly Roger**   The Jolly Roger is a flag that shows a white skull and crossbones against a black background. It was flown by pirate ships when pirates were active, in the 1600s and 1700s.

**KGB**   The KGB was the secret police force in the SOVIET UNION.

**Kidd, Captain**   Captain Kidd was a famous pirate of the 1600s.

**Korean War**   The Korean War was fought in the early 1950s. The United States helped SOUTH KOREA defend itself against an invasion from communist NORTH KOREA. *See also* KOREAN WAR *under "United States History Since 1865."*

**League of Nations**   The League of Nations was an organization established after WORLD WAR I that was the forerunner of the UNITED NATIONS. The League brought about international cooperation on health issues, labor problems, and refugee affairs. Although President WOODROW WILSON was a founder of the League of Nations, the United States never joined it.

**Lenin, V. I.** (LEN-in)   V. I. Lenin was the leader of the communist group that seized power during the RUSSIAN REVOLUTION. He became the first political leader of the SOVIET UNION.

**Livingstone, David**   David Livingstone was a Scottish missionary in AFRICA in the middle 1800s. He explored a large part of central Africa, including many places no European had gone before. Livingstone was a strong opponent of black slavery.

**Louis XIV** (LOOH-ee)   Louis XIV, known as the Sun King, was a king of FRANCE during the 1600s, when France was the most powerful country in EUROPE. He is famous for the absolute power he held over his people and for his support of the arts.

**Mandela, Nelson** (man-DEL-uh)   Nelson Mandela was the most famous leader in the struggle of black South Africans against APARTHEID. In the 1960s, the white government of SOUTH AFRICA sentenced him to life in prison. He was released in 1990, how-

**Nelson Mandela**

ever, and was elected president in 1994. Mandela won the NOBEL PRIZE for peace in 1993.

**Mao Zedong or Mao Tse-tung** (mowd-zuh-DOONG, mowt-tse-tung)  Mao Zedong was the leader of mainland CHINA after he led the communists to victory in the late 1940s. He became a very powerful dictator and controlled every aspect of his people's lives.

**Marie Antoinette** (muh-REE an-twuh-NET) Marie Antoinette was the queen of FRANCE at the time of the FRENCH REVOLUTION. She and the king, Louis XVI, were executed by the revolutionaries.

**Martí, José** (hoh-ZAY mahr-TEE)  José Martí was a Cuban poet in the late 1800s who inspired many Cubans to fight for independence from SPAIN. He was killed in a battle fighting Spanish soldiers.

**Mussolini, Benito** (mooh-suh-LEE-nee)  Benito Mussolini was the political leader of ITALY during WORLD WAR II.

**Nagasaki**  During WORLD WAR II, American forces dropped an ATOMIC BOMB on the Japanese city of HIROSHIMA. Three days later another atomic bomb was dropped on the city of Nagasaki.

**Napoleon** (nuh-POH-lee-uhn) Napoleon Bonaparte was a general and the emperor of FRANCE in the early 1800s. He conquered much of EUROPE before being defeated by the British at the Battle of WATERLOO.

**Nazis** (NAHT-seez)  The Nazis were members of the political party that ruled GERMANY before and during WORLD WAR II. They hated Jews and other groups of people and believed that Germans were superior to all other peoples and should rule the world. Their leader was ADOLF HITLER, whose policies led to the HOLOCAUST.

**Nightingale, Florence**  Florence Nightingale was an English nurse of the 1800s. She became famous for her work tending wounded soldiers and helped establish the modern profession of nursing.

**Normandy**  Normandy is a region of northern FRANCE on the ENGLISH CHANNEL. Its beaches were where the American and British troops landed on D-DAY in WORLD WAR II.

**Pearl Harbor**  On December 7, 1941, the Japanese attacked the United States naval base at Pearl Harbor, HAWAII. After the attack, the United States declared war on JAPAN, which led to direct American participation in WORLD WAR II in EUROPE as well as in ASIA.

**Persian Gulf War**  The Persian Gulf War was fought between the forces of the UNITED NATIONS, which were led by the United States, and those of IRAQ. It began in response to Iraqi president SADDAM HUSSEIN's

**Napoleon.** A painting by Jean-Auguste-Dominique Ingres.

invasion of KUWAIT in August 1990. The United Nations forces expelled Iraqi troops from Kuwait in March 1991.

**Peter the Great**   Peter the Great was a Russian CZAR of the late 1600s and early 1700s who helped unify and modernize his country. He visited the great cities of EUROPE and brought back ideas for how Russian society could be improved. He built the city of ST. PETERSBURG.

**potato famine, Irish**   The Irish potato famine was caused by the failure of potato crops in IRELAND for several years in the 1840s. Many in Ireland starved. During the famine, more than a million Irish came to the United States.

**Reign of Terror**   The Reign of Terror was a phase of the FRENCH REVOLUTION during which many people were executed because they were considered enemies of the Revolution.

**Russian Revolution**   In 1917 and 1918, the Russian people overthrew their government. The Bolsheviks, a communist group, came to power and created the Union of Soviet Socialist Republics (USSR), which was also called the SOVIET UNION. *See also* LENIN, V. I.

**Santa Anna**   Santa Anna was a Mexican general and political leader in the early and middle 1800s. He helped win Mexico's independence from SPAIN, but his army was defeated by the United States in the MEXICAN WAR. It was Santa Anna's soldiers who won a victory over the Texans at the ALAMO.

**Seven Years' War**   The Seven Years' War was a power struggle between the German kingdom of Prussia, which was supported by GREAT BRITAIN, and an alliance that included AUSTRIA, FRANCE, and RUSSIA. It lasted from 1756 to 1763. Prussia and Britain won the war and gained power; Britain took all of CANADA and much of INDIA. Some of the war was fought in NORTH AMERICA, where it was called the French and Indian War.

**slave trade**   In the 1500s, Europeans, with the help of Africans, began to bring people from AFRICA to work as slaves on the farms and plantations of NORTH and SOUTH AMERICA. The slave trade did not end in America and EUROPE until the 1800s, when many European countries passed laws against SLAVERY.

***Sputnik***   *Sputnik* is the name of a Russian SATELLITE that was launched in 1957. It was the first artificial satellite to orbit EARTH. The success of *Sputnik* and other Russian satellites caused the United States to work harder on its own space program.

**Stalin, Joseph** (STAH-lin)   Joseph Stalin was the leader of the SOVIET UNION in the early and middle 1900s, including WORLD WAR II. Notorious for his cruelty, he caused the deaths of millions of his people.

**Teresa, Mother**   Mother Teresa, a Roman Catholic nun who lived in INDIA, won the NOBEL PRIZE for peace in 1979 for helping unfortunate and poor people.

***Titanic***   The *Titanic* was a luxury ocean liner that struck an iceberg and sank during its first voyage, from ENGLAND to NEW YORK, in April 1912. The ship had been considered unsinkable. (*See* image, next page.)

**Toussaint L'Ouverture** (TOOH-san looh-vur-TUHR)   Toussaint L'Ouverture was a Haitian who led a slave revolt against the French in the late 1700s. Later he led the fight for the country's independence. He was finally captured, but he is honored today as one of the founders of HAITI.

**United Nations**   The United Nations, or U.N., is an organization that was formed after WORLD WAR II to promote world peace. Almost all of the nations of the world belong to the United Nations and send representatives to its headquarters in NEW YORK CITY.

The *Titantic*

Queen Victoria

**Victoria, Queen** Queen Victoria was the ruler of GREAT BRITAIN during the late 1800s, now known as the Victorian period. During her lengthy reign, Great Britain became the world's most powerful nation.

**Vietnam War** The Vietnam War, between North and South Vietnam, lasted from the 1950s to 1975. Because North Vietnam was a communist country, the United States sent troops to help the South Vietnamese government. The war ended with the defeat of the South Vietnamese. *See also* VIETNAM WAR *under "United States History Since 1865."*

**Villa, Pancho** (PAHN-choh VEE-uh) Pancho Villa was a Mexican revolutionary leader of the early 1900s. Villa was considered an outlaw by some people, but to others he was a popular hero. When he crossed the border and raided a town in NEW MEXICO, the United States government sent a large force into MEXICO to capture him, but Villa always managed to escape.

**Waterloo** Waterloo is the village in BELGIUM where NAPOLEON was finally defeated at the Battle of Waterloo in 1815.

**Vietnam War.** U.S. Army soldiers prepared to fight.

**Wellington, Duke of** Arthur Wellesley, the First Duke of Wellington, was a British general of the nineteenth century who defeated NAPOLEON at the Battle of WATERLOO.

**World War I** World War I was fought in EUROPE between 1914 and 1918. GREAT BRITAIN, RUSSIA, and FRANCE joined forces against GERMANY and Austria-Hungary, which was an empire made up of a number of eastern European countries. In 1917, the United States entered the war on the side of Great Britain and its allies. World War I was the largest and bloodiest war that had ever been fought in Europe. It was especially shocking because of the use of destructive devices such as airplanes, poison gas, and machine guns. Much of the fighting took place in trenches, or special holes dug by the soldiers. The war ended with the defeat of Germany and Austria-Hungary. *See also* WORLD WAR I *under "United States History Since 1865."*

**World War II** World War II was fought in EUROPE and ASIA between 1939 and 1945. On one side were the AXIS POWERS, GERMANY, ITALY, and JAPAN, and on the other

**World War II.** London, 1940: the dome of St. Paul's Cathedral can be seen through the fire and smoke.

side were the Allies, including the United States, GREAT BRITAIN, the SOVIET UNION, and CHINA. The war began when Germany and Japan invaded neighboring countries. The turning point of the war in Europe came when Allied troops landed in FRANCE on D-Day, June 6, 1944. Germany surrendered early in 1945. Japan gave up several months later, after the United States dropped ATOMIC BOMBS on the Japanese cities of HIROSHIMA and NAGASAKI. *See also* CHURCHILL, WINSTON; DE GAULLE, CHARLES; HITLER, ADOLF; MUSSOLINI, BENITO; PEARL HARBOR; STALIN, JOSEPH. *See also* WORLD WAR II *under "United States History Since 1865."*

**Zapata, Emiliano** (ay-meel-YAH-noh sah-PAH-tuh) Emiliano Zapata was a Mexican revolutionary leader of the early 1900s. He tried to bring about reforms that would take land from the wealthy landowners and divide it among the poor Indian farmers. He was assassinated in 1919. *See also* VILLA, PANCHO.

**Emiliano Zapata**

# United States Geography

Geography is the study of the surface of the earth, its division into regions, and the different characteristics of those regions. This section of the dictionary focuses on the United States. It lists and locates the fifty states and some of the country's territories, the major natural formations, such as mountain ranges and rivers, the different regions of the country, and some of the major cities.

**Adirondack Mountains** (ad-uh-RON-dack) The Adirondacks are a mountain range in northeast NEW YORK STATE.

**Alabama** Alabama is a state in the SOUTH.

**Alaska** Alaska, which is north and west of CANADA, is the largest state.

**Allegheny Mountains** (al-uh-GAY-nee) The Alleghenies are a mountain range extending from northern PENNSYLVANIA to southwest VIRGINIA.

**Annapolis** (uh-NAP-uh-lis) Annapolis is the capital of MARYLAND and the site of the United States Naval Academy.

**Appalachian Mountains** (AP-uh-LAY-chee-uhn) The Appalachians are a mountain chain that extends almost the entire length of the EAST COAST, from QUEBEC, CANADA, to ALABAMA. The Appalachian Trail runs through part of the Appalachian Mountains.

**Arizona** Arizona is a state in the SOUTHWEST.

**Arkansas** (AHR-kuhn-saw) Arkansas is a state in the SOUTH.

**Atlanta** Atlanta is the capital of GEORGIA and the state's most populous city. It is one of the major cities of the SOUTH.

**Badlands** The Badlands, in SOUTH DAKOTA, is an area of barren hills and gullies caused by erosion.

**Blue Ridge Mountains** The Blue Ridge Mountains, part of the APPALACHIAN MOUNTAIN chain, are mostly in VIRGINIA and NORTH CAROLINA.

**Boston** Boston is the capital of MASSACHUSETTS and the largest city in NEW ENGLAND.

**Brooklyn** Brooklyn is a part, or borough, of NEW YORK CITY. The BROOKLYN BRIDGE, between MANHATTAN and Brooklyn, is a famous structure.

**California** California, one of the PACIFIC COAST STATES, is the most populous state. Two of its most important cities are LOS ANGELES and SAN FRANCISCO.

**Cape Canaveral** (kuh-NAV-uhr-uhl) A cape is an area of land that extends out into the water. Cape Canaveral, in FLORIDA, is the site of the John F. Kennedy Space Center, where the space program launches rockets.

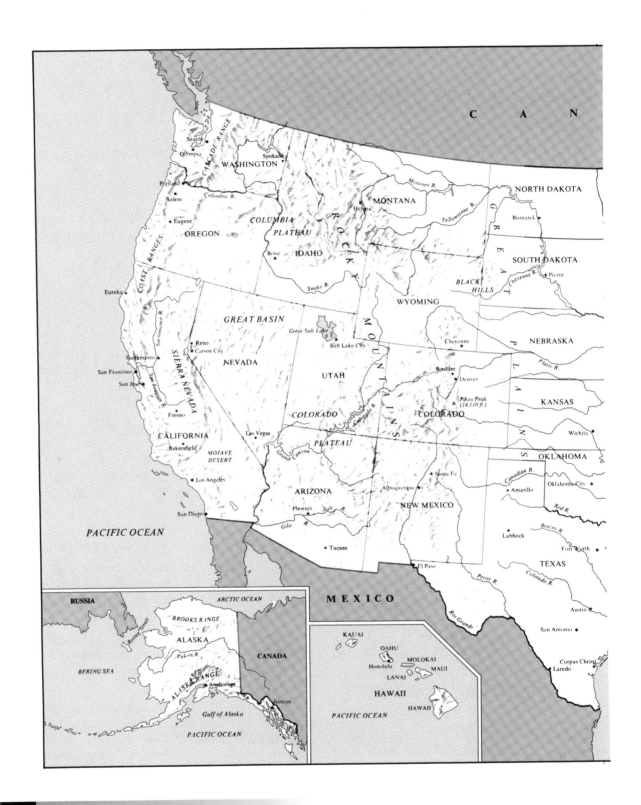

C A N

WASHINGTON

Seattle
Olympia
Spokane

Portland
Salem
Columbia R.
Eugene
OREGON

CASCADE RANGE

COLUMBIA
PLATEAU
Boise
IDAHO

MONTANA
Helena

Yellowstone R.

Missouri R.

NORTH DAKOTA

Bismarck

SOUTH DAKOTA

Pierre
Cheyenne R.

BLACK
HILLS

WYOMING

ROCKY

COAST RANGES

Eureka

Snake R.

GREAT BASIN

Great Salt Lake
Salt Lake City

Sacramento R.

Reno
Carson City

NEVADA

UTAH

Sacramento

San Francisco
San Jose

SIERRA NEVADA

San Joaquin R.

Fresno

CALIFORNIA

Bakersfield

MOJAVE
DESERT

Las Vegas

COLORADO
PLATEAU

Grand Canyon

Colorado R.

Cheyenne

Boulder
Denver

Pikes Peak
(14,110 ft.)

COLORADO

MOUNTAINS

Los Angeles

ARIZONA

Phoenix
Salt R.
Gila R.

San Diego

Tucson

PACIFIC OCEAN

NEW MEXICO

Santa Fe

Albuquerque

El Paso

MEXICO

Rio Grande

GREAT

PLAINS

NEBRASKA

Platte R.

KANSAS

Wichita

OKLAHOMA

Oklahoma City

Red R.

Canadian R.

Amarillo

Lubbock

Brazos R.

Fort Worth

TEXAS

Pecos R.
Colorado R.

Austin

San Antonio

Corpus Christi
Laredo

RUSSIA

ARCTIC OCEAN

BROOKS RANGE

ALASKA

Yukon R.

BERING SEA

Bering Strait

ALASKA RANGE

Anchorage

CANADA

Juneau

Gulf of Alaska

PACIFIC OCEAN

KAUAI

OAHU
Honolulu
LANAI
MOLOKAI
MAUI

HAWAII

PACIFIC OCEAN

HAWAII

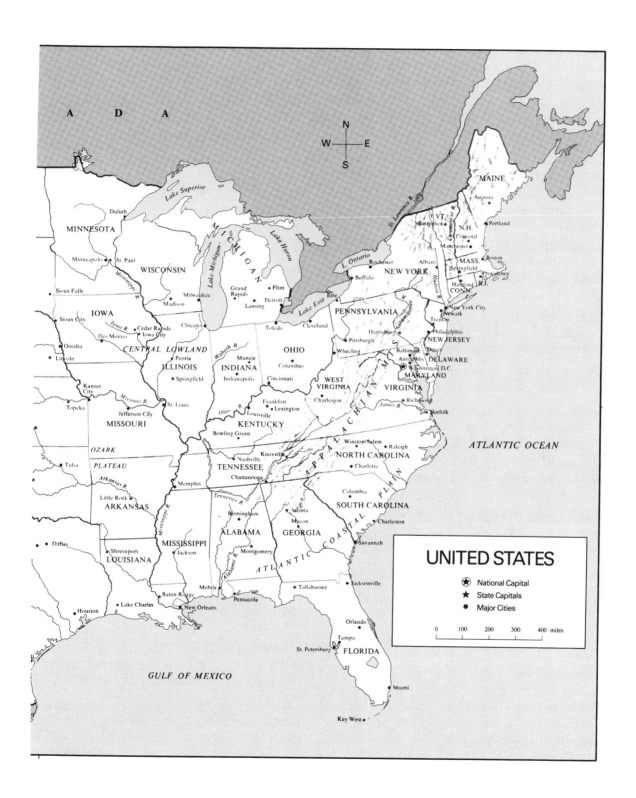

**UNITED STATES**

⬨ National Capital
★ State Capitals
• Major Cities

0   100   200   300   400 miles

**Cape Cod**   Cape Cod is a resort area on the ATLANTIC OCEAN in southeastern MASSACHUSETTS.

**Charleston**   Charleston, SOUTH CAROLINA, is an old seacoast city. Another city named Charleston is the capital of WEST VIRGINIA.

**Chesapeake Bay**   A bay is a part of a larger body of water that is partly enclosed by land. The Chesapeake Bay extends into the land from the ATLANTIC OCEAN; it is bordered by MARYLAND and VIRGINIA.

**Chicago**   (shi-KAH-goh)   Chicago, ILLINOIS, is a major MIDWEST city and the country's third most populous city. On the shores of LAKE MICHIGAN, it is nicknamed the Windy City.

**Colorado**   Colorado is one of the ROCKY MOUNTAIN STATES.

**Colorado River**   The Colorado River, in the SOUTHWEST, is one of the country's longest rivers.

**Columbia River**   The Columbia River is in the PACIFIC NORTHWEST.

**Connecticut**   (kuh-NET-i-kuht)   Connecticut is one of the NEW ENGLAND states and was one of the original thirteen states.

**Continental Divide**   The Continental Divide, or Great Divide, is a series of mountain ranges that stretch from ALASKA to MEXICO. West of the Continental Divide, rivers flow west, toward the PACIFIC OCEAN. East of the Continental Divide, rivers flow east, toward the ATLANTIC OCEAN, or south, toward the GULF OF MEXICO.

**Dallas**   Dallas is a large city in TEXAS and a major city in the SOUTHWEST.

**Death Valley**   Death Valley is a desert valley in eastern CALIFORNIA that is so named because of its harsh climate. In summer, it is one of the hottest places in the United States, and at 280 feet below sea level, it is the lowest point in NORTH AMERICA.

**Delaware**   Delaware is one of the MIDDLE ATLANTIC STATES and was one of the original thirteen states.

**Denver**   Denver is the capital of COLORADO and its largest city. It is the major city of the Rocky Mountain region.

**Detroit**   (di-TROIT)   Detroit, in MICHIGAN, is called the Motor City because it is the center of automobile manufacturing in the country.

**District of Columbia**   *See* WASHINGTON, D.C.

**East Coast**   The East Coast is the name for the part of the country on the ATLANTIC OCEAN.

**Erie Canal**   (EER-ee)   The Erie Canal was a canal (a man-made waterway) in NEW YORK State that connected the ATLANTIC OCEAN to the GREAT LAKES. It was a major transportation and shipping route in the 1800s, in the days before the railroad and automobile, when freight was carried on boats.

**Everglades**   The Everglades is a large, marshy region in southern FLORIDA famous for its wildlife, including alligators.

**Far West**   The Far West is the part of the country west of the ROCKY MOUNTAINS, on the PACIFIC OCEAN.

**Florida**   Florida, a state in the SOUTH, is the southernmost state on the EAST COAST.

**Florida Keys**   The Florida Keys are a long chain of islands off the southern tip of FLORIDA.

**Georgia**   (JAWR-juh)   Georgia is a state of the SOUTH, on the EAST COAST just north of FLORIDA, and was one of the original thirteen states.

**Grand Canyon**   The Grand Canyon is a deep, wide canyon in ARIZONA formed by the COLORADO RIVER. It is known for its spectacular scenery.

**The Grand Canyon**

**Great Lakes**   The Great Lakes are a group of five lakes in the north-central part of the United States along the Canadian border: LAKE SUPERIOR, LAKE MICHIGAN, LAKE HURON, LAKE ERIE, and LAKE ONTARIO. They are the largest group of freshwater lakes in the world.

**Great Plains**   The Great Plains is the vast, flat area of prairie, or grassland, that extends through parts of the MIDWEST, the WEST, and the SOUTHWEST. The prairie has very rich soil and grows vast quantities of corn and wheat.

**Great Salt Lake**   The Great Salt Lake is a large saltwater lake in northern UTAH.

**Great Smoky Mountains**   The Great Smokies are the part of the APPALACHIAN MOUNTAINS along the TENNESSEE-NORTH CAROLINA border. They are named for the smoke-like haze that hangs over them.

**Gulf of Mexico**   A gulf is a large body of ocean that is partly enclosed by land. The Gulf of Mexico is the part of the ATLANTIC OCEAN bordered by the southern coast of the United States and the eastern coast of MEXICO.

**Hawaii** (huh-WHY-ee)   Hawaii, the only state in the PACIFIC OCEAN, is a group of tropical islands far to the southwest of the United States mainland.

**Hollywood**   Hollywood, the traditional center of the movie industry, is part of LOS ANGELES, CALIFORNIA.

**Honolulu** (HON-uh-LOOH-looh)   Honolulu is the capital of HAWAII.

**Houston** (HYOOH-stuhn)  Houston is the largest city in TEXAS and one of the major cities of the SOUTHWEST.

**Hudson River**  The Hudson is a river in NEW YORK State. About 315 miles long, it flows to the ATLANTIC OCEAN past the west side of MANHATTAN Island.

**Idaho** (EYE-duh-HOH)  Idaho is one of the ROCKY MOUNTAIN STATES, famous for its potatoes.

**Illinois** (IL-uh-NOI)  Illinois is a state in the MIDWEST noted for its largest city, CHICAGO.

**Indiana** (IN-dee-AN-uh)  Indiana is a state in the MIDWEST.

**Indianapolis**  Indianapolis is the capital of INDIANA and its largest city.

**Iowa** (EYE-uh-wuh)  Iowa is a state in the MIDWEST.

**James River**  The James River is a river of central VIRGINIA flowing into CHESAPEAKE BAY. Near its mouth, JAMESTOWN was established in the early 1600s as the first permanent English settlement in America.

**Kansas** (KAN-zuhs)  Kansas is a state in the MIDWEST.

**Kansas City** (KAN-zuhs)  Kansas City is a major city in MISSOURI. Another Kansas City sits in northeast KANSAS on the Missouri River, adjacent to Kansas City, Missouri.

**Kentucky**  Kentucky is a state in the SOUTH.

**Lake Erie**  Lake Erie is one of the GREAT LAKES north of OHIO.

**Lake Huron** (HYOOR-uhn)  Lake Huron, one of the GREAT LAKES, is northeast of MICHIGAN.

**Lake Michigan** (MISH-i-guhn)  Lake Michigan is one of the GREAT LAKES, bordered by MICHIGAN to the east and WISCONSIN to the west.

**Lake Ontario**  Lake Ontario, one of the GREAT LAKES, is north of NEW YORK State.

**Lake Superior**  Lake Superior, the largest GREAT LAKE, is north of MICHIGAN.

**Las Vegas**  Las Vegas is a city in NEVADA famous for its entertainment and gambling casinos.

**Long Island**  Long Island is an island east of NEW YORK CITY that contains part of the city and many of its suburbs. The eastern end of the island is also known as a resort area.

**Los Angeles** (laws-AN-juh-luhs)  Los Angeles, in southern CALIFORNIA, is the second most populous city in the United States.

**Louisiana** (looh-EE-zee-AN-uh)  Louisiana is a state in the SOUTH.

**Maine**  Maine, one of the NEW ENGLAND states, is the northernmost state on the EAST COAST.

**Manhattan**  Manhattan is an island and the part of NEW YORK CITY noted for its skyscrapers, theaters, and financial district, known as Wall Street. In the 1600s, Manhattan Island was bought from the Native Americans by Dutch settlers for $24 worth of trinkets.

**Maryland** (MER-uh-luhnd)  Maryland is one of the MIDDLE ATLANTIC STATES and was one of the original thirteen states.

**Massachusetts** (MAS-uh-CHOOH-sits)  Massachusetts is a state in NEW ENGLAND and was one of the original thirteen states.

**Miami** (meye-AM-ee)  Miami is a city in FLORIDA. Miami Beach, just east across Biscayne Bay, is a famous resort town.

**Michigan** (MISH-i-guhn)  Michigan is a state in the MIDWEST. DETROIT is its largest city.

**Middle Atlantic states**  The Middle Atlantic states (PENNSYLVANIA, NEW YORK, NEW JERSEY, DELAWARE, and MARYLAND) are on the EAST COAST. All but Pennsylvania touch

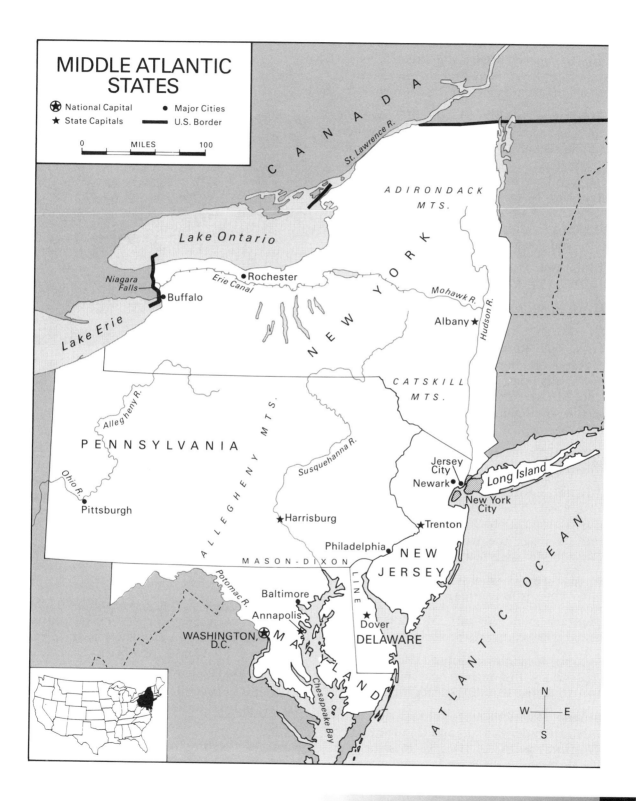

## MIDDLE ATLANTIC STATES

⊛ National Capital    ● Major Cities
★ State Capitals      ▬ U.S. Border

0          MILES          100

CANADA

St. Lawrence R.

ADIRONDACK MTS.

Lake Ontario

NEW YORK

Niagara Falls

●Rochester

Erie Canal

Mohawk R.

Hudson R.

Albany ★

Lake Erie

●Buffalo

CATSKILL MTS.

Allegheny R.

PENNSYLVANIA

ALLEGHENY MTS.

Susquehanna R.

Ohio R.

●Pittsburgh

★Harrisburg

Jersey City

Newark●

Long Island

New York City

★Trenton

Philadelphia●

NEW JERSEY

MASON-DIXON LINE

Potomac R.

Baltimore●

Annapolis★

WASHINGTON, D.C. ⊛

M A R Y L A N D

★Dover

DELAWARE

ATLANTIC OCEAN

Chesapeake Bay

N
W—E
S

the Atlantic Ocean, although Philadelphia is connected with the Atlantic by the Delaware River. This region is the most densely populated area in the country.

**Midwest**  The Midwest, or Middle West, is the vast, mostly flat area in the northern middle section of the United States. Mainly on the Great Plains, it has some of the richest farmland in the world. The Midwest states are North Dakota, South Dakota, Nebraska, Kansas, Minnesota, Wisconsin, Iowa, Missouri, Illinois, Indiana, Michigan, and Ohio.

**Minnesota** (MIN-i-SOH-tuh)  Minnesota is a state in the Midwest.

**Mississippi**  Mississippi is a state in the South.

**Mississippi River**  The Mississippi, in the center of the country, is 2,350 miles long and is an important shipping channel. It runs from Minnesota in the north to Louisiana in the south and empties into the Gulf of Mexico.

**Missouri** (muh-ZOOR-uh; muh-ZOOR-ee)  Missouri is a state in the Midwest.

**Missouri River** (muh-ZOOR-uh; muh-ZOOR-ee)  The Missouri is the longest river in the United States. It flows for 2,565 miles through the West and Midwest and into the Mississippi River.

**Mojave Desert** (moh-HAH-vee)  The Mojave Desert is in southern California.

**Montana** (mon-TAN-uh)  Montana is one of the Rocky Mountain states.

**Mount McKinley**  Mount McKinley, in Alaska, is the highest mountain in the United States. It is 20,320 feet high.

**Mount Rainier** (ray-NEER; ruh-NEER)  Mount Rainier is a mountain in the state of Washington. At 14,410 feet, it is the highest elevation in the state.

**Mount Rushmore.** From left to right: George Washington, Thomas Jefferson, Theodore Roosevelt, and Abraham Lincoln.

**Mount Rushmore**  Mount Rushmore is a high cliff in the Black Hills of South Dakota where the faces of four American presidents (George Washington, Thomas Jefferson, Theodore Roosevelt, and Abraham Lincoln) are carved. Each face is about sixty feet tall.

**Mount Saint Helens**  Mount Saint Helens is an active volcano in the state of Washington. It is 8,363 feet high.

**Mount Whitney**  Mount Whitney is in the Sierra Nevada range of eastern California. At 14,280 feet, it is the highest peak in the 48 lower United States. Mount McKinley is the highest peak in North America.

**Nashville**  Nashville is the capital of Tennessee and the center of the country music industry.

**Nebraska**  Nebraska is a state in the Midwest.

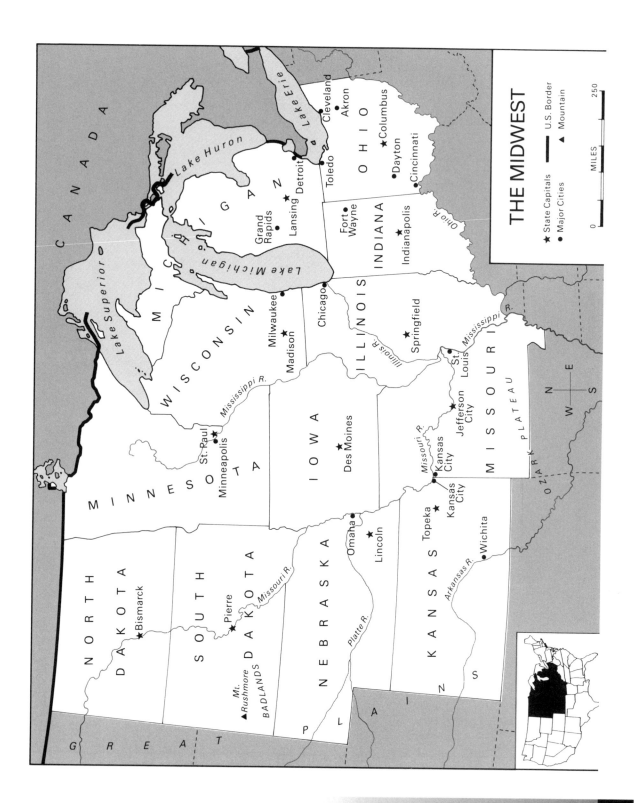

THE MIDWEST

★ State Capitals    —— U.S. Border
• Major Cities    ▲ Mountain

MILES

CANADA

Lake Superior

Lake Huron

Lake Michigan

Lake Erie

MICHIGAN

Cleveland
Akron

OHIO

★ Columbus
• Dayton
Cincinnati

Toledo

Detroit
Lansing
Grand Rapids

Fort Wayne

INDIANA

Indianapolis

Ohio R.

WISCONSIN

Milwaukee ★
Madison

Chicago

ILLINOIS

Springfield ★

Illinois R.

Mississippi R.

St. Louis

Mississippi R.

MISSOURI

PLATEAU

MINNESOTA

St. Paul ★
Minneapolis

IOWA

Des Moines ★

Missouri R.

Kansas City

Jefferson City ★

Kansas City

OZARK

N
W E
S

NORTH DAKOTA

★ Bismarck

SOUTH DAKOTA

Pierre ★

▲ Mt. Rushmore

BADLANDS

Missouri R.

NEBRASKA

Omaha

Lincoln ★

Platte R.

KANSAS

Topeka ★

Wichita

Arkansas R.

GREAT PLAINS

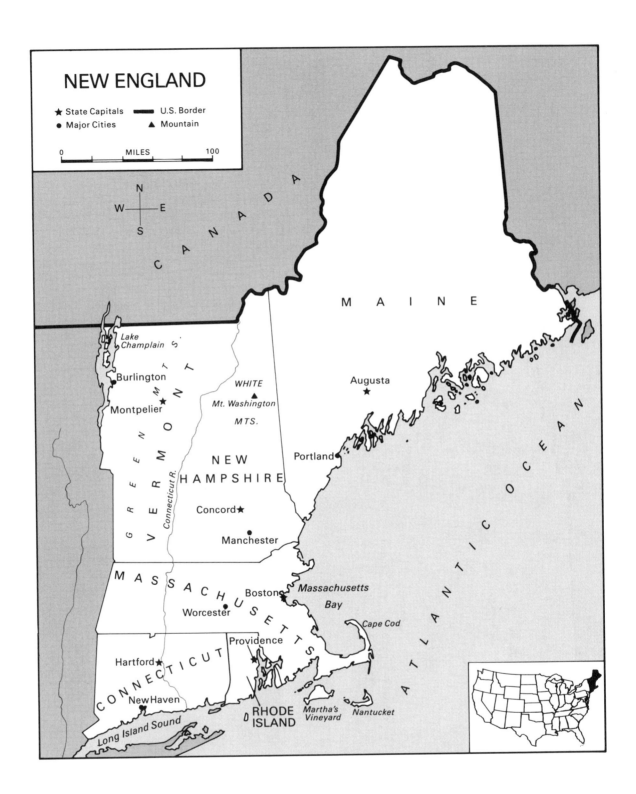

# NEW ENGLAND

★ State Capitals   ━━━ U.S. Border
● Major Cities   ▲ Mountain

0      MILES      100

N
W ✦ E
S

CANADA

MAINE

Lake
Champlain

● Burlington

Montpelier ★

VERMONT

GREEN MTS.

Connecticut R.

WHITE
▲
Mt. Washington

MTS.

Augusta ★

NEW
HAMPSHIRE

Portland ●

Concord ● ★

Manchester ●

ATLANTIC OCEAN

MASSACHUSETTS

Boston ★

Massachusetts
Bay

Worcester ●

Cape Cod

Providence

Hartford ★

CONNECTICUT

New Haven ●

RHODE
ISLAND

Martha's
Vineyard

Nantucket

Long Island Sound

**Nevada** (nuh-VAD-uh)   Nevada is one of the ROCKY MOUNTAIN STATES. Its best-known city is LAS VEGAS.

**New England**   New England is the northeast region of the United States. It is a hilly and forested area, with many picturesque small towns. The New England states are MAINE, NEW HAMPSHIRE, VERMONT, MASSACHUSETTS, CONNECTICUT, and RHODE ISLAND.

**New Hampshire**   New Hampshire is a state in NEW ENGLAND and was one of the original thirteen states.

**New Jersey**   New Jersey is one of the MIDDLE ATLANTIC STATES and was one of the original thirteen states.

**New Mexico**   New Mexico is a state in the SOUTHWEST.

**New Orleans** (AWR-lee-uhnz; AW-luhnz; aw-LEENZ)   New Orleans is a port city in LOUISIANA, near the mouth of the MISSISSIPPI RIVER, known for a yearly festival called MARDI GRAS.

**New York**   New York is a MIDDLE ATLANTIC STATE and was one of the original thirteen states.

**New York City**   New York City, a port city on the ATLANTIC OCEAN, is the most populous city in the United States. It is made up of five boroughs, or parts: the Bronx, BROOKLYN, MANHATTAN, Queens, and Staten Island. New York City is one of the key financial, communications, and arts centers of the world.

**Niagara Falls** (neye-AG-ruh; neye-AG-uh-ruh)   Niagara Falls is a pair of spectacular waterfalls in western NEW YORK State on the Canadian border.

**North Carolina**   North Carolina is a state in the SOUTH and was one of the original thirteen states.

**North Dakota**   North Dakota is a state in the MIDWEST.

**Northeast**   The Northeast is the region of the United States that includes NEW ENGLAND and the MIDDLE ATLANTIC STATES.

**Ohio**   Ohio is a state in the MIDWEST.

**Ohio River**   The Ohio River flows along the southern borders of OHIO, INDIANA, and ILLINOIS before joining the MISSISSIPPI RIVER.

**Oklahoma**   Oklahoma is a state in the SOUTHWEST, north of TEXAS.

**Oregon** (AWR-i-guhn)   Oregon is one of the PACIFIC COAST STATES, north of CALIFORNIA.

**Pacific Coast states**   The Pacific Coast states, on the WEST COAST along the PACIFIC OCEAN, are WASHINGTON, OREGON, and CALIFORNIA. They are known for their scenic mountains and shoreline.

**Pacific Northwest**   The Pacific Northwest is a name for the northwest part of the United States. It includes WASHINGTON, OREGON, and northern CALIFORNIA.

**Pennsylvania** (PEN-suhl-VAYN-yuh)   Pennsylvania is one of the MIDDLE ATLANTIC STATES and was one of the original thirteen

**Niagara Falls**

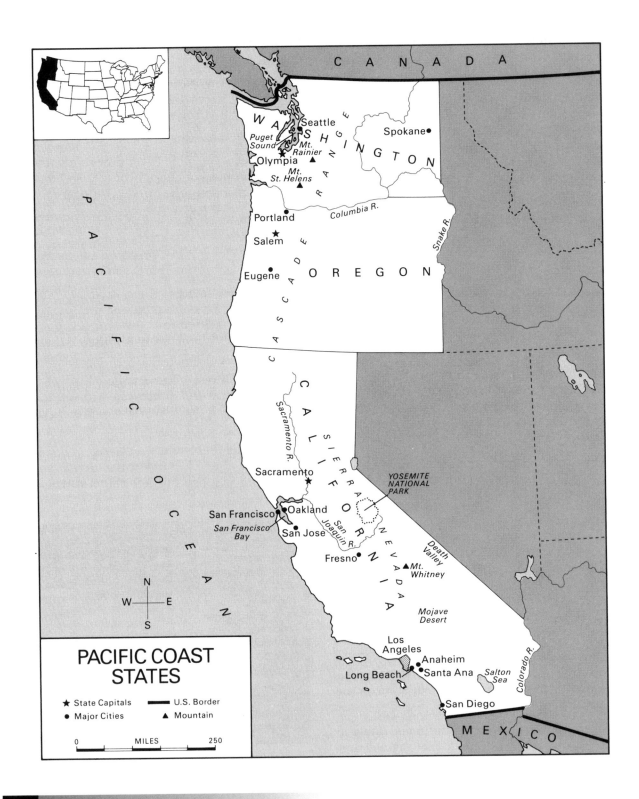

PACIFIC COAST STATES

★ State Capitals    ▬▬ U.S. Border
● Major Cities      ▲ Mountain

0          MILES          250

states. It was named for William Penn, a QUAKER who settled the area when he was granted the land by the king of England.

**Philadelphia** (fil-uh-DEL-fee-uh) Philadelphia is the largest city in PENNSYLVANIA. Noted for its historical sites, it was the capital of the United States for a short time in the late 1700s.

**Pikes Peak** Pikes Peak is a mountain in COLORADO. It is 14,110 feet high.

**Pittsburgh** Pittsburgh is an industrial city in western PENNSYLVANIA known for its steel mills.

**Portland** Portland is the largest city in OREGON and a major city in the PACIFIC NORTHWEST.

**Potomac River** (puh-TOH-muhk) The Potomac River flows between MARYLAND and VIRGINIA to CHESAPEAKE BAY.

**Puerto Rico** (pawr-tuh-REE-koh; pwer-tuh-REE-koh) Puerto Rico, an island southeast of FLORIDA, in the CARIBBEAN SEA, is a commonwealth of the United States. Its people are United States citizens, although they may not vote in national elections.

**Rhode Island** Rhode Island is a state in NEW ENGLAND and was one of the original thirteen states.

**Rio Grande** (REE-oh-GRAND, REE-oh-GRAND-ee) The Rio Grande (Spanish for "Big River"), about 1,885 miles long, is a river in the SOUTHWEST. It flows along the southern border of TEXAS and divides the United States from MEXICO.

**Rocky Mountain states** The Rocky Mountain states are the landlocked states in the western part of the country: IDAHO, MONTANA, WYOMING, NEVADA, COLORADO, and UTAH. They are known for their spectacular mountains and wilderness areas.

**Rocky Mountains** The Rocky Mountains, in the WEST and SOUTHWEST, run from ALASKA in the north, through CANADA, and south to MEXICO.

**Saint Lawrence River** The Saint Lawrence, about 750 miles long, is a river in eastern CANADA that connects the ATLANTIC OCEAN to the GREAT LAKES. Part of it borders NEW YORK State.

**Saint Lawrence Seaway** The Saint Lawrence Seaway is a system of dams and canals in eastern CANADA and along the NEW YORK State border that was built by American and Canadian engineers. The seaway makes it possible for ships to transport goods along the SAINT LAWRENCE RIVER from the ATLANTIC OCEAN to the GREAT LAKES.

**Saint Louis** (saynt-LOOH-uhs) Saint Louis is a major MIDWEST city in MISSOURI on the MISSISSIPPI RIVER. It was called the Gateway to the West in the 1800s because it served as a starting place for wagon trains.

**Salt Lake City** Salt Lake City is the capital of UTAH and is the center of the Church of Jesus Christ of Latter-Day Saints, called the Mormon Church.

**San Andreas Fault** (san an-DRA Y-uhs) The San Andreas Fault, in CALIFORNIA, is where parts of the earth's surface rub each other and cause earthquakes.

**San Francisco** (fruhn-SIS-koh) San Francisco is the largest city in northern CALIFORNIA and is known for the GOLDEN GATE BRIDGE.

**Seattle** (see-AT-l) Seattle is the largest city in WASHINGTON and a major city in the PACIFIC NORTHWEST. (*See* image, page 183.)

**Shenandoah Valley** (shen-uhn-DOH-uh) The Shenandoah, in VIRGINIA, is noted for its scenic beauty and its importance as a site of military action in the CIVIL WAR.

**Sierra Nevada** (see-ER-uh nuh-VAH-duh) The Sierra Nevada is a mountain range in eastern CALIFORNIA.

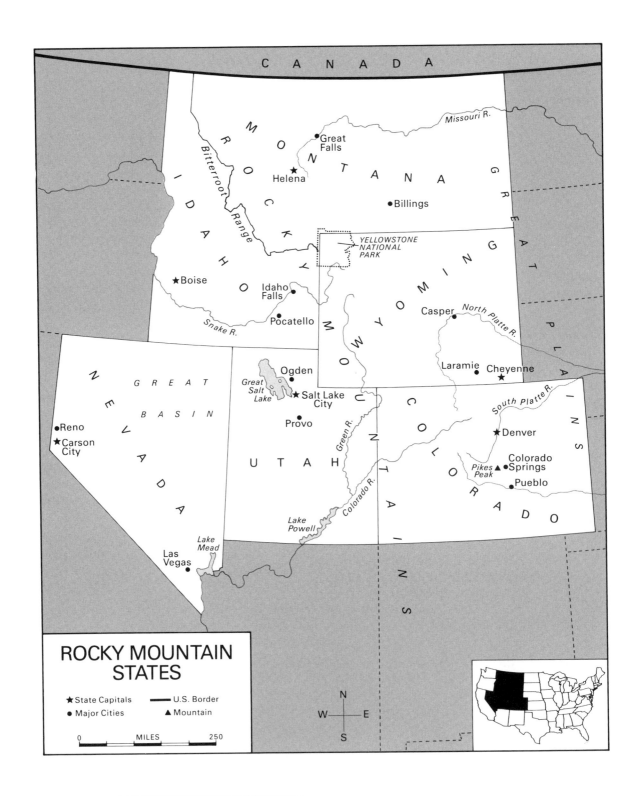

CANADA

**Missouri R.**

MONTANA

●Great Falls

★Helena

●Billings

IDAHO

Bitterroot Range

R O C K Y

YELLOWSTONE NATIONAL PARK

★Boise

Idaho Falls●

Snake R.

●Pocatello

WYOMING

GREAT

Casper●

North Platte R.

Laramie●   Cheyenne★

GREAT PLAINS

NEVADA

GREAT BASIN

Ogden●

Great Salt Lake

★Salt Lake City

Provo●

Green R.

MOUNTAINS

South Platte R.

★Denver

●Reno

★Carson City

UTAH

COLORADO

Pikes Peak ▲ ● Colorado Springs

●Pueblo

Colorado R.

Lake Powell

Las Vegas●

Lake Mead

## ROCKY MOUNTAIN STATES

★ State Capitals      ── U.S. Border

● Major Cities        ▲ Mountain

0 ──── MILES ──── 250

N
W ─●─ E
S

**Seattle Space Needle**

**South** The South is made up of the states in the southeast region of the country: ARKANSAS, LOUISIANA, KENTUCKY, TENNESSEE, WEST VIRGINIA, VIRGINIA, NORTH CAROLINA, SOUTH CAROLINA, MISSISSIPPI, ALABAMA, GEORGIA, and FLORIDA.

**South Carolina** South Carolina is a state in the SOUTH that was one of the original thirteen states.

**South Dakota** South Dakota is a state in the MIDWEST.

**Southwest** The Southwest is the region of the country known for its magnificent desert scenery and oil, gas, and mineral deposits. The southwest states are ARIZONA, NEW MEXICO, OKLAHOMA, and TEXAS.

**Tennessee** Tennessee is a state in the SOUTH.

**Texas** Texas is a state in the SOUTHWEST and, after ALASKA, the biggest state.

**Times Square** Times Square is a section of MANHATTAN, in NEW YORK CITY, where people gather every year to celebrate New Year's Eve.

**Utah** (YOOH-taw) Utah is one of the ROCKY MOUNTAIN STATES.

**Vermont** Vermont is a state in NEW ENGLAND known for its maple syrup.

**Virgin Islands** The Virgin Islands are resort areas in the CARIBBEAN SEA. Some of the islands belong to the United States; others belong to the British Commonwealth.

**Virginia** (vuhr-JIN-yuh) Virginia is a state in the SOUTH that was one of the original thirteen states.

**Washington** Washington is one of the PACIFIC COAST STATES, north of OREGON.

**Washington, D.C.** Washington, D.C., the capital of the United States, is on the POTOMAC RIVER between MARYLAND and VIRGINIA. The initials D.C. stand for District of Columbia, which is a federal district established in the 1800s by acts of CONGRESS.

**West Coast** The West Coast is the name for the part of the United States on the PACIFIC OCEAN.

**West Point** West Point is a small town on the HUDSON RIVER in NEW YORK State where the United States Military Academy (the Army's military college) is located. The school is often referred to as West Point.

**West Virginia** (vuhr-JIN-yuh) West Virginia is a state in the SOUTH.

**Wisconsin** Wisconsin is a state in the MIDWEST known for its dairy products.

**Wyoming** (weye-OH-ming) Wyoming is one of the ROCKY MOUNTAIN STATES.

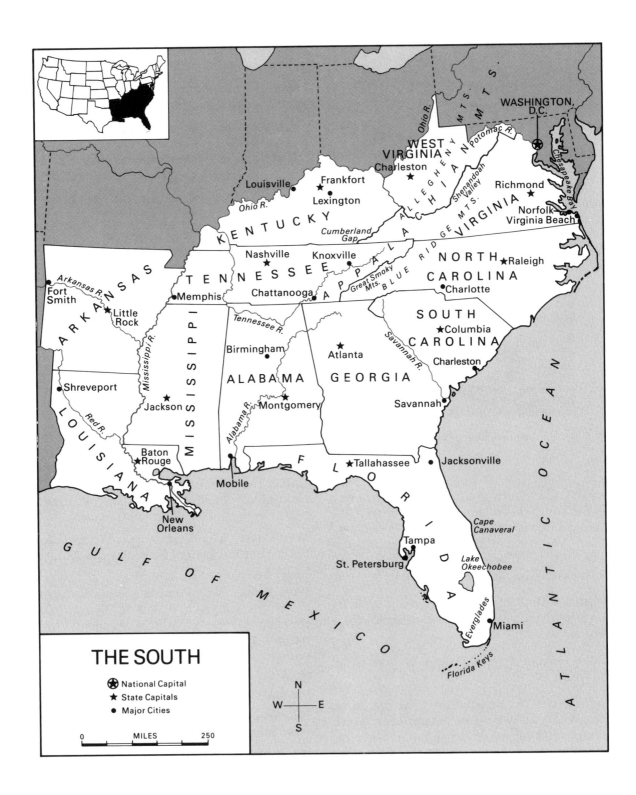

THE SOUTH

National Capital
State Capitals
Major Cities

N
W   E
S

MILES
0         250

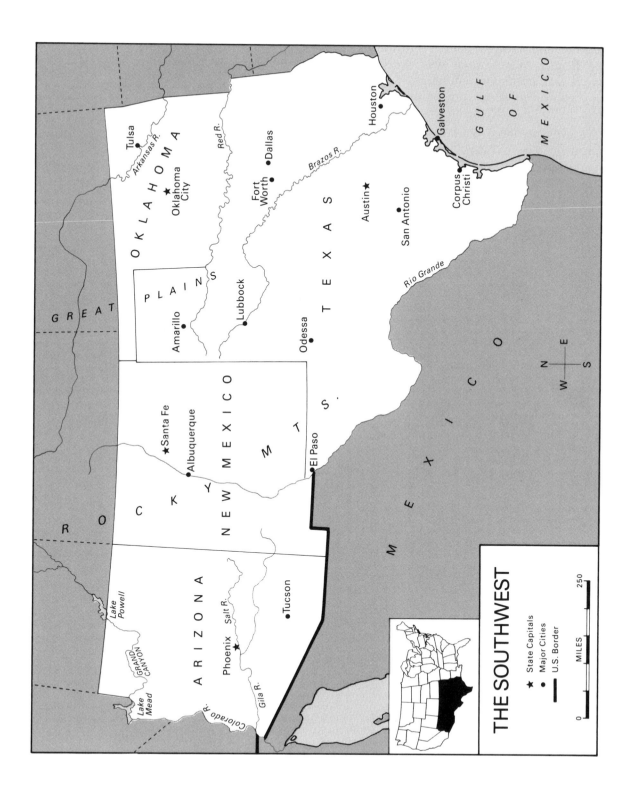

THE SOUTHWEST

State Capitals ★
Major Cities •
U.S. Border ▬

MILES
0    250

**Yellowstone National Park** Yellowstone, in the ROCKY MOUNTAINS, was the first national park in the United States. It is famous for its spectacular scenery, wildlife, and GEYSERS, including Old Faithful.

**Yosemite National Park** (yoh-SEM-uh-tee) Yosemite National Park, in eastern CALIFORNIA, is noted for its views and waterfalls, including Yosemite Falls, the highest waterfall in NORTH AMERICA.

**Yosemite National Park**

# World Geography

Geography is the study of the surface of the earth. Physical geography concerns physical features such as mountains, continents, and oceans. Political geography concerns countries and cities. Few people can name all the nations of the world, but most educated people recognize the names of most countries and have a general idea of where they are. You probably could not name the countries of eastern Africa, but if you came across Kenya in your reading, you should be able to know it is a country in Africa.

Listed below are the continents, countries, important cities, bodies of water, and major land formations of the world as well as the chief mountains and deserts. In many countries, the name of the official language is related to the name of the country; for example, Polish (Poland) and French (France). In some cases where that is not so, we indicate the most frequently spoken language or languages of the country. This edition of the dictionary reflects changes that have occurred in some of the borders and names of countries since the first edition was published.

**Acapulco** (ak-uh-POOL-koh)  Acapulco is a resort city in MEXICO on the PACIFIC OCEAN.

**Aconcagua Mountain** (ak-uhn-KAH-gwuh)  Aconcagua, in ARGENTINA, is the highest peak in the ANDES. At 23,034 feet, it is also the highest mountain in SOUTH AMERICA and the highest in the world outside ASIA.

**Adriatic Sea** (ay-dree-AT-ik)  The Adriatic Sea is an arm of the MEDITERRANEAN SEA. It is bordered by ITALY to the west and north, and the BALKAN peninsula to the east.

**Aegean Sea** (i-JEE-uhn)  The Aegean Sea is the northeast part of the MEDITERRANEAN SEA between GREECE and TURKEY. Many of the famous Greek islands are found there.

**Afghanistan** (af-GAN-i-stan)  Afghanistan is a mountainous country in southern ASIA between IRAN and PAKISTAN. Its capital is Kabul.

**Africa**  Africa is the second largest continent. It is bordered on the north by the MEDITERRANEAN SEA, on the east by the INDIAN OCEAN, and on the west by the ATLANTIC

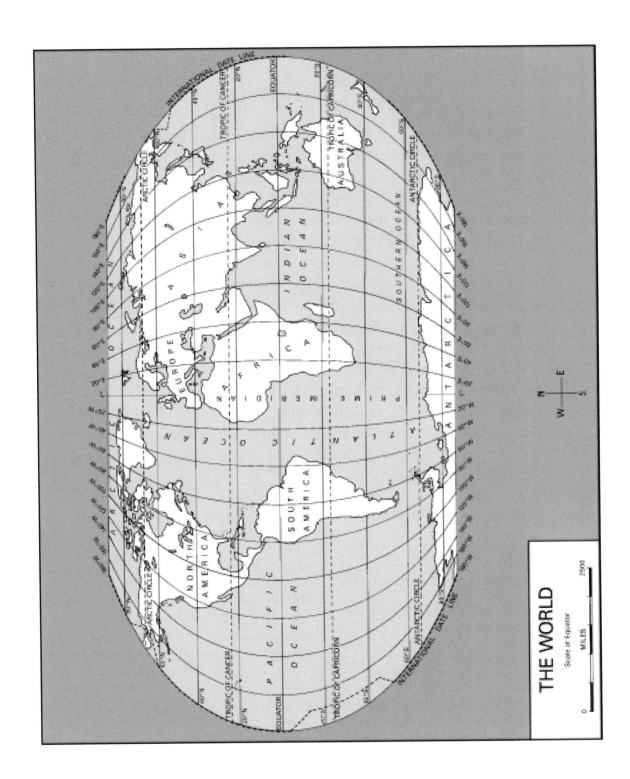

# THE WORLD

Scale at Equator

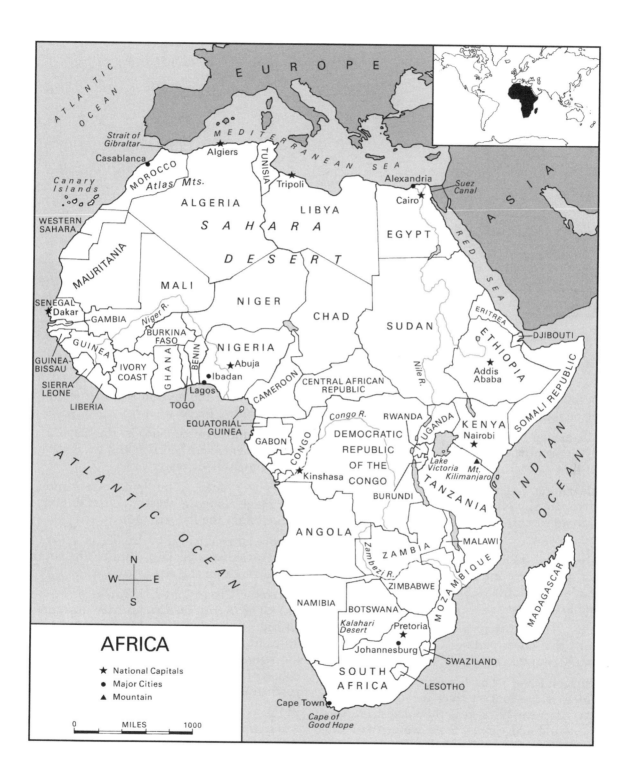

AFRICA

★ National Capitals
● Major Cities
▲ Mountain

0        MILES        1000

**Antarctica.** Camp of U.S. Navy meteorologists.

OCEAN. Many tribal and European languages are spoken there.

**Albania** (al-BAY-nee-uh) Albania, a country in southeast EUROPE, is northwest of GREECE.

**Alexandria** Alexandria is a city in northern EGYPT on the NILE RIVER and the MEDITERRANEAN SEA. It was founded by ALEXANDER THE GREAT.

**Algeria** (al-JEER-ee-uh) Algeria is an Arabic-speaking country in northern AFRICA on the MEDITERRANEAN SEA between MOROCCO and LIBYA.

**Alps** The Alps are a range of high mountains that cover parts of GERMANY, FRANCE, ITALY, SWITZERLAND, and AUSTRIA.

**Amazon River** The Amazon, running 3,900 miles, is the longest river in SOUTH AMERICA. After the NILE, it is the longest river in the world and carries more water than any other river. Most of its length runs west to east in northern BRAZIL. The Amazon River is named after the mythological female warriors called AMAZONS.

**Amsterdam** Amsterdam is the capital of the NETHERLANDS and is noted for its many canals (man-made waterways).

**Andes** (AN-deez) The Andes are a mountain range along the western coast of SOUTH AMERICA on the PACIFIC OCEAN.

**Angola** (ang-GOH-luh) Angola is a Bantu- and Portuguese-speaking country in southwest AFRICA on the ATLANTIC OCEAN.

**Antarctic Circle** (ant-AHRK-tik; ant-AHR-tik) The Antarctic Circle is an imaginary latitude line around the earth about 1,600 miles from the SOUTH POLE and PARALLEL to the EQUATOR. South of this line is the polar region of ANTARCTICA, where it stays cold all year, much colder than in the ARCTIC CIRCLE.

**Antarctica** (ant-AHRK-ti-kuh) Antarctica is the continent at the SOUTH POLE. Most of it is covered with ice.

**Arabia** (uh-RAY-bee-uh) Arabia is a large, oil-rich PENINSULA in southwest ASIA that is bounded on the east by the PERSIAN GULF, on the south by the INDIAN OCEAN, and on the west by the RED SEA. *See also* SAUDI ARABIA.

**Arabian Sea** The Arabian Sea is a part of the INDIAN OCEAN. Its main arms include the Gulf of Oman, to the northwest, and the Gulf of Aden, to the west.

**Arctic Circle** (AHRK-tik; AHR-tik) The Arctic Circle is an imaginary latitude line around the earth about 1,600 miles from the NORTH POLE and PARALLEL to the EQUATOR. North of this line is the polar region of the Arctic, where it stays cold all year.

**Arctic Ocean** The Arctic Ocean surrounds the NORTH POLE. It is the world's smallest ocean and is mostly covered by solid ice, ice floes, and icebergs.

**Argentina** (ahr-juhn-TEE-nuh) Argentina is a Spanish-speaking country in southern SOUTH AMERICA that extends all the way to the tip of the continent on the ATLANTIC side. Its capital and most populous city is Buenos Aires. To the west is CHILE. In Spanish, *argentina* means "of silver," a metal that has been mined there.

**Armenia** Armenia is a country in southwest ASIA, bordered by GEORGIA to the north, AZERBAIJAN to the east, IRAN to the south, and TURKEY to the south and west. Armenia was a part of the SOVIET UNION from 1920 to 1991.

**Asia** Asia is the world's largest continent and is populated by more than half of the world's people. It is bordered on the north by the ARCTIC OCEAN, on the east by the PACIFIC OCEAN, on the south by the INDIAN OCEAN, and on the west by EUROPE. Because Europe and Asia are connected, they are sometimes referred to as Eurasia.

**Athens** Athens is the capital of GREECE and the site of the PARTHENON.

**Atlantic Ocean** The Atlantic Ocean, the second largest ocean in the world, extends from the ARCTIC OCEAN to the SOUTHERN OCEAN. It is east of NORTH and SOUTH AMERICA and west of EUROPE and AFRICA.

**atlas** An atlas is a book of maps.

**Atlas Mountains** The Atlas Mountains are a series of mountain ranges in northwest AFRICA in MOROCCO and ALGERIA.

**Australia** (aw-STRAYL-yuh) Australia, the smallest continent, is bordered on the east by the southern PACIFIC OCEAN and on the west by the INDIAN OCEAN. Its main language is English. Sydney is its most populous city.

**Austria** (AW-stree-uh) Austria is a German-speaking mountainous country in the ALPS of central EUROPE, east of SWITZERLAND. Its most populous city and capital is Vienna.

**Azerbaijan** (az-uhr-beye-JAHN) Azerbaijan is a country in southwest ASIA, south of RUSSIA between the BLACK SEA and the CASPIAN SEA. Azerbaijan declared its independence from the SOVIET UNION in 1991.

**Baghdad** Baghdad is the capital of IRAQ. It is located in central Iraq on both banks of the TIGRIS RIVER.

**Bahamas** The Bahamas is an English-speaking country in the ATLANTIC OCEAN, southeast of FLORIDA, that is made up of hundreds of islands. It was under the control of the UNITED KINGDOM until 1973, when it gained independence.

**Balkan Mountains** The Balkan Mountains are a mountain range in southeast EUROPE.

**Balkans** The countries in the region of the BALKAN MOUNTAINS on the Balkan Peninsula are known as the Balkan countries, or the Balkans: ALBANIA, BULGARIA, BOSNIA AND HERZEGOVINA, CROATIA, MACEDONIA, SERBIA AND MONTENEGRO, SLOVENIA, and parts of GREECE, ROMANIA, and TURKEY.

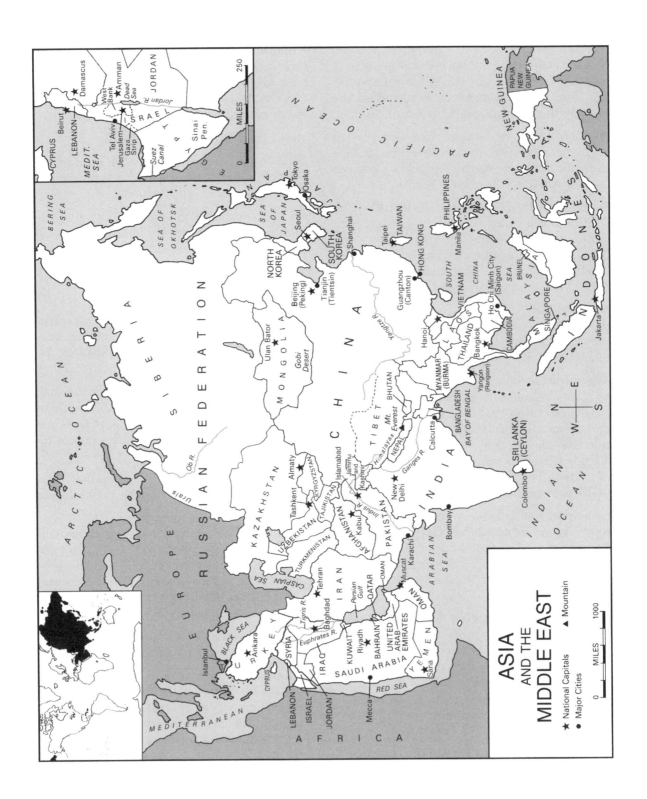

## ASIA AND THE MIDDLE EAST

★ National Capitals ● Major Cities ▲ Mountain

**MILES**
0        1000

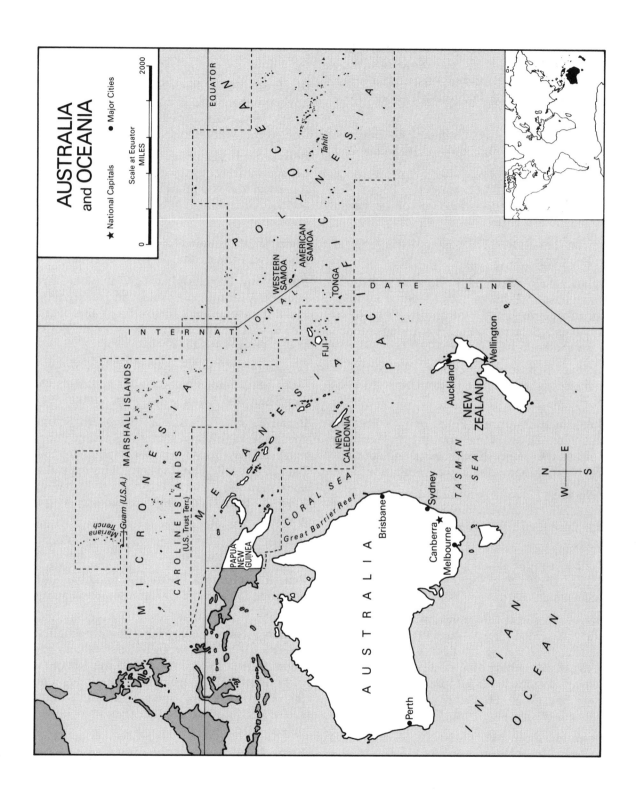

# AUSTRALIA and OCEANIA

★ National Capitals   ● Major Cities

Scale at Equator
MILES

0          2000

EQUATOR

P O L Y N E S I A

Tahiti

P A C I F I C   O C E A N

WESTERN SAMOA

AMERICAN SAMOA

TONGA

INTERNATIONAL   DATE   LINE

FIJI

M E L A N E S I A

NEW CALEDONIA

MICRONESIA

MARSHALL ISLANDS

Guam (U.S.A.)

CAROLINE ISLANDS
(U.S. Trust Terr.)

Mariana Trench

PAPUA NEW GUINEA

CORAL SEA

Great Barrier Reef

Wellington

Auckland

NEW ZEALAND

TASMAN SEA

Brisbane

Sydney

Canberra ★
Melbourne

A U S T R A L I A

Perth

I N D I A N   O C E A N

N
W   E
S

**Baltic Sea**  The Baltic Sea, in northern EUROPE, is bordered by the SCANDINAVIAN countries on the west and RUSSIA and other former republics of the SOVIET UNION on the east.

**Bangkok** (BANG-kok)  Bangkok is the capital of THAILAND and its principal port and commercial center.

**Beijing** (BAY-JING)  Beijing (or Peking) is the capital of CHINA, known for its grand palaces and temples.

**Beirut** (bay-ROOHT)  Beirut is the capital of LEBANON.

**Belarus** (bel-uh-ROOHS)  Belarus is a country in eastern EUROPE. It is bordered by RUSSIA to the north and east and by POLAND to the west. Belarus gained its independence from the SOVIET UNION in 1991.

**Belfast**  Belfast is the capital of NORTHERN IRELAND, which is part of the UNITED KINGDOM.

**Belgium** (BEL-juhm)  Belgium is a French- and Flemish-speaking country in western EUROPE that is north of FRANCE and south of the NETHERLANDS. Its capital is BRUSSELS.

**Belgrade**  Belgrade, on the DANUBE RIVER, is the capital of present-day SERBIA. It was also the capital of the former country of YUGOSLAVIA.

**Bering Sea** (BEER-ing)  The Bering Sea is the part of the PACIFIC OCEAN between ALASKA and SIBERIA.

**Berlin**  Berlin is the capital of reunited GERMANY. Divided after WORLD WAR II into East Berlin, the capital of East Germany, and West Berlin, a part of West Germany, it was reunified along with Germany in 1990. *See also* BERLIN WALL *under "World History Since 1600."*

**Bermuda** (buhr-MYOOH-duh)  Bermuda is an English-speaking group of islands in the ATLANTIC OCEAN, about 600 miles east of the United States. It is a self-governing British colony.

**Black Sea**  The Black Sea lies between EUROPE and ASIA and is almost completely enclosed by land except for a narrow connection to the MEDITERRANEAN SEA.

**Bolivia** (buh-LIV-ee-uh)  Bolivia is a Spanish-speaking country in western SOUTH AMERICA and is named for SIMÓN BOLÍVAR, a South American revolutionary leader and statesman.

**Bonn** (BON)  Bonn, a city on the RHINE RIVER, was the capital of West Germany.

**Bosnia and Herzegovina** (BOZ-nee-uh; hurt-suh-goh-VEE-nuh)  Bosnia and Herzegovina is a BALKAN country in southeast EUROPE. It was a part of the former country of YUGOSLAVIA from 1918 to 1991.

**Bosporus** (BOS-puh-ruhs)  The Bosporus is a strait, or narrow channel, that separates the European and Asian portions of TURKEY.

**Brazil** (bruh-ZIL)  Brazil, in eastern SOUTH AMERICA, is the largest country on the continent. Its two most populous cities are SÃO PAULO, then RIO DE JANEIRO. The capital is the planned, twentieth-century city of Brasília. Brazil's official language is Portuguese.

**Britain**  *See* UNITED KINGDOM OF GREAT BRITAIN and IRELAND.

**British Columbia**  British Columbia is a province in western CANADA, on the PACIFIC OCEAN.

**British Isles**  The British Isles are English-speaking islands in western EUROPE comprising the UNITED KINGDOM and the REPUBLIC OF IRELAND. There are two main islands. One includes ENGLAND, SCOTLAND, and WALES; the other, NORTHERN IRELAND and the Republic of Ireland.

**Brussels**  Brussels is the capital of BELGIUM and the headquarters of NATO (the North

Atlantic Treaty Organization) and the European Union.

**Budapest** (BOOH-duh-pest) Budapest is the capital of HUNGARY. It combines two older towns, Buda and Pest, which faced each other across the DANUBE.

**Buenos Aires** (BWAY-nuhs EYER-iz) Buenos Aires is the capital of ARGENTINA and one of the most populous cities in SOUTH AMERICA.

**Bulgaria** Bulgaria is a BALKAN country in southeast EUROPE, south of ROMANIA.

**Burma** Burma is a country in SOUTHEAST ASIA, south of CHINA. It is now officially known as Myanmar.

**Cairo** (KEYE-roh) Cairo is the capital of EGYPT and the most populous city in AFRICA.

**Calcutta** Calcutta is a city in eastern INDIA.

**Cambodia** (kam-BOH-dee-uh) Cambodia is a country in SOUTHEAST ASIA, south and east of THAILAND.

**Canada** Canada, the country north of the United States, is the world's second largest country in area. Its capital is OTTAWA, in the province of ONTARIO. Its most populous cities are TORONTO, MONTREAL, and VANCOUVER. The languages of Canada are English and, in the province of QUEBEC, French. *See also* CANADIAN PROVINCES AND TERRITORIES.

**Canadian provinces and territories** Canada is made up of ten provinces and three territories. The provinces are Alberta, BRITISH COLUMBIA, Manitoba, New Brunswick, NEWFOUNDLAND and Labrador, NOVA SCOTIA, ONTARIO, Prince Edward Island, QUEBEC, and Saskatchewan. The territories are the Northwest Territories, NUNAVUT, and the YUKON. A province has its own government, while a territory does not.

**Cape of Good Hope** The Cape of Good Hope is a point of land in southern SOUTH AFRICA. It is the southernmost tip of AFRICA.

**Caracas** (kuh-RAH-kuhs) Caracas is the capital and most populous city of VENEZUELA.

**Caribbean Sea** (kar-uh-BEE-uhn; kuh-RIB-ee-uhn) The Caribbean Sea is the part of the ATLANTIC OCEAN bordered by CENTRAL AMERICA, SOUTH AMERICA, and the WEST INDIES. It is also called simply the Caribbean.

**cartography** Cartography is the art or practice of making maps and navigation charts. A person who designs maps is called a cartographer.

**Caspian Sea** The Caspian Sea is the largest saltwater lake in the world. It lies between RUSSIA and KAZAKHSTAN in the north and IRAN in the south.

**Central America** Central America is the name for the narrow strip of land between MEXICO and SOUTH AMERICA. It is sometimes considered part of South America because its people speak Spanish and are culturally related to the people of South America. Geographically, however, it is considered part of NORTH AMERICA. The countries of Central America are Belize, COSTA RICA, EL SALVADOR, GUATEMALA, HONDURAS, NICARAGUA, and PANAMA.

**Ceylon** *See* SRI LANKA.

**Chad** Chad is a landlocked country in north-central AFRICA. French, Arabic, and dozens of African languages are spoken there.

**Chang Jiang** *See* YANGTZE RIVER.

**Chile** (CHIL-ee) Chile is a Spanish-speaking country on the western slopes of the ANDES in southwest SOUTH AMERICA. Long and narrow, it goes along the PACIFIC COAST to the southern tip of South America.

**China** China, in eastern ASIA, has the largest population of any country in the world. Officially, it is called the People's Republic of China. Its capital is BEIJING (Peking).

**Colombia** Colombia is a Spanish-speaking country in northern SOUTH AMERICA, east of PANAMA. It is named for CHRISTOPHER COLUMBUS.

**Congo, Democratic Republic of** The Democratic Republic of Congo is a country in central AFRICA. It used to be called Zaire; before that, it was known as the Belgian Congo. It gained independence from BELGIUM in 1960. Army general Mobutu Sese Seko ruled the country from 1965 to 1997, when he was ousted by rebel forces. Its capital is Kinshasa.

**Congo, Republic of** The Republic of Congo is a country in west-central AFRICA. Its capital is Brazzaville. It gained independence from FRANCE in 1960.

**Congo River** The Congo, in central AFRICA, is the second longest river in Africa. It is 2,900 miles long.

**coordinates** Coordinates show where something is located on a map by giving the LATITUDE and LONGITUDE.

**Copenhagen** (KOH-puhn-hay-guhn) Copenhagen is the capital of DENMARK and its most populous city.

**Costa Rica** (KOS-tuh-REE-kuh) Costa Rica is a Spanish-speaking country in CENTRAL AMERICA, west of PANAMA. Its name means "rich coast" in Spanish.

**Crete** Crete is an island of GREECE. The largest of the Greek islands, it lies south of the Greek mainland, in the MEDITERRANEAN SEA. Its Minoan civilization was one of the earliest civilizations in the world and reached its peak in 1600 B.C.

**Croatia** (kroh-AY-shuh) Croatia is a BALKAN country in southeast EUROPE north and west of BOSNIA AND HERZEGOVINA. Croatia was a part of the former country of YUGOSLAVIA from 1918 to 1991.

**Cuba** (KYOOH-buh) Cuba is a Spanish-speaking island country between the CARIBBEAN SEA and the ATLANTIC OCEAN, south of FLORIDA. Its most populous city is HAVANA.

**Cyprus** (SEYE-pruhs) Cyprus is a Greek- and Turkish-speaking island country in the MEDITERRANEAN SEA, south of TURKEY. Its name comes from the Greek word for copper, which was mined there in ancient times.

**Czech Republic** (CHEK) The Czech Republic is a country in central EUROPE east of GERMANY and south of POLAND. Its capital is PRAGUE. The Czech Republic and SLOVAKIA comprised the former country of Czechoslovakia from 1918 to 1993.

**Danube River** (DAN-yoohb) The Danube is the second longest river in EUROPE. It forms part of the border between several countries, including SLOVAKIA, HUNGARY, ROMANIA, and BULGARIA.

**Dead Sea** The Dead Sea is a salt lake between ISRAEL and JORDAN in southwest ASIA, in what is commonly called the MIDDLE EAST. Its surface is the lowest point on the surface of the earth. It is called dead because its water is too salty for fish to survive.

**Delhi** (DEL-ee) Delhi is a region in INDIA as well as a populous city in this region. *See also* NEW DELHI.

**Denmark** Denmark is a SCANDINAVIAN country in northern EUROPE between the North and the Baltic seas. Its capital is Copenhagen.

**Dominican Republic** (duh-MIN-i-kuhn) The Dominican Republic is a Spanish-speaking country in the WEST INDIES. It is the eastern part of the same island, east of CUBA, that contains HAITI.

**Don River** The Don River is a river in southwest RUSSIA.

**Dublin**  Dublin is the capital of the REPUBLIC OF IRELAND and the birthplace of several famous writers, such as James Joyce and W. B. Yeats.

**East Asia**  East Asia includes CHINA, JAPAN, NORTH KOREA, SOUTH KOREA, and TAIWAN. The term sometimes includes the countries of SOUTHEAST ASIA as well. The region is sometimes called the Far East, though it is only "far" from the Western point of view.

**Ecuador** (EK-wuh-dawr)  Ecuador is a Spanish-speaking country in northwest SOUTH AMERICA. It lies on the EQUATOR, with its west coast on the PACIFIC OCEAN.

**Edinburgh** (ED-n-buh-ruh)  Edinburgh is the capital of SCOTLAND.

**Egypt** (EE-jipt)  Egypt is an Arabic-speaking country in northeast AFRICA, near the region known as the MIDDLE EAST. It was the home of a great ancient civilization, which was ruled by the PHARAOHS. The NILE RIVER flows through it, and the PYRAMIDS and the SPHINX are found there. Its capital is Cairo.

**El Salvador** (SAL-vuh-dawr)  El Salvador is a Spanish-speaking country in CENTRAL AMERICA. Its capital is San Salvador. In Spanish, *salvador* means Savior, a term for JESUS.

**England**  England is a country in northwest EUROPE. Along with SCOTLAND, NORTHERN IRELAND, and WALES, it is part of the UNITED KINGDOM. England is on an island, called GREAT BRITAIN, with Scotland and Wales.

**English Channel**  The English Channel is a very narrow part of the ATLANTIC OCEAN that separates ENGLAND and FRANCE. Strong athletes have swum across the English Channel.

**equator**  The equator is the imaginary line that circles the middle of the EARTH between the two poles and divides it into two halves, the Northern and Southern Hemispheres. It is the zero line of LATITUDE.

**Estonia** (e-STOH-nee-uh)  Estonia is a country in northern EUROPE on the BALTIC SEA. It was a part of the SOVIET UNION from 1940 to 1991.

**Ethiopia** (ee-thee-OH-pee-uh)  Ethiopia is a mountainous country in eastern AFRICA, whose main product is coffee.

**Euphrates River** (yooh-FRAY-teez)  The Euphrates is a river in southwest ASIA, about 1,700 miles long, that flows to the PERSIAN GULF. It was an important center of ancient civilization.

**Eurasia**  *See* ASIA; EUROPE.

**Europe** (YOOR-uhp)  Europe is the continent west of ASIA. It is bordered on the north by the ARCTIC OCEAN, on the south by the MEDITERRANEAN SEA, and on the west by the ATLANTIC OCEAN. Because Europe and Asia are connected, they are sometimes referred to as Eurasia.

**Far East**  *See* EAST ASIA.

**Federal Republic of Germany**  The country of GERMANY is officially named the Federal Republic of Germany.

**Finland**  Finland is a SCANDINAVIAN country in northern EUROPE between SWEDEN and RUSSIA. Its capital is Helsinki.

**France**  France is a large country in EUROPE and the second most populous country on the European continent. Its capital is PARIS.

**Ganges River** (GAN-jeez)  The Ganges, about 1,500 miles long, is a river in INDIA that is sacred to members of the Hindu religion. *See also* HINDUISM. (*See* image, page 199.)

**Gaza Strip** (GAH-zuh)  The Gaza Strip is a small strip of land between EGYPT, ISRAEL, and the MEDITERRANEAN SEA. It is populated mainly by Palestinian refugees.

**Geneva** (juh-NEE-vuh)  Geneva is a city in southwestern SWITZERLAND where many international conferences are held.

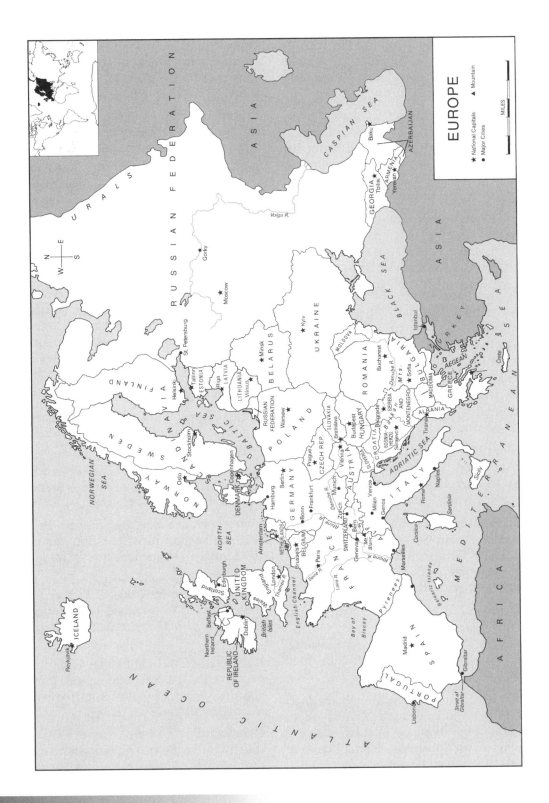

EUROPE

**Ganges River.** Hindu devotees bathe in the Ganges River during a religious festival.

**Georgia**   Georgia is a country on the BLACK SEA. It was a part of the SOVIET UNION from 1922 to 1991.

**Germany**   Germany is a country in central EUROPE bordered on the west by the NETHERLANDS, BELGIUM, and FRANCE; on the east by POLAND and the CZECH REPUBLIC; on the north by DENMARK; and on the south by SWITZERLAND and AUSTRIA. It is the most populous country in Europe. Berlin is its capital. Germany was divided after WORLD WAR II into COMMUNIST East Germany and DEMOCRATIC West Germany and was not reunified until 1990.

**Ghana** (GAH-nuh)   Ghana is a country in western AFRICA. Its official language is English.

**Gibraltar** (ji-BRAWL-tuhr)   Gibraltar is a PENINSULA in southern SPAIN overlooking a narrow sea lane between the ATLANTIC OCEAN and the MEDITERRANEAN SEA. It is located on the Rock of Gibraltar, a huge limestone mass.

**Gobi Desert** (GOH-bee)   The Gobi Desert is in MONGOLIA. Dinosaur eggs have been found there.

**Great Britain**   Great Britain is the island in northwest EUROPE containing ENGLAND, SCOTLAND, and WALES. *See also* UNITED KINGDOM OF GREAT BRITAIN AND IRELAND.

**Greece**   Greece is a BALKAN country on the MEDITERRANEAN SEA in southern EUROPE and the site of a great ancient civilization. Its capital and largest city is ATHENS.

**Greenland**   Greenland is the world's largest island that is not a continent. It is in the northern ATLANTIC OCEAN and is part of DENMARK.

**Greenwich**  *See* LONGITUDE; PRIME MERIDIAN.

**Guam** (GWAHM)  Guam is a territory of the United States located in the western PACIFIC OCEAN.

**Guatemala** (gwah-tuh-MAH-luh)  Guatemala is a Spanish-speaking country in CENTRAL AMERICA.

**Gulf of Mexico**  A gulf is a large body of ocean that is partly enclosed by land. The Gulf of Mexico is the part of the ATLANTIC OCEAN bordered by the southern coast of the United States and the eastern coast of MEXICO.

**The Hague** (HAYG)  The Hague is the seat of government for THE NETHERLANDS. It is located in the western part of that nation, near the NORTH SEA. The city is often the site of international conferences and trials.

**Haiti** (HAY-tee)  Haiti is a French- and Creole-speaking country in the WEST INDIES. It is the western part of the same island, east of CUBA, that contains the DOMINICAN REPUBLIC. Its capital and largest city is Port-au-Prince.

**Havana** (huh-VAN-uh)  Havana is the capital of CUBA.

**Helsinki** (HEL-sing-kee)  Helsinki is the capital of FINLAND. It is the site of many international conferences.

**hemisphere**  A hemisphere is one half of the planet EARTH. *Hemi* means "half" and *sphere* means "a round ball or globe." The earth can be divided into the Northern and Southern Hemispheres. The Northern Hemisphere is the half of the globe north of the EQUATOR; the Southern Hemisphere is the half of the globe south of the equator. The earth can also be divided into the Eastern and Western Hemispheres. The Eastern Hemisphere is the part of the world east of zero LONGITUDE and contains AFRICA, ASIA, AUSTRALIA, and EUROPE. The Western Hemisphere is the part west of zero longitude and contains NORTH AMERICA and SOUTH AMERICA. *See also* LATITUDE; PRIME MERIDIAN.

**Himalayas** (him-uh-LAY-uhz; huh-MAHL-yuhz)  The Himalayas are a mountain range in south-central ASIA. The highest mountains in the world are found there, including the very highest, Mount Everest.

**Holland**  *See* THE NETHERLANDS.

**Honduras** (hon-DOOR-uhs)  Honduras is a Spanish-speaking country in CENTRAL AMERICA.

**Hong Kong**  Hong Kong is a special part of CHINA that has its own economy. Until 1997, it was a British colony. Most of Hong Kong is on an island in the South China Sea off the southeast coast of China.

**Hudson Bay**  Hudson Bay is a sea in northeast CANADA that is almost completely surrounded by land. It connects with the ATLANTIC OCEAN.

**Hungary**  Hungary is a country in central EUROPE. Its capital is Budapest.

**Iceland**  Iceland is an island country in northwest EUROPE in the north ATLANTIC OCEAN, north of ENGLAND and west of NORWAY.

**India**  India is a country in southern ASIA. It is the second most populous country in the world, after CHINA. Numerous languages are spoken there, but Hindi and English are its official languages. Its capital is NEW DELHI.

**Indian Ocean**  The Indian Ocean, the third largest ocean in the world, lies between the ATLANTIC and the PACIFIC OCEANS. It is south of ASIA, east of AFRICA, and west of AUSTRALIA.

**Indochina**  Indochina is the name of a region in SOUTHEAST ASIA that contains MYANMAR (BURMA), THAILAND, LAOS, CAMBODIA, VIETNAM, and parts of MALAYSIA.

**Istanbul.** The Blue Mosque.

**Indonesia** (in-duh-NEE-zhuh) Indonesia is a country in SOUTHEAST ASIA made up of a string of more than thirteen thousand islands.

**Indus River** The Indus is a river in south-central ASIA that flows to the Arabian Sea, a large body of water off INDIA and PAKISTAN. The Indus is about 1,900 miles long. It was the site of an advanced civilization in ancient times.

**international date line** The international date line, the 180th meridian, is the LONGITUDE line where, by international agreement, a day begins and ends. If it is 3:00 P.M. on March 21 east of the line, it is 3:00 P.M. on March 22 west of the line! *See also* LONGITUDE; MERIDIAN.

**Iran** (i-RAN) Iran is a country in the MIDDLE EAST, west of AFGHANISTAN and east of IRAQ. Its capital is Tehran.

**Iraq** (i-RAK) Iraq is a country in the MIDDLE EAST, west of IRAN and east of SYRIA, JORDAN, and SAUDI ARABIA. Its capital is Baghdad. Modern Iraq includes the site of ancient MESOPOTAMIA.

**Ireland** *See* NORTHERN IRELAND; REPUBLIC OF IRELAND.

**Israel** (IZ-ree-uhl) Israel is a country at the eastern end of the MEDITERRANEAN SEA, in the MIDDLE EAST. It is in a region also known as PALESTINE. Its capital and most populous city is JERUSALEM.

**Istanbul** (is-tan-BOOHL) The most populous city in TURKEY, Istanbul is located mostly in the European section of the country and is known for its beautiful domes and towers. In the past, the city was called CONSTANTINOPLE and, before that, Byzantium.

**Italy** Italy is a country in southern EUROPE. On a map, it looks like a boot jutting out into the MEDITERRANEAN SEA. It was the site of the ancient Roman civilization and the home of many great artists. Its capital is ROME.

**Jamaica** (juh-MAY-kuh) Jamaica is an English-speaking island country in the WEST INDIES. It is south of CUBA, in the CARIBBEAN SEA.

**Japan** Japan is a country made up of islands in eastern ASIA, east of KOREA and RUSSIA. Its capital is Tokyo, which is one of the most populous cities in the world.

**Jerusalem** (juh-ROOH-suh-luhm) Jerusalem is the capital of ISRAEL and a holy city for Christians, Jews, and MUSLIMS.

**Johannesburg** (joh-HAHN-uhs-burg) Johannesburg is the largest city in SOUTH AFRICA. It is located in the northeastern part of the country.

**Jordan** Jordan is a country in the MIDDLE EAST.

**Jordan River** The Jordan, about 200 miles long, is a river in northern ISRAEL. It borders Israel and JORDAN.

**Kabul** (KAH-bool, kuh-BOOHL) Kabul is the capital and largest city of AFGHANISTAN. It is located in the eastern part of the country.

**Kalahari** The Kalahari Desert lies across parts of Botswana, Namibia, and SOUTH AFRICA. It is one of the world's largest deserts.

**Kashmir** (KASH-meer) Kashmir is a state in the north of INDIA, bordering PAKISTAN. It is a tourist attraction known for its beauty and is the site of continuing conflict between the two countries.

**Kazakhstan** (kah-zahk-STAHN) Kazakhstan is a country in west-central ASIA, south of RUSSIA and west of CHINA. It was a part of the SOVIET UNION from 1936 to 1991.

**Kenya** (KEN-yuh) Kenya is a Swahili- and English-speaking country in eastern AFRICA, south of ETHIOPIA. Important archaeological discoveries have been made in Kenya, such as the remains of the world's earliest known humans.

**Kilimanjaro** (kil-uh-muhn-JAHR-oh) Kilimanjaro, in TANZANIA, is the highest mountain in AFRICA.

**Korea** *See* NORTH KOREA; SOUTH KOREA.

**Kuwait** (kooh-WAYT) Kuwait is a small, oil-rich country in the MIDDLE EAST. It is south of IRAQ and north of SAUDI ARABIA on the Arabian Peninsula.

**Lake Maracaibo** (mar-uh-KEYE-boh) Lake Maracaibo is a lake in northwest VENEZUELA. It is the largest lake in SOUTH AMERICA.

**Lake Tanganyika** (tan-guhn-NEE-kuh) Lake Tanganyika is a lake in east-central AFRICA between TANZANIA and the REPUBLIC OF CONGO.

**Lake Titicaca** (tit-i-KAH-kuh) Lake Titicaca, a large freshwater lake in SOUTH AMERICA, is in the ANDES on the PERU-BOLIVIA border.

**Lake Victoria** Lake Victoria, in central AFRICA, is the second largest freshwater lake in the world (after LAKE SUPERIOR in the United States). It is a source of the NILE RIVER.

**Laos** (LAH-ohs; lah-AWS) Laos, a country in SOUTHEAST ASIA, lies south of CHINA and west of VIETNAM.

**Latin America** Latin America is a name for the Spanish- and Portuguese-speaking countries of NORTH and SOUTH AMERICA, including MEXICO and the countries of CENTRAL AMERICA. The name Latin America arose because both the Spanish and Portuguese languages developed from Latin, an ancient language. Central America and Mexico are culturally related to South America, though geographically they are part of North America.

**latitude** Latitude is a way of measuring, in degrees, the distance north and south of the EQUATOR. Lines of latitude are imaginary lines around the EARTH that are parallel to the equator and run east and west. A place on the earth can be located on a map by marking the place where its line of latitude and its line of LONGITUDE cross each other.

**Latvia** (LAT-vee-uh) Latvia is a country in northern EUROPE on the BALTIC SEA. Latvia was a part of the SOVIET UNION from 1940 to 1991.

**Lebanon** (LEB-uh-nuhn) Lebanon is a country in the MIDDLE EAST. It lies at the eastern end of the MEDITERRANEAN SEA, north of ISRAEL.

**Libya** (LIB-ee-uh) Libya is a country in northern AFRICA that lies west of EGYPT on the MEDITERRANEAN SEA. Arabic, Italian, and English are widely spoken there.

**Lisbon** (LIZ-buhn) Lisbon is the capital of PORTUGAL and its most populous city.

**Lithuania** (lith-ooh-AY-nee-uh) Lithuania is a country in northern EUROPE on the BALTIC SEA. It was a part of the SOVIET UNION from 1940 to 1990.

**Loire River** (LWAHR) The Loire is the longest river, at 630 miles, in FRANCE.

**London** London is the capital of GREAT BRITAIN. One of the most populous cities of EUROPE, it is the site of BIG BEN. It is on the THAMES RIVER.

**longitude** Longitude is a way of measuring, in degrees, the distance east and west of the PRIME MERIDIAN. The prime meridian is an imaginary line that runs from the North Pole to the South Pole through the city of Greenwich, England, and is zero degrees longitude. Lines of longitude run north and south through the two poles, where they come together. They are farthest apart at the EQUATOR. A place on the EARTH can be found on a map by marking the spot where its line of longitude and its line of LATITUDE cross each other. *See also* LATITUDE; PRIME MERIDIAN.

**Macedonia** (mas-uh-DOH-nee-uh) Macedonia is a BALKAN country in southeast EUROPE. It was a part of the former country of YUGOSLAVIA from 1918 to 1991. Macedonia is also the name of a region of southeast Europe including present-day Macedonia, northern GREECE, and southwest BULGARIA.

**Madagascar** (mad-uh-GAS-kuhr) Madagascar is an island country in the INDIAN OCEAN, off the southeast coast of AFRICA.

**Madrid** (muh-DRID) Madrid is the capital of SPAIN and its most populous city.

**Magellan, Strait of** *See* STRAIT OF MAGELLAN.

**Malaysia** (muh-LAY-zhuh) Malaysia is a country in SOUTHEAST ASIA that lies south of THAILAND. Another large part of the country is located on the island of Borneo to the east.

**Manila** (muh-NIL-uh) Manila is the capital and most populous city of the PHILIPPINES.

**Maracaibo** SEE LAKE MARACAIBO.

**Matterhorn** The Matterhorn is a mountain in the European ALPS between SWITZERLAND and ITALY. It is famous for its distinctive pointed peak and is about 14,600 feet high.

**Mecca** Mecca is a city in western SAUDI ARABIA. The place where MUHAMMAD was born, it is the holiest city in ISLAM. MUSLIMS are supposed to take a hajj, or a pilgrimage to Mecca, at least once during their lifetime.

**Mediterranean Sea** (med-i-tuh-RAY-nee-uhn) The Mediterranean Sea is bordered by southern EUROPE, ASIA, and northern AFRICA. It is the largest inland sea in the world and connects with the ATLANTIC OCEAN through the narrow STRAIT OF GIBRALTAR.

**Mercator projection** (muhr-KAY-tuhr) A Mercator projection is a kind of map that is made by drawing the land masses of the globe on a flat surface. The Mercator projection is easier to look at than a globe because all the major continents can appear on the same map. However, this kind of map makes the northern and southern land masses appear larger than they really are.

**meridian**   A meridian is a line of LONGITUDE.

**Mexico**   Mexico, the country directly south of the United States, borders CALIFORNIA, ARIZONA, NEW MEXICO, and TEXAS. Its capital is MEXICO CITY, one of the largest cities in the world. In ancient times, Mexico was the home of the MAYAN and AZTEC civilizations. Its language is Spanish.

**Mexico City**   Mexico City is the capital and most populous city of MEXICO. With more than eight million people, it is also the most populous city in the world.

**Middle East**   The Middle East is a name used popularly in the Western world to refer to certain countries of western ASIA and the northeast part of AFRICA. It is called "Middle" because, from the Western point of view, it lies between the Western world and the "Far East." The region includes the African countries of EGYPT and LIBYA and the Asian countries of IRAN, IRAQ, ISRAEL, JORDAN, KUWAIT, LEBANON, SYRIA, SAUDI ARABIA, and other countries of the Arabian peninsula. TURKEY and CYPRUS are sometimes considered part of this region. It is also sometimes called the Near East or Mideast.

**Moldova**   (mol-DOH-vuh) Moldova is a country in eastern EUROPE bordering on northeast ROMANIA. Its official language is Romanian. Moldova was a part of the SOVIET UNION from 1940 to 1991.

**Mongolia**   Mongolia is a country in north-central ASIA that lies north of CHINA. It contains the GOBI DESERT.

**Mont Blanc**   Mont Blanc, in the ALPS, stands at 15,700 feet tall and is the highest mountain in western EUROPE.

**Montenegro**   *See* SERBIA AND MONTENEGRO.

**Montreal**   (mon-tree-AWL) Montreal is the second most populous city in CANADA, after TORONTO. It is in the province of QUEBEC, where the principal language is French.

**Morocco**   (muh-ROK-oh) Morocco is a country in the northwest corner of AFRICA, west of ALGERIA, on the ATLANTIC OCEAN and the MEDITERRANEAN SEA.

**Moscow**   MOSCOW is the capital and the most populous city of RUSSIA.

**Mount Everest**   Mount Everest, in the HIMALAYAS of central ASIA, is the highest mountain in the world. It is 29,000 feet high!

**Mount Vesuvius**   (vuh-SOOH-vee-uhs) Mount Vesuvius is an active VOLCANO in southwest ITALY, on the MEDITERRANEAN SEA. One of its earliest recorded eruptions, in A.D. 79, buried POMPEII and Herculaneum. It is still an active volcano.

**Munich**   (MYOOH-nik) Munich, a city in southern GERMANY and the capital of the state of Bavaria, is the most populous city in that region of the country.

**Myanmar**   (MYAHN-mahr) Myanmar, a country of southeast ASIA on the Bay of Bengal, has been the official name of BURMA since 1989.

**Nairobi**   (neye-ROH-bee) Nairobi is the capital and most populous city of KENYA.

**The Netherlands**   The Netherlands (sometimes called Holland) is a Dutch-speaking country in western EUROPE, north of BELGIUM. Its name means "Low Countries" because much of the country is below sea level. Its capital is AMSTERDAM.

**New Delhi**   (DEL-ee) New Delhi, the administrative section of the old city of DELHI, is the capital of INDIA.

**New Zealand** (ZEE-luhnd)   New Zealand is an English-speaking island country in the southern PACIFIC OCEAN, southeast of AUSTRALIA. It includes two islands, South Island and North Island.

**Newfoundland** (NOOH-fuhn-luhnd)   Newfoundland is a province in eastern CANADA, on the ATLANTIC coast.

**Nicaragua** (nik-uh-RAH-gwuh)   Nicaragua is a Spanish-speaking country in CENTRAL AMERICA, north of COSTA RICA.

**Niger River** (NEYE-juhr)   The Niger River, about 2,600 miles long, is the main river of western AFRICA. It is the third longest river in Africa, after the NILE and the CONGO.

**Nigeria** (neye-JEER-ee-uh)   Nigeria is an English-speaking country in west AFRICA.

**Nile River**   The Nile is the longest river in the world and runs for 4,100 miles. It is in AFRICA, mainly in EGYPT and SUDAN, and empties into the MEDITERRANEAN SEA. The Nile River valley in Egypt is the site of one of the first great civilizations.

**North America**   North America is the northern continent with the ATLANTIC OCEAN on its east and the PACIFIC OCEAN on its west. It includes CANADA, the United States, MEXICO, and the countries of CENTRAL AMERICA. It is the third largest continent, after ASIA and AFRICA.

**North Korea** (kuh-REE-uh)   North Korea is a country in eastern ASIA, east of CHINA and west of JAPAN.

**North Sea**   The North Sea is the part of the ATLANTIC OCEAN between GREAT BRITAIN and continental EUROPE.

**Northern Ireland**   Northern Ireland is the part of Ireland that is included in the UNITED KINGDOM. *See also* REPUBLIC OF IRELAND.

**Norway**   Norway is a SCANDINAVIAN country in northern EUROPE, west of SWEDEN,

that is known for its fjords *(see* OSLO). Its capital is Oslo.

**Nova Scotia** (NOH-vuh-SKOH-shuh)   Nova Scotia is a province in eastern CANADA, on the ATLANTIC coast. Its name means "New Scotland" in Latin.

**Nunavut** (NUHN-uh-vuht)   Nunavut is the newest of the CANADIAN PROVINCES AND TERRITORIES. It was part of the Northwest Territories until 1999. It is populated mainly by INUIT peoples.

**Ob River**   The Ob River, about 2,300 miles long, is a principal river of central RUSSIA. It flows through SIBERIA and empties into the ARCTIC OCEAN.

**Oceania** (oh-shee-AN-ee-uh)   Oceania is a name for the thousands of islands in the central and southern PACIFIC OCEAN. Oceania is sometimes referred to as the South Seas.

**Oder River**   The Oder is a river that flows about 560 miles through central EUROPE. It runs through POLAND and GERMANY to the BALTIC SEA.

**Ontario** (on-TAIR-ee-oh)   Ontario is a province of CANADA north of the GREAT LAKES. It includes TORONTO, the country's most populous city, and OTTAWA, the Canadian capital.

**The Orient**   The Orient is a name used popularly in the Western world to refer to the countries of eastern ASIA. It means "the East," from the Latin word for the rising sun, because the sun rises in the east. A word that is sometimes opposed to Orient is *Occident*, meaning "the West."

**Orinoco River** (ahr-uh-NOH-koh)   The Orinoco is a river in VENEZUELA flowing 1,500 miles, partly along the Venezuela-COLOMBIA border, to the ATLANTIC OCEAN.

**Oslo** (OZ-loh)   Oslo is the capital and most populous city of NORWAY and is located on a fjord (FEE-yohrd), a narrow part of a sea between steep slopes.

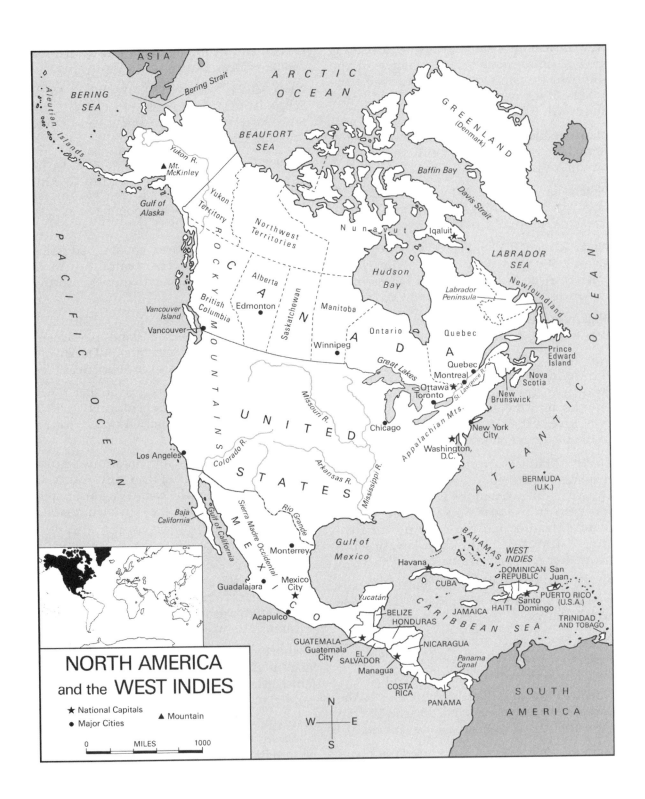

## NORTH AMERICA and the WEST INDIES

★ National Capitals    ▲ Mountain
● Major Cities

0      MILES      1000

N
W   E
S

**Ottawa** (OT-uh-wuh) Ottawa, in the province of ONTARIO, is the capital of CANADA.

**Pacific Ocean** The Pacific is the largest ocean in the world, extending from the ARCTIC OCEAN to the SOUTHERN OCEAN. It is west of NORTH and SOUTH AMERICA and east of ASIA and AUSTRALIA.

**Pacific Rim** The Pacific Rim region includes the nations and islands whose borders lie in the PACIFIC OCEAN. Among these are AUSTRALIA, NEW ZEALAND, JAPAN, and the PHILIPPINES.

**Pakistan** Pakistan is a country in southern ASIA that lies northwest of INDIA. Punjabi, Sindhi, Pashtu, and Urdu are among the many languages spoken there.

**Palestine** Palestine is a region on the eastern shore of the MEDITERRANEAN SEA that comprises parts of modern ISRAEL, JORDAN, and EGYPT. It is often referred to as the HOLY LAND.

**Panama** Panama is the Spanish-speaking CENTRAL AMERICAN country that borders SOUTH AMERICA. At its narrowest point is the PANAMA CANAL, which allows ships to move between the ATLANTIC and PACIFIC OCEANS without going around the southern tip of South America.

**Panama Canal** The Panama Canal, in the CENTRAL AMERICAN country of PANAMA, was built by American engineers in the early 1900s. Ships use the Panama Canal to sail between the ATLANTIC and the PACIFIC OCEANS, avoiding the lengthy journey around the tip of SOUTH AMERICA.

**Papua New Guinea** (PAP-yooh-uh-NOOH-GIN-ee) Papua New Guinea is a tropical country in the western PACIFIC OCEAN north of AUSTRALIA. English is its official language, but hundreds of native languages are also spoken there.

**Paraguay** (PAR-uh-gway) Paraguay is a Spanish-speaking country in central SOUTH AMERICA, north of ARGENTINA.

**Paris** Paris is the capital of FRANCE, on the SEINE RIVER. It is the site of the EIFFEL TOWER.

**Peking** *See* BEIJING.

**Persian Gulf** (PUR-zhuhn) The Persian Gulf is an inlet of the INDIAN OCEAN, between IRAN to the north and SAUDI ARABIA to the south. It is bordered by several other Arab countries as well.

**Peru** (puh-ROOH) Peru is a Spanish-speaking country in western SOUTH AMERICA on the PACIFIC OCEAN, south of ECUADOR. It was the home of the old civilization of the INCAS.

**Philippines** (FIL-uh-peenz) The Philippines is a Filipino- and English-speaking country made up of more than seven thousand islands in the southwest PACIFIC OCEAN. Its capital and most populous city is Manila.

**Poland** Poland is a country in central EUROPE, between GERMANY on the west and BELARUS on the east. Its capital is Warsaw.

**Polynesia** (pol-uh-NEE-zhuh) Polynesia is a group of thousands of islands in the central and southern PACIFIC OCEAN. Its name means "many islands." HAWAII is in Polynesia.

**Portugal** (PAWR-chuh-guhl) Portugal is a country in southwest EUROPE on the ATLANTIC OCEAN, west of SPAIN. Its capital is Lisbon.

**Prague** (prahg) Prague is the capital of the CZECH REPUBLIC and its most populous city.

**prime meridian** The prime meridian is an imaginary line that runs from the NORTH to the SOUTH POLE through the city of Greenwich, England. The prime meridian is the first meridian (*prime* means "first") because all the others are numbered from it. *See also* LONGITUDE.

**Pyrenees** (PEER-uh-neez)  The Pyrenees are a mountain range in EUROPE between FRANCE and SPAIN.

**Quebec** (kwi-BEK)  Quebec is a province in eastern CANADA. Most of the people in Quebec have French ancestors, and the principal language is French.

**Red Sea**  The Red Sea is a long, narrow sea between the Arabian Peninsula and AFRICA. It is joined to the MEDITERRANEAN SEA by the SUEZ CANAL in EGYPT.

**relief map**  A relief map is a map that shows the physical features of the land, such as mountains and deserts, by using various colors, shading, and contour lines.

**Republic of Ireland**  The Republic of Ireland is an English-speaking country in northern EUROPE. Its capital is Dublin. *See also* NORTHERN IRELAND.

**Rhine River**  The Rhine is a major river flowing about 820 miles in central EUROPE. It carries more boat traffic than any other river in the world.

**Rhodesia**  *See* ZIMBABWE.

**Rhone River** (ROHN)  The Rhone is a river flowing 500 miles in southern EUROPE. It empties into the MEDITERRANEAN SEA in southern FRANCE.

**Ring of Fire**  The Ring of Fire is an extensive area of volcanic activity that corresponds roughly to the borders of the PACIFIC OCEAN. Volcanic eruptions and earthquakes often occur in this zone.

**Rio de Janeiro** (REE-oh-day-zhuh-NAIR-oh)  Rio de Janeiro is a populous city in BRAZIL. It is sometimes called simply Rio. Rio is famous for its yearly carnival, featuring parades of people with spectacular costumes.

**Rock of Gibraltar**  *See* GIBRALTAR.

**Romania** (roh-MAY-nee-uh)  Romania (or Rumania) is a BALKAN country in southeast EUROPE, east of HUNGARY and south of UKRAINE.

**Rome**  Rome is the capital of ITALY and is known for its ancient ruins and the VATICAN. The TIBER RIVER flows through Rome.

**Rumania**  *See* ROMANIA.

**Russia**  Russia, the world's largest country in area, stretches from eastern EUROPE across northern ASIA to the PACIFIC OCEAN. It was the most powerful republic of the former SOVIET UNION. In fact, the entire Soviet Union was sometimes called Russia. Its capital and largest city is Moscow. *See also* UNION OF SOVIET SOCIALIST REPUBLICS.

**Rwanda** (roo-AHN-duh)  Rwanda is a country of eastern AFRICA. Its landscape is known for magnificent mountains and deep valleys. Rwanda gained its independence from BELGIUM in 1962, but it has long been marked by ethnic strife between the Hutu and Tutsi peoples.

**Sahara**  The Sahara is the largest desert in the world. It lies in northern AFRICA.

**Saint Lawrence River**  *See* SAINT LAWRENCE RIVER *under "United States Geography."*

**Samoa**  Samoa is a nation of islands in the southern PACIFIC OCEAN.

**São Paulo** (SOUN-POW-looh)  São Paulo, BRAZIL, is the most populous city in SOUTH AMERICA and one of the largest cities in the world.

**Saudi Arabia** (SOU-dee-uh-RAY-bee-uh)  Saudi Arabia is an oil-rich, Arabic-speaking country in the MIDDLE EAST.

**Scandinavia** (skan-duh-NAY-vee-uh)  Scandinavia is the name of a group of neighboring

**The Sahara Desert**

countries of northern EUROPE: DENMARK, FINLAND, ICELAND, NORWAY, and SWEDEN.

**Scotland** Scotland is an English-speaking region north of ENGLAND on the island of GREAT BRITAIN. It is part of the UNITED KINGDOM.

**Seine** (SEN) The Seine is a river flowing 480 miles in FRANCE. It travels through Paris and eventually empties into the ATLANTIC OCEAN at the ENGLISH CHANNEL.

**Serbia and Montenegro** (SUR-bee-uh, MON-tuh-NEG-roh) Serbia and Montenegro is a country in southeastern EUROPE, with ALBANIA to the south, BOSNIA AND HERZEGOVINA to the west, and ROMANIA to the east. Formerly a part of Yugoslavia, the country became a federation of two republics in 2003. Its capital is Belgrade.

**Shanghai** (shang-HEYE) Shanghai is the most populous city in CHINA and one of the largest cities in the world.

**Siberia** (seye-BEER-ee-uh) Siberia is a large northern region in the eastern part of RUSSIA.

**Sicily** (SIS-uh-lee) Sicily is the largest island in the MEDITERRANEAN SEA. Part of ITALY, it is off the southern tip of Italy's "boot."

**Singapore** Singapore is an island country in SOUTHEAST ASIA, between MALAYSIA and INDONESIA. It is one of the world's biggest and busiest ports.

**Slovakia** (sloh-VAH-kee-uh) Slovakia is a country in central EUROPE, south of POLAND. It was a part of the former country of Czechoslovakia.

**Slovenia** (sloh-VEE-nee-uh) Slovenia is a BALKAN country in southeast EUROPE, north of CROATIA. It was a part of the former country of Yugoslavia.

**South Africa** South Africa is the country at the southern tip of AFRICA. *See also* APARTHEID; NELSON MANDELA.

**South America** South America is a continent in the Southern Hemisphere with the ATLANTIC OCEAN on its east and the PACIFIC OCEAN on its west. Its main languages are Spanish and Portuguese.

**South Korea** (kuh-REE-uh) South Korea is a country on a PENINSULA in eastern ASIA, south of NORTH KOREA and west of JAPAN. Its capital is Seoul.

**South Seas** The South Seas is a name for the southern part of the PACIFIC OCEAN, which contains many of the POLYNESIAN islands, including SAMOA and TAHITI.

**Southeast Asia** Southeast Asia is a name that refers to the countries that lie southeast of CHINA: MYANMAR (BURMA), THAILAND, LAOS, CAMBODIA, VIETNAM, MALAYSIA, SINGAPORE, INDONESIA, and the PHILIPPINES.

**Southern Ocean** The Southern Ocean surrounds ANTARCTICA. It is the fourth largest

CARIBBEAN SEA

N. AMER.

Lake Maracaibo

Caracas

GUYANA

SURINAME

FRENCH GUIANA

VENEZUELA

Medellín

★ Bogotá

COLOMBIA

★ Quito

ECUADOR

Guayaquil

Amazon R.

B R A Z I L

ANDES

Lima

PERU

Lake Titicaca

La Paz

BOLIVIA

Brasília ★

PARAGUAY

Paraná R.

São Paulo

Rio de Janeiro

Asunción ★

Paraná R.

URUGUAY

Valparaíso

Aconcagua

ANDES

ARGENTINA

Santiago

CHILE

Buenos Aires

Montevideo

Patagonia

PACIFIC OCEAN

ATLANTIC OCEAN

Falkland Islands (U.K.)

N
W        E
S

Strait of Magellan

Tierra del Fuego

Cape Horn

**SOUTH AMERICA**

★ National Capitals
● Major Cities
▲ Mountain

0          MILES          1000

ocean in the world. It is also the newest ocean. The International Hydrographic Association named it, and marked its boundaries, in spring 2000.

**Soviet Union**   The Soviet Union is another name for the former country of the UNION OF SOVIET SOCIALIST REPUBLICS (USSR), or RUSSIA.

**Spain**   Spain is a country in southwest EUROPE, east of PORTUGAL and south of FRANCE, at the western end of the MEDITERRANEAN SEA. Its capital is Madrid.

**Sri Lanka** (sree-LAHNG-kuh)   Sri Lanka is an island country off the southeast coast of INDIA that is noted for its tea. It used to be called Ceylon.

**steppes**   The steppes are vast grassy plains found in southeast EUROPE, SIBERIA, and central NORTH AMERICA.

**Stockholm**   Stockholm is the capital of SWEDEN and where the NOBEL PRIZES are awarded each year. The NOBEL PRIZE for Peace, however, is awarded in OSLO, NORWAY.

**Strait of Magellan** (muh-JEL-uhn)   The Strait of Magellan is a channel just north of the southern tip of SOUTH AMERICA that joins the ATLANTIC and PACIFIC OCEANS. *See also* MAGELLAN, FERDINAND.

**Sudan** (soo-DAN)   The Sudan is a country in northeastern AFRICA, south of EGYPT.

**Suez Canal** (sooh-EZ)   The Suez Canal, in EGYPT, connects the MEDITERRANEAN SEA and the RED SEA. Ships use it to travel from the Mediterranean Sea to the INDIAN OCEAN, avoiding the lengthy journey around the AFRICAN continent.

**Sweden** (SWEED-n)   Sweden is a SCANDINAVIAN country in northern EUROPE, east of NORWAY. Its capital is Stockholm.

**Switzerland**   Switzerland is a small country in central EUROPE that lies in the ALPS. It is known for its neutrality, that is, its refusal to take sides in any arguments between other countries. Switzerland's most populous city is Zurich. Its capital is Bern.

**Sydney** (SID-nee)   Sydney is the most populous city in AUSTRALIA.

**Syria** (SEER-ee-uh)   Syria is a country in the MIDDLE EAST. It lies at the eastern end of the MEDITERRANEAN SEA, north of LEBANON and west of IRAQ.

**Tahiti** (tuh-HEE-tee)   Tahiti is an island in POLYNESIA, famous for its natural beauty.

**Taiwan** (TEYE-WAHN)   Taiwan, also called the Republic of China, is a Chinese-speaking island country in the PACIFIC OCEAN in eastern ASIA, east of CHINA. It was once named Formosa and was part of China.

**Tanganyika**   *See* LAKE TANGANYIKA.

**Tanzania** (tan-zuh-NEE-uh)   Tanzania is a Swahili- and English-speaking country in

**Sydney.** Sydney Opera House.

eastern AFRICA, south of KENYA, on the INDIAN OCEAN.

**Tehran** (te-RAHN)  Tehran is the capital of IRAN.

**Tel Aviv** (TEL-uh-VEEV)  Tel Aviv is a large city in ISRAEL.

**Thailand** (TEYE-land)  Thailand is a country in SOUTHEAST ASIA. Part of INDOCHINA, it lies south of MYANMAR (BURMA) and LAOS and north of CAMBODIA and MALAYSIA. Thailand was formerly called Siam. Its capital is Bangkok.

**Thames** (TEMZ)  The Thames is a river flowing 210 miles through southern ENGLAND, including London. It is the principal commercial waterway for England.

**Tiber River** (TEYE-buhr)  The Tiber, about 250 miles long, is a river in central ITALY that flows through ROME.

**Tibet** (ti-BET)  Tibet is a region in the HIMALAYAS in southwest CHINA.

**Tigris River** (TEYE-gris)  The Tigris, about 1,150 miles long, is a river in southwest ASIA flowing through IRAQ to the EUPHRATES RIVER. It was an important center of ancient civilization.

**Titicaca**  *See* LAKE TITICACA.

**Tokyo** (TOH-kee-oh)  Tokyo is the capital and most populous city of JAPAN. It is also one of the largest cities in the world.

**Toronto** (tuh-RON-toh)  Toronto is the most populous city in CANADA as well as the capital of the province of ONTARIO.

**Tropic of Cancer**  The Tropic of Cancer is an imaginary line around the EARTH in the NORTHERN HEMISPHERE. It is about 1,600 miles north of and PARALLEL to the EQUATOR and marks the northern boundary of the tropical regions, where it stays hot all year.

**Tropic of Capricorn**  The Tropic of Capricorn is an imaginary line around the EARTH in the Southern Hemisphere. It is about 1,600 miles south of and PARALLEL to the EQUATOR and marks the southern boundary of the tropical regions, where it stays hot all year.

**Turkey**  Turkey is a country between the BLACK SEA and the MEDITERRANEAN SEA, lying mostly in southwest ASIA and partly in southeast EUROPE. It is part of a region that historically, since ancient times, was called Asia Minor. Its most populous city is Istanbul.

**Uganda** (yooh-GAN-duh)  Uganda is a country in eastern AFRICA, west of KENYA.

**Ukraine** (yooh-KRAYN)  Ukraine is a country in eastern EUROPE. It was a part of the SOVIET UNION from 1922 to 1991.

**Union of Soviet Socialist Republics (USSR)**  The Union of Soviet Socialist Republics, also known as the SOVIET UNION and popularly as Russia, is a former country of eastern EUROPE and western and northern ASIA. The Soviet Union came to an end officially in 1991.

**United Kingdom of Great Britain and Ireland (U.K.)**  The United Kingdom of Great Britain and Ireland is an English-speaking country in northwest EUROPE made up of ENGLAND, SCOTLAND, WALES, and NORTHERN IRELAND, which are united under one government, based in LONDON. Great Britain is officially the name of the island that contains England, Scotland, and Wales, but sometimes Great Britain, or simply Britain, is used to refer to the United Kingdom as a whole.

**Ural Mountains** (YOOR-uhl)  The Urals are a mountain range in RUSSIA that divide EUROPE and ASIA.

**Uruguay** (YOOR-uh-gweye)  Uruguay is a Spanish-speaking country on the ATLANTIC OCEAN, on the east coast of SOUTH AMERICA. It lies south of BRAZIL and east of ARGENTINA.

**Vancouver** (van-KOOH-vuhr) Vancouver, BRITISH COLUMBIA, is the most populous city in western CANADA.

**Vatican City State** Vatican City State is a tiny nation located within the city of ROME. It is the seat of the ROMAN CATHOLIC CHURCH and the home of the POPE.

**Venezuela** (VEN-UH-ZWAY-LUH) Venezuela is a Spanish-speaking country in northern SOUTH AMERICA. It is at the northern tip of the continent on the CARIBBEAN SEA.

**Venice** (VEN-is) Venice is a city in northeastern ITALY. It is built on islands in the Adriatic Sea, which is a part of the MEDITERRANEAN SEA between ITALY and the BALKAN Peninsula. The islands are connected largely by canals, and people and goods are carried by boats, most notably the traditional long, black gondolas.

**Victoria** *See* LAKE VICTORIA.

**Victoria Falls** Victoria Falls is a 355-foot-high waterfall on the Zambezi River in south-central AFRICA on the ZIMBABWE-Zambia border.

**Vienna** (vee-EN-uh) Vienna is the capital and most populous city of AUSTRIA.

**Vietnam** (vee-et-NAHM) Vietnam is a country in SOUTHEAST ASIA. It lies south of CHINA. Its capital is Hanoi.

**Volga** The Volga, in western RUSSIA, is the longest river in EUROPE.

**Wales** (waylz) Wales is a region west of ENGLAND on the island of GREAT BRITAIN. It is part of the UNITED KINGDOM.

**Warsaw** Warsaw is the capital of POLAND and its most populous city.

**West Indies** The West Indies are the group of islands east and south of FLORIDA and north of SOUTH AMERICA that lie between the ATLANTIC OCEAN and the CARIBBEAN SEA. They were visited by Columbus in 1492. Among the islands are the BAHAMAS, CUBA, JAMAICA, and PUERTO RICO.

**Yangtze River** (YANG-see) The Yangtze, in CHINA, is the longest river in ASIA, flowing 3,400 miles. The Chinese call it the Chang Jiang.

**Yellow River** The Yellow River, about 3,000 miles long, is a river in northern CHINA. It is named for the yellow deposits that it carries to its delta. The Chinese name is Huang He or Huang Ho.

**Yucatán** (yooh-kuh-TAN) The Yucatán is a region in southern MEXICO that was the home of the ancient MAYAN civilization. It is also a PENINSULA that includes parts of GUATEMALA and HONDURAS.

**Yugoslavia** (yooh-goh-SLAH-vee-uh) The former country of Yugoslavia was a union of six REPUBLICS: BOSNIA AND HERZEGOVINA, CROATIA, MACEDONIA, Montenegro, Serbia, and SLOVENIA. In 2003, the former Yugoslavia was renamed SERBIA AND MONTENEGRO.

**Yukon River** The Yukon River, about 2,000 miles long, flows through CANADA's YUKON TERRITORY and the state of ALASKA. It empties into the BERING SEA. It was a main route to the Klondike during the GOLD RUSH of the 1890s.

**Yukon Territory** (YOOH-kon) The Yukon Territory is in northwest CANADA, east of ALASKA. Thousands of people rushed to the Yukon Territory in the 1890s, when gold was discovered in the Klondike mining district.

**Zaire** (zeye-EER) *See* CONGO, DEMOCRATIC REPUBLIC OF.

**Zimbabwe** (zim-BAHB-way) Zimbabwe is a country in southern AFRICA that used to be called Rhodesia. English is its official language.

**Zurich** (ZOOR-ik) Zurich is the largest city in SWITZERLAND.

# Mathematics

Mathematics is a way of thinking that often uses numbers and symbols instead of words. A typical statement in mathematics is 2 + 2 = 4 (two plus two equals four). Most statements in mathematics can be expressed as equations, although many scientists in different fields use advanced mathematics. For example, an astronomer uses mathematical equations to discover how far certain stars are from the earth or from each other. Almost everyone uses basic arithmetic like addition and subtraction in everyday life. When we shop, we use numbers to compare prices. In sports, we use numbers to compare players or teams. For example, calculating a batting average is a mathematical operation.

Here we define the basic mathematical terms and operations that most people find useful. Knowing them is especially helpful if you want to learn more advanced scientific and mathematical ideas.

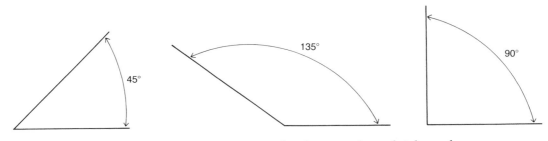

**Angle.** From left to right: acute angle, obtuse angle, and right angle.

**acute angle** An acute angle is an ANGLE that measures less than a RIGHT ANGLE, that is, less than 90 DEGREES (90°).

**addition** Addition is one of the four basic operations of ARITHMETIC (along with SUBTRACTION, MULTIPLICATION, and DIVISION). Its symbol is the plus sign: +. To add two numbers means to combine them to get a total number, which is called the SUM. For example, the sum of 7 and 5 is 12; 7 + 5 = 12 (seven plus five equals twelve).

**angle** An angle is created when two lines meet at the same point. The resulting angle is always measured in DEGREES. *See also*

ACUTE ANGLE; ARC; OBTUSE ANGLE; RIGHT ANGLE.

**arc** An arc is a part of the CIRCUMFERENCE of a CIRCLE and is measured in DEGREES. Any ANGLE can form an arc on the circumference when the two lines of the angle are RADII of the circle. A full circle has 360 degrees.

**area** Area is the amount of surface contained by a figure, such as a RECTANGLE, a SQUARE, or a CIRCLE. Area is measured in units such as the square inch, which is an area the size of a square with sides 1 inch long. Some common units of area are:

  square inch (abbreviated as sq in or in²)
  square foot (sq ft or ft²) = 144 square inches
  square yard (sq yd or yd²) = 9 square feet
  acre = 4,840 square yards
  square mile (sq mi or mi²) = 640 acres

Area can also be measured using the METRIC SYSTEM:

  square centimeter (sq cm or cm²)
  square meter (sq m or m²) = 10,000 square centimeters
  square kilometer (sq km or km²) = 1,000,000 square meters

**arithmetic** Arithmetic is a kind of mathematics that studies how to solve problems with numbers and no VARIABLES in them. The four basic operations of arithmetic are ADDITION, SUBTRACTION, MULTIPLICATION, and DIVISION.

**average** The average of a set of numbers is found by adding them together and dividing the sum by the number of separate numbers in the set. Thus, the average of 5, 6, and 4 is 5, because the sum of 5, 6, and 4 is 15 and there are 3 numbers in the set: 15 ÷ 3 = 5 (fifteen divided by three equals five). An average is one way to describe a set of numbers. For example, to find out the average height of the people in your class, you would measure each person, add up all the heights, and divide the sum by the number of people. The answer would be the average height of the people in your class. *See also* MEAN.

**bar graph** A bar graph is a kind of chart used to compare DATA. For example, if you know the average life span of different animals and want to present the information in a way that is easy to see at a glance, you can make a bar graph.

**bell curve** A bell curve is a type of graph that is shaped like a bell, with a line that peaks in the middle and slopes at each end. It is also called a "normal distribution," because it shows how things in the world are distributed, with most individuals falling near the middle where the curve is high, and few individuals falling at the ends where the curve is low.

**braces** Braces { } are symbols that indicate a SET. *Compare* PARENTHESES.

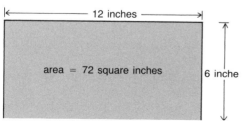

**Area**

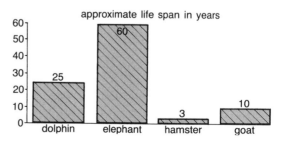

**Bar graph.** The approximate life span of several animals, shown in years.

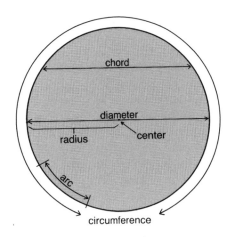

**Circle.** A circle and its parts.

**cardinal number**  A cardinal number, such as 1, 5, or 75, indicates the quantity but not the order of things. A cardinal number is not followed by *th. Compare* ORDINAL NUMBER.

**chord**  A chord is a straight line joining two POINTS on the same curve or CIRCLE.

**circle**  A circle is a round, closed, PLANE (flat) figure. All the POINTS on its CIRCUMFERENCE are the same distance from the center.

**circumference**  The circumference is the edge or boundary of a CIRCLE.

**common denominator**  A common denominator is a MULTIPLE shared by the DENOMINATORS of two or more FRACTIONS. For example, 6 is a common denominator of the fractions ½ (or ³⁄₆) and ⅓ (or ²⁄₆) because 6 is a multiple of both 2 and 3. In order to add or subtract fractions, you must find their LEAST COMMON DENOMINATOR. For example, ½ + ⅓ = ³⁄₆ (or ½) + ²⁄₆ (or ⅓) = ⁵⁄₆.

**compute**  To compute is to solve problems that use numbers. ADDITION, SUBTRACTION, MULTIPLICATION, and DIVISION all involve computation. *See also* COMPUTER.

**cone**  A cone is a three-dimensional figure that rises from a circular base to a single POINT (called an apex) at its top. *See also* SOLID.

**congruent**  Congruent figures are identical in size and shape. A TRIANGLE that is congruent with another triangle will occupy the same amount of space.

**coordinates**  The two numbers that define the position of a POINT on a LINE GRAPH are called coordinates. One number represents vertical distance from the ZERO point, the other horizontal distance. The coordinates define the point where the vertical and horizontal lines cross. *See also* ORDERED PAIR.

**cube**  In geometry, a cube is a three-dimensional figure that has six square faces. A pair of dice are cubes. In multiplication, when you cube a number, you multiply the number by itself three times. This is sometimes called raising the number to its third POWER. The operation of cubing is indicated by the use of an EXPONENT: $2^3 = 2 \times 2 \times 2$. In the expression $2^3$, the exponent is 3 and is always placed halfway above the line. *See also* SOLID.

**cylinder**  A cylinder is a rounded three-dimensional figure that has a flat, circular face at each end, such as a rolling pin or a hockey puck.

**data**  Data are facts that have been collected but not interpreted. For instance, to find out how long the average cat lives, you would have to collect data on the life spans of many cats.

**decimal**  A decimal is a FRACTION written according to the decimal number system. (*Decimal* means "based on the number 10.") Decimals, which are sometimes called decimal fractions, are expressed using a DECIMAL POINT and the PLACE VALUES tenths, hundredths, thousandths, and so on. The fraction ½ is the decimal .5 or ⁵⁄₁₀; the fraction ¼ is 0.25 or ²⁵⁄₁₀₀. In a decimal, each place value to the right of the decimal point has ¹⁄₁₀ (one-tenth) the value of the place immedi-

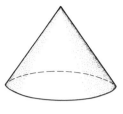

**Cone**

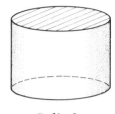

**Cylinder**

ately to its left. The numbers on a simple hand calculator appear in decimals.

**decimal point**   A decimal point looks like a period [.] and is used to mark the PLACE VALUE in a number that contains a value lower than 1. For example, in the number 3.45 (or $3^{45}/_{100}$), the decimal point tells you that the 3 is in the *ones* place, the 4 is in the *tenths* place, and the 5 is in the *hundredths* place. If the decimal point was moved and the number was written as 34.5 ($34^{5}/_{10}$), the 3 would be in the *tens* place, the 4 in the *ones* place, and the 5 in the *tenths* place.

**degree**   A degree is a unit of measurement for ANGLES and ARCS and is indicated by a small circle (°) raised halfway above the line. We often write 90 degrees as 90°. A CIRCLE measures 360 degrees; a RIGHT ANGLE measures 90 degrees.

**denominator**   A denominator is the bottom number of a FRACTION and indicates the number of parts needed to make a whole unit. In the fraction $^{2}/_{3}$, the denominator is

3 ($^{3}/_{3}$ = 1). *See also* COMMON DENOMINATOR; NUMERATOR.

**diagonal**   In a four-sided plane (flat) figure, a diagonal is a straight line from one corner of the figure to the opposite corner.

**diameter**   The diameter of a CIRCLE is a straight line across the circle through its center. *See also* CIRCUMFERENCE; RADIUS.

**difference**   The difference between two numbers is the answer you get when you subtract the smaller from the larger. The difference between 7 and 4 is 3, because 7 − 4 = 3. *See also* SUBTRACTION.

**digit**   A digit is a single number from 0 to 9 that occupies one place. A number such as 1,368 is a four-digit number because it uses four digits in four places. The number 1,000 is also a four-digit number, even though three of the digits are the same number. The number 5 is a single-digit number; 45 is a two-digit number. The value of a digit depends on its PLACE VALUE with respect to the DECIMAL POINT.

**dimension**   Dimension is the indication of how far something extends in space. A line has one dimension: LENGTH. A SQUARE has two dimensions: length and width. (One-dimensional and two-dimensional objects are PLANES.) Real objects, and the objects that are called SOLIDS in GEOMETRY, have three dimensions: length, width, and height, such as a CUBE.

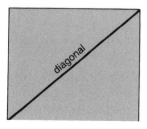

**Diagonal**

**dividend**   A dividend is a number that is to be divided. In the expression $16 \div 2 = 8$ (or or $^{16}\!/_2 = 8$), 16 is the dividend. *See also* DIVISOR.

**division**   Division is one of the four basic operations of ARITHMETIC (along with MULTIPLICATION, ADDITION, and SUBTRACTION). Its symbol is $\div$, which means "divided by." To divide is to determine how many times one quantity is contained in another. Therefore, to divide is to determine how many times you have to subtract a number to reach zero. For example, $6 \div 3 = 2$, because you subtract 3 from 6 two times to reach ZERO. This problem may also be represented as $^6\!/_2 = 3$. When you divide a larger number by a smaller number, you get a whole number ($8 \div 2 = 4$) or a mixed number ($8 \div 3 = 2^2\!/_3$). When you divide a smaller number by a larger number, you get a fraction ($3 \div 8 = ^3\!/_8$). *See also* DIVIDEND; DIVISOR; QUOTIENT; REMAINDER.

**divisor**   A divisor is the number that divides the DIVIDEND. In the expression $20 \div 4 = 5$, 4 is the divisor. *See also* QUOTIENT; REMAINDER.

**ellipse**   An ellipse is a closed, oval, PLANE (flat) figure that is not as round as a CIRCLE. The ORBITS of the PLANETS are ellipses.

**equation**   An equation is a statement that two different numbers or mathematical expressions are equal to each other. For example, $3 + 12 = 15$ is an equation. Equations use the equals sign: =.

**equilateral triangle**   An equilateral triangle is a TRIANGLE that has three sides of equal LENGTH and three ANGLES of equal size. Because the angles of a triangle always add up to 180 DEGREES, each angle of an equilateral triangle is 60 degrees.

**estimate**   An estimate is a rough guess at a number. If someone asks how long it will take you to read a story and you say, "About 30 minutes," you have made an estimate. Es-

**Ellipse**

timates can help you solve problems. If you add 9.26 and 4.21, you can estimate that the answer will be around 13, because $9 + 4 = 13$.

**even number**   An even number is a number that can be divided by 2 without leaving a REMAINDER. The numbers 2, 4, 6, 8, 10, and so on, can be divided evenly by 2 and are thus even numbers. *Compare* ODD NUMBER.

**exponent**   An exponent is the small number to the right and above the main number that shows how many times the number is to be multiplied by itself. For instance, in the expression $2^3$, 3 is the exponent, or the number of times that 2 is to be multiplied by itself. Thus, $2^3 = 2 \times 2 \times 2 = 8$. The expression $2^3$ is read aloud as "two to the power of three," "two to the third," or "two exponent three." *See also* POWER.

**factor**   In multiplication, a factor is a number that is being multiplied. In the expression $3 \times 9 = 27$, the factors are 3 and 9. *See also* GREATEST COMMON FACTOR.

**formula**   A formula is a general mathematical expression that can be applied in particular cases. For example, to calculate the AREA (a) of a SQUARE, you multiply the LENGTH of one side (s) of the square by itself. Thus, the formula for the area of a square is $a = s^2$. No matter how large the square is, if you multiply the length of one side by itself, you will get its area. A formula is usually written as an EQUATION. *Compare* VARIABLE.

**fraction** A fraction is a number that expresses a part of a whole. In the fraction ⅔, 3 is the DENOMINATOR, which is the number of equal parts that make the whole. The number 2 is the NUMERATOR, which is the number of parts you are talking about. If you have two apples to divide among three people, each person would get a fraction of an apple, or ⅔ (two-thirds) of an apple. Fractions are sometimes expressed as DECIMALS: ⁴⁄₁₀ = 0.4. Sometimes numbers greater than 1 are called fractions when they are written as fractions. For example, ³⁄₂ (or 1½) is sometimes called a fraction. *See also* IMPROPER FRACTION.

**geometry** Geometry is the mathematical study of shapes (such as TRIANGLES), three-dimensional figures or SOLIDS (such as CUBES and CYLINDERS), and positions in space (such as POINTS).

**greatest common factor** (GCF) The greatest common factor is the biggest number that is a common FACTOR of two or more numbers. For example, the numbers 8 and 12 have common factors of 1, 2, and 4. Therefore, their greatest common factor is 4.

**hexagon** A hexagon is a PLANE (flat) figure with six straight sides.

**horizontal** A horizontal line is PARALLEL to the earth's surface or the bottom of a page; it goes across rather than up and down. *Compare* VERTICAL.

**hypotenuse** The hypotenuse is the longest side of a RIGHT TRIANGLE and is opposite the RIGHT ANGLE.

**improper fraction** An improper fraction is a fraction in which the NUMERATOR is greater

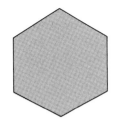

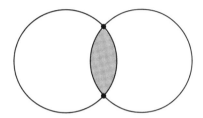

**Hexagon and Intersect.** Dots indicate where the lines intersect; shading highlights the intersecting area.

than or equal to the DENOMINATOR, as in ⁹⁄₅ or ⁵⁄₄.

**infinity** Infinity refers to a set of numbers that goes on without end, for example: 1, 2, 3, 4, and so on. The symbol for infinity is ∞.

**integer** Integers are the set of numbers that includes ZERO and the NEGATIVE NUMBERS but not FRACTIONS. The set of integers includes 0, 1, 2, 3, and so on; it also includes −1, −2, −3, and so on. An integer is also called a WHOLE NUMBER.

**intersect** In geometry, two figures are said to intersect when they cross each other. The POINTS where they cross are their intersections. The place where two roads cross is also called an intersection.

**isosceles triangle** An isosceles TRIANGLE has two straight sides of equal LENGTH and two ANGLES of equal size.

**least common denominator** (LCD) The least common denominator is the smallest number that can be divided evenly by two DENOMINATORS. For example, with the fractions $\frac{1}{9}$ and $\frac{1}{12}$, the least common denominator is 36. Fractions with different denominators must be renamed with a common denominator before they are added or subtracted: $\frac{1}{9} + \frac{1}{12} = \frac{4}{36} + \frac{3}{36} = \frac{7}{36}$.

**least common multiple** (LCM) The least common multiple is the smallest number that is a common MULTIPLE of two or more numbers. For example, with the numbers 8 and 12, the least common multiple is 24. To find the least common multiple of two numbers, you must first find their GREATEST COMMON FACTOR. Next, multiply the numbers together, and divide the PRODUCT by the greatest common factor: $8 \times 12 = 96 \div 4 = 24$.

**length** Length is the straight-line distance from one point to another. Some common units for measuring length are:

inch (in)
foot (ft) = 12 inches
yard (yd) = 3 feet
mile (mi) = 5,280 feet

Length can also be measured using the METRIC SYSTEM:

millimeter (mm) = 0.1 centimeter
centimeter (cm) = 0.39 inch
meter (m) = 100 centimeters or 39 inches
kilometer (km) = 1,000 meters or 0.6 mile

**line** In geometry, a line is something that has LENGTH but no width. It has only one dimension (its length) and extends infinitely in both directions. On a PLANE (flat) surface, a straight LINE SEGMENT is the shortest distance between two points. A line is labeled with letters and may be written: line AB or $\overline{AB}$.

**line graph** A line graph is a chart that shows DATA clearly and simply. For example, if you want to show how the cost of milk has

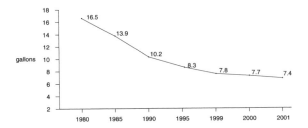

**Line graph.** Showing the decrease in the consumption of plain whole milk per person (in gallons) over twenty-one years.

changed over the past twenty years, you can use a line graph.

**line segment** A line segment is part of a LINE. In theory, a line can go on forever. Therefore, when we draw a line, we are really drawing a part of a line, or a line segment. A line segment is labeled line segment AB or $\overline{AB}$.

**lowest common denominator** See LEAST COMMON DENOMINATOR.

**lowest terms** A FRACTION is in lowest terms when its NUMERATOR and DENOMINATOR cannot both be divided evenly by any whole number greater than 1. The fraction $\frac{4}{8}$ is not in lowest terms because its numerator (4) and its denominator (8) can each be divided by 4, yielding $\frac{1}{2}$, which is in lowest terms because no number except one can divide both numerator (1) and denominator (2). Finding lowest terms is also known as *reducing* or *simplifying* the fraction.

**mean** A mean is the same as an AVERAGE and is found by adding a set of amounts and dividing their SUM by the number of different amounts in the set. The mean of $8 + 4 + 3$ is the sum (15) divided by the number of items (3): $15 \div 3 = 5$, which is the mean.

**median** When a set of numbers is arranged in order from the least to the greatest, the median is the middle number. In the set 1, 3, 5, 7, 9, the median is 5. For an even number of items, the median is midway between the two middle numbers. The median divides the DATA into two equal parts. *Compare* MEAN.

**metric system**   The metric system is used to weigh and measure things by scientists and by people in most of the countries in the world. Everything in the metric system is based on the meter, which is about three feet long. Weight is defined by the gram, which is the weight of one cubic centimeter of water. (A centimeter is one-hundredth of a meter.) Area is defined by square meters. A unit of VOLUME is the liter, which is 1,000 cubic centimeters, about one quart.

**mixed number**   A mixed number is a number that includes a WHOLE NUMBER and a FRACTION, as in $4\frac{2}{3}$.

**multiple**   A multiple is a quantity into which another quantity can be divided with zero REMAINDER. The numbers 4 and 8 are multiples of 2. A DIVIDEND is a multiple of a DIVISOR if there is zero remainder. *See also* LEAST COMMON MULTIPLE.

**multiplication**   Multiplication is one of the four basic operations of ARITHMETIC (along with DIVISION, ADDITION, and SUBTRACTION). Its symbol is the "times" sign: ×. Multiplication is like addition because you add the same number a certain number of times. For example, $2 \times 3 = 3 + 3$; $5 \times 6 = 6 + 6 + 6 + 6 + 6$; $5 \times 6$ also equals $5 + 5 + 5 + 5 + 5 + 5$. When you multiply numbers, you get their PRODUCT. The product of 2 and 3 is 6 because $2 \times 3 = 6$.

**negative number**   A negative number is less than ZERO (0) and is written with a minus sign in front of it: $-3$. A negative number often stands for a measurement that is below a certain reference point. For instance, in the CENTIGRADE temperature scale, a temperature of $-24°C$ is 24 degrees below zero, or the freezing point of water. *Compare* POSITIVE NUMBER. *See also* OPPOSITE NUMBER.

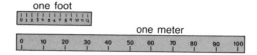

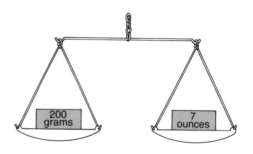

**Metric system.** One gallon is approximately 3.75 liters; one foot is just under one third of a meter; 200 grams equals 7 ounces.

**numeral**   A numeral is a symbol that stands for a number. The numeral 4 stands for the number four. In the past, people used different symbols for numbers from the ones we use now. For example, the ancient Romans wrote the number three as III. ROMAN NUMERALS are sometimes used today, but today we usually use symbols called *Arabic numerals*, so named because they were first taught to Europeans by Arabs. The Arabic numerals are: 1, 2, 3, 4, 5, 6, 7, 8, 9, and 0.

**numerator**   A numerator is the top part of a FRACTION and the number that is divided by the DENOMINATOR. Therefore, a numerator is a DIVIDEND and a denominator is a DIVISOR. In the fraction $\frac{2}{3}$, the numerator is 2.

**obtuse angle** An obtuse angle is an ANGLE greater than 90 DEGREES (90°) and less than 180 degrees (180°).

**octagon** An octagon is a PLANE (flat) figure with eight straight sides.

**odd number** An odd number is a number that cannot be divided evenly by two. The numbers 1, 3, 5, 7, 9, 11, and so on, are odd numbers. *Compare* EVEN NUMBER.

**opposite number** Any two numbers whose sum is ZERO are opposite numbers to each other. Thus, 3 and −3 are opposite numbers because −3 + 3 = 0. The opposite number of −5 is 5. Zero's opposite number is itself, because 0 + 0 = 0. *See also* NEGATIVE NUMBER.

**ordered pair** An ordered pair is a pair of numbers that represents a position on a LINE GRAPH. For example, (8, 3) is an ordered pair because 8 tells you how far the POINT is to the right of 0 and 3 tells you how far the point is above 0. These numbers are sometimes called COORDINATES.

**ordinal number** An ordinal number indicates the order of a thing in a series: first (1st), second (2nd), third (3rd), twenty-fifth (25th), and so on. After 1st, 2nd, 3rd, and larger numbers with these quantities, like 21st, 22nd, and 23rd, ordinal numbers use the *th* ending. *Compare* CARDINAL NUMBER.

**parabola** (puh-RAB-uh-luh) A parabola is a shape in GEOMETRY that is made of a single bend with a line at each end going off to an infinite (endless) distance. An object that is thrown away from EARTH, and then pulled back by GRAVITY—such as a ball—follows the shape of a parabola.

**parallel** Parallel lines are lines that never meet. They extend in the same direction and always remain the same distance from each other, like railroad tracks.

**parallelogram** A parallelogram is a PLANE (flat) figure with four straight sides. The sides opposite each other are PARALLEL and

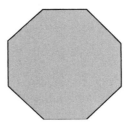

**Octagon**

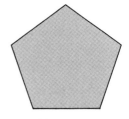

**Pentagon**

the same LENGTH. SQUARES, RECTANGLES, and RHOMBUSES are all parallelograms.

**parentheses** Parentheses ( ) are used in mathematics to show that the operation inside the parentheses should be treated as a single quantity. In the equation 2 × (3 + 2) = 10, the digits (3 + 2) should be treated as a single quantity, which is 5. *Compare* BRACES.

**pentagon** A pentagon is a PLANE (flat) figure with five straight sides.

**percent** Percent is a way of expressing a number as a FRACTION of 100. (*Percent* means "by hundreds.") The symbol for percent is %. To express the number ½ as a percentage, you change it to a fraction of 100. Thus, ½ = $^{50}/_{100}$, which as a percentage is

A          B

**Parallel.** Line segment AB is parallel to line segment CD.

written as 50%. To express 200 as a percentage, you would calculate that $200 = {}^{200}\!/_{100}$, or 200%. Similarly, $\frac{1}{3} = 33\frac{1}{3}\%$, because $\frac{1}{3}$ of $100 = 33\frac{1}{3}$. The fraction $\frac{1}{4} = {}^{25}\!/_{100}$, or 25%.

**perimeter** A perimeter is the distance around the edge of a multisided figure. For example, if each of the four sides of a SQUARE measures 2 inches, its perimeter is 8 inches.

**perpendicular** Two straight lines are perpendicular when they form a RIGHT ANGLE (an angle that measures 90 DEGREES).

**pi** Pi is the RATIO of the CIRCUMFERENCE of a CIRCLE to its DIAMETER. *Pi* is the name of a Greek letter that is written as the symbol $\pi$. The actual number is approximately 3.14159 and is used in many calculations.

**pie chart** A pie chart, or graph, is a way to represent percentages or FRACTIONS. A pie chart is also called a CIRCLE graph because it is circular. This pie chart shows that Mike spends $\frac{1}{2}$ (50%) of his money on food, $\frac{1}{4}$ (25%) on school supplies, and the remaining $\frac{1}{4}$ (25%) on toys.

**place value** Each DIGIT is given a place value, depending on where it is in a number with more than one digit. In the number 7,324, 4 is in the *ones* place; it equals $4 \times 1$. The number 2 is in the *tens* place; it equals $2 \times 10$. The number 3 is in the *hundreds* place; it equals $3 \times 100$. The number 7 is in the *thousands* place; it equals $7 \times 1,000$. Higher place values are ten thousands, hundred thousands, millions, billions, and so on. Lower place values are ten-thousandths, hundred-thousandths, and so on. *See also* DECIMAL POINT.

**plane** In geometry, a plane is a flat area. One-dimensional figures, such as LINES, and two-dimensional figures, such as RECTANGLES, exist in planes. Anything three-dimensional, such as a CUBE or a CONE, exists in space, not in a plane. *Compare* SOLID. *See also* DIMENSION.

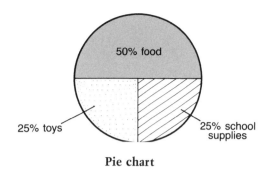

**Pie chart**

**point** In geometry, a point represents a position but has no size. A point is represented by a small dot, like the period at the end of this sentence.

**polygon** A polygon is a many-sided PLANE figure, such as a PENTAGON or an OCTAGON. (*Poly* means "many" in Greek.)

**polyhedron** In geometry, a polyhedron is a three-dimensional figure, such as a CUBE or a PYRAMID, that is bounded by polygons.

**positive number** A positive number is a number greater than 0. *Compare* NEGATIVE NUMBER.

**power** In mathematics, power refers to the number of times a number is to be multiplied by itself. For instance, 2 to the power of 3 (or $2^3$) equals $2 \times 2 \times 2$. The symbol that shows to what power a number is raised is called an EXPONENT. In the expression $2^3$, the exponent is 3.

**prime number** A prime number is a number that cannot be divided evenly by any number except itself and 1. The number 4 is not a prime number because it can be divided evenly by 1, 2, and 4. But 3 is a prime number because it can only be divided evenly by 1 and 3.

**probability** Probability is the chance that a particular thing will happen. For instance, the probability of a coin landing heads up is $\frac{1}{2}$ (1 out of 2, or 50%), because it is one of two possible outcomes.

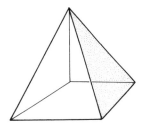
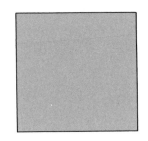
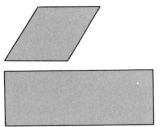

**Pyramid and Quadrilateral.** Left: square. Right, top to bottom: rhombus and rectangle.

**product**  A product is the result of MULTI-PLICATION. For example, 6 is the product of 2 and 3 because $2 \times 3 = 6$. *See also* MULTIPLE.

**proportion**  A proportion is a RATIO or a comparison of ratios and can be expressed as a FRACTION. For example, ½ is the proportion 1 to 2. It can be compared with the proportion 5 to 10, or ⁵⁄₁₀. These proportions (or ratios or fractions) are all the same, since they can all be reduced to ½.

**pyramid**  A pyramid is a three-dimensional figure whose base is a POLYGON and whose sides are TRIANGLES that come to a point at the top. *See also* SOLID; PYRAMIDS *under "World History to 1600."*

**Pythagorean theorem** (puh-THAG-uh-REE-uhn)  The Pythagorean theorem is a statement in GEOMETRY that, in a RIGHT TRIANGLE, the SQUARE of the LENGTH of the HYPOTENUSE is equal to the SUM of the squares of the lengths of the two other sides. This statement is often shown as the EQUATION $a^2 + b^2 = c^2$.

**quadrilateral**  A quadrilateral is a PLANE (flat) figure with four straight sides. RECTANGLES, SQUARES, and RHOMBUSES are quadrilaterals.

**quotient**  A quotient is the result of DIVISION. For example, when 10 is divided by 2, the quotient is 5, because $10 \div 2 = 5$. This problem may also be represented as $^{10}\!/_2 = 5$ or $2\overline{)10}^{\,5}$.

**radius**  The radius of a CIRCLE is the length of a straight LINE drawn from the center to the CIRCUMFERENCE. The radius is half the DIAMETER. The plural of radius is RADII.

**rate**  A rate is a way of comparing two different kinds of quantities. Rates use RATIOS. If Bill walked 8 miles in 2 hours, you can find his rate of speed by dividing the number of miles he walked by the number of hours he walked. The rate is ⁸⁄₂ miles per hour, or 4 miles per hour.

**ratio**  A ratio is a way of comparing two numbers by dividing one by the other. For example, the ratio of 2 to 3 is ⅔. The ratio of 6 to 3 is ⁶⁄₃, or 2. If there are 15 boys and 10 girls in your class, the ratio of boys to girls is 15 to 10. In LOWEST TERMS, ¹⁵⁄₁₀ is ³⁄₂; therefore, the ratio of boys to girls is 3 to 2.

**reciprocal**  If you multiply one number by another and get 1 for an answer, the numbers being multiplied are reciprocals. The reciprocal of 2 is ½, because $2 \times \frac{1}{2} = 1$. To get the reciprocal of a FRACTION, you simply flip it over, switching the positions of the NUMERATOR and the DENOMINATOR. Thus, the reciprocal of ⅔ is ³⁄₂, because $\frac{2}{3} \times \frac{3}{2} = \frac{6}{6} = 1$. (A fraction whose NUMERATOR and DENOMINATOR are equal, such as ⁶⁄₆, will always equal 1. Such a fraction is its own reciprocal.)

**rectangle**  A rectangle is a PLANE (flat) figure with four straight sides that form four RIGHT

ANGLES. The sides opposite each other are PARALLEL and of equal LENGTH.

**remainder** The remainder is the number left over when one number is divided by another. For example, when you divide 9 by 2, you get a QUOTIENT of 4 with a remainder of 1.

**repeating decimal** A repeating decimal is a DECIMAL with a DIGIT or pattern of digits that repeats itself forever to INFINITY. The numbers 9.14141414 and 1.33333 are repeating decimals. The answers to some division problems are repeating decimals; for example, 28 divided by 3 gives an answer of 9.333333.

**rhombus** A rhombus is a PARALLELOGRAM that has four straight sides of the same LENGTH but no RIGHT ANGLES. A diamond shape is a rhombus.

**right angle** A right angle is an ANGLE that measures 90 DEGREES (90°) and is formed when two PERPENDICULAR lines meet.

**right triangle** A right triangle is a TRIANGLE in which two sides meet to form a RIGHT ANGLE.

**Roman numerals** Roman numerals are the numbers used by the ancient Romans, which resemble the letters of our alphabet. Some common Roman numerals are:

| | | |
|---|---|---|
| I = 1 | VI = 6 | XI = 11 |
| II = 2 | VII = 7 | L = 50 |
| III = 3 | VIII = 8 | C = 100 |
| IV = 4 | IX = 9 | D = 500 |
| V = 5 | X = 10 | M = 1,000 |

**rounding** Rounding is something you do to a number when it does not need to be exact. In many cases, an approximate number (one that is almost exact) is enough. For example, 68,823 people attended a football game. If you were talking to a friend, you would probably round the number up to the nearest thousand and say that about 69,000 people were at the game. Numbers with decimals are often rounded to the next highest whole number when the decimal is .5 or greater or to the same whole number when the decimal is less than .5. For example, 5.63 would be rounded to 6.00; 5.44 to 5.00. *See also* PLACE VALUE.

**scale** A scale is a RATIO that shows the size relationship between a diagram and the real thing it represents. For instance, on a map, the scale might be 1 inch = 10 miles. This means that 1 inch on the map represents 10 miles on the land.

**scalene triangle** A scalene triangle is a TRIANGLE that has no sides of the same LENGTH or ANGLES of equal measure.

**set** A set is a group of things with a common property and is indicated by BRACES: { }. For instance, a set of fruits is {oranges, pears, apples}. A set of odd numbers is {−3, −1, 1, 3}.

**solid** In geometry, a solid is a three-dimensional figure such as a CUBE, a CONE, or a PYRAMID. *Compare* PLANE.

**sphere** A sphere is a three-dimensional round figure, such as a basketball. Every point on a sphere is the same distance from its center.

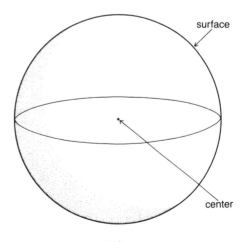

surface

center

**Sphere**

**square** In geometry, a square is a RECTAN-GLE with four straight sides of equal LENGTH. Each side meets with another side to form a RIGHT ANGLE. In arithmetic, to square a number is to multiply it by itself once. For example, 3 squared ($3^2$) is $3 \times 3$, which equals 9. The operation of squaring is indicated by using the EXPONENT 2, as in the expression $3^2$.

**square root** The square root of any number is the number that, when squared (multiplied by itself once), gives the original number as a product. The symbol for square root is $\sqrt{\ }$. The square root of 4 ($\sqrt{4}$) is 2 because 2 squared ($2^2$ or $2 \times 2$) equals 4. The square root of 9 ($\sqrt{9}$) is 3 because $3^2$ equals 9.

**subtraction** Subtraction is one of the four basic operations of ARITHMETIC (along with ADDITION, MULTIPLICATION, and DIVISION). It is the opposite of addition, because instead of adding one number to another, you take one number away from another. The symbol for subtraction is the minus sign: $-$. When you subtract one number from another you find the DIFFERENCE between them. The difference between 12 and 5 is 7; $12 - 5 = 7$.

**sum** A sum is the answer to an ADDITION problem. For example, 8 is the sum of 5 and 3 because $5 + 3 = 8$. *Compare* DIFFERENCE.

**surface area** The surface area of a figure is the measure of its surface expressed in square units, such as square inches or square miles. *See also* AREA.

**symmetry** If a figure can be divided into two parts that are mirror images of each other, the figure has symmetry or is symmetrical. For example, regular figures such as CIRCLES and SQUARES are symmetrical.

**trapezoid** A trapezoid is a PLANE (flat) figure with four straight sides. Only two of the sides are PARALLEL to each other.

**triangle** A triangle is a PLANE (flat) figure with three straight sides. *See also* EQUILAT-

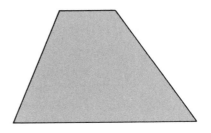

**Trapezoid**

ERAL TRIANGLE; ISOSCELES TIRANGLE; RIGHT TRIANGLE; SCALENE TRIANGLE.

**variable** A variable is a symbol whose value can change in a FORMULA or EQUATION. It is usually represented by a letter. For instance, the AREA of a SQUARE is the square of the LENGTH of one side. The formula is $a = s^2$ where $a$ is a variable that stands for area and $s$ is a variable that stands for the length of a side.

**vertical** A vertical line is straight up and down and is PERPENDICULAR to a HORIZONTAL line.

**volume** In geometry, volume is the measure of space occupied by a SOLID figure, such

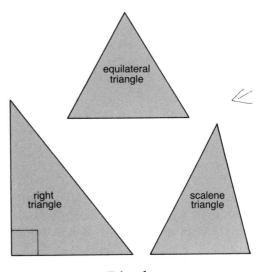

**Triangle**

as a CUBE. It is measured in units such as the cubic inch, which is the amount of space inside a cube with edges 1 inch long. Some common units of volume are:

cubic inch (cu in or in$^3$)
cubic foot (cu ft or ft$^3$) = 1,728 cubic inches
cubic yard (cu yd or yd$^3$) = 27 cubic feet

Some metric units of volume are:

cubic centimeter (cu cm or cm$^3$)
cubic meter (cu m or m$^3$) = 1 × 10$^6$ cubic centimeters or 1.3 cubic yards

The volume of a liquid is often measured in ounces:

fluid ounce (fl oz) = 1.8 cubic inches
pint (pt) = 16 fluid ounces
quart (qt) = 2 pints
gallon (gal) = 4 quarts

The most common metric liquid measurement is the liter (l); 1 liter is a little less than 1 quart. *See also* METRIC SYSTEM.

**weight** Weight is the measure of how heavy something is. Some common units of weight are:

ounce (oz) (the weight of 1 ounce of water by volume)
pound (lb) = 16 ounces
ton = 2,000 pounds

Some common metric units of weight are:

milligram (mg) = 0.001 gram
centigram (cg) = 0.01 gram (the weight of 1 cubic centimeter of water)
gram (g) = 100 centigrams or 0.035 ounces
kilogram (kg) = 1,000 grams or 2.2 pounds

**whole number** A whole number is an INTEGER.

**zero** Zero (0) is the number that, when added to another number, does not change it. Thus, 3 + 0 = 3. If any number is multiplied by 0, the answer is 0: 3 × 0 = 0.

# Physical Sciences

The basic ideas of chemistry, physics, and astronomy are presented here. In the next section, "Earth Sciences and Weather," important concepts from other physical sciences are introduced.

In modern science, the borderline between chemistry and physics has become fuzzy. *Chemistry* is basically the science of what things are made of, what identifies them, and how they change. *Physics* is basically the study of matter and motion. *Astronomy* uses both physics and chemistry to investigate the sun, moon, stars, and planets.

The physical sciences encompass the most enormous things that exist (stars and planets in space), but they also are concerned with the tiniest things—molecules, atoms, and parts of atoms, which are all too small to be seen with the naked eye. These sciences help us understand our place in the universe and how everything around us works. Every year scientists are finding out more about the world of the past and the world of the present.

---

**acid** In CHEMISTRY, an acid is the opposite of a BASE or ALKALI. When an acid and base come together, they counteract each other and make a SALT plus water. An acid tastes sour. Strong acids can be dangerous. Vinegar is a weak acid.

**alkali** (AL-kuh-leye) In CHEMISTRY, an alkali is a strong BASE, the opposite of an ACID. Strong alkalis can be dangerous. Ammonia is an alkali.

**alloy** (AL-oy) An alloy is a material made by mixing metals together. It is designed to be stronger or last longer than the individual metals. Bronze is an alloy usually made of copper and tin.

**aluminum** Aluminum is a lightweight silver metal that does not rust easily, like iron. Airplanes are often made of aluminum because it is both light and strong. Drinking cans, aluminum foil, and other household products are also made of aluminum.

**Andromeda galaxy** (an-DROM-uh-duh) The Andromeda galaxy is the GALAXY that is closest to the MILKY WAY. It was given this name because the stars of the CONSTELLATION Andromeda appear to surround it. The galaxy is about 2.2 million light years from EARTH and is visible to the naked eye.

**asteroid**   An asteroid is a very small PLANET that revolves around the SUN.

**astronomy**   Astronomy is the science of heavenly bodies, such as the SUN, the MOON, the STARS, and the PLANETS.

**atom**   An atom is the smallest particle of any ELEMENT that can still be recognized as that element. Atoms combine to form MOLE-CULES. *See also* ELECTRON; NEUTRON; NU-CLEUS; PROTON; QUARK.

**atomic number**   The atomic number of an ELEMENT is the number of PROTONS that are normally found in an ATOM of that element. The higher the number, the heavier the atom is.

**base**   In CHEMISTRY, a base is the opposite of an ACID. When an acid and a base come together, they react to produce a SALT plus water. If you mix vinegar (an acid) with bicarbonate of soda (a base), you will get a salt that is different from table salt. *See also* AL-KALI.

**The Big Bang Theory**   The Big Bang Theory is the idea that the UNIVERSE was created billions of years ago in a single explosion that threw MATTER in all directions. This could explain why distant GALAXIES appear to be moving away from EARTH. The Big Bang Theory is widely accepted but has yet to be proven.

**Big Dipper**   The Big Dipper is a CONSTELLA-TION (group of STARS) that people have observed since ancient times. Its stars make a pattern in the sky that resembles a cup with a long handle for dipping. The direction north can be determined almost exactly by the NORTH STAR, which can be found by following the pointer stars of the Big Dipper, the two stars on the far end of the bowl of the dipper.

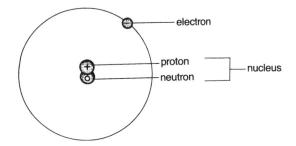

**Atom.** A diagram of a hydrogen atom.

**black hole**   A black hole is a massive celestial object having such a strong gravitational pull that nothing can escape it, not even LIGHT.

**boiling point**   The boiling point is the TEM-PERATURE at which something boils, or begins to change from a LIQUID to a GAS. Every liquid has a definite boiling point. *See also* CONDENSATION POINT.

**buoyancy**   Buoyancy is the tendency of something to float on a FLUID because of its power to exert an upward force on objects. A balloon floats on air, which is a fluid. A cork has buoyancy when it is resting on water. A buoy is a float attached by a long line to the bottom of a lake or ocean; it helps sailors know where they are.

**carbon**   Carbon is a chemical ELEMENT used by all living things to make their CELLS.

**carbon dioxide**   Carbon dioxide is a colorless, odorless gas that does not burn. Each molecule of carbon dioxide is composed of two atoms of OXYGEN and one atom of CAR-BON and is symbolically represented by $CO_2$. Carbon dioxide is present in the ATMO-SPHERE, formed when any carbon-containing fuel is burned, and exhaled from an animal's lungs during RESPIRATION. It is used by plants during PHOTOSYNTHESIS.

**catalyst** (KAT-uh-list)   In CHEMISTRY, a catalyst is a substance that helps a chemical re-

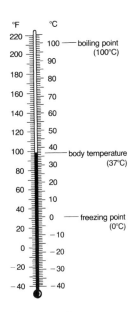

**Celsius.** Celsius readings are on the right; Fahrenheit readings are on the left.

action to occur; it is usually not itself changed by the reaction.

**Celsius scale** (SEL-see-uhs) The Celsius scale is used to measure TEMPERATURE in scientific work and in most countries except the United States. On the Celsius scale, water freezes at 0 degrees (0°C) and boils at 100 degrees (100°C). An example of a temperature below the freezing point is −8°C. *See also* CENTIGRADE. *Compare* FAHRENHEIT SCALE.

**centigrade** The centigrade TEMPERATURE scale is the CELSIUS SCALE. Centigrade, from the Latin word for one hundred (*centum*), means "divided into one hundred parts." The Celsius scale divides the range of temperature between water's freezing and boiling points into 100 degrees.

**centrifugal force** (sen-TRIF-uh-guhl) Centrifugal force causes an object going around in a circle to move away from the center. If you whirl a bucket of water in a circle, cen-

trifugal force will tend to keep the water in the bucket.

**chain reaction** A chain reaction is a process that keeps going by itself once it is started. A bad forest fire is a chain reaction. After the fire starts, the flames from one tree set the next tree on fire, and so on, until something stops it. The term also refers to a nuclear chain reaction, when the NUCLEUS of an ATOM splits and releases high-energy particles. These particles split the centers of other atoms, which then split others as the reaction keeps going. Nuclear chain reactions release tremendous amounts of ENERGY.

**change of phase** MATTER can exist as a SOLID, a LIQUID, or a GAS. When something changes from one of these forms (or phases) to another, it goes through a change of phase. For instance, when water freezes, it goes through a change of phase from a LIQUID to a SOLID.

**chemical energy** Chemical energy is the energy stored in a chemical substance. Sometimes this energy is released in a chemical reaction, which occurs when one substance is changed into another. Fire is one kind of chemical reaction.

**chemistry** Chemistry is the study of MATTER, especially at the level of ATOMS and MOLECULES.

**combustion** Combustion means burning. In CHEMISTRY, things that combust take on OXYGEN.

**comet** A comet is an object that usually circles the SUN in an extremely long ORBIT. It can be seen from EARTH only when its orbit takes it close to the sun. When material is boiled off from the sun's heat, a tail forms on the comet.

**compound** A compound is a substance whose MOLECULES have two or more ELEMENTS.

**condensation point**  The condensation point is the TEMPERATURE at which a GAS condenses to a LIQUID. Every substance has a definite condensation point. *See also* BOILING POINT.

**conduction**  Conduction is the spread of ENERGY through a medium without any change to that medium. For example, a steel pot is a good medium for the conduction of heat energy. Heat can spread through a steel pot without changing the pot itself.

**constellation**  A constellation is an easily recognized group of STARS in the sky that form a picture. These patterns have been observed since ancient times and have been named for the mythical figures and objects they resemble. For instance, the constellation Leo (Latin for "lion") looks somewhat like a lion.

**Copernicus, Nicolaus**  Nicolaus Copernicus was a Polish astronomer of the late 1400s and early 1500s who argued that the EARTH and all other PLANETS revolve around the SUN. *See also* SOLAR SYSTEM.

**crystal**  A crystal is a SOLID in which the ATOMS or MOLECULES are arranged in a tight, orderly pattern. Snowflakes and grains of salt are crystals.

**Curie, Marie**  Marie Curie was a French chemist of the late 1800s and early 1900s. She was born in Poland and, with her husband, Pierre Curie, discovered the naturally occurring radioactive ELEMENT radium. She was the first major female scientist of modern times. *See also* RADIOACTIVITY.

**density**  Density is the relative heaviness of objects, or put another way, the measure of the amount of MASS for each unit of VOLUME of a substance.

**distillation**  Distillation is the process of boiling a LIQUID and condensing the vapor. Drinking water and salt can be produced from sea water by distillation.

Marie Curie

**Earth or the earth**  Earth is the planet on which we live. It orbits the SUN, making one revolution (complete turn) per year. It also rotates (turns on its own axis), making one rotation per day. Earth is one of nine PLANETS in our SOLAR SYSTEM. *See also* EARTH *under "Earth Sciences and Weather."*

**eclipse** (i-KLIPS)  An eclipse occurs when one heavenly body blocks light traveling from the SUN to another heavenly body. An eclipse of the sun occurs when the MOON passes between the sun and the EARTH (so that the sun cannot be seen or can be seen only in part). An eclipse of the moon occurs when the earth passes directly between the sun and the moon (so that a shadow moves across the surface of the moon).

**Einstein, Albert** (EYEN-steyen)  Albert Einstein was a brilliant scientist of the early 1900s who won the NOBEL PRIZE in physics. His ideas about converting mass to ENERGY proved correct when ATOMS were first split. The explosive energy of splitting atoms is the power in the ATOMIC BOMB. (*See* image, next page.)

**electron**  An electron is a very small, light particle that revolves around the NUCLEUS of

**Albert Einstein.** Writing out the equation for the density of the Milky Way in 1931.

an ATOM. Electrons have a negative electric charge. When free electrons flow through a wire or other CONDUCTOR, ELECTRICITY results.

**element**  An element is a substance that cannot be broken down into simpler substances. The ATOMS of each element have a unique structure. Some common elements are aluminum, hydrogen, iodine, iron, mercury, nitrogen, oxygen, sodium, and zinc. *See also* PERIODIC TABLE.

**energy**  Energy is the ability to do WORK. To a scientist, work is done when a FORCE is used to move an object. For example, gasoline is a source of energy. When it is burned in a car engine and the car moves, the energy has been turned into work.

**equilibrium** (EE-kwuh-LIB-REE-uhm) Equilibrium means balance. In chemical reac-

tions, an equilibrium is reached when no further measurable change occurs.

**equinox**  An equinox is a time when day and night are of equal length. There are two equinoxes in a year. At an equinox, the SUN is directly over EARTH'S EQUATOR. The vernal, or spring, equinox occurs about March 22. The autumnal, or fall, equinox occurs about September 21.

**evaporation**  Evaporation occurs when a LIQUID turns into a GAS, or evaporates.

**experiment**  In science, an experiment is a strict, highly controlled test of an idea. Experiments are often carried out in laboratories.

**extraterrestrial**  (ek-struh-tuh-RES-tree-uhl) An extraterrestrial object is one that comes from outer space. Meteorites are one type of extraterrestrial object.

**Fahrenheit scale** (FAIR-uhn-heyet) Fahrenheit is the TEMPERATURE scale most commonly used in the United States. In the Fahrenheit scale, water freezes at 32 degrees (32°F) and boils at 212 degrees (212°F). The normal temperature of the human body is 98.6°F. *Compare* CELSIUS SCALE; CENTIGRADE.

**fluid**  A fluid is something that flows; it includes both LIQUIDS and GASES.

**force**  A force is a push or a pull on something. *See also* ENERGY; GRAVITY; WORK.

**freezing point**  The freezing point is the TEMPERATURE at which something freezes, or changes from a LIQUID to a SOLID. Every substance has a definite freezing point. *Compare* MELTING POINT.

**friction**  Friction is the FORCE that slows down a moving object when it rubs against a surface. If you shove a pencil or a shoe across the floor, friction will keep it from going very far. Carpeting produces more friction than a bare floor.

**Galaxy.** The Whirlpool Galaxy.

**galaxy**   A galaxy is an enormous group of STARS. The galaxy that contains our SUN is called the MILKY WAY. The universe contains billions of galaxies.

**Galileo**   (gal-uh-LEE-oh,   gal-uh-LA Y-oh) Galileo Galilei was an Italian scientist of the early 1600s. He improved the original TELESCOPES and was one of the first to use them for ASTRONOMY. He saw the moons of JUPITER and the mountains on the moon. He also believed, like COPERNICUS, that EARTH revolves around the SUN.

**gas**   Matter can exist as a SOLID, a LIQUID, or a gas. A gas has no particular shape and can expand indefinitely, and its molecules are farther apart than those of a liquid or a solid. Air and steam are both gases.

**gravity**   Gravity is the force that pulls objects toward each other. The EARTH'S gravity pulls everything on earth toward the center of the earth. Thus, objects fall toward the ground. The SUN'S gravity keeps the PLANETS in their ORBITS. Gravity was first explained by ISAAC NEWTON.

**Halley's comet**   (HAL-ee)   Halley's comet is the most famous COMET in the study of astronomy. It appears approximately every 76 years and is named after Edmond Halley, a British astronomer of the late 1600s and early 1700s who first predicted the comet's regular reappearance.

**helium**   Helium is a chemical ELEMENT that is usually found in the form of a GAS. Because helium is lighter than air, it is sometimes used to fill balloons.

**H₂O**   $H_2O$ is the scientific symbol for a water MOLECULE. Two ATOMS of hydrogen (H) and one atom of oxygen (O) join to form a molecule of water.

**hydrocarbons**   ORGANIC compounds that contain only CARBON and HYDROGEN. Many hydrocarbons, such as gasoline and methane, are used as fuels.

**hydrogen**   Hydrogen is the lightest ELEMENT. Each MOLECULE of water is composed of two ATOMS of hydrogen and one atom of OXYGEN. The symbol for the water molecule is $H_2O$. There are many more hydrogen atoms than any other kind in the UNIVERSE.

**inertia**   (i-NUR-shuh)   Inertia is a resistance to change in motion: that is, the tendency of an object to keep moving in the same path or to stay still if it is not moving.

**infrared radiation**   (in-fruh-RED)   Infrared radiation is invisible light at the opposite end of the SPECTRUM from ULTRAVIOLET RADIATION. It is felt as heat, and much of the heat from the SUN comes from its infrared light.

**inorganic**   *Inorganic* is a descriptive term for compounds that generally do not contain CARBON and that are usually not found in living things. *Compare* ORGANIC.

**ions**   (EYE-uhn)   An ion is an ATOM or a group of atoms that has an electrical charge. Positive ions lack one or more ELECTRONS, while negative ions have a surplus of electrons.

**Jupiter**   Jupiter is the largest PLANET in the SOLAR SYSTEM and the fifth major planet from the SUN. It is composed mostly of GASES.

**lens** A lens is a piece of curved glass or plastic that can bend light rays. Lenses are used in cameras, projectors, eyeglasses, TELESCOPES, and MICROSCOPES.

**light** Light is a form of ENERGY that is visible to the human eye. It is made up of waves, called electromagnetic waves, that travel at about 186,282 miles per second. *See also* SPECTRUM.

**light year** A light year is the distance traveled by light in a year, about six trillion miles. Distances between objects in outer space are often measured in light years. *See also* SPEED OF LIGHT.

**liquid** MATTER can exist as a SOLID, a GAS, or a liquid. In a liquid, the molecules are close together but loosely connected, so that they move around. A liquid takes the shape of its container. Water and milk are both liquids.

**litmus** (LIT-muhs) In CHEMISTRY, litmus is a special kind of powder that is used to tell whether a SOLUTION is an ACID or a BASE. Litmus paper is paper that has been treated with litmus powder. Acids turn blue litmus paper red; bases turn red litmus paper blue.

**magnet** A magnet is a device, usually made of iron, that creates a magnetic field. When a wire moves through a magnetic field, it makes ELECTRICITY. When electricity passes through a wire, it makes a magnetic field. These facts are the basis of GENERATORS. Magnets have positive and negative poles. Opposite poles attract each other; like poles repel each other.

**Mars** Mars is the fourth major planet from the SUN. Because it appears to be red, it is sometimes called the red planet. Mars has been, and continues to be, the focus of space research by NASA.

**mass** The mass of a substance is the amount of MATTER contained in a physical body. Mass is different from WEIGHT because

it remains the same regardless of the force of gravity.

**matter** Matter is anything taking up space that you can see, hear, feel, touch, or taste. Air, stone, water, wood, skin, and the EARTH itself are all examples of matter.

**melting point** The melting point is the TEMPERATURE at which something melts, or changes from a SOLID to a LIQUID. Every substance has a definite melting point. *Compare* FREEZING POINT.

**Mercury** Mercury is the PLANET in our SOLAR SYSTEM closest to the SUN. Mercury is also a silvery metal that is LIQUID at room temperature; it is used in thermometers to measure the body TEMPERATURE of a person.

**meteor** (MEE-tee-uhr) A meteor is a chunk of stone or metal that enters the EARTH'S ATMOSPHERE from outer space. When a meteor plows through the atmosphere, it burns up, making a streak of light across the sky, often called a "falling star" or a "shooting star."

**meteorite** A METEOR that falls to earth is called a meteorite.

**Milky Way** The Milky Way is the GALAXY that contains our SOLAR SYSTEM.

**Mitchell, Maria** Maria Mitchell was an American astronomer and educator who lived in the mid-1800s. She is known for her

**Mars.** Photograph of the surface of the planet.

study of SUNSPOTS and for her discovery of a COMET, which now bears her name.

**molecule** (MOL-uh-kyoohl)  A molecule is a tiny structure that is made up of two or more ATOMS.

**moon**  A moon is a natural SATELLITE of a planet, like EARTH. The earth's moon revolves around the earth as the earth revolves around the SUN. It takes one month for the moon to revolve around Earth. Once a month the whole moon is visible as a round ball. At other times, only part of the moon is visible. It is described as a "half moon" when it looks like a disk sliced in half. It is described as a "crescent moon" when only its curved edge is visible. The dark patches on the moon's surface are craters, or large pits. In 1969, NEIL ARMSTRONG became the first person to walk on the moon.

**Neptune**  Neptune is the eighth PLANET from the SUN in the SOLAR SYSTEM.

**neutron** (NOO-tron)  A neutron is an electrically neutral subatomic particle of MATTER that is one of the building blocks of the NUCLEUS, or center, of an ATOM. It is more than a thousand times heavier than an ELECTRON.

**neutron star**  A neutron star is a celestial body made up almost entirely of an extremely dense mass of NEUTRONS. Neutron stars have a powerful gravitational pull.

**Newton, Isaac**  Sir Isaac Newton was a great English scientist and mathematician of the 1600s and 1700s. He is said to have discovered GRAVITY when he saw an apple fall from a tree.

**nitrogen**  Nitrogen is a chemical ELEMENT that is abundant in the earth's ATMOSPHERE. It is a necessary part of all plant and animal TISSUES.

**North Star** (Polaris)  The North Star is found in the pattern of stars called the Little Dipper. You can find it by following the pointer stars in the BIG DIPPER. The North Star shines almost directly above the NORTH POLE and therefore always seems to stand very close to true north in the NORTHERN HEMISPHERE. The other stars seem to turn around the North Star because the EARTH spins on an AXIS that runs through the North and South Poles.

**nucleus** (NOO-klee-uhs)  The nucleus of an ATOM is the part in the center that contains most of its MASS. The ELECTRONS of the atom revolve around this nucleus.

**orbit**  To orbit something means to go around it. EARTH orbits the SUN, and the MOON orbits Earth. The force of GRAVITY keeps Earth and the moon in their orbits.

**organic**  Organic is a descriptive term for COMPOUNDS that are often found in living things. ORGANIC molecules are composed of atoms of CARBON to which atoms of HYDROGEN, NITROGEN, and OXYGEN may be attached. *Compare* INORGANIC.

**oxidation**  (OK-si-DAY-shuhn)  Oxidation occurs when a substance combines with OXYGEN. The most familiar form of oxidation is rust, which is a COMPOUND of oxygen and iron. When foods such as apples or potatoes turn brown on exposure to the air, they have undergone oxidation.

**oxygen**  Oxygen is an ELEMENT that makes up an important part of the air we breathe. Plants, animals, and most other organisms depend on oxygen to live.

**periodic table**  The periodic table is a chart of all the known ELEMENTS. The horizontal rows on the chart show the elements in order of increasing ATOMIC NUMBER. The vertical rows group elements that share certain chemical properties.

**phases of matter**  MATTER can exist as a SOLID, a LIQUID, or a GAS at different TEMPERATURES and under different pressures. For example, water can be a liquid, a solid (ice), or a gas (steam or water vapor). The different forms of matter are called phases. See also CHANGE OF PHASE.

**physics** Physics is the science that studies MATTER and motion and the way they interact.

**planet** A planet is a heavenly body that orbits a STAR. The planets in our SOLAR SYSTEM orbit the star we call the SUN. Unlike stars, planets do not give off light. EARTH is a planet.

**Pluto** Pluto is the PLANET in our SOLAR SYSTEM whose orbit takes it farthest from the SUN. It was discovered in 1930.

**Polaris** *See* NORTH STAR.

**proton** (PROH-ton) A proton is an elementary particle that is found in the NUCLEUS of an ATOM. It has a positive electric charge. Protons are about a thousand times heavier than ELECTRONS, and with NEUTRONS, they make up most of an atom's mass.

**quarks** (KWAHRKS) Quarks are the particles that make up the PROTONS and NEUTRONS in the NUCLEUS of an ATOM. They are the most basic known building blocks of all MATTER.

**quasars** (kway-zahrz) Quasars are the most distant celestial objects that can be seen from EARTH.

**radiation** Radiation is the general name for ENERGY that is sent out in particles or waves. It includes various kinds of light, including kinds that cannot be seen, such as INFRARED, ULTRAVIOLET, and X-RAYS.

**radioactivity** Radioactivity is a property of certain substances that causes them to decay naturally, or change, over time. As they decay, they release ENERGY. Uranium and plutonium are radioactive substances.

**reflection** Reflection occurs when LIGHT bounces off a surface. A mirror is a good reflector of light.

**refraction** Refraction occurs when LIGHT bends as it passes through a clear substance like air or water. The denser the substance, the more the light bends.

**salt** In CHEMISTRY, a salt is a COMPOUND that is produced by the reaction between an ACID and a BASE. The chemical name of table salt is sodium chloride.

**satellite** In ASTRONOMY, a body that orbits a larger body is called a satellite. EARTH's natural satellite is the MOON. There are also many artificial satellites orbiting Earth. They transmit television signals, gather information about space, survey military installations, and help predict the weather.

**Saturn** Saturn is the second-largest major PLANET, sixth from the SUN, in our SOLAR SYSTEM. It is distinguished by the colored rings that surround it. These rings are huge bands of icy particles in ORBIT around the planet.

**scientific method** Scientists have developed certain special research procedures. Taken together, they are called the scientific method. One important part of the scientific

**Satellite.** The Hubble telescope in orbit.

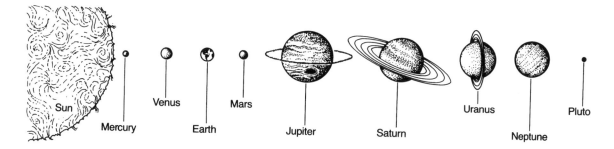

**Solar system.** The planets are shown in their relative sizes and distances from the sun.

method is the rigorous testing of ideas by EX-PERIMENTS. An untested idea is not considered scientifically sound.

**solar system**  The solar system is made up of the SUN and the nine PLANETS that revolve around it: MERCURY, VENUS, EARTH, MARS, JUPITER, SATURN, URANUS, NEPTUNE, and PLUTO. The solar system also includes the planets' MOONS or SATELLITES and objects such as ASTEROIDS and COMETS. *Solar* means "of the sun."

**solid**  MATTER can exist as a solid, a GAS, or a LIQUID. In a solid, MOLECULES are locked together. Unlike a gas or a liquid, a solid has a fixed size and shape. A rock, an ice cube, and a piece of cloth are all solids.

**solution**  In CHEMISTRY, a solution is a uniform mixture, usually a LIQUID. If you dissolve salt in water, you will get a salt solution.

**spectrum**  The visible spectrum consists of the different colors of LIGHT, from red to violet. A RAINBOW is a visible spectrum. The entire spectrum consists of radio waves, microwaves, infrared light, visible light, ultraviolet light, x-rays, gamma rays, and cosmic rays. *See also* INFRARED RADIATION; ULTRAVIOLET RADIATION.

**speed of light**  Light travels at about 186,262 miles per second when there is nothing to slow it down. Light from the SUN takes about eight minutes to reach EARTH; light from the MOON takes about a second and a half to reach Earth.

**star**  A star is a heavenly body that gives off LIGHT, such as the SUN. The sun looks bigger than other stars only because it is much closer to the EARTH. At night, many other stars are visible as tiny points of light. *See also* CONSTELLATION; SUPERNOVA; WHITE DWARF.

**sun**  The sun is the STAR at the center of the SOLAR SYSTEM. It is an enormous ball of burning gases, about 4.5 billion years old, thousands of times the size of EARTH. The nine PLANETS of the system, including Earth, revolve around the sun. All life on Earth depends on light from the sun.

**sunspot**  A sunspot is a dark spot that appears on the surface of the SUN due to magnetic storms. Sunspots can cause disturbances in EARTH's atmosphere, interfering with radio and television communication.

**supernova** (sooh-puhr-NOH-vuh)  A supernova is a large, dying STAR that suddenly explodes. When it does so, it becomes extremely bright.

**telescope**  A telescope is an instrument that can be used to see objects that are very far away because it makes them appear larger. (In Greek, *tele* means "far away," as in *telephone* and *television*.) Telescopes are used to

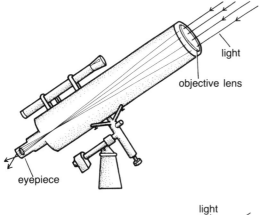

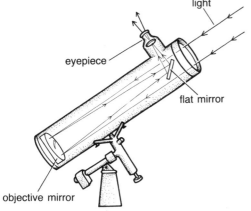

Telescope. Refracting telescope (top) and reflecting telescope (bottom).

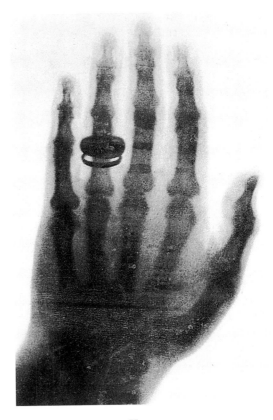

**X-ray**

study the STARS and the PLANETS. *Compare* MICROSCOPE *under "Technology."*

**ultraviolet radiation** Ultraviolet radiation is the invisible LIGHT beyond violet in the light SPECTRUM. Ultraviolet rays from the SUN can cause sunburn and eye damage.

**universe** The universe is the sum of all MATTER and ENERGY, including EARTH and the stars, galaxies, and other matter in outer space.

**Uranus** (YOOR-uh-ness, yoo-RAY-ness) Uranus is the seventh major PLANET from the SUN in the SOLAR SYSTEM. It was the first planet discovered in modern times (1781).

**vacuum** A vacuum is space with no MATTER or air in it. You can make a vacuum by pumping the air out of an airtight container.

**Venus** Venus is the PLANET in the SOLAR SYSTEM that is closest to EARTH. Venus is the second major planet from the SUN.

**watt** A watt is the basic unit of power. Light bulbs are rated in watts according to the amount of ELECTRICITY they use. A 100-watt bulb uses more electricity (and hence costs more to use) than a 40-watt bulb.

**white dwarf** A white dwarf is what a STAR like our SUN turns into at the end of its life cycle, when it has used up its fuel. A white dwarf collapses upon itself and becomes extremely dense (*see* DENSITY).

**x-rays** X-rays are a penetrating kind of LIGHT with extremely short wavelengths that can pass through solid objects. X-rays are at the very far end of the SPECTRUM, beyond ultraviolet light. *See also* X-RAY *under "Medicine and the Human Body."*

# Earth Sciences and Weather

Many kinds of scientists study the earth and its weather. Those who study the earth's history and structure are called *geologists*. They examine fossils, rocks, and minerals. Other scientists, called *meteorologists*, study the weather. They examine the causes of weather conditions and how weather can be predicted. Other earth sciences include *oceanography*, which is concerned with water and the oceans, and *geography*, which studies the surface of the earth.

**acid rain**    Acid rain is rain or other PRECIPITATION that contains ACIDS that form in the ATMOSPHERE when coal, gasoline, or oil is burned in automobiles, factories, and utilities. Acid rain is a form of AIR POLLUTION that damages trees, plants, and soil and pollutes rivers and lakes, killing fish and other aquatic life.

**aftershock**    An aftershock is a less powerful quake that occurs after an EARTHQUAKE.

**air pollution**    Air pollution is caused when harmful gases and particles are released into the air, making it so polluted that it threatens people's health. Exhaust fumes from cars and trucks and smoke from FACTORIES, power plants, and incinerators that burn trash are major causes of air pollution. *See also* POLLUTION; SMOG.

**aquifer**    An aquifer is an underground layer of sand, gravel, or spongy rock that collects large amounts of water and through which water flows easily.

**atmosphere**    The atmosphere is the layer of GAS that surrounds a PLANET. The EARTH'S atmosphere is made up of about 80% NITROGEN and 20% OXYGEN, with small amounts of other gases.

**atmospheric pressure**    Atmospheric pressure is the weight of the air pressing against a surface. Atmospheric pressure changes slightly from day to day. It also decreases as elevation increases.

**axis**    The EARTH'S axis is the imaginary line around which the earth spins. It lies between the NORTH and SOUTH POLES and goes through the center of the earth.

**axis of rotation**    The axis of rotation is the imaginary straight line through an object, such as the EARTH, around which that object seems to rotate.

**barometer**    A barometer is a device for measuring ATMOSPHERIC PRESSURE.

**Carson, Rachel**    Rachel Carson was an American scientist of the twentieth century who wrote a number of books, including *Silent Spring*, about the dangers of POLLUTION and artificial substances to the natural environment.

**Cirrus clouds**

**cave**  A cave is a naturally formed hollow or passage under the earth or in the side of a hill or mountain with an opening to the surface. A very large cave is known as a cavern.

**cirrus clouds** (SIR-uhs)  Cirrus clouds are feathery, white clouds that float high in the sky, usually visible before a change in the WEATHER.

**climate**  The climate of a region is its weather pattern over a long period: its heat and cold, moisture and dryness, clearness and cloudiness, and wind and calm. Regions near the EQUATOR tend to have hot climates; those near the POLES, cool ones.

**clouds**  Clouds are masses of condensed water or ice particles floating in the air. Four types of clouds are CIRRUS, CUMULUS, STRATUS, and THUNDERHEADS.

**coal**  Coal is a black or brown rock found in the ground consisting largely of CARBON. It can be dug up, or mined, and used as FUEL. Coal is formed when layers of earth build up for millions of years over the remains of plants and animals. *See also* FOSSIL FUELS.

**cold front**  A front is a place in the air where two very large bodies of air meet. A cold front is the place where cold air pushes out warm air. *Compare* WARM FRONT.

**conservation**  Conservation is the preservation or protection of the EARTH'S NATURAL RESOURCES. A person who believes in or works for conservation is a conservationist.

**continent**  A continent is a huge land mass. The EARTH has seven continents: AFRICA, ANTARCTICA, ASIA, AUSTRALIA, EUROPE, NORTH AMERICA, and SOUTH AMERICA.

**continental drift**  The term *continental drift* describes the fact that the CONTINENTS move, very slowly, across EARTH'S surface.

**continental shelf**  A continental shelf is the area along the coastline of a CONTINENT where the OCEAN is only a few hundred feet deep. The continental shelves are often rich in MINERAL resources and marine life.

**coral reef**  A coral reef, created by the skeletal deposits of corals, is found at or near the

**Coral reef**

surface of tropical waters. A coral is a kind of slow-growing INVERTEBRATE animal that does not move, but instead attaches itself to the OCEAN floor. Coral reefs provide food and shelter for a variety of sea life. They are some of the world's most diverse ECOSYSTEMS. The largest coral reef is the Great Barrier Reef of Australia.

**core** The core is the center of the EARTH and consists of hot metals, such as iron and nickel.

**crust** The crust is the outer layer of the EARTH and is made chiefly of rock. It includes the CONTINENTS and the OCEAN bottom.

**cumulonimbus clouds** *See* THUNDERHEADS.

**cumulus clouds** (KYOOH-myuh-luhs) Cumulus clouds are large, white, fluffy clouds that begin low in the sky and rise up very high.

**cyclone** A cyclone is a storm or winds moving around a calm central area of low ATMOSPHERIC PRESSURE. In the SOUTHERN HEMISPHERE, the winds of a cyclone rotate in a clockwise direction, while in the NORTHERN HEMISPHERE these winds rotate in a counterclockwise direction.

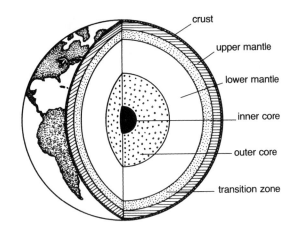

**Earth.** A cutaway view showing the earth's layers.

**Cumulus clouds**

**delta** A delta is an area of fertile land that forms at the mouth of a river from soil that has been washed away from other regions and deposited at the mouth. It is called a delta because it resembles the triangular shape of the Greek letter *delta*.

**desert** A desert is a dry region that is often covered by sand and that has few, if any, plants.

**dew** Dew is small water drops that form on cool surfaces when WATER VAPOR in the air is cooled to its CONDENSATION POINT.

**earth** The earth is the PLANET on which we live and is the third planet from the SUN. It is a large ball made up of several layers of rock and minerals. The outer layer is called the CRUST. Beneath it is the MANTLE, which is a thick layer of rock. Below it is the CORE, or center of the earth, which is made of hot metal. Almost three-fourths of the earth's surface is covered by water. Rock and soil cover the rest. A layer of air called the ATMOSPHERE surrounds the earth.

**earthquake** An earthquake makes the ground move or shake. It is caused by the movement of PLATES, which are vast, rigid masses of rock underneath the EARTH's surface. *See also* AFTERSHOCK; EPICENTER; FAULT; RICHTER SCALE.

**ecosystem**   An ecosystem is a collection of plants, animals, and the ENVIRONMENT in which they live.

**El Niño** (NEEN-yoh)   El Niño is a warming of surface water in the eastern and central PACIFIC OCEAN. It occurs when cold water does not rise to the surface. An El Niño usually happens every four to twelve years. It causes unusual weather, such as heavy rains in western SOUTH AMERICA and drought in eastern AUSTRALIA and INDONESIA.

**environment**   The environment is the set of external conditions that affect the internal growth and development of organisms. Weather and living space, other organisms, and food, along with their complex interactions, make up the environment. People who work to preserve clean and healthy conditions in the environment are called environmentalists. *See also* CONSERVATION; POLLUTION.

**epicenter**   An epicenter is the location on the EARTH's surface directly above the point underground where an EARTHQUAKE begins. This underground point of origin is called the focus.

**equator**   The equator is the imaginary line that circles the earth halfway between the NORTH and SOUTH POLES. This line divides the earth into the NORTHERN and SOUTHERN HEMISPHERES.

**erosion**   Erosion occurs when soil and rocks are worn down and moved around by water, wind, or GLACIERS. Gullies created by heavy rain are a common example of erosion.

**fault**   A fault is a crack in the EARTH's surface, usually just below the CRUST. Faults occur where two PLATES meet and grind against each other. EARTHQUAKES occur along fault lines when the plates move, causing the soil and rocks above the fault to shift.

**Fossils.** A fossil of a young dinosaur.

**fossil fuels**   The fossil fuels coal, oil, and natural gas are created over millions of years from the remains of animals and plants.

**fossils**   Fossils are formed from the remains of prehistoric animals and plants and are preserved in rock or other materials. Many prehistoric animals and plants are now extinct; fossils are the only traces we have of these species of animals and plants.

**geology**   Geology is the study of how the EARTH is put together and what it is made of. Geologists study surface rocks and minerals as well as the layers underneath the earth's surface. Geologists learn, among other things, how mountains are formed and what causes EARTHQUAKES.

**geyser**   A geyser is a hot spring that blasts water and steam into the air, like a fountain. Some geysers erupt every few minutes, while others may not erupt for years.

**glacier**   Glaciers are large sheets of ice that do not melt. They move like very slow rivers pulled by their own weight. Many valleys on our continent were carved out by glaciers long ago, when the climate was colder.

**global warming**   Global warming is the idea that EARTH's temperature is increasing due to the GREENHOUSE EFFECT. Whether global warming is actually happening is a source of scientific debate.

**grassland** A grassland is an area, such as a prairie or meadow, that is covered with grass or similar plants. Grasslands are often areas where food can be grown easily.

**greenhouse effect** The greenhouse effect is the heating of the ATMOSPHERE due to the presence of CARBON DIOXIDE and other GASES. Without these gases, heat from the SUN would return to space. With these gases, heat from the sun is trapped, and EARTH's ATMOSPHERE is warmed. This is similar to what happens in a greenhouse, where glass traps the heat from the sun and warms the air.

**groundwater** Groundwater is water that is soaked up by the soil and that slowly moves beneath the earth's surface. Groundwater fills the wells and springs that provide water to many communities.

**gulf** A gulf is a sea or ocean that is partially surrounded by land.

**Gulf Stream** The Gulf Stream is a warm current in the ATLANTIC OCEAN that is driven north along the coast of NORTH AMERICA by winds from the TROPICS. (A current is a flow of water in the ocean that moves in a definite direction in relation to the water around it.)

**hail** Hail is frozen rain in the form of small balls called hailstones. Sometimes hailstones become quite large, even as big as baseballs, and cause damage.

**hard water** Water that has MINERALS dissolved in it is called hard water. Soft water has few minerals in it. In the mountains, the water is soft because it has not run very far across the EARTH. Lower down, near sea level, the water tends to be hard because it has had a chance to dissolve minerals. Hard water does not make soapsuds easily.

**humidity**  *See* RELATIVE HUMIDITY.

**hurricane** A hurricane is a large and powerful storm originating in the TROPICS, with fast, circular winds and heavy rains. A hurricane that occurs in the western part of the PACIFIC OCEAN is called a typhoon. The calm center region of a hurricane is called the eye.

**ice age** An ice age is a period far back in the EARTH's history when most of the land was covered by GLACIERS. There have been several ice ages.

**iceberg** An iceberg is a large mass of ice in the ocean, a piece of a GLACIER that has broken off and floated out to sea. Most of the ice in an iceberg is under water, leaving only the "tip of the iceberg" visible. Sometimes we use this expression to mean that the most important part of something is hidden or not obvious.

**igneous rock** (IG-nee-uhs) Igneous rocks are made from very hot liquid MATTER that has cooled and hardened. Granite is an igneous rock.

**isthmus** (IS-muhs) An isthmus is a narrow strip of land that connects two larger land masses.

**jet stream** The jet stream is a strong, usually swift current of wind that most often blows from west to east at altitudes of 10 to 15 miles.

**lava** Lava is hot, melted rock that comes from a VOLCANO or a crack in the earth's surface. When cool, it forms an IGNEOUS rock that is also called lava.

**lightning** Lightning is electricity that is released from CLOUDS when a large amount of static ELECTRICITY has built up in them. It shoots from the clouds in bright, jagged streaks or in large flashes of light. Lightning causes THUNDER.

**magma** Magma is red-hot rock under the CRUST of the EARTH. When it erupts through

**Lightning**

the surface of the earth, it becomes more fluid and is called LAVA.

**mantle** The mantle is the layer of rock below the EARTH'S surface that surrounds the CORE, or center, of the earth. It is more than two thousand miles thick.

**Marianas Trench** (mair-ee-AN-uhs) The Marianas Trench is a deep valley in the floor of the PACIFIC OCEAN, near the PHILIPPINES. This trench is the deepest place on the EARTH'S surface.

**meridian** A meridian is an imaginary circle passing through any place on the EARTH'S surface and through the NORTH and SOUTH POLES.

**metamorphic rock** Metamorphic rock is made when one kind of rock is changed into another kind of rock exposure to extreme heat and pressure. For example, marble is a metamorphic rock that comes from limestone.

**meteorology** Meteorology is the study of WEATHER and CLIMATE. A meteorologist is someone who studies meteorology and attempts to predict the weather.

**mineral** Minerals are the various chemical COMPOUNDS that make up ROCKS. A mineral is pure and uniform, made of only one kind of material. Most rocks are made of several kinds of minerals.

**monsoon** A monsoon is a wind system that affects the weather in a large area. A monsoon that occurs every year in SOUTHEAST ASIA causes extremely heavy rains in spring and summer.

**mountain** A mountain is a raised portion of the EARTH'S surface, usually quite high and rocky, that forms when material is lifted or folded upward by movements beneath the earth's CRUST, such as when PLATES collide or volcanoes erupt.

**Muir, John** John Muir was an American naturalist of the 1800s and early 1900s who was born in SCOTLAND. He was an early crusader for CONSERVATION and the establishment of national parks and reservations.

**natural gas** Natural gas is a FUEL that is found under the ground. It can be burned to provide heat and energy. *See also* FOSSIL FUELS.

**natural resources** A natural resource is any material that can be taken from the EARTH and used. Trees, oil, and water are examples of natural resources. Some kinds of resources are nonrenewable; that is, they cannot be replaced once they are used up. Coal and oil are nonrenewable because they take millions of years to form. Water and cotton are renewable resources, since water can be collected or cleaned and used again and cotton can be planted and harvested each year.

**Nimbus clouds**

**nimbus clouds**   Nimbus clouds are the dark gray clouds that produce rain or snow. They are often called rain clouds.

**North Pole**   The North Pole is the northern end of the earth's AXIS OF ROTATION.

**Northern Hemisphere**   The Northern Hemisphere is the half of the earth that is north of the EQUATOR. CANADA, the United States, MEXICO, FRANCE, INDIA, EGYPT, and NIGERIA are some of the many nations that are part of this hemisphere.

**northern lights**   The northern lights are bright and colorful lights that appear to swirl and soar in the night sky. They occur when particles from the SUN meet ATOMS in the upper ATMOSPHERE near the NORTH POLE. The scientific name for the northern lights is *aurora borealis* (uh-RAWR-uh bawr-ee-AL-is).

**ocean**   The ocean is the mass of salt water that covers about 72 percent of the EARTH'S surface. Oceanic divisions are known by specific names such as the ATLANTIC OCEAN, the PACIFIC OCEAN, and the INDIAN OCEAN. *See also* SEA.

**oil**   Oil is a LIQUID FUEL that forms beneath the EARTH'S surface. It is used to make a number of products, including gasoline and asphalt. *See also* FOSSIL FUELS.

**ore**   Ore is a MINERAL that contains a commercially useful material, such as gold or uranium.

**ozone**   Ozone is a form of OXYGEN present in the ATMOSPHERE, especially after a thunderstorm. In the upper atmosphere, ozone acts as a screen, protecting living things from exposure to excessive amounts of ultraviolet radiation. A region of high ozone concentration, called the ozone layer, exists above the EARTH at altitudes between 10 and 15 miles. During the past decade or so, the destruction of atmospheric ozone by various chemical compounds has caused a thinning of this layer, particularly above the POLAR REGIONS, forming what is known as the ozone hole.

**paleontologist** (pay-lee-uhn-TOL-uh-jist)   A paleontologist is a scientist who studies ancient forms of life, especially as they appear in FOSSILS.

**peninsula**   A peninsula is a long section of land that extends into the water. In Latin it means "almost island."

**plate**   A plate is a vast area of rigid rock just below the EARTH'S surface. The CONTINENTS and some of the OCEAN's floor rest on plates, which are as large as or larger than continents.

**plateau** (pla-TOH)   A plateau is a flat area high above the surrounding land.

**polar regions**   The polar regions are the areas around the NORTH and SOUTH POLES. It stays cold all year in these areas.

**pole**   A pole is an imaginary point at each end of the EARTH'S AXIS. *See also* NORTH POLE; SOUTH POLE.

**pollution**   Pollution is caused when substances that are harmful to life are released into the air or water or onto the land. Pollution often hurts or kills fish and animals and can endanger people's health as well. *See also* AIR POLLUTION.

**precipitation** Precipitation is water that falls from the air as rain, sleet, or snow.

**prevailing westerlies** Prevailing westerlies are winds that blow west-to-east in the EARTH'S TEMPERATE ZONES.

**rain forest** *See* TROPICAL RAIN FOREST.

**rainbow** A rainbow is a curve of colored light in the sky caused by sunlight shining through droplets of water in the air. The droplets break up the sunlight into colored bands of violet, indigo, blue, green, yellow, orange, and red.

**recycling** Recycling is a process of treating discarded materials, such as newspapers or aluminum cans, in order to extract usable substances and create new materials or products.

**relative humidity** Relative humidity is the amount of water in the air compared to the amount of water the air can hold. If the air is holding all the water it possibly can, the relative humidity is 100%. If the air is holding only half the amount of water possible, the relative humidity is 50%.

**Richter scale** (RICK-tuhr) The Richter scale is used to measure the intensity of EARTHQUAKES. It shows how much ENERGY has been released by the quake.

**rock** A rock is a mass of mineral matter. The CRUST of the EARTH is composed of rock. *See also* IGNEOUS ROCK; METAMORPHIC ROCK; SEDIMENTARY ROCK.

**San Andreas Fault** (SAN an-DRAY-uhs) The San Andreas Fault is a long crack in the CRUST of the EARTH along the west coast of CALIFORNIA. Many EARTHQUAKES occur along this fault.

**sea** A sea is a very large body of salt water that is completely or partially surrounded by land. *Sea* is sometimes used to refer to the mass of salt water called OCEAN.

**sedimentary rock** (sed-uh-MEN-tuh-ree) Sedimentary rock is formed when layers of material from SEDIMENTATION are pressed together and hardened. Shale and limestone are examples of sedimentary rock. Sedimentary rocks often contain FOSSILS.

**sedimentation** Sedimentation occurs when particles of rock and other materials fall to the bottom of rivers, lakes, or oceans. The particles form layers of mud and debris called sediment.

**seismograph** (seyez-muh-graf) A seismograph is an instrument that detects EARTHQUAKES and measures their strength. *See also* RICHTER SCALE.

**smog** Smog (a combination of the words *smoke* and *fog*) is the dirty fog or haze that forms when AIR POLLUTION combines with moisture in the air.

**soil** Soil consists of small particles of MINERALS and organic debris mixed with water on the surface of the EARTH. It is formed by wind, water, freezing, thawing, the actions of plants and small animals, and the WEATHERING of rocks.

**solar energy** Solar energy is energy from the SUN that comes to EARTH in the form of light. The term can also be used to mean the process of taking energy from the sun to generate heat or electricity for human use.

**South Pole** The South Pole is the southern end of the earth's AXIS OF ROTATION.

**Southern Hemisphere** The Southern Hemisphere is the half of the EARTH that is south of the EQUATOR. CHILE, SOUTH AFRICA, AUSTRALIA, NEW ZEALAND, and ANGOLA are some of the nations that are part of this hemisphere.

**Stalactites and stalagmites.** The Luray Caverns, Virginia.

**stalactites** (stuh-LAK-teyets)  Stalactites are cylindrical or conical MINERAL deposits projecting downward from the roof of a CAVE and formed by dripping mineral water.

**stalagmites** (stuh-LAG-meyets)  Stalagmites are cylindrical or conical MINERAL deposits formed upward from the floor of a cave by mineral water that drips down from above.

**stratus clouds**  (STRAY-tuhs, STRAT-uhs) Stratus clouds hang low in the sky and look like a smooth layer of fog.

**temperate zone**  A temperate zone is an area of the EARTH where the weather changes from season to season. The temperate zones are between the POLAR REGIONS, where it stays cold all year, and the TROPICS, where it stays hot. Most of the United States is in a temperate zone.

**thunder**  Thunder is the sound caused when LIGHTNING heats the air. The heated air expands so rapidly that it pushes the air out in a shock wave, which we hear as thunder.

**thunderheads**  Thunderheads are dense clouds that rise high into the sky in huge columns. They often produce thunderstorms, hailstorms, rain, or snow. They are sometimes called thunderstorm clouds, but their technical name is cumulonimbus clouds.

**tidal wave**  A tidal wave is an unusually large, high movement of water onto a seashore. It is often caused by a large storm and can be very destructive.

**tides**  Tides are regular changes in the height of the OCEAN: two high tides and two low tides occur each day in most parts of the world. They are caused primarily by the force of the MOON'S GRAVITY on the water, but the SUN and other factors also affect them.

**topographic map**  A topographic map shows an area's surface features, such as its rivers, mountains, and valleys.

**topsoil**  Topsoil is the thin layer of soil containing ORGANIC matter and nutrients where plants get most of their food. EROSION can destroy valuable farmland when topsoil is washed away.

**tornado**  A tornado is a violent storm in which the wind moves upward in a narrow, circular funnel. The winds in a tornado move fast enough to destroy buildings and uproot trees. Tornadoes are common in the MIDWEST.

**tropical rain forest**  A tropical rain forest is a region where the weather is hot and wet all year. This climate supports many kinds of plants and trees as well as a large variety of animals and insects.

**Tornado.** Tornado near Iron Ridge, Wisconsin.

**tropics**   The tropics are the areas north and south of the EQUATOR where the weather stays hot all year.

**tsunami** (tsoo-NAH-mee)   A tsunami is a TIDAL WAVE, usually caused by an under-sea EARTHQUAKE or the eruption of a VOL-CANO.

**tundra**   The tundra is the vast, flat, cold area in the northern regions of the EARTH where no trees grow. Tundra is found in

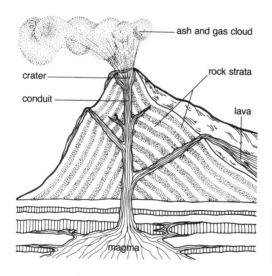

**Volcano.** A cross-section of an erupting volcano (left) and a photograph of Mount St. Helens erupting on May 18, 1980.

Lapland and in regions OF ALASKA, CANADA, and RUSSIA.

**typhoon**   A typhoon is a type of tropical CYCLONE that occurs in the western parts of the PACIFIC OCEAN.

**volcano**   A volcano is a mountain created by the flow of melted rock through an opening in the EARTH's surface. It is active when it can still erupt and release LAVA, hot gases, and dust. It is extinct when it has not erupted for millions of years. *See also* MAGMA.

**warm front**   A front is a place in the air where two very large bodies of air meet. A warm front is the place where warm air pushes out cold air. *Compare* COLD FRONT.

**water cycle**   The water cycle is the process in which water from the OCEAN evaporates into the air and then falls back to the EARTH as rain, hail, or snow. The water then flows into rivers, which return it to the ocean, and the cycle begins again.

**water vapor**   Water vapor is water in the air that has changed into a GAS.

**weather satellite**   A weather satellite is a device that orbits the EARTH. It carries instruments that detect the different kinds of weather on the earth's surface and transmits the information back to meteorologists (people who study the weather).

**weathering**   Weathering occurs when ROCKS are broken down to form soil. It is caused by rain, ice, and plant roots that break apart the rocks.

# Life Sciences

Many important and useful terms are employed in the scientific study of living things. The life sciences include *zoology*, which is the study of animals, and *botany*, which is the study of plants. *Biology* is another name for the life sciences. In the next section of this dictionary, we explain terms that relate to medicine and the human body.

**algae** Algae are red, green, or brown ORGANISMS that lack structures such as roots, stems, and leaves, grow mainly in water, and range in size from single cells to large marine plants called seaweeds.

**amphibians** (am-FIB-ee-uhns) Amphibians are animals that live both in water and on land. When they are young, most amphibians breathe water by means of gills; as they grow older, they lose their gills and develop lungs for breathing air. Frogs and toads are amphibians.

**anatomy** The anatomy of a plant or animal is its structure.

**animals** Like PLANTS, animals are organisms (living things). Animals differ from plants because they can move by themselves and do not perform PHOTOSYNTHESIS. Animals are divided into two groups: VERTEBRATES and INVERTEBRATES. Vertebrates are animals with backbones, such as mammals, reptiles, amphibians, birds, and fish. Invertebrates are animals without backbones, such as insects and mollusks.

**arthropods** (AHR-thruh-podz) Arthropods are animals with jointed legs and segmented bodies. INSECTS, spiders, and CRUSTACEANS are all arthropods.

**asexual reproduction** (ay-SEK-shooh-uhl) Asexual reproduction is the kind in which it is not necessary to have two parents to produce a living thing. It is very common among plants. Asexual reproduction can also occur among certain other life forms, such as SINGLE-CELLED organisms, which may reproduce by dividing themselves.

**bacteria** Bacteria are MICROORGANISMS that reproduce by splitting into two cells that then grow to full size. Or they reproduce by producing tiny, one-celled reproductive bodies called spores that develop into new organisms. Some types of bacteria are useful to humans, such as the bacteria that live in the stomach and aid digestion, while other types of bacteria are disease-causing PATHOGENS. A single organism is called a bacterium.

**balance of nature** The balance of nature is a term for the way all parts of nature rely on one another. If one kind of animal becomes

**Bird.** A pelican, a large and very inquisitive bird.

EXTINCT, the lives of other animals and plants are changed, and the balance of nature is upset.

**biology** Biology is the science that studies living things. Botany (the study of plants) and zoology (the study of animals) are branches of biology.

**birds** Birds are VERTEBRATES with wings and feathers. They are WARM-BLOODED and lay eggs. Eagles, pigeons, chickens, ducks, sparrows, and parakeets are all birds.

**botany** Botany is the branch of biology that studies plants.

**carnivore** (KAHR-nuh-vawr) A carnivore is an animal that eats meat. Some plants, such as the Venus's-flytrap, are also carnivores. *Compare* HERBIVORE; OMNIVORE.

**cell** A cell is the smallest part of any living thing that is able to function by itself. Plants

and animals are made up of tiny units called cells.

**cell membrane** The cell membrane is the thin structure that surrounds the PROTOPLASM of a cell and regulates the passage of materials such as nutrients and waste products in and out of the cell.

**cell wall** The cell wall is the rigid outer layer of a plant cell that surrounds the CELL MEMBRANE. It is composed mainly of a stringy organic material called cellulose.

**chlorophyll** (KLAWR-uh-fil) Chlorophyll is the substance in green plants that gives them their color and helps in the process of PHOTOSYNTHESIS.

**chloroplast** A chloroplast is a small, green CHLOROPHYLL-containing structure found in plant CELLS and in some MICROORGANISMS.

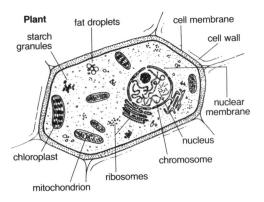

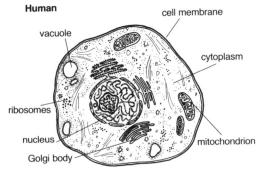

**Cell.** Plant cell (top) and human cell (bottom) as they appear under an electron microscope.

The process of PHOTOSYNTHESIS occurs in chloroplasts.

**chromosome** (KROH-muh-sohm) A chromosome is a part of the NUCLEUS of a CELL. Chromosomes carry the chemical "instructions," or DNA, for reproduction of the cell. *See also* GENE; HEREDITY; X-CHROMOSOME; Y-CHROMOSOME.

**classification** Classification is a way of organizing living things. In BIOLOGY, ORGANISMS are classified in decreasingly general categories known as kingdom, phylum, class, order, family, genus, and species. For example, a domesticated dog is classified as belonging to the animal kingdom, the phylum of chordates, the class of mammals, the order of carnivores, the family of canids, the genus *Canis*, and the species *Canis familiaris*.

**cloning** The term *cloning* usually refers to scientists creating a living thing that is an exact copy of another living thing. A clone has the same GENES as its parent. The first MAMMAL to be cloned successfully, a sheep named Dolly, was born in SCOTLAND in 1996. Since then, mice, monkeys, pigs, horses, and other animals also have been cloned. There is a major debate on the ethical aspects of cloning, especially as it applies to humans.

**cold-blooded animal** A cold-blooded animal's temperature changes according to the TEMPERATURE of its surroundings. Thus, if a cold-blooded animal lives in a cold place, its body will be cold; if it lives in a warm place, its body will be warm. Fish and reptiles are cold-blooded animals. *Compare* WARM-BLOODED ANIMAL.

**Crick, Francis** Francis Crick is a twentieth-century British scientist who worked with JAMES D. WATSON on the discovery of the DOUBLE HELIX of DNA.

**crustaceans** (kru-STAY-shuhn) Crustaceans are a kind of ARTHROPOD that have shells. Crabs, lobsters, shrimp, and crayfish are crustaceans.

**cytoplasm** (SEYE-tuh-plaz-uhm) The cytoplasm is the cellular material that surrounds the NUCLEUS and is itself surrounded by the CELL MEMBRANE.

**Darwin, Charles** Charles Darwin, a great English scientist of the 1800s, is known for his theory of EVOLUTION.

**deciduous** Trees and shrubs that lose their leaves in the autumn are deciduous. Oaks, elms, and maples are deciduous trees. *Compare* EVERGREEN.

**dinosaur** Dinosaurs were REPTILES that lived millions of years ago and are now extinct. Some types of dinosaurs were small, but others were larger than elephants. (*See* illustration, next page.)

**DNA** DNA (deoxyribonucleic acid) is a large MOLECULE that is different for each SPECIES of living thing. An important part of a GENE, it helps determine the particular traits of each living thing. *See also* DOUBLE HELIX; CRICK, FRANCIS; RNA; WATSON, JAMES D.

**dormancy** Many plants, such as tulips and corn, are dormant for part of each year. During this dormancy the flowers, stems, and leaves die, but the roots or bulbs live under-

**Crustacean.** A crab scrambles across rock.

**Dinosaur.** From left to right: Triceratops (30 feet long), Tyrannosaurus (50 feet long), and Stegosaurus (29 feet long).

ground, storing NUTRIENTS for the next growing season.

**double helix** A double helix forms the shape of the DNA MOLECULE. A helix is a three-dimensional spiral in the shape of a spring. A DNA molecule consists of two intertwined helixes.

**ecology** Ecology is the science that studies the relationship between living things and their ENVIRONMENT, or surroundings.

**egg** An egg is a female reproductive cell in a plant or an animal. *See also* FERTILIZATION; REPRODUCTION; SPERM.

**embryo** (EM-bree-oh) An embryo is a very young plant or animal. The embryos of many plants are contained in their SEEDS. The embryo of a human being is carried inside the mother before birth.

**evergreen** Trees and shrubs that stay green in the winter are evergreens. Pines, cedars, and spruces are evergreen trees. *Compare* DECIDUOUS.

**evolution** Evolution is the process by which living things evolve, or change form, from one generation to the next. According to CHARLES DARWIN's theory of evolution, all existing forms of life evolved from earlier forms.

**extinct** An extinct plant or animal SPECIES is one that has disappeared from the EARTH. A species that is at risk for becoming extinct is said to be endangered. A species that is at risk for becoming endangered is said to be threatened.

**fertilization** Fertilization is part of the process of sexual REPRODUCTION in animals and plants. In humans and many other animals, an EGG and a SPERM join to form a new CELL that grows into an EMBRYO. In some plants, POLLEN grains must enter the PISTIL of a flower; from this union, FRUIT eventually grows.

**fish** Fish are COLD-BLOODED VERTEBRATES that live in water. They move by using their fins and breathe with organs called gills. They generally lay eggs, although some bear their young alive. Trout, salmon, sharks, minnows, goldfish, eels, and sea horses are all fish.

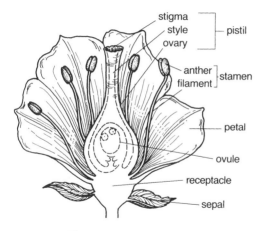

**Flower.** A cross-section.

**flower**  A flower is a plant part that produces SEEDS and sometimes FRUIT. It is often colorful to attract insects, which then cover the PISTIL with POLLEN from the STAMEN.

The fertilized egg in the pistil makes the seed. In most plants, both stamen and pistil are in the same flower. *See also* FERTILIZATION.

**food chain**  A food chain is a series of plants and animals that are linked together because they feed on each other. For instance, if the sap of a plant is eaten by an insect, and the insect is eaten by a bird, and the bird is eaten by a cat, then the plant, the insect, the bird, and the cat are parts of the same food chain.

**fruit**  In some plants, the fruit is the part of the plant that comes from the FLOWER after it is FERTILIZED. The fruit usually contains SEEDS. Some foods that we commonly think of as vegetables, such as tomatoes, eggplants, and squash, are really fruits.

**fungus**  A fungus is an ORGANISM that lives by feeding off other plants or animals, alive

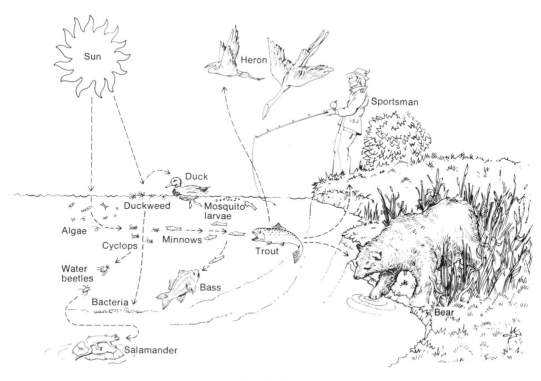

**Food chain**

or dead. Mushrooms, molds, yeasts, and mildew are all types of fungus. The plural of *fungus* is *fungi*.

**gene**   A gene is part of a CHROMOSOME in a CELL. It determines which traits will be passed on from parents to children. For instance, your parents' genes determined the color of your eyes. *See also* DNA.

**genetics**   Genetics is the study of the principles of HEREDITY and the variation of inherited characteristics among similar or related ORGANISMS.

**genome project**   The U.S. Human Genome Project was a government project with international support that examined the human genome. A genome is all the information contained in the DNA for a living thing. The genome project identified about 30,000 GENES in human DNA; then it organized and studied the information. The project lasted from 1990 until 2003.

**Goodall, Jane**   Jane Goodall is a modern British scientist who is best known for her study of the behavior and social patterns of chimpanzees in Africa. Her books include *My Friends the Wild Chimpanzees.*

**habitat**   The place where an animal or plant normally lives is called its habitat.

**herbivore**   (HUR-buh-vawr)   A herbivore is an animal that eats only plants. Cattle, sheep, and horses are herbivores. *See also* CARNIVORE; OMNIVORE.

**heredity**   The passing of traits from parents to children is called heredity in both plants and animals. If you have received a trait through heredity, you are said to have "inherited" it. For instance, you may have inherited the color of your hair from your mother.

**hibernation**   Some animals, like woodchucks, spend the entire winter sleeping. While they are sleeping, they are said to be hibernating or in hibernation. Hibernating animals store up fat before the cold season in order to nourish their bodies.

***Homo sapiens***   *Homo sapiens* is the scientific Latin name for humans as a species of animal.

**hybridization**   Hybridization is the process of cross-breeding plants or animals of different varieties, strains, or species. Hybridization is used extensively in agriculture to produce new forms of hardy, disease-resistant plants.

**insects**   Insects are small INVERTEBRATE animals. They have six legs and long feelers

**Jane Goodall**

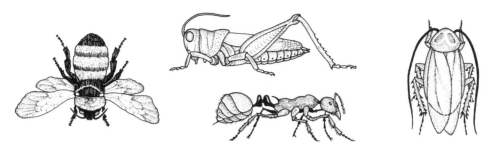

**Insect.** Bumblebee (left), grasshopper (top center), ant (bottom center), and cockroach (right).

called antennae. Ants, bees, grasshoppers, and cockroaches are all insects.

**instinct** Instinct is a way of behaving that is inherited (passed on through HEREDITY) rather than learned or taught. For instance, birds do not teach each other how to build nests; their instinct serves as a guide.

**invertebrates** (in-VUR-tuh-bruhts) Animals without backbones, like INSECTS and MOLLUSKS, are invertebrates. *Compare* VERTEBRATES.

**kingdom** Scientists organize living things into kingdoms, based on their similarities and differences. It is generally said that there are five kingdoms: ANIMALS, PLANTS, MONERA (BACTERIA and certain ALGAE), FUNGI, and PROTOCTISTA (SINGLE-CELLED and other simple ORGANISMS). *See also* CLASSIFICATION.

**mammals** Mammals are warm-blooded VERTEBRATES with hair who make milk to feed their young. Cows, dogs, elephants, giraffes, horses, mice, and human beings are all mammals. Although porpoises and whales live in the sea, they are also mammals.

**McClintock, Barbara** Barbara McClintock was an American scientist of the twentieth century who is best known for her study of GENES. Her studies, particularly of corn, showed that genetic material could shift position on a CHROMOSOME from generation to generation. Her work was a major contribution to DNA research.

**meiosis** (meye-OH-sis) Meiosis is the division of a parent CELL into four "daughter" cells, each with half the GENES of the parent. It is a major process in sexual REPRODUCTION and produces an endless number of variations in the offspring.

**Mendel, Gregor** Gregor Mendel, a nineteenth-century biologist and monk in AUSTRIA, discovered the laws of HEREDITY by experimenting with pea plants.

**Mesozoic** (mez-uh-ZOH-ik) The Mesozoic era of geologic time lasted from about 250 million years ago to about 65 million years ago. During this era, the DINOSAURS appeared and became extinct. The Mesozoic is also known as "The Age of Reptiles."

**metamorphosis** (met-uh-MAWR-fuh-sis) When an animal completely changes its form, it is said to undergo metamorphosis. Metamorphosis occurs when a caterpillar changes into a butterfly. (*See* illustration, next page.)

**microorganisms** Microorganisms are ORGANISMS that are so small they can be seen only with the aid of a MICROSCOPE.

**mitochondrion** (meye-tuh-KON-dree-uhn) A mitochondrion is a MICROSCOPIC structure found in the CYTOPLASM of most living CELLS. It contains ENZYMES that act to

**Metamorphosis.** The metamorphosis of a butterfly from egg to larva (caterpillar) to pupa to butterfly.

change food to ENERGY that can be used by the cell. Any one cell contains many mitochondria.

**mitosis** (meye-TOH-sis) Mitosis is the division of a single CELL into two identical "daughter" cells. It begins when DNA in the parent cell reproduces itself; it ends with the two cells having exactly the same GENES. Mitosis is an important process in REPRODUCTION. *Compare* MEIOSIS.

**mollusk** Mollusks are INVERTEBRATE animals with soft bodies that are often covered by hard shells. Clams, snails, scallops, and squid are all mollusks.

**Monera** (muh-NEER-uh) The kingdom of Monera is made up of single-celled organisms, such as BACTERIA, that do not have a cell NUCLEUS. They are the most primitive living things.

**mutation** A mutation is a change in the GENES or CHROMOSOMES of a living thing that can be inherited by that organism's offspring.

**natural selection** Natural selection is the principle that only ORGANISMS best able to survive in their ENVIRONMENT tend to survive and reproduce, passing their genetic characteristics to their offspring. These offspring will, in turn, survive and reproduce, as will their offspring, thus increasing the propor-

tion of these characteristics with each generation. This principle is fundamental to EVOLUTION as described by CHARLES DARWIN.

**nucleus** Inside each CELL of an ORGANISM is a tiny round body called the nucleus. It controls the activities of the cell and contains the CHROMOSOMES.

**omnivore** (OM-nuh-vawr) An animal that eats both meat and plants is called an omnivore. Human beings and bears are omnivores. *Compare* CARNIVORE; HERBIVORE.

**organism** An organism is a living thing. All plants and animals are organisms.

**Pavlov, Ivan** Ivan Pavlov was a Russian scientist of the nineteenth century. He experimented with dogs to show what he called a conditioned response. For example, when he rang a bell and presented food to a dog, the food caused the dog to produce a natural flow of SALIVA. After he repeated this process several times, the dogs would salivate merely at the sound of the bell, without food being offered.

**photosynthesis** Photosynthesis is a process that takes place in green plants when the plant uses the ENERGY in sunlight to make food for itself. During photosynthesis, CARBON DIOXIDE is taken from the air and OXYGEN is released into it. CHLOROPHYLL plays an important part in photosynthesis.

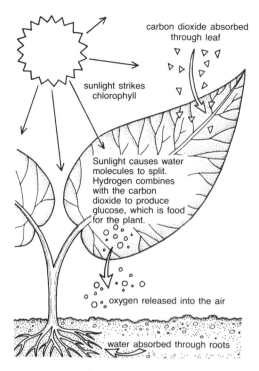

**Photosynthesis**

**pistil**  The pistil is the part of a flower that contains the egg cells. In order for the flower to reproduce, these cells must be fertilized by POLLEN. *See also* FERTILIZATION; STAMEN.

**plants**  Like animals, plants are organisms (living things). Plants are different from animals, however, because they cannot move by themselves and because they can usually make their own food. Green plants use PHOTOSYNTHESIS to make their food. Trees, bushes, grass, and flowers are plants; so are moss and seaweed. Some plants like corn, wheat, and rice provide human beings with food.

**pollen**  Pollen is a powder produced by the STAMEN of flowering plants. It fertilizes the egg cells in the PISTIL so that the plant can make SEEDS and reproduce. *See also* FERTILIZATION.

**Protoctista** (pruh-TOHK-tis-tah)  The kingdom of Protoctista includes ORGANISMS, usually SINGLE-CELLED ones, whose CELLS include a NUCLEUS. It includes very simple organisms, such as the amoeba.

**protoplasm**  (PROH-tuh-plaz-uhm)  Protoplasm is a jellylike substance forming the living MATTER in all plant and animal CELLS. It is made up of PROTEINS, FATS, and other substances dissolved and suspended in water. A cell's protoplasm includes the NUCLEUS and CYTOPLASM.

**protozoa**  (proh-tuh-ZOH-uh)  Protozoa are SINGLE-CELLED organisms that can only be seen with a MICROSCOPE. They are classified in the kingdom of PROTOCTISTA. The best known of the protozoa is the amoeba (uh-MEE-buh).

**reproduction**  When plants or animals produce offspring, the process is called reproduction. There are two types of reproduction: asexual and sexual. ASEXUAL REPRODUCTION requires only one parent. For example, a tiny animal called an amoeba reproduces by dividing in two. SEXUAL REPRODUCTION requires the union of a SPERM and an EGG to form a new cell. This new cell eventually becomes an animal or plant. *See also* FERTILIZATION.

**reptiles**  Reptiles are a group of VERTEBRATES whose bodies are covered with scales. Snakes, lizards, turtles, and alligators are all reptiles. Like AMPHIBIANS, reptiles are COLD-BLOODED ANIMALS, but, unlike amphibians, reptiles always have lungs.

**RNA**  RNA is one of a group of MOLECULES similar in structure to a single strand of DNA. It carries information from DNA in a cell's NUCLEUS into the body of the CELL and is important in the production of PROTEINS.

**seed**  A seed is the small EMBRYO of a plant. It usually contains some food that can be used when it starts to grow. The seed is usually protected by a covering that must be wet before it will grow. *See also* FRUIT.

**sexual reproduction**   Sexual reproduction is the creation of a new living thing by two parents. Almost all animals reproduce sexually through the union of a SPERM and an EGG to form a new CELL. Some plants, such as flowering plants and ferns, may also reproduce sexually. *See also* FERTILIZATION.

**single-celled**   An ORGANISM that is single-celled is made up of only one cell. BACTERIA and PROTOZOA are some single-celled organisms.

**species**   Individual plants and animals that belong to exactly the same biological CLASSIFICATION are said to belong to the same species. All human beings belong to the species *Homo sapiens.*

**sperm**   A sperm is a male reproductive cell in a plant or an animal. *See also* EGG; FERTILIZATION; REPRODUCTION.

**stamen**   (STAY-muhn)   The stamen is the part of a flower that produces POLLEN. *See also* FERTILIZATION; PISTIL.

**vertebrates**   (vur-tuh-bruhts)   Animals with backbones, like mammals and reptiles, are vertebrates. *Compare* INVERTEBRATES.

**warm-blooded animal**   A warm-blooded animal's body temperature does not change when the surrounding temperature changes. Thus, whether the air is hot or cold, the temperature of a warm-blooded animal stays the same. Mammals and birds are warm-blooded animals. *Compare* COLD-BLOODED ANIMAL.

**Watson, James D.**   James D. Watson is a modern American scientist who worked with FRANCIS CRICK on the discovery of the DOUBLE HELIX of DNA.

**X-chromosome**   The X-chromosome is associated with female sex characteristics. The X- and Y-CHROMOSOMES are called sex chromosomes because they determine what sex a living thing will be. At FERTILIZATION, each parent supplies one sex chromosome to the new organism. The mother's EGG always supplies an X-chromosome, while the father's SPERM can supply either an X- or a Y-chromosome. If two X-chromosomes are paired, the offspring will be female. If the pairing consists of an X- and a Y-chromosome, the offspring will be male.

**Y-chromosome**   The Y-chromosome is associated with male sex characteristics. *See* X-CHROMOSOME.

**zoology**   (zoh-OL-uh-jee)   Zoology is the science that studies animals.

# Medicine and the Human Body

The human body is one of nature's most complicated creations. It is easier to enjoy your life if you are healthy, and it is easier to stay healthy if you know something about how your body is put together and how it works. You can learn to eat the right foods, exercise, and recognize the kinds of things in the body that sometimes go wrong. You can also learn how your physical condition affects your mental health. The following terms will be useful as you learn more about your health and well-being.

**abdomen** (AB-duh-muhn) In humans and other MAMMALS, the abdomen is the front part of the body from below the chest to just above where the legs join, containing the STOMACH, INTESTINES, and other life-sustaining ORGANS.

**adolescence** Adolescence is the time of life between childhood and adulthood when a young person grows and changes physically, emotionally, and mentally. *See also* PUBERTY.

**aerobic** (air-OH-bik) Aerobic means "with OXYGEN." Aerobic exercise increases the HEART rate and pumps OXYGEN throughout the body. It strengthens the heart, LUNGS, and MUSCLES. Running, bicycling, and swimming are some forms of aerobic exercise.

**AIDS** AIDS stands for *a*cquired *i*mmune *d*eficiency *s*yndrome. It is a disease of the IMMUNE SYSTEM that is caused by the human immunodeficiency VIRUS, or HIV. The virus attacks WHITE BLOOD CELLS, making it difficult for the body to fight INFECTION. AIDS is an EPIDEMIC that has infected tens of millions of people worldwide. Many scientists today are hopeful that AIDS can be managed by new medicines. *See also* IMMUNITY.

**alcoholism** Alcoholism is a disease in which people cannot control their desire to drink alcohol.

**allergy** An allergy results when the body reacts badly to outside substances such as POLLEN, dust, animals, or certain foods. People with allergies develop symptoms such as sneezing and rashes.

**Alzheimer's disease** (AHLTS-heye-muhrz) Alzheimer's disease is a NONCOMMUNICABLE DISEASE of the NERVOUS SYSTEM marked by a deterioration of memory and other mental faculties.

**anorexia nervosa** (an-uh-REK-see-uh nur-VOH-suh) Anorexia nervosa is an eating disorder in which a person refuses to eat and tries to lose extreme amounts of weight. People with anorexia usually believe that they are fat even when they are dangerously thin. Anorexia can cause severe damage to the body and may result in death if not medically treated.

**antibiotics**  Antibiotics are drugs that control diseases by killing the BACTERIA that cause them.

**antibodies**  Antibodies are substances made by the body that fight disease-causing germs (such as VIRUSES) by attaching themselves to the germs and making them harmless until they can be removed from the body.

**antigen** (AN-ti-juhn)  An antigen is a substance that stimulates the body's production of ANTIBODIES. Certain BACTERIA, VIRUSES, foreign blood cells, and cells from transplanted TISSUES can all act as antigens in the body.

**antihistamine**  (an-tee-HIS-tuh-meen)  An antihistamine is any of several DRUGS that block the production or action of histamine, a substance the body produces in response to external agents such as POLLEN. When activated, histamine causes symptoms such as a runny nose, watery eyes, and sneezing.

**antiseptic**  An antiseptic is a substance that stops the growth and activity of MICROORGANISMS that cause INFECTION.

**aorta** (ay-AWR-tuh)  The aorta is the largest ARTERY. Blood leaves the heart through the aorta and circulates throughout the body. *See also* CIRCULATORY SYSTEM.

**appendix**  The appendix is a small saclike ORGAN attached to the large INTESTINE. It has no known function. If the appendix becomes infected, it causes an illness called appendicitis. When this happens, the appendix must be removed by surgery.

**artery**  An artery is a type of BLOOD VESSEL that carries blood away from the heart to other parts of the body. *See also* CIRCULATORY SYSTEM.

**arthritis**  Arthritis is INFLAMMATION of TISSUES in a JOINT or joints, usually resulting in pain and stiffness.

**asthma** (AZ-muh)  Asthma is a respiratory disease characterized by difficulty in breathing, coughing, and a tightness of the chest. Various substances to which a person has an ALLERGY can cause an asthma attack.

**attention deficit disorder** (ADD)  attention deficit disorder, or ADD, is a disorder in which a person has a hard time keeping focused. Someone with ADD may find it hard to sit still or to pay attention for very long.

**baby teeth**  The baby teeth are the first set of teeth to appear in a child. They fall out one by one as the permanent teeth grow in.

**bacteria**  Bacteria are tiny, one-celled organisms (or living things). You can see them by using a MICROSCOPE. Most bacteria are harmless. Some bacteria live in your intestines and help to digest food. Others cause INFECTIONS, such as tetanus and tuberculosis, when they enter the body.

**balanced diet**  A balanced diet contains all the kinds of food that a person needs to stay healthy. It includes PROTEINS, CARBOHYDRATES, FATS, VITAMINS, and MINERALS. Proteins build TISSUES such as MUSCLES. Carbohydrates and fats provide ENERGY. Vitamins and minerals help the body to function normally. *See also* RDA.

**bicuspids**  Bicuspids are the smaller, flat teeth in the inner part of the mouth. They are used to grind food.

**Blackwell, Elizabeth**  Elizabeth Blackwell was an American physician of the 1800s and early 1900s who was born in ENGLAND. The first woman in the United States to receive a medical degree, she helped found an in-

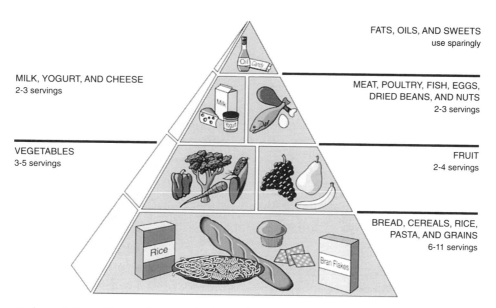

**Balanced diet.** Dietary "pyramid" chart showing the six food groups and the ideal number of daily portions of each.

firmary for women and children and a medical college for women in NEW YORK CITY.

**blood**   Blood is the red fluid that carries OXYGEN and food to various parts of the body. Blood also removes waste products that build up after CELLS use oxygen and food. *See also* CIRCULATORY SYSTEM, PLASMA, PLATELETS, RED BLOOD CELLS, WHITE BLOOD CELLS.

**blood pressure**   Blood pressure is the measure of how hard the blood presses against the walls of the ARTERIES. If a person's blood pressure gets too high, it can cause damage to the HEART or other parts of the body.

**blood type**   Human BLOOD is divided into four main types, known as A, B, AB, and O. These types differ with respect to the presence or absence of certain PROTEINS on the surface of blood cells. In most cases, the proteins on the blood cells of one type of blood will act as ANTIGENS, producing ANTIBODIES when they come in contact with blood cells carrying proteins from a different blood group. To prevent this reaction during blood transfusions, the type of a blood donor is

carefully analyzed to make sure it matches the type of the person into whom the blood is to be transfused. Because blood type is inherited, the search for the perfect blood donor often begins within the recipient's own family.

**blood vessels**   Blood vessels are the tubes that carry BLOOD through the body. They are made of TISSUES and MUSCLES. *See also* ARTERY; CAPILLARY; VEIN.

**bone**   A bone is one of the pieces of hard and dense material supporting the rest of the body. For example, your arm has three main bones, one in the upper arm and two in the lower arm. The system of bones in the body is called the SKELETAL SYSTEM.

**brain**   The brain is the very complex ORGAN inside the head that controls the rest of the body. It receives information from the SENSES and controls movement. It is also the center of thought and feeling. *See also* CEREBRUM; CRANIUM; NERVOUS SYSTEM. (*See* illustration, next page.)

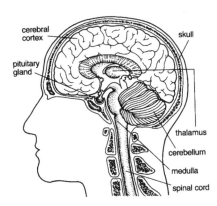

**Brain.** A cutaway view.

Labels: cerebral cortex, skull, pituitary gland, thalamus, cerebellum, medulla, spinal cord

**bulimia** (boo-LEE-mee-ah) Bulimia is an eating disorder in which a person "binges" — eats a lot, all at once, while feeling out of control. A binge is usually followed by feelings of guilt or depression. A person with bulimia may force herself to throw up.

**caffeine** Caffeine is a DRUG found in many soft drinks, chocolate, coffee, and tea that increases the activity of the BRAIN and NERVOUS SYSTEM. Too much caffeine can make you nervous or irritable.

**cancer** Cancer is a disease in which CELLS in the body grow without stopping and destroy other parts of the body. Some kinds of cancer can be controlled if they are discovered early enough.

**canine teeth** (KAY-neyen) The canine teeth are the sharp, pointed teeth near the front of the mouth on either side of the INCISORS. Canine teeth are used to bite and tear food. They are also called eye teeth.

**capillary** Capillaries are tiny BLOOD VESSELS that connect ARTERIES and VEINS. They are important because they let food MOLECULES and OXYGEN pass from the blood to the body's cells through their thin walls. They also pick up waste products that build up when oxygen and food are used by the cells. *See also* CIRCULATORY SYSTEM.

**carbohydrates** Carbohydrates are foods that supply energy. Sugars and starches are carbohydrates. Some of the most common carbohydrate foods are bread, noodles, potatoes, and rice. *See also* BALANCED DIET.

**cartilage** Cartilage is soft, flexible TISSUE in the JOINTS. Parts of the nose and ears are also made of cartilage. Because cartilage can stand up to pressure, it helps to protect parts of the body from shock.

**cavity** A cavity is a hole in the surface of a tooth.

**cerebrum** (SER-uh-bruhm, sur-REE-bruhm) The cerebrum is the largest part of the BRAIN and is the center of thought, feeling, and remembering. It also controls the body's movements.

**chicken pox** Chicken pox is a COMMUNICABLE DISEASE that is caused by a VIRUS. It often causes fever and blisters.

**cholesterol** (kuh-LES-tuh-rawl) Cholesterol is a fatty substance that is important in METABOLISM and HORMONE production. Cholesterol is found in blood, egg yolks, and seeds. In excessive amounts, cholesterol is thought to cause diseases that involve the HEART and BLOOD VESSELS, especially arteries.

**circulatory system** The circulatory system is made up of BLOOD, BLOOD VESSELS, and the HEART. The heart pumps the blood through the body. Blood moves from the heart through the ARTERIES. The arteries get smaller as the blood gets farther from the heart. The blood then moves into tiny CAPILLARIES. The thin walls of the capillaries allow food MOLECULES and OXYGEN to pass into the CELLS and allow waste products to move from the cells into the blood. The blood then travels through VEINS that get larger as the blood is carried back to the heart.

**communicable disease** A communicable disease is a disease that one person can catch

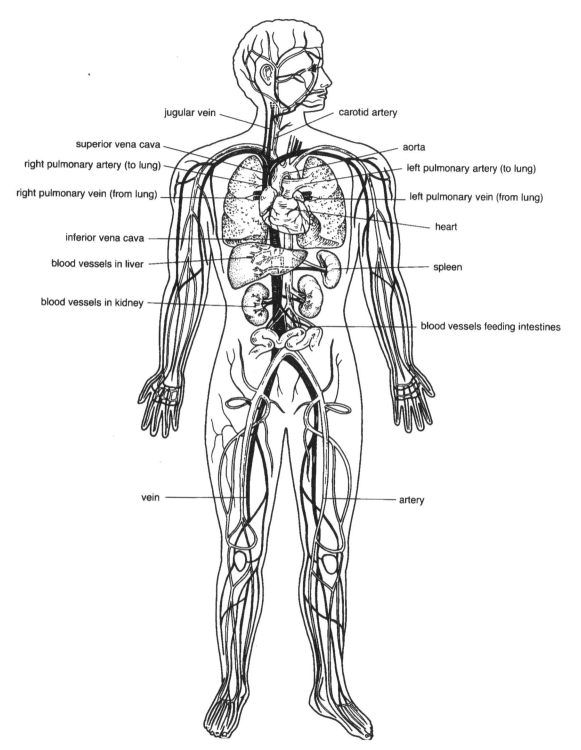

**Circulatory system.** In this illustration, veins are black and arteries are white.

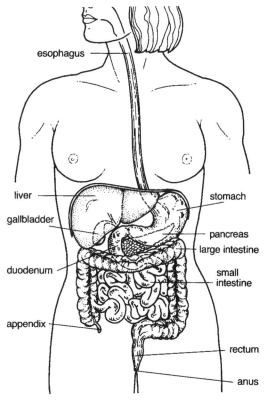

esophagus

liver

gallbladder

duodenum

appendix

stomach

pancreas

large intestine

small intestine

rectum

anus

**Digestive system**

from another. It is also called a contagious disease. These diseases are caused by tiny germs, such as BACTERIA and VIRUSES. Germs spread from person to person through the air or physical contact. Colds and the flu are common communicable diseases. *Compare* NONCOMMUNICABLE DISEASE.

**cornea** (KAWR-nee-uh) The cornea is the clear piece of TISSUE that protects the front of the eye.

**CPR** CPR stands for cardiopulmonary resuscitation, an emergency procedure that uses HEART massage and mouth-to-mouth resuscitation to restore normal breathing and circulation in a person whose heart has stopped functioning.

**cranium** (KRAY-nee-uhm) The cranium is the set of bone plates in the head that protect the BRAIN. It is also called the skull.

**digestion** Digestion is the process of breaking down food so that it can be used by the body.

**digestive system** The digestive system is the group of ORGANS that take in food and break it down so that it can be used by the body. It includes the digestive tract (the mouth, THROAT, STOMACH, and small and large INTESTINES), GLANDS, and other ORGANS, such as the LIVER and gallbladder. When food is swallowed, it enters the stomach. The stomach mixes food and digestive juices together. The juices break down the food, which then passes into the small intestine, where more digestion takes place. Waste products then pass through the large intestine and finally leave the body through the anus. *See also* SALIVA.

**Drew, Charles** Charles Drew was an African-American surgeon of the early 1900s who developed a way to preserve blood PLASMA for transfusion, the transfer of blood from one person to another.

**drug** A drug is a chemical that causes changes in the way the body works. Some drugs are medicines prescribed by doctors to help people get well. Other drugs are found in foods or drinks. CAFFEINE is a drug that is found in some soft drinks and in chocolate, tea, and coffee; alcohol is a drug found in beer, wine, and other liquors. Still other drugs, like marijuana and heroin, are illegal substances; it is against the law to sell or use them. They also can cause permanent damage to the body. Many drugs are habit-forming; that is, people may begin to feel that they need to take them.

**eardrum** The eardrum is a round piece of TISSUE at the end of the ear canal (which leads from the opening to the inner part of the ear). The eardrum is like the tightly

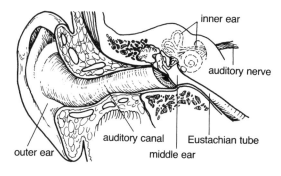

**Ear**

stretched skin of a drum. Sound causes it to vibrate. The eardrum passes along the vibrations to the inner ear, which passes them to the BRAIN as nerve impulses. The brain then makes sense of these impulses, causing us to hear.

**enzyme**  An enzyme is a PROTEIN produced in living cells that aids in bringing about changes in other chemical substances without being changed itself.

**epidemic**  An epidemic is an outbreak of a disease that spreads quickly and infects many people at the same time.

**esophagus** (i-SOF-uh-guhs)  The esophagus is the tube that connects the THROAT with the STOMACH for the passage and digestion of food. *See also* DIGESTIVE SYSTEM.

**eye**  The eye is the ORGAN of sight. *See also* CORNEA; IRIS; LENS; OPTIC NERVE; PUPIL; RETINA.

**farsightedness**  Farsightedness is an eye problem that causes distant objects to appear distinct while nearby objects look fuzzy. *Compare* NEARSIGHTEDNESS.

**fat**  A fat is an ORGANIC compound that is found in plant and animal TISSUES and that serves as a reserve source of ENERGY. In humans, fats also help the body absorb certain VITAMINS. Fats are often divided into two types, known as SATURATED FATS and UNSATURATED FATS. *See also* BALANCED DIET.

**Fleming, Alexander**  Alexander Fleming was a Scottish scientist who discovered the antibiotic PENICILLIN in 1928.

**food poisoning**  Food poisoning is an illness resulting from eating food that has become contaminated with toxic substances or illness-causing organisms. Food poisoning can be serious or even fatal, as in botulism, an illness caused by poisons produced by bacteria that grow in improperly canned or preserved food.

**germs**  Germs are microorganisms that can cause disease or INFECTION. *See also* PATHOGENS.

**gland**  A gland is an ORGAN in the body that makes a substance that the body uses. Saliva, sweat, and tears are made by glands.

**heart**  The heart is a muscular ORGAN in the middle of the chest that pumps BLOOD through the body. The sound made by the repeated, rhythmic action of the heart as it pumps blood is called the heartbeat.

**heart attack**  A heart attack occurs when the heart muscle does not get enough blood. Heart attacks damage the heart and are sometimes fatal.

**hemoglobin** (HEE-muh-gloh-bin)  Hemoglobin is the complex ORGANIC substance that contains iron and that gives RED BLOOD CELLS their characteristic color. Hemoglobin carries OXYGEN to the cells of the body.

**hormone**  A hormone is a chemical produced by certain GLANDS. Hormones travel through the blood and control bodily processes such as growth and DIGESTION.

**immune system**  The immune system is a system in the body that works to prevent and to fight illness and INFECTION. The WHITE BLOOD CELLS are an important part of this system. Some white blood cells produce ANTIBODIES that fight disease-causing germs. MUCUS, fevers, and sneezing are some other examples of the immune system at work.

**immunity** Immunity is the ability to resist disease or INFECTION. When your body produces enough ANTIBODIES to kill the GERMS that cause a particular disease, you are said to be immune to that disease.

**immunization** Immunization is the process of bringing about IMMUNITY by VACCINATION, that is, by the injection of ANTIBODIES into the body. Schoolchildren are often required by law to be immunized against certain diseases, such as smallpox and diphtheria.

**incisors** (in-SEYE-zuhrz) Incisors are the sharp, flat-edged teeth at the front of the mouth (four on the top and four on the bottom) that are used for biting food.

**infection** An infection happens when BACTERIA, VIRUSES, or other harmful GERMS grow and reproduce in the body. Cuts in the skin can become infected if they are not kept clean. Colds, the flu, pneumonia, and other diseases are also caused by infections.

**infectious disease** SEE COMMUNICABLE DISEASE.

**inflammation** Inflammation is the response of a part of the body to injury, irritation, or INFECTION, characterized by redness, swelling, soreness, and heat.

**influenza** (in-flooh-EN-zuh) Influenza is a COMMUNICABLE DISEASE caused by VIRUSES and characterized by fever, INFLAMMATION of the RESPIRATORY SYSTEM, headache, irritation of the DIGESTIVE SYSTEM, and muscular pain. It is commonly called the flu.

**intestines** The intestines are long tubes in the body below the STOMACH. After food is mixed with digestive juices in the stomach, it goes into the small intestine, where it is digested further. Waste products then pass into the large intestine and finally leave the body. *See also* DIGESTIVE SYSTEM.

**iris** (EYE-ris) The iris is the colored part of the eye. It controls the amount of light that is let into the eye by making the pupil (the dark opening of the eye) larger or smaller. If a room is dark, the eye needs more light to see, so the iris makes the pupil larger to let in more light. If it is bright, the iris makes the pupil smaller to let in less light.

**Jenner, Edward** Edward Jenner was a British physician of the late 1700s and early 1800s. He was the first to discover the medical uses of VACCINATION.

**jet lag** Jet lag is a temporary disruption of the body's rhythms, such as eating and sleeping times, caused by rapid travel through several time zones by airplane.

**joint** A joint is a place in the body where two BONES meet. Movable joints such as the knee and the elbow allow body parts to move.

**kidneys** The kidneys are a pair of ORGANS that filter liquid waste products out of the BLOOD. They are near the lower part of the back.

**lens** The lens is the part of the eye that focuses light rays onto the RETINA. It is just behind the dark opening of the eye called the PUPIL.

**ligament** A ligament is a band of TISSUE that fastens bones together at the JOINTS.

**liver** The liver is a large ORGAN near the STOMACH that removes waste from the BLOOD and produces digestive juices.

**lungs** The lungs are a pair of ORGANS that allow us to breathe. They are in the chest on either side of the HEART. In the lungs, OXYGEN inhaled from the air is transferred to the BLOOD while CARBON DIOXIDE is removed from the blood and exhaled. *See also* RESPIRATORY SYSTEM.

**lymph nodes** The lymph nodes are numerous small, rounded structures located along the small vessels known as the lymphatic system. Lymph nodes supply certain WHITE BLOOD CELLS to the body and filter out harmful BACTERIA and foreign particles from the lymph fluid.

**malnutrition** Malnutrition occurs when the body is weakened because it does not get enough of the foods it needs. Malnutrition can also be caused by diseases that keep the body from properly using the food that it does get. *See also* BALANCED DIET.

**marrow** Marrow is the soft TISSUE inside BONE. RED BLOOD CELLS form in bone marrow.

**measles** Measles is a disease caused by a virus that makes a rash of pink or red spots break out all over the skin. It is contagious, which means that a person who has it can easily give it to another person. Rubella, a contagious disease that causes a rash, is sometimes called German measles.

**menopause** (MEN-uh-pawz) Menopause is the period in a woman's life during which MENSTRUATION ceases, occurring usually between the ages of 45 and 55.

**menstruation** (men-strooh-AY-shuhn) Menstruation is the periodic discharge of the blood-enriched lining of the UTERUS that occurs in women who are not pregnant about every four weeks from PUBERTY to MENOPAUSE.

**metabolism** Metabolism is the sum of chemical and physical processes that occur within living cells. In humans, metabolism is related to a person's intake and use of food. People with a high metabolism can generally eat more without gaining weight.

**minerals** Minerals are substances in food that keep the body working correctly. They help keep teeth and BONES strong and also maintain MUSCLES and BLOOD cells. Calcium is an example of a mineral.

**molars** Molars are the large, flat teeth at the back of the mouth that are used to grind food.

**mucus** Mucus is a dense, sticky liquid in the mouth, nose, throat, and lungs. It keeps dust and germs from getting far inside the body.

**mumps** Mumps is a contagious disease caused by a VIRUS that affects the GLANDS at the back of the throat. Its symptoms include swelling and soreness.

**muscles** Muscles are the TISSUES that make body parts move. Voluntary muscles are muscles that you control, like the ones in your arms and legs. Involuntary muscles, like the HEART and the muscles in the STOMACH, work whether or not you are aware of them.

**nearsightedness** Nearsightedness is an eye problem that affects the way a person sees. A nearsighted person can see nearby objects clearly, but distant objects appear fuzzy. *Compare* FARSIGHTEDNESS.

**nerves** Nerves are fibers that connect the rest of the body to the BRAIN. They make actions possible by carrying messages, called electrical impulses, from the brain and the SPINAL CORD to the rest of the body.

**nervous system** The nervous system is made up of the BRAIN, the SPINAL CORD, and the NERVES and controls the body's ORGANS, movements, and SENSES. Messages from one part of the body to another are sent by way of the nervous system, from the brain along the spinal cord to the nerves. The nerves send the messages to the MUSCLES or the organs. Messages are also sent from the body back to the brain along the same path. (*See* illustration, next page.)

**neuron** (NOOR-on, NYOOR-on) A neuron is a nerve cell. Neurons transmit electric signals throughout the NERVOUS SYSTEM.

**noncommunicable disease** A noncommunicable disease is one that is not caused by germs and cannot be caught from another person. Some noncommunicable diseases are caused by substances in the ENVIRONMENT.

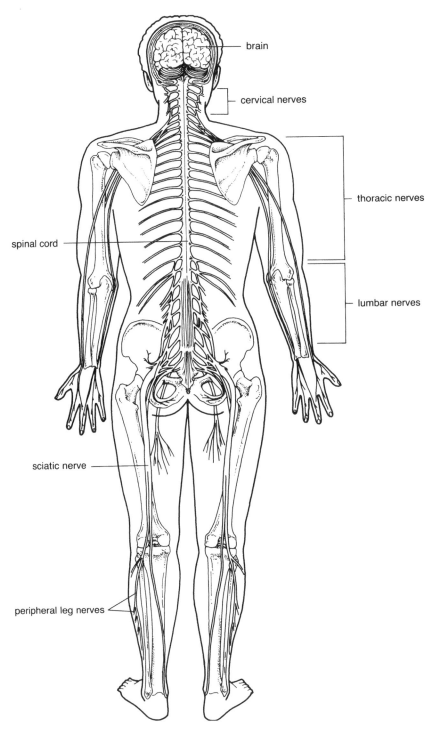

brain

cervical nerves

thoracic nerves

spinal cord

lumbar nerves

sciatic nerve

peripheral leg nerves

**Nervous system**

For example, CANCER may be caused by smoking cigarettes. Other noncommunicable diseases are inherited, or passed down to children in their GENES. Still others are present in the body when a person is born; these are called congenital diseases. *Compare* COMMUNICABLE DISEASE.

**nutrients**  Nutrients are the substances in food that provide ENERGY and help the body to grow and stay healthy. *See also* BALANCED DIET.

**nutrition**  Nutrition is the study of the foods people need to stay healthy. *See also* BALANCED DIET.

**olfactory nerves** (ol-FAK-tuh-ree, ohl-FAK-tuh-ree)  The olfactory nerves are high inside the nose and sense the various odors and flavors we can detect. *See also* TASTE BUDS.

**optic nerve**  The optic nerve connects the eye to the BRAIN. It carries messages from the eye to the brain, which the brain interprets, enabling us to see.

**organ**  An organ is a part of the body that does a specific job. The HEART, STOMACH, and eyes are organs.

**Pasteur, Louis** (pas-TUR, pah-STEUR)  In the nineteenth century Louis Pasteur helped prove that many diseases are caused by small organisms such as BACTERIA. His name was given to the process known as *pasteurization*, in which fluids such as milk are heated in order to kill harmful bacteria.

**pathogen** (PATH-uh-juhn)  Pathogens are disease-causing agents, such as certain MICROORGANISMS and VIRUSES. The common term for pathogens is *germs*.

**pediatrician**  A pediatrician is a doctor who takes care of babies, children, and teenagers.

**penicillin**  Penicillin was the most important early ANTIBIOTIC to be discovered that did not harm the body. Penicillin is produced by molds such as the ones that grow on bread.

**permanent teeth**  The permanent teeth are those that grow in after children lose their BABY TEETH. When permanent teeth remain healthy, they will last a lifetime. The body cannot replace them if they fall out or are damaged. *See also* BICUSPIDS; CANINE TEETH; INCISORS; MOLARS.

**pharmacist**  A pharmacist is a person who has been trained to give out DRUGS prescribed by a doctor. *See also* PRESCRIPTION DRUG.

**plasma** (PLAZ-muh)  Plasma is the part of the BLOOD that carries blood CELLS. It is often used to replace the blood a person loses in an accident or during an operation.

**platelets**  Platelets are microscopic flat disks that are found in BLOOD and that aid in the clotting of blood.

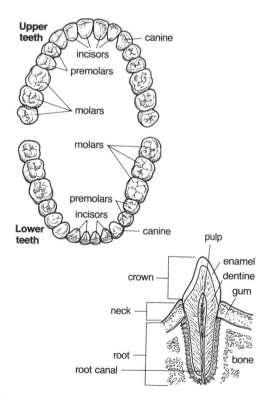

**Permanent teeth.** The teeth of an adult human (left) and a cross-section of an incisor (right).

**pneumonia** (noo-MOHN-yuh) Pneumonia is a COMMUNICABLE DISEASE that causes inflammation of the LUNGS. Once a very dangerous disease, pneumonia can now often be cured with ANTIBIOTICS such as PENICILLIN.

**prescription drugs** Prescription drugs are medicines prescribed by a doctor. When you are sick, the doctor examines you and decides which drugs will help you get well. A note from your doctor, called a prescription, tells the PHARMACIST what kind of drug to sell you and how much of it you should take.

**proteins** Proteins are the parts of food that help the body repair itself and grow. Eggs, meat, fish, cheese, and foods made from soybeans have proteins in them. *See also* BALANCED DIET.

**psychiatrist** A psychiatrist is a doctor who helps people with mental or emotional problems. A psychiatrist is permitted to prescribe DRUGS.

**psychologist** A psychologist is a person who helps people with mental or emotional problems. Unlike psychiatrists, psychologists are not doctors and cannot prescribe drugs.

**puberty** Puberty is the time in life when children's bodies start to become like adults' bodies. During puberty, children begin to mature sexually; that is, they develop the ability to have children. *See also* ADOLESCENCE; REPRODUCTIVE SYSTEM.

**pupil** The pupil is the dark opening in the eye through which light enters the eye.

**rabies** (RAY-beez) Rabies is a very dangerous COMMUNICABLE DISEASE. People catch it if they are bitten by an animal that is infected with the disease. A vaccine to prevent rabies was developed by LOUIS PASTEUR.

**RDA** RDA stands for recommended daily allowance. The result of study by various scientific groups, RDAs are amounts of various PROTEINS, VITAMINS, and MINERALS that are considered necessary to the proper functioning of the body. Most people meet the RDAs through their daily intake of food, although occasionally additional amounts of certain substances, such as calcium and iron, are needed. Such additional amounts are known as supplements. *See also* BALANCED DIET.

**red blood cells** Red blood cells are the cells in the blood that contain HEMOGLOBIN.

**reproductive system** The reproductive system is the group of GLANDS and ORGANS that allow people to reproduce, that is, to have children. The female reproductive glands are called the ovaries; they produce egg cells. The male reproductive glands are called the testes; they produce sperm cells.

**respiration** Respiration is the action of breathing. When you inhale, or breathe in, OXYGEN is taken into the body and used by the CELLS. Cells produce CARBON DIOXIDE as a waste product, which is released from the body when you exhale, or breathe out.

**respiratory system** (res-puh-ruh-tawr-ee) The respiratory system is the mechanism that allows you to breathe. It is made up of the LUNGS and the tubes that connect your nose and mouth to the lungs. The lungs pull air into the body to get OXYGEN. They transfer the oxygen to the bloodstream and remove CARBON DIOXIDE from the BLOOD. The lungs then push the carbon dioxide out of the body and pull in fresh oxygen. They also act as filters to prevent germs and dust in the air from getting into the bloodstream.

**retina** The retina is a layer of TISSUE at the back of the eye. Light rays are focused onto the retina, where they form an image. The retina then transmits the image along the OPTIC NERVE to the BRAIN.

**ribs** The ribs are the series of curved BONES in the chest that are attached to the SPINAL COLUMN. Ribs protect the organs in the chest, such as the LUNGS and HEART.

**saliva** (suh-LEYE-vuh) Saliva is the fluid produced by the GLANDS in the mouth. It keeps the mouth moist and softens food so that it can be chewed and swallowed.

**saturated fats** Saturated fats are so named because they are saturated with all the HYDROGEN ATOMS they need. Saturated fats are usually SOLID at room temperature and are found in butter, milk, and animal products. Eating too many saturated fats increases the likelihood of heart disease.

**senses** The five principal senses tell the BRAIN what is happening in the outside world: sight, hearing, touch, taste, and smell. The body also learns what is going on inside through senses such as hunger, thirst, and tiredness. The senses send messages to the brain so it can tell the body how to react. For example, if you touch something that is too hot, your brain "tells" your hand to pull away before it is badly burned. If you have not eaten for a long time, your sense of hunger "tells" you that your body needs food.

**shock** Shock occurs when a person's ORGANS do not get enough BLOOD because the blood's circulation is too slow. It is sometimes caused by an accident or a serious illness. A person in shock must be kept warm until medical help arrives.

**skeletal system** The skeletal system, or skeleton, is the system of BONES that supports the body and holds it together. Some parts of the skeletal system protect internal ORGANS. The CRANIUM protects the BRAIN; the SPINAL COLUMN protects the SPINAL CORD; the rib cage protects many of the organs in the chest. (*See* illustration, next page.)

**skin** The skin is the outer layer of the human body. It helps to protect the inside of the body and keep the body's temperature at the proper level. Skin also keeps the body in touch with the outside world by sensing heat and cold and by allowing us to feel things.

**spinal column** The spinal column, also called the backbone, or spine, is a series of linked BONES that protect the SPINAL CORD.

**spinal cord** The spinal cord is a long piece of nerve TISSUE that runs from the BRAIN down through the backbone and connects the brain to the NERVES. The backbone, or SPINAL COLUMN, protects the spinal cord from injury.

**stomach** The stomach is the place where food goes when it is swallowed. The stomach mixes food and digestive juices together. The juices break down the food so that it can be used by the body. The food then moves into the small intestine, where further digestion takes place. *See also* DIGESTIVE SYSTEM.

**stroke** A stroke is a sudden loss of BRAIN function caused by a blockage or rupture of a BLOOD VESSEL to the brain and marked by loss of muscular control, loss of sensation or consciousness, dizziness, or slurred speech.

**taste buds** The taste buds are groups of cells in the tongue. They sense the chemicals in food and send information about them to the BRAIN, allowing us to notice

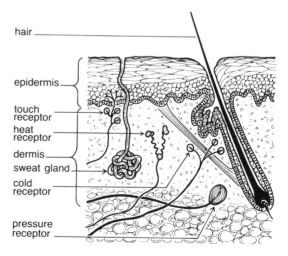

**Skin.** A cutaway view of the layers of human skin.

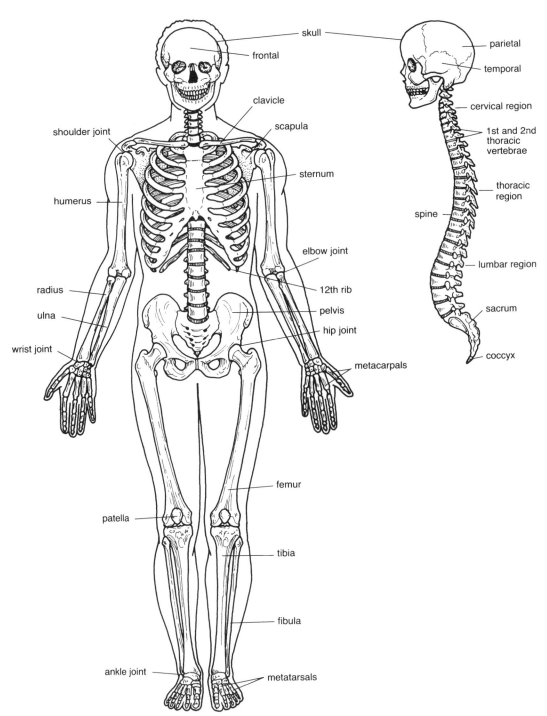

**Skeleton.** A frontal view of the adult skeletal system (left) and a profile of the adult skull and spine (right).

tastes that are bitter, salty, sweet, or sour. *See also* OLFACTORY NERVES.

**teeth**   *See* BABY TEETH; PERMANENT TEETH.

**tendons**   Tendons are the strong pieces of TISSUE that connect the MUSCLES to the BONES.

**throat**   The throat is the part of the digestive tract that forms a passage between the rear of the mouth and the ESOPHAGUS.

**tissues**   Tissues are groups of CELLS that act together to perform a specific job.

**tonsils**   The tonsils are two oval masses of TISSUE located on each side of the THROAT, either or both of which may often be the site of INFECTION or INFLAMMATION, especially in young children. An inflammation of the tonsils is called tonsillitis.

**unsaturated fats**   Unsaturated fats are so called because they can take up more HYDROGEN ATOMS. Unsaturated fats, which are often LIQUID at room temperature, are found in oils such as peanut and soybean and in foods such as peanut butter, olives, and other plant products. They are healthier to eat, in moderation, than are saturated fats.

**uterus**   (YOOH-tuh-ruhs)   The uterus is a hollow muscular ORGAN of the female REPRODUCTIVE SYSTEM in which the fertilized EGG implants and develops from EMBRYO to fetus.

**vaccination**   (vak-suh-NAY-shun)   Vaccination is a method that doctors use to protect the body against disease. They inject a small amount of a weakened or dead VIRUS, called a VACCINE, into the body, which then produces ANTIBODIES to fight the virus. The antibodies stay in the body and protect it against the disease caused by that particular virus.

**vaccine**   (vak-SEEN)   A vaccine is a substance that causes the body to make ANTIBODIES. Vaccines are usually weak or dead VIRUSES or BACTERIA. *See also* VACCINATION.

**vein**   A vein is a BLOOD VESSEL that carries blood back to the HEART. *See also* CIRCULATORY SYSTEM.

**virus**   (VEYE-ruhs)   A virus is an extremely small organism that often causes disease. Viruses cannot be seen without using a very powerful MICROSCOPE.

**vitamins**   Vitamins are the substances in foods that help the body to use other food groups, such as carbohydrates and proteins. Although the body needs only small amounts of vitamins each day, they do many things to keep the body healthy. Foods that are rich in vitamins include green, yellow, and red vegetables as well as fruits, meats, and some grains, such as bread and cereals. *See also* BALANCED DIET.

**white blood cells**   White blood cells are the cells in the blood that help the body fight disease. They surround and kill GERMS or other harmful substances that enter the body.

**x-ray**   An x-ray is a form of ENERGY like LIGHT. X-rays can go through many surfaces that stop light. Doctors use x-rays to take pictures of the inside of the body so that they can see things that may be wrong.

# Technology

Technology concerns inventions and techniques that affect every part of your life. You already know many examples of modern technology. Cars and airplanes allow us to travel faster and farther than used to be possible; furnaces and air conditioners keep us comfortable in any weather; movies and television entertain us; computers make many kinds of work faster and easier. Examples of modern technology such as ovens and heaters are in almost every home in the industrial nations of the world.

Technology is not just another word for machines, however. A book is an example of technology; so are a pen and paper. The invention of writing was a major advance in technology. For thousands of years the wheel has been used to move things, the plow has been used to till fields, and axes and knives have been used to break things apart.

This section does not attempt to mention every important invention and technological discovery. Instead, it notes some terms, ideas, and machines that will help you understand the modern technology that affects your life each day. It also names a few people who have helped create the technology of the modern age.

**alternating current** An alternating current, also called AC, is an ELECTRIC CURRENT that regularly changes direction. AC is created by GENERATORS. Most homes in the United States use alternating current. *Compare* DIRECT CURRENT.

**ampere** An ampere measures the rate of ELECTRON flow in an electric circuit. *See also* VOLTAGE; WATT.

**amplifier** An amplifier is a device that takes a weak electric signal and makes it stronger without changing its pattern. Amplifiers are used in stereo systems, electric guitars, and some loudspeakers.

**Apollo Program** The Apollo Program was a project of the National Aeronautics and Space Administration (NASA), designed to put a person on the moon. In 1969, during

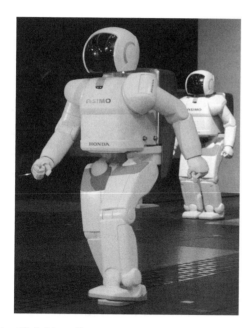

**Artificial intelligence.** Walking robots are just one example of artificial intelligence at work.

the eleventh Apollo mission, Neil Armstrong became the first person to walk on the moon.

**artificial intelligence** (AI)  Artificial intelligence is the ability of COMPUTERS, robots, and other devices to perform activities that are thought to require intelligence. Some examples of this ability are solving problems, telling objects apart, and responding to voice commands.

**assembly line**  An assembly line is a way of putting products together by a series of individual tasks. A car, for example, moves through a number of workstations. At each station, workers do something, such as bolt a door onto the car or put in the engine. Each person on an assembly line has one special job and repeats it over and over again. HENRY FORD perfected the assembly line.

**astronaut**  An astronaut is a person trained to serve as a member of the crew of a spacecraft.

**automation**  Automation is the use of machines rather than people to do a job. For example, a THERMOSTAT automatically keeps a room's TEMPERATURE the same, so you do not have to adjust the heat yourself. Automation is also used to do jobs more quickly or accurately than people can do them.

**axle**  *See* WHEEL AND AXLE.

**battery**  A battery is a device that makes ELECTRICITY through chemical action.

**Bell, Alexander Graham**  Alexander Graham Bell was a Scottish-born inventor of the late 1800s and early 1900s. He invented the telephone in the late 1800s.

**cable television**  In a cable television system, television signals are transmitted by cable to subscribers who pay for the service.

**capacity**  *See* VOLUME.

**CD-ROM**  CD-ROM stands for COMPACT DISK, *read only memory*. It is a disk used for storing large amounts of information that can be read, but not changed, by a computer PROGRAM.

**Alexander Graham Bell.** Calling Chicago from New York City in 1892.

**cell phone** (cellular phone)   A cell phone is a portable telephone that uses wireless cellular technology. In a cellular phone network, a large area is divided into smaller areas called cells. Within each cell, a wireless telephone sends signals to and from an antenna in a cell tower, which connects to a telephone network.

**circuit**   A circuit is the path that an ELECTRIC CURRENT travels. Computers contain very complicated circuits.

***Columbia* space shuttle**   The U.S. space shuttle *Columbia* was the first reusable spacecraft. It first launched in 1981. On its twenty-eighth mission, in 2003, the *Columbia* broke up as it reentered EARTH'S ATMOSPHERE. All seven crew members were killed.

**compact disk**   A compact disk is a transparent, plastic disk containing a thin, internal metallic layer that records digital data (data that is in 0s and 1s) in the form of tiny bits that can be read by a small LASER.

**computer**   A computer is an electronic device that stores information and follows instructions very rapidly to do a great variety of tasks. *See also* HARD DRIVE; HARDWARE; LAPTOP; SOFTWARE.

**computer virus**   A computer virus is a PROGRAM that enters a COMPUTER. Some viruses are mild and only cause disruptive messages to appear on the screen. Others are destructive and can wipe out a computer's memory. Computer viruses are spread most often over the INTERNET.

**concave lens**   A concave lens is a LENS that is curved inward toward its center and is thicker at the edges than at the center. *Compare* CONVEX LENS.

**conductor**   A conductor is a substance that can carry an ELECTRIC CURRENT or other forms of ENERGY such as heat. Metals such as copper and silver are good conductors of heat and electricity. *Compare* INSULATOR.

A compact computer, also called a PDA (personal digital assistant).

**convex lens**   A convex lens is a LENS that is curved outward, away from the center, and is thinner at the edges than at the center. *Compare* CONCAVE LENS.

**cyberspace**   Cyberspace is the imaginary space in which computer information is exchanged between computers and within computer networks.

**database**   A database is an organized collection of information that can be searched, changed, sorted, and retrieved by the use of various COMPUTER programs. The pieces of information in a database are called data.

**digital signal**   A digital signal is one in which the original information is converted into smaller units of information, called bits, before being transmitted. A compact disk, for example, stores its sound in digital form.

**direct current** (DC)   A direct current is an ELECTRIC CURRENT that flows in one direction. BATTERIES produce a direct current. *Compare* ALTERNATING CURRENT.

**DNA fingerprinting**   DNA fingerprinting is a technique in which the DNA of a person is compared with DNA that is found in a sample or taken from another person. It provides evidence that can be used in criminal trials or to identify remains. DNA fingerprinting does not use fingerprints, but, as with a fingerprint, just a little DNA can identify a person.

**DVD**   DVD stands for *digital versatile disk* or *digital video disk*. DVDs are often used for storing movies, music, or computer data. They have better sound and picture quality than compact disks or videotapes because they hold more information.

**Edison, Thomas A.**   Thomas A. Edison was an American inventor of the late 1800s and early 1900s who perfected the electric light bulb and the phonograph, an early form of the record player.

**electric current**   An electric current is the flow of ELECTRONS along a material, such as a wire, that can carry them. *See also* ALTERNATING CURRENT; CONDUCTOR; DIRECT CURRENT.

**electricity**   Electricity is a form of ENERGY caused by the movement of tiny particles called ELECTRONS. Electricity is used to create light, heat, and power. It also occurs in nature, for example, as LIGHTNING.

**electronic file**   An electronic file is a sequence of data that is given a name and that can be changed, stored, and retrieved by a COMPUTER.

**electronics**   Electronics is a use of ELECTRICITY that employs special control devices, such as TRANSISTORS, small SWITCHES, and AMPLIFIERS, that make electricity perform complex tasks. Some electronic devices are COMPUTERS and DVD players.

**e-mail** (electronic mail)   E-mail is an abbreviation for electronic mail, a message sent electronically from one COMPUTER user to another computer user within a NETWORK or on the INTERNET. It makes it possible for two people at different ends of the world to communicate at high speed.

**engineering**   Engineering is the use of scientific knowledge for practical purposes.

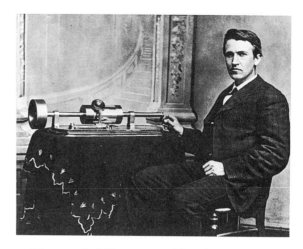

**Thomas A. Edison.** Seated beside his tinfoil phonograph.

Engineers design and build all kinds of useful items, from tiny calculators to huge dams and bridges.

**fax**   A fax is an image that is sent from one electronic device to another. The image is translated into data by the sending machine and retranslated into an image by the receiving machine, which then prints it out.

**fuel**   Fuel is anything that can be burned or consumed to make ENERGY. Wood, gasoline, oil, and food are fuels.

**fulcrum**   A fulcrum is the point on which a LEVER rests.

**Fulton, Robert**   Robert Fulton was an American engineer and inventor of the late 1700s and early 1800s. He invented the steamboat in the early 1800s.

**gear**   A gear is a simple machine, a wheel with teeth cut in it that makes it easier to move another object. Many turns of a small gear make one turn of a large gear. The relative size of the gears determines how hard it is to turn the wheel. Most hand drills and can openers use gears.

**generator**  A generator is a machine that, when turned rapidly, produces ELECTRICITY. Small generators make power for a single machine or house. Large generators the size of buildings provide electricity for cities and states.

**global positioning system** (GPS)  A global positioning system is a United States military satellite system that is now available to the public. It allows anyone who has a GPS receiver to locate her position on the earth's surface to within a few feet.

**hard drive**  Most of the memory of a personal COMPUTER is stored on the hard drive, which is made up of hard disks inside the computer. Information in the hard drive remains stored even when the computer is turned off.

**hardware**  In COMPUTER terminology, hardware is the wiring, devices, and physical parts that make up a computer system. *See also* SOFTWARE.

**home page**  A home page is the first screen containing information on an INTERNET WEB SITE, usually including a greeting to visitors to the site; general information about a subject, person, or organization; and connections, called links, to other files.

**hydroelectric power**  Hydroelectric power is created when ENERGY from running water is turned into ELECTRICITY in a GENERATOR in a hydroelectric plant. Hydroelectric power plants can use natural waterfalls, artificial waterfalls created by dams, running water in rivers, or waves to turn the TURBINES of generators.

**inclined plane**  An inclined plane is a slanted surface, or ramp, that makes it easier to move objects to a higher place or let them roll down again. People use inclined planes to load things into trucks because it is easier to roll or carry an object up an inclined plane than to lift it off the ground.

**information superhighway**  The information superhighway is a term that describes all of the cables, satellites, and HARDWARE that allow information to be transferred quickly over large distances. It is sometimes used as another name for the INTERNET.

**insulator**  An insulator is a substance that does not easily carry ELECTRICITY or heat. Wood and rubber are good insulators. *Compare* CONDUCTOR.

**internal combustion engine**  An internal combustion engine burns FUEL inside the engine itself, as in a car engine. In other engines, such as STEAM ENGINES, the burning occurs outside the engine. Internal combustion engines usually burn FOSSIL FUELS and are often a major cause of AIR POLLUTION.

**Internet**  The Internet is a global communication NETWORK that allows almost all computers worldwide to connect and share information.

**Inclined plane**

**Laptop**

**irrigation** Irrigation is the process of bringing water to land that would otherwise be too dry to grow crops.

**jet engine** A jet engine creates a high-speed rush of GASES by compressing and burning fuel and air. The enormous thrust of the gases pushing out behind the engine moves it forward. *See also* ROCKET ENGINE.

**laptop** A laptop is a small, portable personal COMPUTER that can run on a BATTERY.

**laser** A laser is a device that makes a highly concentrated beam of light. The beam is so powerful that it can be used to cut metal. It is also so narrowly focused that it can be used to perform delicate surgery.

**lens** A lens is a piece of curved glass or plastic that can bend light rays. Lenses are used in cameras, projectors, eyeglasses, TELE-SCOPES, and MICROSCOPES.

**lever** A lever is a bar or pole or similar object that rests on a point called a FULCRUM. It is a simple machine that makes it easier to move objects. For example, you can raise a person of your own size who is sitting on a seesaw (which is a lever) much more easily than you could by yourself. (*See* illustration, next page.)

**mass media** The mass media are the methods of communication used in modern society to reach large numbers of people at the same time. They include television, newspapers, movies, radio, the INTERNET, books, and magazines.

**mass production** Mass production is the fastest and least expensive way of making many identical things. For example, a cookie factory can make and pack thousands of cookies in the time it would take you to make and pack a small batch.

**microscope** A microscope is an instrument that usually uses LENSES to make small, close objects appear larger. It can be used to see objects too small to be seen with the eye. Common microscopes use lenses; other types of microscopes use ELECTRONS, X-RAYS, or other kinds of radiation. *Compare* TELESCOPE.

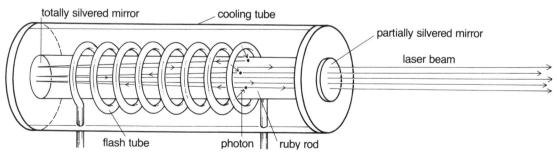

**Laser**

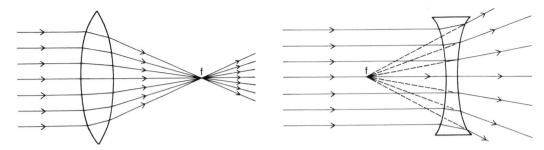

**Lens.** Light passing through a double-convex lens (left), and light passing through a double-concave lens (right). The "f" indicates the focus (or focal point).

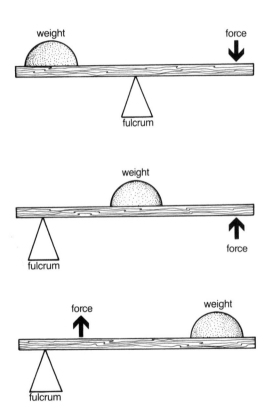

**Lever.** From top to bottom: First-class lever, with the fulcrum between the weight and the force (for example, removing a nail with a claw hammer); second-class lever, with the weight between the fulcrum and the force (for example, lifting the handles of a wheelbarrow); third-class lever, with the force between the fulcrum and the weight (for example, bending one's elbow).

**microwave**   A microwave is a kind of EN-ERGY. It is commonly used in microwave ovens, which can cook food much faster than ovens that use heat. Microwaves are light waves that are longer than infrared waves and shorter than radio waves.

**Morse, Samuel F. B.**   Samuel F. B. Morse was an American artist and inventor of the nineteenth century. He invented the TELEGRAPH in the mid-1800s. He also devised the MORSE CODE.

**Morse code**   The Morse code is a set of short and long signals ("dots" and "dashes") that stand for letters and numbers. For instance, SOS, the signal for emergencies, is [ . . . - - - . . . ]. Morse code was invented to send messages over a TELEGRAPH, but it can also be transmitted by radio and with flashes of light.

**network**   A network is a group or system of COMPUTERS that is connected so that users can exchange information and access a variety of DATABASES. *See also* INTERNET.

**nuclear energy**   Nuclear energy is ENERGY that comes from the NUCLEUS, or center, of an ATOM when part of its matter is converted to energy. It is the most powerful energy source known. A nucleus changes matter to energy when it splits apart or when it fuses with another nucleus. *See also* CHAIN REAC-TION *under "Physical Sciences."*

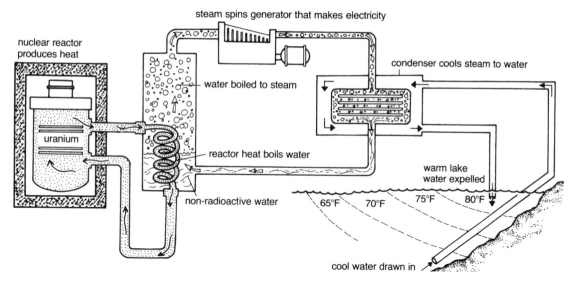

steam spins generator that makes electricity

nuclear reactor produces heat

water boiled to steam

condenser cools steam to water

uranium

reactor heat boils water

warm lake water expelled

non-radioactive water

65°F    70°F    75°F    80°F

cool water drawn in

**Nuclear reactor**

**nuclear reactor** A nuclear reactor is a device that produces NUCLEAR ENERGY in a gradual, controlled way to make ELECTRICITY.

**nuclear weapons** Nuclear weapons create powerful explosions by producing NUCLEAR ENERGY suddenly in a CHAIN REACTION. They also release deadly radioactive particles into the air. Some nuclear weapons, such as atomic and hydrogen bombs, can destroy a city with a single blast. *See also* CHAIN REACTION; RADIOACTIVITY *under "Physical Sciences."*

**patent** A patent is a legal document that says that no one may use, make, or sell a person's invention without permission. The government issues a patent when a person applies for it and the invention is accepted as a new product.

**PC** PC is an abbreviation for personal COMPUTER.

**piston** A piston is a solid CYLINDER set inside a hollow tube that is slightly bigger than the cylinder, allowing it to move back and forth. The pressure from expanding GASES or

**Nuclear weapons.** The "mushroom" cloud that formed over Nagasaki, Japan, on August 9, 1945, after the United States dropped an atomic bomb on the city.

from LIQUIDS under pressure moves the cylinder forward. Then the pressure is released and the piston moves back. The piston is attached to a rod that transfers the back-and-forth movement where it is needed. Most car engines use pistons.

**program** In COMPUTER terminology, a program is a set of instructions that directs a computer to carry out certain operations. A general term for computer programs is SOFTWARE.

**pulley** A pulley is a simple machine made of a wheel with a rope moving around it. Several pulleys working together make it easier to raise and lower heavy objects.

**radar** Radar is an ELECTRONIC device that uses radio waves to find objects too far away to be seen. It works by bouncing the radio waves off the objects and receiving the waves that are reflected back. Radar equipment tracks the movement of objects and can determine their speed, as used by highway police. Airplanes and airports use radar to find objects in the sky.

**refinery** A refinery is a factory where natural materials are purified and made into useful products. An oil refinery takes crude oil and turns it into FUEL.

**resistance** In an electric CIRCUIT, resistance slows down or stops the movement of ELECTRONS, converting their flow into WORK or heat. Resistance is measured in ohms.

**rocket engine** A rocket engine moves by creating a fast rush of GASES. The force of the gases pushing out behind the engine moves it forward. A rocket engine is different from a JET ENGINE because it needs no air to burn its FUEL. All the chemicals it burns are inside the rocket. Because rockets do not need to mix fuel with air, they can be used in outer space, where there is no air. The first people to make rockets are thought to have been the Chinese, who propelled bamboo tubes with gunpowder centuries ago.

**screw** A screw is a simple machine that works like an INCLINED PLANE twisted into a spiral. Wood screws and drills use the screw's action to move into or through a surface. The propellers that move planes and boats are called screws because they use the same spiral action to move through the air and water.

**short circuit** A short circuit occurs when wires in a CIRCUIT that are not supposed to touch are brought into contact. Because there is little RESISTANCE, the amount of ELECTRIC CURRENT in the circuit increases and becomes high enough to generate a dangerous amount of heat. Short circuits can cause fires.

**software** In COMPUTER terminology, software refers to the PROGRAMS and instructions that a computer can run. *See also* HARDWARE.

**solar cell** A solar cell is a device that converts ENERGY from the sun into electrical energy. Solar cells provide power for artificial satellites.

**solar power** Solar power is ENERGY that comes from the SUN. Solar energy comes to EARTH in the form of LIGHT. Special materials can change solar energy into usable heat or electricity. *See also* SOLAR CELL.

**sonic boom** A sonic boom is the loud sound made when an airplane travels faster than the speed of sound.

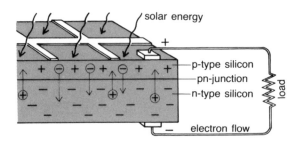

**Solar cell**

**space shuttle**  The space shuttle is a vehicle, built by NASA, that can fly into space with passengers and cargo and return to EARTH. Unlike earlier space vehicles, the space shuttle can be used again and again.

**space station**  A space station is an artificial SATELLITE that orbits EARTH and is designed to allow people to stay in space. Eventually, space stations may be permanent habitats where people can live and work and where scientific experiments can be carried out for further explorations of outer space.

**static electricity**  Static electricity is the name for electrical charges that are not moving in a CIRCUIT. (The word *static* means "not moving.") The shock you get when you walk across a thick carpet on a dry day and then touch a doorknob is caused by static electricity. It also makes some kinds of clothes cling together after they come out of a dryer.

**steel**  Steel is a strong and durable metal made by purifying iron and mixing it with other materials. It is used to make machines and large buildings.

**supersonic**  Supersonic means "faster than the speed of sound." Airplanes that travel faster than the speed of sound are called supersonic planes.

**switch**  A switch is a device that can open or close an electric CIRCUIT.

**telegraph**  The telegraph was the first device that used ELECTRICITY to send messages over long distances. It was invented by SAMUEL F. B. MORSE in the mid-1800s. The first telegraphs used a key that sent electrical impulses along a wire. The impulses could be heard on the other end of the wire as a series of clicking sounds. Telegraph operators used the MORSE CODE to spell out messages using the clicks.

**temperature**  Temperature is the measure of how hot or cold a substance is. Its temper-

**Space shuttle.** The launch of the *Columbia* space shuttle.

ature is related to how fast its MOLECULES are moving. For example, when water molecules are heated, they move faster and faster until they become steam. When the water molecules get colder, they slow down until they become ice.

**thermostat**  A thermostat is an automatic device that senses and controls TEMPERATURE. In a room, it keeps the temperature the same by sending signals to the furnace. The thermostat will turn on the furnace when the temperature gets too low and turn it off when the temperature gets high enough.

**transformer**  A transformer is a device used to transfer electrical ENERGY from one CIRCUIT to another.

**transistor**  A transistor is a tiny device that is operated by one ELECTRIC CURRENT to influence another one. It can act as a small AMPLIFIER. Transistors are used in small electronic devices (for example, portable radios) and in COMPUTERS.

**turbine** A turbine is a wheel with fins. A fan, for example, is a turbine. The wheel can be moved by water, heated air, or steam. Many GENERATORS use turbines.

**VCR** VCR stands for videocassette recorder, a device that electronically records or plays back the images and sound on a VIDEOTAPE. *See also* DVD.

**videotape** A videotape is a magnetic tape used to record visual images and associated sound for later playback. A videotape and the case that contains it is called a videocassette. *See also* DVD.

**volt** *See* VOLTAGE.

**voltage** Voltage signifies the force that moves ELECTRONS in a CIRCUIT. The higher the voltage, the more electrical CURRENT will flow in the circuit. *Compare* AMPERE; RESISTANCE; WATT.

**water power** Water power is provided by moving water, such as a waterfall. *See also* HYDROELECTRIC POWER.

**watt** A watt is a unit of electrical power that combines VOLTS and AMPERES.

**Watt, James** James Watt was a Scottish engineer and inventor of the 1700s and early 1800s. He improved the steam engine in the 1700s. His engine was the first one that was efficient enough to be used widely in industry.

**Web page** A Web page is a document with its own address on the INTERNET.

**Web site** *See* WEB PAGE.

**wedge** A wedge is a simple machine made of two planes that meet to form a sharp edge.

**Eli Whitney.** Whitney's cotton gin.

Wedges such as axes and knives make it easier to break things apart.

**wheel and axle** A wheel and axle is a simple machine made of a wheel turning around a rod. The wheels on a car or a wagon use the wheel and axle to make it easier to move things.

**Whitney, Eli** Eli Whitney was an American inventor of the late 1700s and early 1800s. He invented the cotton gin in the late 1700s. The cotton gin was a machine that removed the seeds from cotton plants much faster than people could do it by hand.

**work** In science, work is what happens when a FORCE is used to move an object through a distance.

**World Wide Web** *See* INTERNET.

# Illustration Credits

## Literature

**Jane Austen** Bettmann/Corbis **Brer Rabbit** From *Uncle Remus and His Friends*, by Joel Chandler Harris **Emily Dickinson** Stock Montage, Inc. **Dracula** Dust jacket of 1901 edition of *Dracula* published by Archibald Constable & Co., Ltd. **The Fox and the Grapes** Bettmann/Corbis **Gulliver's Travels** Stock Montage, Inc. **The Hare and the Tortoise** Bettmann/Corbis **Harry Potter** Reuters NewMedia, Inc./Corbis **Humpty Dumpty** Bettmann/Corbis **King Arthur** From *Stories of Legendary Heroes*, selected and arranged by E.M. Tappan. Drawing by Daniel Maclise. **Little Red Riding Hood** Bettmann/Corbis **Oliver Twist** Bettmann/Corbis **Rapunzel** From *Household Stories from the Bros. Grimm.* Courtesy of the Boston Public Library, Alice M. Jordan Collection. **William Shakespeare** By permission of the Folger Shakespeare Library **Mark Twain** Bettmann Archive/Corbis **Alice Walker** AP/Wide World Photos **Phillis Wheatley** Art Resource, NY/National Portrait Gallery, Smithsonian Institution, Washington, D.C. **Laura Ingalls Wilder** Bettmann/Corbis

## Mythology

**Adonis** *Venus and Adonis*, by Titian. National Gallery of Art, Washington, Widener Collection. **Athena** Bettmann/Corbis **Centaur** Alinari/Art Resource, NY **Cupid** Stock Montage, Inc. **Diana** Library of Congress **Freya** Bettmann/Corbis **Hercules** Courtesy, Museum of Fine Arts, Boston, C.P. Perkins Collection **Pegasus** Bettmann/Corbis **Trojan Horse** Bettmann/Corbis **Zodiac** Bettmann/Corbis

## Music, Art, and Architecture

*American Gothic* Grant Wood's *American Gothic*, friends of the American Art Collection, 1930.934, photograph copyright © The Art Institute of Chicago. All rights reserved. **Baroque** Angelo Hornak/Corbis **The Beatles** Norman Parkinson Library/Fiona Cowan/Corbis **Beethoven** AKG/Photo Researchers, Inc. **Big Ben** British Tourist Authority **Eiffel Tower** Pierre Berger/Photo Researchers, Inc. **Ella Fitzgerald** Bettmann/Corbis **Golden Gate Bridge** Royalty-Free/Corbis **Gothic** Richard List/Corbis **Impressionism** Geoffrey Clements/Corbis **Leaning Tower of Pisa** Peter Menzel/Stock, Boston **Lincoln Memorial** United States Department of Agriculture, neg. no.BN-36272 *Mona Lisa* Photo Researchers, Inc. **Parthenon** Bettmann/Corbis **Elvis Presley** Corbis **Pyramids** George Holton/Photo Researchers, Inc. **St. Peter's Basilica** David Ball/Corbis **Statue of Liberty** Photograph © by Peter Menzel/Stock, Boston **Taj Mahal** Art Resource, NY **Tepee** State Historical Society of North Dakota/Frank B. Fiske, Neg. no. 5530 *Venus de Milo* Alinari/Art Resource, NY **Washington Monument** Dennis Degnan/Corbis **Frank Lloyd Wright** Photograph by David Heald/© The Solomon R. Guggenheim Foundation, NY

## The Bible

**Adam and Eve** Courtesy, Museum of Fine Arts, Boston, Centennial gift of Landon T. Clay **Books of the Bible** Copyright © 1991 by Houghton Mifflin Company. Adapted and reprinted by permission from *The American Heritage Dictionary, Second College Edition* **Daniel in the lions' den** Bettmann/Corbis **Dead Sea Scrolls** Bettmann/Corbis **Jonah** Bettmann/Corbis *The Last Supper* Stock Montage, Inc. **Mary** *The Small Cowper Madonna*, Raphael. National Gallery of Art, Washington; Widener Collection **Moses** Library of Congress **Noah** The Walters Art Museum, Baltimore **Plagues of Egypt** Bettmann/Corbis

## Religion and Philosophy

**Amish** Hulton-Deutsch Collection/Corbis **Buddha** David S. Strickler/Index Stock Imagery **Confucius** From *1993 Information Please Almanac*, copyright © 1992 by Houghton Mifflin Company. Reprinted by permission. *Jesus Healing the Sick* Bettmann/Corbis **Martin Luther** H. Armstrong Roberts, Inc. **Mecca** AP/Wide World Photos **Menorah** Bettmann/Corbis **Pope John Paul II** AP/Wide World Photos **Prayer rug** Hulton-Deutsch Collection/Corbis **Saint** Burstein Collection/Corbis **Socrates** Francis G. Mayer/Corbis **Star of David** From *Symbols, Signs and Signets*, Dover Publications, copyright © 1950 by Ernest Lehner **Torah Scroll** Topham/The Image Works **Totem poles** SEF/Art Resource, NY **Western Wall** Jan Lukas/Photo Researchers, Inc.

## United States History to 1865

**Clara Barton** Bettmann/Corbis **Boston Massacre** Courtesy of The Bostonian Society/Old State House **The Declaration of Independence** National Archives and Records Administration **Frederick Douglass** Bettmann/Corbis **Benjamin Franklin** Stock Montage, Inc. **Stonewall Jackson** Corbis **Abraham Lincoln** Library of Congress **Mayflower** Courtesy of the Pilgrim Hall Museum, Plymouth, Massachusetts **Navajos** Department of Library, Archives and Public Records, Research Library, Arizona State Capitol **Sacajawea** Bettmann/Corbis **Slavery** University of Maryland, Baltimore County, Photography Collections, acsn. No. 76-13-002 **The Original Thirteen Colonies** Map copyright © 2004 by Mary Reilly **Harriet Tubman** Sophia Smith Collection, Smith College, neg. no. SATH **George Washington** Bettmann/Corbis

## United States History Since 1865

**Susan B. Anthony** Schlesinger Library, Radcliffe College **Civil rights movement** Photograph © by Matt Herron/Black Star **Dust Bowl refugee family** Bettmann/Corbis **Amelia Earhart** AP/Wide World Photos **Flapper** Bettmann/Corbis **Lou Gehrig** Bettmann/Corbis **Great Depression** Library of Congress **Michael Jordan** AP/Wide World Photos

**John F. Kennedy** John F. Kennedy Library, photo no. AR7595B **Kentucky Derby** Reuters NewMedia, Inc./Corbis **Martin Luther King, Jr.** UPI/Corbis-Bettmann Newsphotos **Pearl Harbor** National Archives and Records Administration **Prohibition** Library of Congress **Franklin D. Roosevelt** AP/Wide World Photos **Sitting Bull** Bettmann/Corbis **Woodrow Wilson** Bettmann/Corbis **Tiger Woods** Photographed by Chris Trotman. Copyright © Duomo/Corbis **World Trade Center** AP/Wide World Photos **Wright Brothers** Bettmann/Corbis

## Politics and Economics

**Capitol Hill** Library of Congress **Dictatorship** Bettmann/Corbis *E pluribus unum* The Great Seal of the United States of America, as it appears on the back of an American dollar bill. Department of the Treasury, Bureau of Engraving and Printing **Pentagon** AP/Wide World Photos **Uncle Sam** Stock Montage, Inc. **The White House** Royalty-Free/Corbis

## World History to 1600

**Aztecs** George Holton/Photo Researchers, Inc. **Christopher Columbus** Library of Congress **Elizabeth I** Scala/Art Resource, NY **Hieroglyphics** Foto Marburg/Art Resource, NY **Incas** Ira Kirschenbaum/Stock, Boston **Joan of Arc** Giraudon/Art Resource, NY **Ming Dynasty** Robert Fried/Stock, Boston **Roman Empire** Jacques Chazaud **Samurai** The Granger Collection, New York **Stonehenge** Copyright © Topham/The Image Works **Tutankhamen** Hulton Archive/Getty Images, Inc. **Vikings** Culver Pictures

## World History Since 1600

**Berlin Wall** Reuters/Corbis-Bettmann Archive **Concentration camps** National Archives and Records Administration, neg. no. 208-AA-206K-31 **D-Day** U.S. Army Photo **Anne Frank** AP/Wide World Photos **Mahatma Gandhi** AP/Wide World Photos **Adolf Hitler** Mary Evans Picture Library/Photo Researchers, Inc. **Nelson Mandela** AP/Wide World Photos **Napoleon** Giraudon/Art Resource, NY **The *Titanic*** Stock Montage, Inc. **Queen Victoria** Bettmann/Corbis **Vietnam War** UPI/Corbis-Bettmann Archive **World War II** Library of Congress **Emiliano Zapata** Brown Brothers

## United States Geography

**United States** Mary Beth Norton et al., *A People and a Nation: A History of the United States, Second Edition.* Copyright © 1986 by Houghton Mifflin Company. Adapted and reprinted with permission. **The Grand Canyon** Grant Heilman Photography, Inc. **Middle Atlantic States, The Midwest** Jacques Chazaud **Mount Rushmore** Leonard Lee Rue III/Photo Researchers, Inc. **New England** Jacques Chazaud **Niagara Falls** New York State Department of Economic Development **Pacific Coast States, Rocky Mountain States** Jacques Chazaud **The Seattle Space Needle** Charles E. Rotkin/Corbis **The South, The Southwest** Jacques Chazaud **Yosemite National Park** National Archives and Records Administration, neg. no. 57-PS-28

## World Geography

**The World, Africa** Jacques Chazaud, updated by Mary Reilly 2004 **Antarctica** The Granger Collection, New York **Asia and the Middle East,** Jacques Chazaud, updated by Mary Reilly 2004 **Australia and Oceania,** Jacques Chazaud **Europe** Jacques Chazaud, updated by Mary Reilly 2004 **Ganges River** Reuters/Corbis-Bettmann Archive **Istanbul** H. Armstrong Roberts, Inc. **North America and the West Indies** Jacques Chazaud, updated by Mary Reilly 2004 **The Sahara Desert** H. Armstrong Roberts, Inc. **South America** Jacques Chazaud **Sydney Opera House** CDRPHOTO/Corbis

## Mathematics

**Angle, Area, Bar graph, Circle, Cone, Cylinder, Diagonal, Ellipse, Hexagon, Intersect, Metric system, Octagon, Parallel, Pentagon, Pie chart, Pyramid, Quadrilateral, Sphere, Trapezoid, Triangle** Laurel Cook Lhowe **Line graph** Copyright © 2004 Houghton Mifflin Company

## Physical Sciences

**Atom, Celsius** Laurel Cook Lhowe **Marie Curie** Hulton-Deutsch Collection/Corbis **Albert Einstein** AP/Wide World Photos **Galaxy** Ewing Galloway, Inc. **Mars** NASA **Satellite** Denis Scott/Corbis **Solar system, Telescope** Laurel Cook Lhowe **X-ray** Bettmann/Corbis

## Earth Sciences and Weather

**Cirrus clouds** Copyright © Vincent J. Schaefer **Coral reef** Stephen Frink/Corbis **Cumulus clouds** Copyright © Vincent J. Schaefer **Earth** Laurel Cook Lhowe **Fossils** Bucky Reeves/Photo Researchers, Inc. **Lightning** Ed Carlin/Index Stock Imagery **Nimbostratus clouds** Copyright © Vincent J. Schaefer **Stalactites and stalagmites** Virginia Division of Tourism **Tornado** UPI/Corbis-Bettmann Newsphotos **Volcano** (drawing) Laurel Cook Lhowe (photograph) AP/Wide World Photos

## Life Sciences

**Bird** Courtesy of Holly Hartman **Cell** Laurel Cook Lhowe **Crustacean** Marko Modic/Corbis **Dinosaur, Flower** Laurel Cook Lhowe **Food chain** Copyright © 1984 by Houghton Mifflin Company. Adapted and reprinted by permission from *Spaceship Earth: Earth Science*, Rev. Ed. **Jane Goodall** UPI/Corbis-Bettmann Archive **Insect, Metamorphosis, Photosynthesis** Laurel Cook Lhowe

## Medicine and the Human Body

**Balanced diet** Hans & Cassady, Inc., Westerville, Ohio **Brain, Circulatory system, Digestive system, Ear, Nervous system, Permanent teeth, Skeleton, Skin** Laurel Cook Lhowe

## Technology

**Artificial intelligence** Corbis **Alexander Graham Bell** Stock Montage, Inc. **Computer, handheld** © Ellen Senisi/The Image Works **Thomas A. Edison** Collections of Greenfield Village and the Henry Ford Museum, Dearborn, Michigan, neg. no. B34599 **Inclined plane** Barbara Rios/Photo Researchers, Inc. **Laptop** Christa Renee/Stone/Getty Images, Inc. **Laser, Lens, Lever, Nuclear reactor** Laurel Cook Lhowe **Nuclear weapons** United States Air Force Photo **Solar cell** Laurel Cook Lhowe **Space shuttle** AFP/Corbis **Eli Whitney** Stock Montage, Inc.

# Index

Hel, **48**
Helen of Troy, **48**, 50, 52
Helium, **233**
Helix, double, **254**
Hell, **90**
"Hello, Dolly," 55
Helping verb, 13
Helsinki, 197, **200**
Hemings, Sally, **106**
Hemingway, Ernest, **27**
Hemisphere, **200**
Hemoglobin, **267**, 272
Henry, Patrick, 105
Henry VIII, 145, **149**
Hephaestus, **48**
Hera, **48**
Herbivore, **256**
Herculaneum, 153, 204
Hercules, **48**, *49*
"Here We Go 'Round the Mulberry
    Bush," **62**
Heredity, **256**, 257
Hermes, **48**
Hermitage, 65
Hero, **27**
Heroin, 266
Heroine, **27**
"He's Got the Whole World in His
    Hands," **62**
Hexagon, *219*
"Hey Diddle Diddle," **27**
Hiawatha, **27**
Hibernation, **256**
Hickok, Wild Bill, **123**
"Hickory, Dickory, Dock," **27**
Hidalgo, Miguel, **162**
Hieroglyphics, 148, **149**, *149*
Himalayas, **200**
Hinduism, **90**, 197, *199*
Hines, Gregory, 71
Hip-hop, **62**
Hiroshima, 118, 126, 131, 134, **162**,
    164, 168
Histamine, 262
History, U.S.: before 1865, 99–116;
    since 1865, 117–34
History, world: before 1600, 144–57;
    since 1600, 158–68
Hit the nail on the head, **8**
Hitch your wagon to a star, **3**
Hitler, Adolf, *138*, **162**, *162*, 164
HIV, 261
H₂O, **233**
*Hobbit, The* (Tolkien), 40
*Holes* (Sachar), 37
Holiday, Billie, 57
Holland, 204
Hollywood, **173**
Holocaust, **162**
Holy Land, **79**, 147, 207
Holy Roman Empire, 146, **149–50**
"Home on the Range," **62**
Home page, **280**
Homer, **27**, 33, 50
Homer, Winslow, **62**
*Homo sapiens*, **256**

Homonyms, **14**
Honduras, 195, **200**
Honest Abe, **106**
Hong Kong, **200**
Honolulu, **173**
Hoover, J. Edgar, **123**
Hopis, **106**
Horizon (art), **62**
Horizontal, **219**, 226
Hormone, **267**
"Hot Cross Buns," **27**
"Hound Dog," 67
House of Representatives, 137, **139**,
    139
"House That Jack Built, The," **27–28**
Houses of Parliament, 57
Houston, **174**
*How the Grinch Stole Christmas*
    (Seuss), 25, 37
Howe, Julia Ward, 56
Huang He (Huang Ho), 213
*Huckleberry Finn, The Adventures of*
    (Twain), **28**, 40
Hudson, Henry, **150**
Hudson Bay, **200**
Hudson River, **174**
Hughes, Langston, 26, **28**
Hull House, 117, 130
Human body, 261–75
Human Genome Project, 256
Human immunodeficiency virus, 261
Humidity, 247
"Humpty Dumpty," 19, **28**, *28*
*Hunchback of Notre Dame, The*
    (Hugo), **28**
Hundred Years' War, **150**, 151
Hungary, 195, **200**
Huns, **150**
Hurricane, **244**
Hurston, Zora Neale, 26, **28**
Hush, little baby, **62**
Hussein, Saddam, **162**, 164
Hutchinson, Anne, **106**, 116
Hutu, 208
Hybridization, **256**
Hydrocarbons, **233**
Hydroelectric power, **280**
Hydrogen atom, *229*, 235, 273, 275
Hymn, **62**
Hypotenuse, **219**, 224
"I came, I saw, I conquered," **150**
I have a dream, **123**, 125, *126*
"I Hear America Singing" (Whitman),
    42
*I Know Why the Caged Bird Sings*
    (Angelou), 19, 23
I only regret that I have but one life to
    lose for my country, **106**
"I think I can, I think I can," 30
Ibn Batuta, **150**
Icarus, 46, **48**
Ice Age(s), **150**, 244
Iceberg, **244**
Iceland, **200**, 209
Icons, **90**
Idaho, 110, **174**, 181

Idioms, 6–11
If at first you don't succeed, try, try
    again, **3**
If the shoe fits, wear it, **3**
If wishes were horses, then beggars
    would ride, **3**
Igloo, **62**
Igneous rock, **244**
"Ike," 122
*Iliad* (Homer), 27, **28**, 52
Illinois, **174**, 176
Imagery, **28**
Immigration, **139**
Immune system, **267**
Immunity, **268**
Immunization, **268**
Impeachment, 119, 125, **139**
Imperative sentence, **14**
Import, **140**
Impressionism, **62**, *62*
Improper fraction, **219**
In hot water, **8**
Incas, 147, **150–51**, *150*, 151, 153, 207
Incisors, **268**, *271*
Inclined plane, **280**, *280*
Indefinite article, 13
Independent clause, 13
India, 146, **151**, 161, **200**
Indian Ocean, **200**
Indian removal policy, **106**
Indiana, **174**, 176
Indianapolis, **174**
Indians of North America: Algonquins,
    **100;** Apaches, **100,** 122; Arapahos,
    **100,** 110; Blackfeet, **101,** 110; Chero-
    kees, **102,** 106, 112, 113; Cheyennes,
    **102,** 110; Creeks, **103,** 106; Dakota
    (Sioux), **112;** Delawares, **103–4;**
    Hopis, **106;** Iroquois League, **106;**
    Massachusetts, 108; Navajos, **109,**
    *110;* Plains Indians, 100, 101, 102,
    **110,** 134; Pueblos, 106, **111,** 147;
    Seminoles, 106; Shawnees, **112;** Sho-
    shones, 111, **112;** Sioux, 102, 110,
    **112,** 120, 130
Indirect object, **14**
Indochina, **200**
Indonesia, **201**, 209
Indus River, **201**
Indus Valley civilization, 150
Industrial Revolution, **162–63**
Inertia, **233**
Infection, 262, 267, **268**
Infectious disease, 264
Infinity, **219**, 225
Inflammation, **268**
Inflation, **140**
Influenza, **268**
Information superhighway, **280**
Infrared light, 237
Infrared radiation, **233**, 236
Ingres, Jean-Auguste-Dominique, *164*
Inorganic, **233**
Insect, 251, **256–57**, *257*
Instinct, **257**
Instruments, musical, **65**

Portland, **181**
Portugal, **207**
Poseidon, **51**
Positive number, **223**
Possessive, **16**
Pot calling the kettle black, the, **10**
Potato famine, Irish, **165**
Potomac River, **181**
Potter, Beatrix, 34
Powell, Colin, **128**
Power (mathematics), 216, 218, **223**
Power (physics), 238
Powhatan, 110, **111**
Practice makes perfect, **4**
Practice what you preach, **4**
Prague, 196, **207**
"Praise to the Lord, the Almighty," 62
Prayer, **94**
Prayer rug, **94**, *94*
Precipitation, 240, **247**
Predicate, **16**
Prefix, **16**
Preposition, **16**
Prepositional phrase, **16**
Prescription drugs, **272**
President, **141**, 143
Presley, Elvis, **67**, *67*, 68
Prevailing westerlies, **247**
*Pride and Prejudice* (Austen), 19
Priest, **94**, 95
Primary colors, **67**
Prime meridian, 203, **207–8**
Prime number, **223**
Prince Edward Island, 195
"Princess and the Peam, The"
  (Andersen), 19, **35**
Printmaking, **67**
Probability, **223**
Procrastination is the thief of time, **4**
Prodigal son, **84**
Product (mathematics), 220, 221, **224**
Program (computer), **284**, 284
Prohibition, **128**, *128*
Prokofiev, Sergei, 67
Prometheus, **51**
Promised Land, 78, 79, 80, 82, **84**
Pronoun, **16**
Proof of the pudding is in the eating,
  The, **4**
Propaganda, **141**
Propeller, 284
Proper noun, **16**
Proportion (art), **67–68**
Proportion (mathematics), **224**
Prose, **35**
Proserpina, **51**
Protein, 262, **272**
Protestant churches, 87, 90, 92, **94,**
  154
Protoctista, 257, **259**
Proton, 229, **236**
Protoplasm, 252, **259**
Protozoa, **259**, 260
Proverbs, 1–5
Psalm, Twenty-third, **85–86**
Psalms, **85**

Psyche, **51**
Psychiatrist, **272**
Psychologist, **272**
Ptolemy, **153**
Puberty, 269, **272**
Pueblos (people), 106, **111**, 147
Puerto Rico, 130, 153, **181**, 213
Pulitzer Prizes, **35**
Pulley, **284**
Punctuation marks, **16**
Punic Wars, 146, **153**
Punjabi, 207
Pupil, **272**
Purim, **94–95**
Puritans, 106, 108, 110, **111**, 116, 160
"Puss-in-Boots," **35**
Pygmalion, **51**
Pyramid (geometry), **224**, *224*
Pyramids, **68**, *68*, 148, **153**, 197
Pyrenees, **208**
Pythagorean theorem, **224**
Quadrilateral, **224**, *224*
Quakers, **95**, **111**
Quarks, **236**
Quartet, **68**
Quasars, **236**
Quebec, 195, 204, **208**
Question mark, **16**
*Quixote, Don* (Cervantes), 21
Quotation marks, **17**
Quotient, **224**, 225
Qur'an, 91
Rabbi, **95**
Rabies, **272**
Radar, **284**
Radiation, 233, **236**
Radii, 224
Radio waves, 237, 284
Radioactivity, **236**
Radius, 214, **224**
Ragtime, 63
"Rain, Rain, Go Away," **35**
Rain forest, 248
Rainbow, 237, **247**
Raining cats and dogs, **10**
Raleigh, Sir Walter, **111**
Ramadan, **95**
Randolph, A. Philip, **128**
Rap (music), 62, **68**
Raphael, *82*
"Rapunzel," **35**, *36*
Rate, **224**
Ratio, 223, **224**, 225
"Raven, The" (Poe), **35**
RDA, **272**
Read between the lines, **10**
Reagan, Ronald, 118, **128**
Reciprocal, **224**
Recommended daily allowance, 272
Reconstruction, **128**
Rectangle, 222, **224–25**
Recycling, **247**
Red blood cells, 267, 269, **272**
Red Cross, American, 101
Red Sea, 78, **208**
Red Sea, parting of the, **85**

Redcoat, **111**
Reducing (fraction), 220
Refinery, **284**
Reflection, **236**
Reformation, 88, **153–54**
Refraction, **236**
Reggae, **68**
Regular verb, **17**
Reign of Terror, 161, **165**
Reincarnation, 90, **95**
Relative humidity, **247**
Relief map, **208**
Religion and philosophy, 87–98. *See
  also* Bible
Remainder, 221, **225**
Rembrandt, **68**
Remember the Alamo!, 100, **111**
Renaissance, **154**
Renewable resources, 245
Repeating decimal, **225**
Reproduction, 251, 258, **259**
Reproductive system, **272**, 275
Reptiles, **259**
Republic, **141**
*Republic, The* (Plato), 94
Republic of China, 211
Republic of Ireland, 194, 197, **208**
Republican party, 137, **141**
Reservation (American Indian), 110,
  **111**, 112
Resistance (electricity), **284**
Respiration, **272**
Respiratory system, **272**
Rest (music), **68**
Resurrection, **85**, 90, 91
Resuscitation, 266
Retina, 268, **272**
Revere, Paul, **111**
Revolution, French, 159, 165
Revolution, Russian, 163, **165**
Revolutionary War (American), **111;**
  battles, 107, 111, 112, 116; causes
  and start of, 101, 102, 110, 112; lead-
  ers, 100, 103, 104, 106, 107, 110, 116;
  soldiers and armies, 103, 109, 111
*Rhapsody in Blue* (Gershwin), 60
Rhine River, **208**
Rhode Island, 113, 116, 179, **181**
Rhodesia, 212
Rhombus, 222, **225**
Rhone River, **208**
Rhyme, **35–36**
Rhyme scheme, **36**
Rhythm, **68**
Ribs, **272**, *274*
Richard the Lion-Hearted, 148, **154**
Richter scale, **247**
Right angle, 219, 223, **225**
Right triangle, 219, 224, **225**
"Ring Around the Rosies," **68**
Ring of Fire, **208**
Rio de Janeiro, 194, **208**
Rio Grande, **181**
"Rip Van Winkle," **36**
RNA, **259**
"Road Not Taken, The" (Frost), 24

DATE DUE

AG 5 .N335 2004

The new first dictionary of
cultural literacy

| DATE | ISSUED TO |
|------|-----------|
|      |           |
|      |           |
|      |           |
|      |           |
|      |           |

AG 5 .N335 2004

The new first dictionary of
cultural literacy